INTERNATIONAL HEALTH

INTERNATIONAL HEALTH

PAUL F. BASCH

NEW YORK • OXFORD UNIVERSITY PRESS • 1978

Copyright © 1978 by Oxford University Press, Inc.

Library of Congress Cataloging in Publication Data

Basch, Paul F
  International health.

  Bibliography: p.
  Includes index.
  1. World health. I. Title. [DNLM: 1. World health. WA540.1 B298i]
RA441.B37   362.1'09'04   78-5082
ISBN 0-19-502328-5
ISBN 0-19-502329-3 pbk.

Printed in the United States of America

PREFACE

Human numbers and needs are now greater than they have ever been, but less than they will be tomorrow. People and microbes and ideas all travel, faster and farther than at any time in the past. The world is becoming one community, and we have much to learn from others. It is mostly for these reasons that I have written this book, not only for students and practitioners of medicine but for those in the social sciences, the world of commerce, private and public agencies, and others who find the health of mankind a subject of continuing concern. This volume is not a compendium of data, nor is it a manual of methods and procedures; it is intended to provide a broad basis for understanding the current global situation regarding health and to focus many diffuse elements into a more coherent pattern.

What is international health? On a technical level we may seek a systematic comparison of the factors that affect the well-being of the peoples of the world, and of the steps that can be taken for its improvement. On an intuitive level we may feel that mankind's health–whatever that may be–somehow abstracts and crystallizes the totality of human experience. From any viewpoint we know that this is a diverse and complex subject.

I have selected for discussion topics providing a general background as well as specific issues of current interest. Where these are by nature controversial, I have tried to present a variety of outlooks and approaches. I am sensitive to the many shortcomings of this book and to the limitations of my own knowledge, experience, and abilities. My background is in zoology and parasitology, with several years of field work in tropical countries, some training in epidemiology and public health, and a decade of laboratory research (mostly on schistosomiasis) and teaching. In a work planned to be comprehensive without being encyclopedic, my decisions to include this or omit that will inevitably differ from the choices that might have been made by others, but I trust that the needs of most people will be met within these covers. Nevertheless, I hope that this book will stimulate its readers to probe deeply into the references cited and into other published sources, to become more involved in the problems of international health, and, above all, to go out and see for themselves the great variety of the human experience. While I have written primarily for readers in the United States, I hope that this book does not present such an "American bias" that it cannot be used profitably elsewhere.

Some friends and colleagues have commented on drafts of sections of this book, but I have not always taken their advice. Therefore the errors and imperfections in these pages are my responsibility alone. My wife and children have gracefully accepted my preoccupation while this work was taking form, and I thank them for their forbearance. Patty Ford, who transformed kilograms of paper, tape, clips, and graphite into a perfect typescript, deserves and gets my gratitude.

PAUL F. BASCH
Stanford, California
April 1978

Contents

1. Nature   3
2. The Past   45
3. Development   78
4. Culture   132
5. Information   167
6. Policy   219
7. Medicine   270
8. Community   321

   Index   373

INTERNATIONAL HEALTH

NATURE 1.

Not many years ago, in a native reserve in a certain country, a number of cases of severe amebic dysentery came to the attention of medical authorities. Among a population of roughly 1,000, more than 100 people had had clinical amebiasis severe enough to warrant hospitalization over a span of nine years. There had been eight deaths, two of which occurred in small children. One-third of the total population carried pathogenic amebae in their bowels. Conditions of nutrition and sanitation were grossly deficient. A picture such as this would not seem unusual in any of dozens of tropical countries. But this did not occur in a tropical country—it happened in northern Saskatchewan, Canada, in a closely knit population of native American Indians (Eaton, 1968). How strange it seems to hear of endemic amebic dysentery in the far North, when our preconceptions hold it to be a "tropical disease." And yet the causative organism, *Entamoeba histolytica,* was first described in 1875 in St. Petersburg, Russia, from a patient residing in Arkhangelsk near the Arctic Circle.

To understand the health conditions of mankind, to see them accurately and objectively, one must be willing to cast aside preconceptions. The notion of "tropical diseases," for example, is largely misleading. Malaria, yellow fever, cholera, and smallpox have ravaged North America and Europe. Tens of thousands died of cholera in New York City after the Civil War. Hundreds of thousands perished in Europe at the same time, and to emphasize the constant threat, some dozens have died of cholera in Italy and Portugal in the 1970s. Yellow fever struck repeatedly in the United States during the eighteenth and nineteenth centuries; in one outbreak in Philadelphia 10% of the population died. The most recent epidemic in an American city struck New Orleans in 1905. Malaria was endemic in the southern states until the 1940s. Smallpox was last notified in the United States in 1949, and minor introductions have occurred in Europe since that date, although this disease is now almost eradicated.

It seems reasonable to ask how it is that these diseases have come and gone from the industrialized countries and whether they might one day return with the same intensity. What is it, in fact, that determines the presence of these, and other less dramatic diseases at any particular time and place? The answers are surely complex, but we can start by exploring the associations between geographic location and health and the nature of interactions between humans and their environment.

THE NATURAL ENVIRONMENT

The study of localities in relation to disease and health was well established by the time of Hippocrates, about the fifth century BC, not only in Greece but in all countries for which we have an adequate historical record from those days. The Hippocratic text entitled "Airs, Waters, Places" begins:

Whoever wishes to pursue properly the science of medicine must proceed thus: First, he ought to consider what effects each season of the year can produce; for the seasons are not at all alike, but differ widely both in themselves and at their changes. The next point is the hot winds and the cold, especially those that are universal but also those that are peculiar to each particular region. . . . For with the seasons, men's diseases, like their digestive organs, suffer change.

More recently, Stallones (1971) has stated it this way: "Disease is embedded in the environments of man, and the greatest improvement in human health may be expected from an understanding and modification of the factors that favor disease occurrence."

Geological substrate

The soil is important to human health primarily because of its chemical makeup, affecting man directly through water for drinking and cooking, and less directly by way of the vegetable food and the other plants that may or may not, grow in it.

Major Minerals The most important element for human health that is frequently absent from soils is iodine, a deficiency of which may lead to endemic goiter or endemic cretinism. These conditions have been known for many centuries. Langer (1960) mentions ancient Chinese writings dating from several centuries BC in which goiter is described and attributed to the quality of the water. More remarkably, seaweed (which is rich in iodine) was mentioned as an efficacious remedy for goiter in a treatise on herbs and roots attributed to Shen-Nung (third millenium BC). Many other authors of antiquity, from India to Egypt to Rome, knew of goiter. Pliny (First century AD) said that swelling of the throat of men and swine was caused mostly by the water they drink. Goiter was common in pre-Columbian America; it was seen by the Spaniards among the Incas in the high Andes (Fierro-Benitez et al., 1969). The recent prevalence of endemic goiter was exhaustively described by Kelly and Snedden (1960); the most notorious goitrous centers of the world are in high mountains: the Pyrenees, Alps, Himalayas, and Andes where the terrain has been subjected to flooding or glaciation and leaching of iodine. Few countries are entirely free from goiter.

Another halogen well known for its relation to health is fluorine, whose effects on tooth enamel are reflected in the prevalence of dental caries. In England, for example, York has 0.2 parts per million in the drinking water, while Hartlepool has from 1.5 to 2 ppm. In 381 children from York the mean number of cavities was 11.5, and a similar group from Hartlepool had 5.5 (Jackson et al., 1973). Fluoride supplementation of drinking water commonly reduces the incidence of cavities, but in excess this element is extremely harmful. In certain areas, notably in India, high concentrations are accompanied by severe skeletal abnormalities in those who must drink the water. In the Punjab natural waters are known with up to 14 ppm of fluorine. Sing et al. (1962) have described the heavy, rough, chalky white bone structure characteristic of chronic fluorosis. Ligaments, membranes, and cartilages become calcified. Children in parts of Uttar Pradesh may have severe crippling from osteosclerosis, and they usually exhibit the dental mottling and discoloration commonly associated with excess fluorine intake (Teotia et al., 1971).

Another element in the geological substrate whose excess is directly associated with health is arsenic, responsible for blackfoot disease in Taiwan (Hopps, 1971) and a chronic poisoning syndrome in Chile and Argentina (Astolfi, 1971).

The human requirement for dietary iron makes this element extremely important in prevention of anemia, a serious problem of worldwide dimensions. Berg (1973) has pointed out that in Latin American countries 29% to 63% of pregnant women are anemic, while in India the proportion is as high as 80%. Anemia owing to iron deficiency is mostly due to factors other than an iron-poor soil. Loss or destruction of red blood cells by hookworm and malaria is often accompanied by inadequate consumption of iron-rich foods (liver, green leafy vegetables). Where iron cooking pots are used, anemia is rare because sufficient iron is transferred to the foods from the pot.

A remarkable association of geologic substrate with disease has been reported by Price (1976): gross swelling of the lower legs (elephantiasis), which occurs in up to 87 per thousand adults in parts of Ethiopia, is specifically related to distribution of a heavy red clay soil of basaltic origin. The soil is rich in colloidal iron oxide, alumina, and silica on which are adsorbed metallic ions known to be toxic to human tissue. When wet, the soil sticks firmly to the skin, and it is presumed that elephantiasis results from irreversible damage to lymphatic channels by chronic absorption of toxic ions. Lymph node biopsies of elephantiasis patients have shown significant concentrations of the same metals that occur in the soil substrate. It is significant that only habitually barefoot farmers are affected. The relationship between the elephantiasis and soil type was confirmed by observations in Kenya, Rwanda, and northwest Tanzania where similiar conditions occur. In one region prevalence of this condition fell from 60 per 1,000 adults on the volcanic highlands to 0.1 on the sandy lowlands, a distance of about 30 km. Filarial infections were ruled out as a cause of this elephantiasis.

Trace Elements And Elusive Correlations The so-called trace elements, such as copper, manganese, magnesium, and molybdenum, may be required in very small amounts for proper functioning of various enzyme systems. Associations have been suggested between soil and water chemistry and diseases such as cancer, multiple sclerosis, and sarcoidosis, but these are difficult to evaluate in view of the large chance for statistical artifact. Studies made in various countries have suggested an inverse correlation between mortality from cardiovascular disease and hardness of drinking water, in particular the calcium, magnesium, and sodium ions. No specific causal relationships have yet been determined (Masironi et al., 1973).

The potential importance of trace elements is emphasized in a report by Sandstead and six others (1967) from Egypt. These workers observed many boys in poor villages who appeared to suffer from lack of pituitary secretion, showing severe growth retardation and hypogonadism. Forty such boys aged 12 to 20 were put on a good hospital diet (after being treated for intestinal worms), and some were also given iron or zinc sulfate. These boys were compared in their growth and development with untreated village boys. Average growth (in inches) reported for one year were: untreated, 0; hospital diet only, 1.8; diet plus iron, 2.9; diet plus zinc, 5.0. Sexual maturation of the boys given zinc was also stimulated. It was suggested by the authors that zinc is a limiting nutrient for growth. Fortunately, frank zinc deficiency appears to be uncommon.

Radioactivity All living organisms are continually exposed to ionizing radiation from three sources: the minute inherent natural radioactivity within the body originating from inhaled air and ingested food and water; cosmic radiation; and decay of naturally radioactive minerals in the earth's crust. The amount of natural radiation to which people are exposed varies from place to place depending largely upon the isotopic composition of the substrate (and, for cosmic radiation, on altitude). Substrate radioactivity is often reflected in water supplies. Within the United States, for instance, raw water in Tacoma, Washington, has a Radium—226 content of about .002 picocuries per liter, while Joilet, Illinois, has 6.54, a range of 3270 times. Mineral springs in Europe, South America, and elsewhere may contain 100 picocuries per liter of ^{226}Ra. Soils in regions of the state of Minas Gerais, Brazil, have so much natural radioactivity that plants growing there will leave a perfect picture of themselves when placed on photographic paper in a darkroom. Parts of Kerala, southern India, also have extensive deposits of radioactive monazite sands (Eisenbud, 1973), which are sometimes intentionally applied to the body as cures for various illnesses.

Health consequences of ionizing radiation may be considered under two categories: those affecting the individual, and those affecting genetic material in the gametes and therefore transmissible to offspring. If oncogenic and mutagenic effects of ionizing radiation vary with dosage it seems reasonable to look for increases in malignancies or in genetic defects in areas of high natural substrate radioactivity. Numerous such investigations have been made, but no firm linkage has been established between substrate radioactivity and either cancer or genetic abnormality.

Latitude And The Seasons

The position of the noonday sun at most places on earth makes an annual migration along a north-south path. At the solstices (June 21 and December 22) the sun is at its furthest north and south limits; at the equinoxes (March 21 and September 23) the sun is at the midpoint of its path. This annual shift is caused by the 23°27′ tilt of the polar axis in relation to the plane of rotation. As the earth circles the sun, the direct rays appear overhead at noon at a slightly different point each day, to a

Figure 1-1

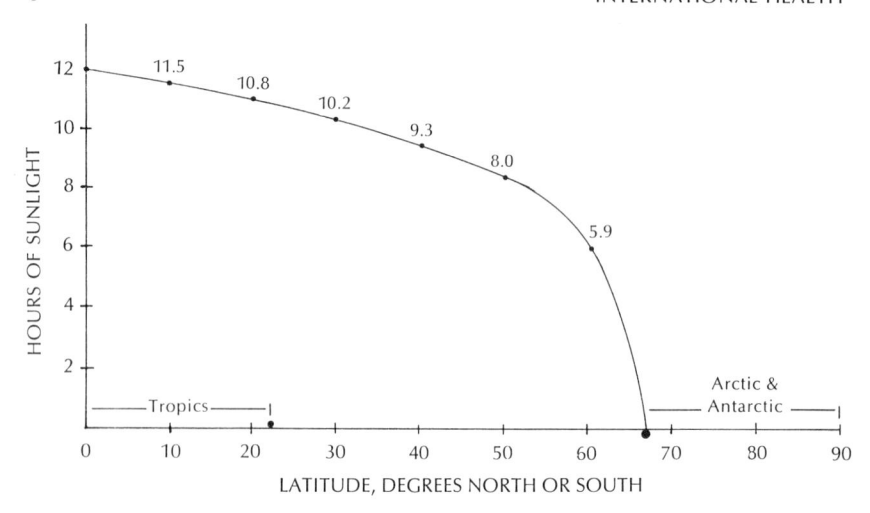

The shortest day of the year at various latitudes.

limit of 23°27′ north latitude (the Tropic of Cancer) at the northern summer solstice and the corresponding southern limit (the Tropic of Capricorn) at the northern winter solstice. The two tropics thus mark the limits of latitude at which the sun is ever directly overhead at noon. The word *tropic* is derived from the Greek *tropos,* meaning "turning," because the sun appears to "turn" back and forth at these imaginary lines. As one proceeds into higher latitudes north or south, the sun appears to make a smaller arc in the sky, never appearing directly overhead. This arc, and the consequent duration of daylight, become smaller and smaller in northern latitudes as the winter solstice approaches (Fig. 1-1), and the situation is reversed south of the equator. At 66°30′ north, daylight reaches zero on that day; this is the Arctic Circle. At the corresponding latitude to the south, there are 24 hours of daylight on the same date. At latitudes nearer the poles the extent of continuous darkness or light becomes slowly greater.

Although the tropical and arctic regions are defined by the geometry of the earth's movements vis-à-vis the sun, the two words bring to mind primarily heat and cold. While it is undeniably true that most localities between Cancer and Capricorn tend towards high temperatures, a study of Table 1-1 shows that other factors such as altitude play an important role in determining the overall climate at any particular place.

Altitude

The study of the effects of altitude on humans has received great impetus in recent years through programs to put humans into space. There has been a virtual avalanche of reports and publications on physiological adaptations to rapid altitude changes and to prolonged residence under conditions of relative hypoxia. Atmospheric pressure and, correspondingly, the partial pressure of oxygen in inspired air decline with increased elevation. Physiological mechanisms to deal with these changes have been investigated in the field primarily in Peru, where in some areas people live and work at extreme altitudes. One of the chief adaptations found is increased pulmonary ventilation. In residents of Morococha, a mining town at 4,540 meters (14,900 feet), this factor exceeds by 40% the degree of ventilation found in sea level residents on a body-weight basis, with basal metabolism at the same level in the two populations (Hurtado, 1964). Table 1-2, adapted from Hurtado's data, shows the substantial differences in many hematologic characteristics between residents of Lima, at sea level, and of Morococha. These physiological adaptations are directed towards more efficient use of the relatively scarce oxygen at high altitudes. Along with these characteristics, peoples native to high altitudes may show evidence of right ventricular enlargment and *pulmonary* hypertension in the presence of reduced systemic arterial pressure. The virtual absence of *systemic* hypertension appears to be correlated with a lack of ischemic heart disease among native high altitude populations, although a relatively high incidence of congenital heart diseases may be present (World Health Organization, 1969).

Persons who travel suddenly from sea level to high altitudes, to such cities as Quito, Ecuador, and La Paz, Bolivia, may develop increased heart rate, insomnia, headache, hyperventilation, and other signs of respiratory distress. Although these abate within a few weeks in normal subjects, acclimatization even after long exposure does not reach the level of adaptation found in locally born people (Folk, 1974).

Chronic mountain sickness (Monge's disease) can occur even in lifelong residents of high altitudes. Peñaloza, Sime, and Ruiz (1971) have studied 10 male native subjects with chronic mountain sickness in Cerro de Pasco, Peru, at 4,375 meters (14,350 feet) elevation. These persons had lost their acclimatization and showed average hematocrit levels of 79% and hemoglobin of almost 25 grams/100 ml, both extraordinarily high values. The amount of oxygen in their arterial blood was, neverthe-

Table 1-1. Typical temperature and rainfall data, by months, for selected localities in the tropics, recent years

Locality	Lat./Alt.	Data	Jan	Feb	Mar	Apr
Belém,	01°28'N	TM	32	32	32	32
Brazil	24M	Tm	23	23	23	23
		P	308	360	292	287
Brasilia,	15°47'S	TM	28	28	28	28
Brazil	1158M	Tm	18	18	18	17
		P	92	451	225	149
Colón,	09°12'N	TM	28	28	29	30
Panama	0M	Tm	24	25	23	22
		P	75	7	70	225
Freetown,	08°30'N	TM	31	32	33	33
Sierra	11M	Tm	22	23	23	22
Leone		P	13	2	12	56
Mombasa,	04°03'S	TM	33	34	34	34
Kenya	16M	Tm	23	23	24	23
		P	25	18	64	195
Nairobi,	01°16'S	TM	27	28	27	26
Kenya	1821M	Tm	9	10	11	13
		P	38	65	124	211
Quito,	00°12'S	TM	22	22	23	24
Ecuador	2818M	Tm	5	6	5	4
		P	83	219	84	59
Singapore	01°18'N	TM	32	33	33	33
	10M	Tm	21	21	22	22
		P	252	173	193	188

Abbreviations:
Alt. altitude above mean sea level at meteorological station. (Localities at or below 24 M are seaports)
Lat. latitude at meteorological station
M   meters
N   north
P   precipitation
R   range from lowest average monthly minimum to highest temperature
S   south
T   total annual precipitation
Tm   average minimum temperature
TM   average maximum temperature

Source: Compiled and calculated from various sources.

May	Jun	Jul	Aug	Sep	Oct	Nov	Dec	Year
33	33	34	34	33	34	34	35	13R
23	22	22	21	21	21	21	21	
354	123	186	177	103	26	74	41	2331T
26	25	26	29	30	28	27	25	17R
15	14	13	15	17	18	17	17	
28	0	0	7	49	81	315	272	1669T
29	29	28	29	29	29	28	28	9R
21	21	22	22	21	22	22	23	
665	286	461	652	290	615	1081	468	4895T
33	32	31	31	31	31	31	31	12R
22	21	21	21	22	21	21	22	
160	302	890	902	610	309	132	41	3492T
31	31	29	29	30	31	33	33	14R
22	21	21	20	21	22	23	23	
320	119	89	64	64	86	97	61	1202T
24	24	24	25	27	27	26	26	20R
11	9	8	8	8	9	10	10	
157	46	15	23	30	53	109	87	956T
23	22	24	24	26	23	24	26	22R
6	5	4	4	3	5	4	6	
93	30	20	4	65	187	35	29	908T
33	33	33	33	33	33	33	32	12R
22	22	22	22	22	22	22	22	
174	172	170	196	178	208	254	256	2414T

less, far lower than in asymptomatic persons in the same town. Neuropsychiatric signs are also a frequent feature of Monge's disease. The cure is simple: removal of the patient to sea level reverses the clinical picture. This option hardly exists for the poor.

Acute and chronic mountain sickness are of interest as perhaps the best examples of a complex pathologic process attributable to well-understood factors in the physical environment. Still, the apparent absence of this disease among residents of the Himalayas presents an intriguing mystery. Pediatric high altitude heart disease has, however, been

Table 1-2. Selected mean hematologic values in native residents of Lima and Morococha, Peru

	Lima (sea level)	Morococha (4,540 meters)
Body weight, kilograms	63	53
Blood volume/kg body weight, cc	79.6	100.5
Plasma volume/kg body weight, cc	42.0	39.2
Red cell volume/kg body weight, cc	37.2	61.1
Hemoglobin/kg body weight, g	12.6	20.7
Red blood cells/cu mm blood ($\times$ 10^6)	5.11	6.44
Hematocrit % red blood cells	46.6	59.5
Respiratory rate/min	14.7	17.3

Source: Adapted from Hurtado, 1964.

reported to be relatively common among residents of high plateaus (to 4,700 m) in Chinghai Province, China (Lin and Wu, 1974).

The relentless hypoxia at high elevations results in certain morphological adaptations in man. McClung (1969) has shown that the average birth weight of infants is lower in Peruvian towns at high altitudes as compared with Lima at sea level, but both the surface area and weight of placentas are greater in the mountain populations.

Barometric pressure is not the only climatic factor to vary inversely with altitude. Air temperature decreases with elevation at a rate of 1°C per 140 meters in the Alps, 165 meters in the Caucasus, and 195 meters in the Equatorial Andes; in consequence the duration of cold seasons is extended. In the Alps, for instance, the period with mean temperature above freezing is six months at 2,000 meters but only two months at 3,100 meters (Hesse, Allee, and Schmidt, 1951). One result of this temperature decline is that habitats at increasing altitude tend to resemble those at increasing latitude so that eventually the tree line and snow line are reached in either direction. The influence of the altitude-temperature relationship is readily seen in Table 1-1. Singapore, Mombasa, Belém, Nairobi, and Quito are all within a few degrees of the equator. The climates of the first three, in Asia, Africa, and Latin America, are remarkably similar—warm and wet. Nairobi is considerably cooler, and Quito cooler still. Note the difference between Mombasa and Nairobi, a scant 400 kilometers (250 miles) apart horizontally but almost 2 kilometers apart vertically. At this latitude day length is practically uniform and month-to-month variations are small at all five localities.

Direct Effects of Climate on Health

Many aspects of climate, such as relative humidity, wind, ionization, and barometric pressure, are not included in Table 1-1. Effects of these factors are more subtle and widespread than such obvious climatic hazards as frostbite or heatstroke. Changes in humidity and pressure can trigger arthritic attacks, affect the pain of corns on the feet due to increased pressure against shoes, and have psychological effects. High humidity retards the loss of heat by reducing the evaporative cooling effect of sweating. High temperatures increase the need for water. Under desert conditions most people can tolerate a water deficit of 5% of body weight; they become very listless with a 10% deficit, and a 15% water deficit can be fatal at only 30°C (86°F). Sweat losses of more than 2 liters daily may be encountered in hot climates, and the continual dermal loss of mineral ions, especially sodium, potassium, chloride, and sulfate, can be significant. The total nitrogen loss may exceed 5 grams daily (Edman, 1964), and more than 1.7 grams of amino acids may be lost in one day's perspiration.

The amount of exposure to sunshine is directly associated with production of vitamin D in the skin. Ultraviolet wavelengths of 275 to 300 nm are most important in this activity. In areas where both dietary vitamin D and sunlight are lacking, rickets may result. In some far northern communities in the U.S.S.R., school children are exposed to artificial ultraviolet light during the long winter period of darkness. On the other hand, excessive exposure to sunlight is a contributing factor to skin cancers at unprotected sites on the body.

The totality of human endeavors has repercussions upon health, and almost all aspects of life are affected by climate. Compare the uniform temperature at sea level near the equator with the dramatic seasonal changes at higher latitudes. In Singapore or Freetown (Table 1-1) the entire annual range of temperatures may be spanned within any single day. In Toronto or Moscow, however, there is no mistaking June for January. The diurnal and annual pattern of activities, the customs, the sports, and the entertainments of temperate zone populations are all correlated with the annual cycle of the seasons. From the design and construction of houses to the types of clothing worn, climatic and seasonal influences are of overriding importance, and their repercussions on the distribution and the intensity of infectious and nutritional diseases can hardly be overestimated. The pervasive effects of these basic environmental parameters extend even to the organization and administration of health services, which must be adapted to local conditions if they are to be effective.

CORRELATION OF PHYSICAL AND BIOTIC ENVIRONMENTS

The combination of soil and climate determines the particular associations of plants, animals, and microorganisms potentially present at any locality. Evolution, migration, passive dispersal, and introduction establish the actual types present at any particular location and time. Long-term environmental changes such as continental movements and glaciations are important in these processes but beyond the scope of this book. Smaller-scale changes such as the southward extension of the Sahara desert have enormous influences upon nutrition, infectious diseases, and behavior of the inhabitants.

Here we will consider some of the characteristic associations between disease-producing agents and local environments in areas not greatly modified by human activities. Large-scale environmental changes and their effects on the distribution of disease-producing agents will be discussed in the next chapter.

The Soil as Reservoir of Disease-Producing Agents

Spores of many potentially pathogenic fungi may be recovered from the soil in many parts of the world. Ajello (1956) examined more than a thousand soil samples from the United States, Canada, Venezuela, Peru, and Nigeria, recovering a number of systemic and cutaneous fungi. *Histoplasma capsulatum,* a fungus producing a disease somewhat resembling tuberculosis, was identified in more than 70 samples. Some fungi are closely associated with particular kinds of environments. The agent of San Joaquin Valley Fever (coccidioidomycosis) is restricted to semiarid habitats in North, Central, and South America.

Other agents associated with soil are spore-forming bacteria, such as those producing tetanus, and certain normally free-living protozoa only recently recognized as pathogens. Some amebae of the genera *Naegleria* or *Acanthamoeba* are able to enter through the nasal mucosa of people swimming in ponds or lakes and can produce a rapidly fatal infection of the brain and spinal cord. This amebic meningoencephalitis has been reported from North America, Europe, and Australia, and will undoubtedly be found elsewhere if it is sought.

In contrast to the small number of known cases of amebic meningoencephalitis is the enormous number of human infections with soil-transmitted helminths. The large roundworm *Ascaris,* the whipworm *Trichuris,* and the hookworms *Necator* and *Ancylostoma* are all but ubiquitous among the population in many tropical countries.

An interesting example of the relationship between soil, climate, season, parasite, and human host has been provided by Gelpi and Mustafa (1967). These authors, working in Saudi Arabia, noted that a certain type of acute, transitory respiratory disease occurred repeatedly in the local population during the spring months, principally in March and April. The sharp seasonal incidence suggested some airborne allergen, but foreign residents in the region, breathing the same air, were unaffected. In this region the total rainfall of 50 to 75 mm (2 to 3 inches) per year occurs between late November and mid February; the air temperature at this period is relatively low, rising to 46° to 48°C (115° to 120°F) during July and August. Eggs of *Ascaris* were rapidly dried and killed in the sandy soil at higher temperatures, but could survive during the brief cooler period. Fecal contamination of vegetable gardens or other plots led to swallowing of some viable eggs during this period, and pneumonitis resulted from migration of the larval *Ascaris* worms through the lungs, a normal part of their life cycle. Patients with respiratory symptoms began to have *Ascaris* eggs in their stools a short time later, when the worms had matured. Since adult worms live for a year or more, they can bridge the gap between one transmission cycle and the next within the intestine of their human lost. Foreign residents, who did not eat the vegetables harboring *Ascaris* eggs, remained free from infection. In regions of the world where the soil is cooler and more moist, transmission of *Ascaris* is continuous throughout the year.

Soil, Climate, and Vegetation

Germination of seeds, growth of plants, formation of flowers, setting of pollen, ripening of fruit, and nutritional value of the crop are determined to a great extent by soil chemistry, temperature, moisture, and photoperiod, as well as by the genetic characteristics of the plant. It is clear that in areas of little sunlight, particularly in higher latitudes during the winter, the type and amount of plant growth is severely limited. Persons in these areas who are dependent upon the environment for their daily food must make dramatic seasonal adjustments in their diet. Aykroyd (1970) has described how the fisherfolk of Newfoundland and Labrador, lacking fresh vegetables over the long winter months, survived mainly on white bread and as a consequence suffered from beriberi. This severe nutritional disease results from a lack of thiamine, which is lost from overmilled flour. Tuberculosis was also increasing, and infant mortality was unacceptably high. A law passed in 1944 required the addition of vitamin A to margarine, and of niacin, iron, thiamine, riboflavin, and calcium to white flour. Within a decade these changes, together with other improvements, caused infant mortality to decline by 63%, stillbirths by 59%, tuberculosis by 81%, and beriberi to disappear (Berg, 1973).

Domestic animals share seasonal cycles with their human companions and are subject to similar climatic stress. Cows fed on hay during the winter produce milk with less vitamin A and D than grass-fed animals (Tromp, 1963). The consequent reduction in vitamin D intake of dairy consumers comes just when the vitamin is most needed because of restricted sunlight.

Seasonal malnutrition is not restricted to higher latitudes. Hughes and Hunter (1970) have shown how subsistence agriculture, using inefficient methods in an area of unreliable rainfall, has affected the inhabitants of the Nangodi region in northern Ghana. The active adult community lost, on average, 6.5% in body weight during the "hungry season" as compared to the time of the year when food was more abundant. Seasonal availability of specific foods at any locality, such as fish, vitamin A-rich fruits like papaya, or citrus fruits, may induce recurrent deficiencies in particular nutrients. Small children after weaning are particularly susceptible to these nutritional deficiencies.

Water- and Airborne pathogens

The hazards of drinking water in areas with poor sanitation are a frequent source of anxiety to the traveler. Water poses an even greater threat to the local populations in these regions, who have no alternative to contaminated sources. Surface waters adequately treated, or uncontaminated water from protected boreholes, springs, or sanitary wells are usually considered safe to drink. In less-developed countries two-thirds of the population live in rural areas (some 1,700 million people in 1970) and the great majority of these people have neither safe water supply nor adequate excreta disposal (Pineo and Subramanyam, 1975). The situation is little better for the hundreds of millions living in nearby cities. Recent statistics of the World Health Organization have shown that only 28% have waterborne sewerage, and almost one-third of urban dwellers in developing countries have no sanitation facilities at all. The world water conference held in Argentina in 1977 reflected these concerns.

The principal diseases transmitted by fecally contaminated water are listed in Table 1-3. These generally strike hardest at infants after weaning and at young children for whom the complex of enteric diseases, combined with malnutrition, represents the great killer in most tropical areas. Even in the industrialized countries, outbreaks of enteric disease are not infrequent. Resort areas, where limited water and sewerage systems are strained by large seasonal influxes of tourists, are particularly vulnerable to such outbreaks. In recent years epidemic typhoid fever has occurred in Zermatt, Switzerland, and Aspen, Colorado, and large outbreaks of giardiasis, hepatitis, and other listed diseases have been reported from widely separated areas.

A combination of water- and airborne pathogens has been cited by Poskitt (1972) as underlying the seasonal recurrence of malnutrition seen

Table 1-3. Principal diseases of man transmitted by fecal contamination of water

Disease	Causative organism
Typhoid fever	*Salmonella typhi*
Dysentery	
Bacillary	*Shigella*, various types
Amebic	*Entamoeba histolytica*
Gastroenteritis	
Bacterial	Pathogenic *Escherichia coli*, *Proteus*, others
Viral	Enteroviruses: ECHO, Polio, Coxsackie, etc.
Hepatitis	Hepatitis virus
Leptospirosis	*Leptospira*, various types, of animal origin
Cholera	*Vibrio cholerae*
Giardiasis	*Giardia lamblia*

at a rural pediatric clinic in Uganda. In this area the wet weather during the rainy season encourages crowding inside houses, with the increased interpersonal contact presumably responsible for the spread of measles (whose virus may survive better in moist atmospheres), lower respiratory tract infections, and diarrhea. The diarrhea and illness in marginally nourished children may lead to development of clinical malnutrition, which reaches a peak at the end of the rainy season. An identical observation has been reported by Waldmann (1973) in the Transvaal, South Africa.

We commonly think of illnesses caused by airborne pathogens as acute febrile episodes. It may seem strange to place heart disease in this category, accustomed as we are in the West to viewing cardiac problems as chronic illnesses of older people. Cruickshank (1976) offers a different perspective: "Any doctor who has walked the paediatric wards of hospitals in the cities of warm climate countries, e.g., Singapore, Hong Kong, Lagos, Calcutta, Mexico City, is immediately impressed with the number of school age patients with rheumatic fever or rheumatic heart disease . . . surveys among school children reveal prevalence rates of rheumatic heart disease ranging from one to 20 percent." Rheumatic fever, and the heart valve damage that sometimes ensues, are caused by group A hemolytic streptococci that are transmitted by inhalation or by contaminated milk or food. In certain countries, heart disease may also follow infection with the protozoan *Trypanosoma cruzi* or the schistosome worms, described below and in Table 1-6. Other widely distributed and locally common heart diseases such as endomyocardial fibrosis may have a viral origin (Shaper, 1974), as may a multitude of other conditions, including cancers, conventionally considered "chronic diseases."

Local Faunas and Human Health

Man is by far the most widely distributed large mammal on earth, in part owing to his capability to modify local environments to make them more habitable. Animals are unable to do this and are consequently more at the mercy of climatic factors. The exploitation and domestication of animals for food, fiber, skins, labor, and companionship has been a common theme in most human societies. To some degree all human populations are at risk of traumatic attack or transmission of infectious disease from animals. It is essential that a broad definition be given to the word "animal" so that birds, reptiles, fishes, and invertebrates (particularly insects) are included. Throughout history, the biting flies have been indirectly responsible for a very large proportion of human illnesses and deaths.

Ecological Differention   Table 1-4 provides data on some specific relationships between man and animals in four Peruvian villages. *San Antonio* is a lowland jungle village, strung out along the bank of a large river. The climate is hot and wet and wildlife abounds. *Cachicoto* is in the montaña or upland forest, in an area containing banana groves, coffee and coca fields, plus much tropical flora. The climate is hot and wet but rainfall is much less than in San Antonio. *Yacango* is in an arid zone of bare, grass-covered hills with irrigated fields. The climate is cool and dry, and many people sleep in straw shelters. *Pusi*, at a very high elevation, has sparse vegetation and few trees. The village is in the foothills near Lake Titicaca. The climate is cold and dry, often below freezing at night during the long dry season. Note (in Table 1-4) the great differences between these four localities in the nature of animal bites from various sources.

Vector-Borne Diseases

No group of diseases is so closely correlated with environmental conditions as those requiring an insect vector for transmission. Both the insect and the agent must be functional at a certain minimal level in order for the infection to pass from one host to another. A good example is pro-

Table 1-4. Recalled history of animal bites in the male populations, four localities in Peru, 1965

Locality	Elevation[a]	Rat	Snake	Dog	Vampire bat	Louse	Triatoma
San Antonio	377	5.1	16.6	4.3	0	0	0
Cachicoto	2,130	11.0	10.3	12.8	18.6	0	0
Yacango	6,150	1.9	0	16.4	0	0	61.7
Pusi	11,500	4.9	0	47.9	0	96.5	0

Percent of persons ever bitten by:

[a] In feet.

Source: Adapted from Buck et al., 1968.

vided by malaria, which is not a single entity but rather a collective term for several distinct febrile diseases, each caused by one of a group of closely related parasites. The malarias occur in many local variants, each transmitted by a specific anopheline mosquito vector. The three principal factors controlling malaria transmission are temperature, humidity, and rainfall (Pampana, 1963).

For *Plasmodium vivax,* the organism causing benign tertian malaria, the mosquito phase of the life cycle is completed in 7 days at 28°C (83°F), 15 days at 22°C (72°F), 30 days at about 18°C (64°F), and 55 days at 16°C (61°F). Below 15° or 16°C, no development takes place, and temperatures of 30° to 32°C (86° to 90°F) are inhibitory or lethal. The most dangerous malaria parasite, *Plasmodium falciparum,* requires a minimum of 21.6°C (70°F) for transmission; where this temperature is not achieved owing to latitude, altitude, or season, *P. falciparum* poses little threat, but *P. vivax* infections may occur at slightly lower temperatures.

Mosquitoes, as heterothermal animals, unable to regulate their internal temperature, are greatly influenced not only by heat but also by relative humidity. Since they do not survive well in dry air, malaria transmission may not occur if the average monthly relative humidity is below 60%, even if temperatures are favorable. The combined effects of temperature and humidity must be considered, and transmission of malaria may be as seasonal in tropical areas with long dry spells (e.g., interior west Africa) as in temperate regions. Rainfall, besides increasing relative humidity, provides water for mosquito breeding and is thus of considerable significance in itself. Where temperatures are consistently warm and rainfall sufficient throughout the year, malaria poses a threat the year round (See Table 1-1 for likely areas).

Data such as those just described are essential for planning control campaigns for insect-transmitted diseases. Intimate familiarity with environmental and entomological conditions must be gained for each separate locality, and it is not enough to look at national or even regional data. Table 1-5 shows how the threat of malaria decreases with elevation in Peru, while typhus shows the opposite distribution. Typhus is transmitted by lice, which are associated with unchanged clothing and lack of bathing, both to be expected in cold climates. Moreover, people may sleep close together for warmth, providing an opportunity for lice to move from one host to another. Typhus is endemic in mountainous regions of Mexico, Central and South America, the Balkans, eastern Europe, Africa, and Asia wherever similar conditions exist. Thus, the association between typhus, lousiness, and altitude is a clear one.

Table 1-5. Percentages of males[a] having had certain vector-borne diseases, four localities in Peru, 1965

Locality	Malaria	Yellow fever	Typhus
San Antonio (Río Marañon)	25.3	1.1	0
Cachicoto (montaña)	13.3	1.8	0
Yacango (coastal area)	12.6	0	1.0
Pusi (Lake Titicaca)	0.7	0	8.4

[a]Percentages are age-adjusted. See Chap. 5.

Source: Adapted from Buck et al., 1968.

Triatoma (Table 1-4) is a fairly large insect, often known as a "kissing bug" because of its habit of biting the face of sleeping persons. In Central and South America this bug is the vector of a protozoan parasite, *Trypanosoma cruzi,* the causative agent of American trypanosomiasis or Chagas' disease. Whereas lice reside on or close to the human body, triatomid bugs spend most of their day in thatching, cracks in walls, or other parts of poorly constructed houses, coming out primarily to take a blood meal from an unwary vertebrate. In Yacango, 85% of homes housed *Triatoma* (Buck et al., 1968), no doubt attributable to the construction of homes and the favorable climate. Some 15.5% of blood samples from inhabitants of this village showed positive serological tests for infection with *T. cruzi,* substantially more than in the other three localities.

Table 1-6 lists a number of important vector-borne diseases of man. A thorough discussion of all these diseases is not possible within the limits of this book, although many will be mentioned in passing. Each is subject to environmental restrictions, as are those few discussed above. In many cases the reasons underlying geographic distributions are well established. In others much work remains to be done. Yellow fever is such a disease: the virus (hence the disease) is now found only in the Western Hempisphere and Africa. There is no evidence that yellow fever has ever become established in the Asian tropics, even though many Asian mosquitoes are good vectors when experimentally infected in the labora-

Table 1-6. Some major vector-borne and zoonotic diseases of man

Disease	Mode	Animals usually involved	Vector	Distribution
Yellow fever	V	Monkeys, marsupials	Aedes mosquitoes	Africa, C & S America
Viral encephalitis	V	Rodents, birds, horses, monkeys	Mosquitoes or ticks	Many types; temperate and tropical areas
Dengue	V	Man	Aedes mosquitoes	Pacific, SE Asia, Caribbean, S Amer
Rabies	D	Dogs, wild mammals		Cosmopolitan
Influenza	D,I	Swine, birds, man		Cosmopolitan
Typhus	V	Rodents, man	Lice	Africa, Asia, C & S Amer, Balkans
Murine typhus	V	Rodents	Fleas	Cosmopolitan
Scrub typhus	V	Rodents	Mites	Asia, S Asia, N Australia
Q fever	D,I	Cattle, sheep, goats, birds		Cosmopolitan
Spotted fevers	V	Rodents, other mammals	Ticks	Several types; Australia, N & S Amer, Africa, India
Psittacosis	D,I	Birds		Cosmopolitan
Anthrax	D,I	Cattle, goats, horses, swine		E Medit, Asia, Caribbean, L Amer
Brucellosis	D,I,M	Cattle, goats, sheep, swine		Cosmopolitan
Plague	D,V,I	Rodents, man	Fleas	Widespread

Disease	Mode	Reservoir	Vector	Distribution
Relapsing fever	V	Rodents	Ticks or Lice	Asia, Africa, Mid-East, S Amer, Europe
Tuberculosis	D,M	Man, cattle, goats, cats, dogs, swine		Cosmopolitan
Leishmaniasis	V	Dogs, wild animals	Sand flies	Asia, India, Africa, C & S Amer
Malaria	V	Man	Anopheles mosquitoes	Mainly in tropics
Chagas' disease	V	Small mammals, dogs	Triatomids bugs	C & S Amer
Sleeping sickness	V	Large mammals, cattle	Tsetse flies	Tropical Africa
Filariasis	V	Primates, cats, dogs	Mosquitoes	Widespread in tropics
Trichinosis	E	Swine, bear		Widespread, temperate areas
Hydatid disease	E	Sheep, dogs		E Medit, N Zealand, S Amer, Europe, Calif
Tapeworms	E	Cattle, swine, dogs		Cosmopolitan
Schistosomiasis	V	Man, cattle, rodents, swine, primates	Snails	Asia, Africa, Mid-East, Caribbean, S Amer

Abbreviations:
D   Direct
E   Eating (ingestion)
I   Inhalation
M   Milk
V   Vector-borne
Z   Zoonosis

tory. It seems unreasonable to expect that no introduction has ever occurred, and no explanation for the absence of this disease in Asia can yet be provided.

Zoonoses and Animal Reservoirs of Disease

Zoonoses are diseases of other animals, particularly mammals and birds, transmissible to man. Whereas some contemporary human diseases, such as measles or syphilis, are not known to occur naturally in other species, a great many pathogens of mankind are shared with wild and domesticated animals. The nonhuman species harboring those infections are reservoirs of the diseases in question; a vector may or may not be involved, depending upon the particular disease and circumstances. More than 150 zoonoses are now recognized (World Health Organization, 1967). The effects on human history of afflictions such as yellow fever, typhus, and African sleeping sickness are incalculable, and the great plague epidemics that swept through Europe in the Middle Ages carried off millions and left many areas virtually deserted.

No area of the world is free of zoonotic diseases. Mosquito-borne viral encephalitis may occur in epidemic proportions in Asia from the eastern U.S.S.R. through Korea and Japan southward to the great archipelagoes of the Philippines and Indonesia. In Japan, infection with Japanese encephalitis virus can spread rapidly in wild birds. *Culex* mosquitoes, which feed on birds, also are attracted to pigs. The pigs, kept near human habitations, are important amplifiers of the virus, which can cause large-scale outbreaks in man by mosquito passage.

Wild birds are not only reservoirs of viral and other diseases, but they may be important in natural spread of disease agents by virtue of their migratory habits. Millions of birds make the round trip between temperate and tropical areas each year: between North and South America, Europe and Africa, Asia and Africa, Central Asia and Sri Lanka, and other distant places. Viruses and rickettsiae may travel with them, either in their own blood and tissues or within the mites, ticks, lice, or other ectoparasites that ride along in or under the feathers. These ectoparasites and the microorganisms within them may be transferred from one end of the flight range to the other, or left at any stopping place in between. Hoogstraal (1961) has provided an account of these bird- and tick-borne infections, which may be responsible for dramatic new outbreaks of disease. In Mysore, India, for example, an unknown, virulent, and often fatal disease of man and monkeys appeared suddenly in 1957.

An agent, called Kyasanur Forest virus, was isolated from monkeys, squirrels, and other small mammals, which share certain species of vector ticks with forest birds. The virus is a member of the RSS (Russian Spring-Summer Encephalitis) group, and it is strongly suspected that a migrating bird from the North introduced the virus or perhaps a parent form from which it arose by local mutation. Many similar cases have been reported.

Migrating birds may also carry other pathogens, including bacteria and helminth (worm) parasites. A case in point is schistosome dermatitis, also known as swimmer's itch, bather's eruption, or by less restrained names. This condition may produce numerous itchy red papules in the skin of persons bathing or otherwise coming in contact with contaminated water. In addition to the birds (commonly ducks) and the disease agent, another organism is required. Rather than a tick, as in the previous example, a particular aquatic snail is needed for dissemination of the infection. The birds have in their blood vessels adult worms of a type closely related to those causing an important human disease, schistosomiasis. Eggs of the worms find their way to the water in the birds' droppings and release a swimming larva that enters the snail and causes production of thousands of larvae of a second type. These normally enter a bird and continue the cycle, but they may also wriggle into the skin of a human bather. When these larvae, lodged in the wrong host, die and disintegrate, the skin reaction is highly noticeable. The snails, permanent residents in the water body, may in times past have themselves been introduced by other migrating birds. In this way a parasite may be established far from its ancestral home. Outbreaks of schistosome dermatitis are common in the Great Lakes area of North America, in California, and in other parts of the world situated along the flyways of migrating ducks.

Of all other mammals, rodents seem most intimately related to human health and disease. The historical association of disease outbreaks with wild and domiciliated rodents (i.e., living around human habitations but not intentionally kept by man) is well established, and is by no means a thing of the past. Gerbils, rats, mice, squirrels, prairie dogs, and even guinea pigs have been incriminated as natural carriers of plague, which can occur in 200 or more species of rodents in Asia, Africa, and the Americas (World Health Organization, 1974). Humans often become involved by intruding into the wild (or sylvatic) rodent-flea-rodent cycle. Each year in the southwestern United States cases of plague occur, typically in tourists who play with dying ground squirrels believing them to be "tame," or in residents of Indian reservations who hunt the bigger rodents for food or skins.

The large area bounded roughly by Japan, northern Australia, and Pakistan is home territory for scrub typhus or Tsutsugamushi disease, a rickettsial infection notable for its focal distribution and seasonal nature in some parts of its range. As with plague, this disease is spread through intrusion of man into the natural disease patterns of wildlife and the carriage to him of the infectious agent, in this case within tiny larval mites.

Even the modern city dweller is not completely sheltered from zoonotic diseases. Tapeworms or trichinae from rare pork sausage, salmonellae from poultry or pet turtles, psittacosis from pet birds, and rabies from man's best friend serve as a constant reminder that the metropolis is separated from natural disease cycles by a thin and often penetrable veneer.

What is the point of this excursion into medical ecology? Merely this: most people feel that there is room for improvement in the health of mankind. But we cannot improve people's health without first recognizing the underlying factors, and we must start at the very beginning. For many—indeed most—people in the world today, control over their environment is minimal. When rains fail to come, they starve; and when the rains fail to stop, they starve again. Biting insects and fecal contamination are inescapable aspects of daily life, and the agents that they transmit pose a continuing menace to health and to life itself. In all countries there is a growing sensitivity to environmental deterioration. We will look at these problems in their various aspects throughout this book, and weigh proposed courses of action. It is clear that thinking about health must be grounded in an ecological viewpoint, for it is only from this direction that preventive measures can be taken.

THE HUMAN DIMENSION

It is obvious that environmental factors can affect the health of people only through their interactions with the human machine. Because the genetic makeup of any species provides the instrument upon which all outside factors impinge, an understanding of environmental forces and adaptations to them can help to reveal the inner workings of the body in relation to health and disease. This viewpoint provides the groundwork for much current discussion about the causes of certain chronic and degenerative diseases. Human habitats and characteristics are extremely diverse; attempts to correlate the prevalence of disorders with environmental and genetic factors have been limited only by the ingenuity of investigators. Many diseases, as shown on Table 1-7, are known to be under direct genetic control, but the degree to which hereditary factors influence susceptibility to others (Table 1-8) poses a great challenge to epidemiologists.

Human Genetic Adaptations

Among the billions of people on earth, no two are alike in all respects. The number of combinations of genetic characters is astronomical: a

Table 1-7. The ethnicity of disease: Some simply inherited disorders

Ethnic group	Relatively high frequency	Relatively low frequency
Ashkenazi Jews	Familial dysautonomia Pentosuria Tay-Sachs disease	Phenylketonuria
Mediterranean peoples (Italians, Greeks, Sephardic Jews)	Thalassemia (mainly β) G6PD deficiency, Mediterranean type Familial Mediterranean fever	Cystic fibrosis
Africans	Hemoglobinopathies, especially Hb S, Hb C, α- and β-thalassemia, persistent Hb F G6PD deficiency, African type Adult lactase deficiency	Cystic fibrosis Hemophilia Phenylketonuria Wilson's disease E_1^a (pseudocholinesterase deficiency) Pi^z (α_1-antitrypsin deficiency)
Japanese (Koreans)	Acatalasia Oguchi's disease Dyschromatosis universalis hereditaria	
Chinese	α-thalassemia G6PD deficiency, Chinese type Adult lactase deficiency	
Armenians	Familial Mediterranean fever	G6PD deficiency
Finns	Congenital nephrosis	Phenylketonuria Krabbe's disease
Norwegians	Cholestasis-lymphedema	
Eskimos	E_1^s (pseudocholinesterase deficiency)	

Source: McKusick, 1973.

Table 1-8. The ethnicity of disease: Some disorders with complex genetics or in which genetic factors are not proved

Ethnic group	High frequency	Low frequency
Ashkenazi Jews	Hypercholesterolemia Diabetes mellitus Polycythemia vera Kaposi's sarcoma Ulcerative colitis and regional enteritis Pemphigus vulgaris Leukemia	Cervical cancer Tuberculosis Alcoholism Pyloric stenosis
Irish	Major central nervous system malformations (anencephaly, encephalocele)	
Northern Europeans	Pernicious anemia	
Chinese	Nasopharyngeal cancer	
Japanese	Cleft lip-palate Cerebrovascular accidents Gastric carcinoma Gallbladder carcinoma (in females) Thrombosis of hepatic vein due to septum or membrane (in females) Pulseless disease (in females)	Otosclerosis Acne vulgaris Breast cancer Chronic lymphatic leukemia
Filipinos	Hyperuricemia (in U.S.)	
Polynesians (Hawaiians)	Clubfoot Coronary heart disease Diabetes mellitus	
Africans	Polydactyly Prehelical fissure Sarcoidosis Tuberculosis Hypertension Esophageal cancer Uterine fibroids Corneal arcus Cervical cancer Ainhum Keloids Lupus erythematosus, systemic	Major central nervous system malformations (anencephaly, encephalocele) Multiple sclerosis Skin cancer Osteoporosis and fracture of hip and spine Pediculosis capitis Polycythemia vera

Ethnic group	High frequency	Low frequency
		Pyloric stenosis Gallstones Psoriasis Emphysema Chronic myeloid leukemia Legg-Perthes disease
American Indians and Mexicans	Gallbladder disease Diabetes mellitus Tuberculosis Cleft lip-palate	Duodenal ulcer
American Indians, Lapps, and North Italians	Congenital dislocation of hip	
Icelanders	Glaucoma	
Eskimos	Salivary gland tumors Otitis, deafness	

Source: McKusick, 1973.

recent estimate (Cavalli-Svorza, 1974) credits each parent with donation of about 5 billion nucleotide pairs to the innocent offspring. As a consequence of small but calculable probabilities of molecular copying errors, every person differs from both parents (i.e., has mutations) on the order of 10 to 100 times. It is to a great extent these differences that provide grist for the evolutionary mill. About one-third of neutral mutations are lost to posterity because they are not passed on to offspring; about one-third are passed to one descendant, and the remainder to more than one. An advantageous mutation, (the altered form of a gene which renders its possessor more likely to survive) may spread widely in a population with the passage of generations. Conversely, disadvantageous characters are less likely to become established in a population. Mutations leading to selectively neutral characters (if indeed there are any such) may distribute themselves in populations according to the rules governing random probabilities. Cavalli-Svorza (1974) suggests an average of about 200,000 differences between any two persons both considered to be Caucasian, or

African, or Oriental, with only a slight higher number of differences between two people from different major groups. The survival value of any particular characteristic (other than an obviously lethal one) has meaning only in the context of a defined environment, and there is no doubt that the variety of selective forces in different regions of the world has been crucial in generating the diversity found among present-day human populations.

The term *natural selection* probably brings to mind some primeval struggle with "survival of the fittest" as part of the picture, but what is really meant in the present context is differential rates of reproduction. The characteristics most crucially concerned are those determining survival to and through the fertile years and those affecting success of the reproductive process itself. Early childhood is the most vulnerable period, and it is at this time that the force of mortality has historically been greatest. Adaptations increasing chances for survival to puberty are therefore highly significant. Because it takes two to reproduce and pass on their particular genomes, the procedure of mate selection becomes extremely important. Adaptations that facilitate the mating process are in this way just as much a feature of natural selection as are those related to physical survival. The plumage of birds and colorful callosities of certain primates, as well as odors, sounds and songs, and behavior patterns of many animals have been interpreted in this way by naturalists since the time of Darwin. Mate selection in human populations is a diverse and complex process, and one subject to numerous behavioral (cultural) influences. The concept of natural selection in mankind must therefore be expanded to include a cultural as well as an environmental component. A further dimension is added by the hazards of chance and genetic drift in small, isolated colonies of human beings. This aspect will be discussed again in the next chapter.

Genetic Diseases A "genetic" disease is a disease only when it is expressed phenotypically as such. One universal defect in mankind is absence of the enzyme gulonolactone oxidase, resulting in inability to synthesize ascorbic acid (vitamin C). Almost all mammals other than primates possess this enzyme and are able to traverse the pathway of biochemical steps from glucose to ascorbic acid. In consequence, extended dietary deprivation does not induce scurvy in them, and they have no requirement for vitamin C in the diet. Somewhere in an early ancestral primate a mutation occurred so that functional gulonolactone oxidase was no longer produced. With a diet rich in fruits the loss did not confer a disadvantage—rather, it may have been beneficial because of the saving in metabolic energy previously expended in production of an "unnecessary" substance. Many thousands of years after the original mutation, adventurous descendants of that primate put out to sea for months, or suffered prolonged crop losses, and came down with symptoms of scurvy. The time had finally come for the mutation to show its effect.

Other contemporary examples may be given of interactions between heredity and environment resulting in widespread disease states. One of the best known of the inheritable traits is the gene for production of hemoglobin S, a variant of normal hemoglobin differing by a single amino acid and controlled by a simple Mendelian factor. In individuals receiving this gene from both parents, a serious disease, sickle-cell anemia, occurs. When one parent donates the S gene and the other a factor for normal hemoglobin, a milder form of disease is seen, known as sickle-cell trait. The hemoglobin S gene is distributed in a broad band across Africa south of the Sahara and north of the Zambesi and Kunene Rivers, also in the Malagasy Republic (Madagascar), parts of the Middle East, India, and the Mediterranean littoral (Lehmann, 1974). The gene was introduced into the Western Hemisphere through the slave trade. It is the most widespread and clinically important of the dozens of known hemoglobin variants. Many investigators have suggested that this "molecular disease" has become widespread by virtue of the partial protection conferred by the trait towards infection with malignant tertian (falciparum) malaria. In an area of high endemicity of this condition, the variant hemoglobin (elsewhere a clearly unfavorable characteristic) appears to be selected for by differential mortality because those persons, particularly small children, possessing conventional hemoglobin are more likely to die of falciparum malaria. This illustration shows the intimacy of the partnership between the two environments on either side of the human skin and the evolutionary bartering, so to speak, of one disease for another.

A third example of a genetically determined disease, showing interactions of heredity, environment, and cultural traits, is favism. Fava beans (*Vicia fava*) are grown extensively for human food in parts of the Middle East and North Africa, where they may account for a substantial proportion of dietary protein. Some people, usually males, who eat the beans develop a disease characterized by fatigue, pallor, jaundice, and hemoglobin in the urine resulting from acute hemolytic anemia. Death from kidney failure may occur. The disease occurs principally in young children, often in weanlings upon their first exposure to the beans. Cases tend to cluster in families, and the incidence of favism varies considerably from one population to another.

Favism is related to the sex-linked genetic deficiency of glucose-6-phosphate dehydrogenase (G6PD), an enzyme of red blood cells, and to a consequent failure in the pentose phosphate pathway through which glucose is metabolized in red cells. Several forms of G6PD deficiency can occur and expression of the disease is complex, depending upon the particular genetic makeup, the form and degree of consumption of fava beans, and available medical attention. The disease usually shows a characteristic seasonal distribution with a peak at harvesting time when the fresh beans come onto local markets. Several authors have suggested that susceptible individuals may become ill just by walking through a field of fava plants in flower and inhaling the pollen. Cases have occurred in nursing G6PD-deficient infants whose normal mothers have eaten the beans: the toxic factor can cross into breast milk.

Several different varieties of fava beans are grown in producing countries, and the mode of preparation varies from place to place. Beans are sometimes eaten raw, or boiled with or without the skin, dried and stewed, or made into flour and incorporated in baked goods. The toxic factor appears to be concentrated in the skin, is heat stable, and diminishes with prolonged storage. Therefore, differences in food handling and preparation may be directly associated with differences in the expression of the disease of favism. A good review of this major Middle Eastern health problem was published by Belsey (1973).

Untangling Heredity and Environment

Disease is not randomly distributed among human beings. This deceptively simple statement is the underpinning of epidemiology, and has enormous significance for the field of international health. Recognition of the obvious inhomogeneities in health status of different individuals and groups leads to related avenues of investigation. The first is descriptive, noting the occurrence of ill health, investigating the circumstances and answering the questions *who, what, where,* and *when?* Without this information no rational assessment can be made of the relative impact of conditions and diseases. The second is analytical, building upon the descriptive data and interpreting them in the light of physiological, genetic, psychological, and other knowledge to form hypotheses of causality of disease, answering the question *why?* Why does the incidence of a disease vary by age, sex, ethnicity, activity, and occupation—and by educational, social, or financial status? In some cases the relationships are fairly straightforward; in others, particularly the malignant and degenerative diseases, a very large amount of work still needs to be done, but in all cases the analytic approach leads towards an explanation of what causes the condition in question. A knowledge of causality can then direct efforts aimed at prevention. This logical sequence is self-evident and would not merit lengthy discussion here were it not for the crucial role that international health studies have played in all its phases. In many situations comparative studies in different countries are indispensable because the variety of conditions encountered is unavailable in any one of them. The association of various risk factors with atherosclerosis is a good example. Diet and serum lipids, hypertension, cigarette smoking, diabetes, psycho-social relationships, heredity, and other factors have been assessed and compared in many different localities. For example, the International Atherosclerosis Project (McGill, 1968) has evaluated the degree of atherosclerosis of the aorta and coronary arteries in more than 31,000 persons autopsied between 1960 and 1965 in 15 cities in North America, Europe, Asia, Africa, and Latin America. This study found that, with respect to the severity of atherosclerotic disease, "the differences related to geographic location seem more prominent than racial or sex differences. This finding . . . supports the prevalent opinion that severe atherosclerosis is primarily due to environmental conditions." Severity of atherosclerosis was found to be associated with the proportion of total calories derived from dietary fat, and with serum cholesterol concentration. No association was found with water hardness. Extensive comparisons of risk factors in atherosclerosis are still in progress in various studies.

It is not only for heart disease, stroke, and cancer that wide-ranging studies are needed. Infectious disease control has also relied heavily on international comparisons. It is clearly not enough, for instance, to say that tuberculosis is caused by infection with tubercle bacilli. Such infection is a necessary, but not a sufficient condition for production of clinical disease, and indeed most people infected with tubercle bacilli never have symptoms or show signs of tuberculosis. Other factors, having to do with innate and acquired characteristics of each particular person, must determine the course of infection and severity of expression of any resultant disease.

Numerous attempts have been made to evaluate the relative contributions of heredity and environment to particular aspects of health. At one extreme lie the conditions known to be inherited according to Mendelian principles; the frequencies for relevant alleles vary from one population to another (Table 1-7). Environment plays relatively little part in the expression of many of these conditions, although some may be ameliorated by appropriate medical attention. At the other extreme are diseases such as rabies or botulism; trauma from aircraft accident, fire, or disaster; and similar hazards against which an individual's genetic makeup offers little protection. Between the extremes lies the great number of tendencies, conditions, and diseases that form the bulk of ill health in human populations.

Blood Factors and Infectious Diseases Of all human hereditary characteristics, blood factors are among the most commonly studied because the logistics of sample collection, storage, and analysis are well adapted to this sort of investigation. Blood contains many discrete factors, distinguishable by fairly straightforward techniques, unchanging during the life of the individual, and inherited according to relatively well-understood genetic rules. At present we know about sixty different systems of genetic polymorphisms in blood types, and gene frequencies for any or all of these may vary widely from one population to another. Many investigators have attempted to correlate the relative proportions of certain alleles with prevalence of specific diseases. Examples of such statistical associations are blood group A with carcinoma of the stomach; and group O with duodenal ulcer and hemorrhage in women taking contraceptives (Mourant, 1973). The example of hemoglobins and falciparum malaria has already been mentioned, but more subtle associations are being sought among the "polymorphisms where none of the variants has any obvious effect on health, but where... in certain extreme environments, such as exposure to certain infections, one allele is more favoured than another" (Mourant, 1973). Once again malaria may serve as an example. Wood (1974) has suggested that *Anopheles gambiae* mosquitoes feed more often on persons of blood group O than on those with the other ABO phenotypes. Therefore, Wood postulates, in areas where malaria is a continuous threat a difference in number of bites represents a potential difference in malarial infection rates and "in determining whom to bite and whom to spare the anopheline... may act as a critical agent of selection."

Differences in the distribution of blood factors from one population to another not only may influence the diseases occurring in those populations but also may reflect past and present experience with various infectious agents. This is true for the blood-group factors such as the A and B antigens carried on the surface of the red cells, the hemoglobins inside them, and the multitude of substances found in the fluid plasma. In a comparison of Nigerian and Swiss blood donors (Houba and Rowe, 1973), it was found that the amount of a certain serum protein, the immunoglobulin IgE, was very different in the two populations. In Switzerland 64% of the donors had no detectable IgE and the highest level seen was 1,600 international units (I.U.). In Ibadan 78% of donors had between 2,000 and 20,000 I.U., a highly signficant difference. Previous investigators had suggested that high levels of IgE occur in infections with various worm parasites such as *Ascaris, Trichuris,* and hookworms, and this interpretation seems valid. The biological role of IgE and the possible heritability of the capacity to make it are as yet unknown. Comparative international studies in populations having different burdens of worm parasites are likely to provide information about this substance, and to help elucidate the basic workings of the immune system in man.

Ethnicity It is difficult and perhaps unrewarding to define ethnic groups, but insofar as these have objective reality, the attempt will inevitably be made. MacMahon and Pugh (1970) suggest that they are "groups of persons who have a greater degree of homogeneity than the population at large with respect to present-day customs and/or biological inheritance." Some disorders of complex origin, varying in frequency in different ethnic groups, have been tabulated by McKusick (Table 1-8).

Incidence rates for specific diseases are often compared when different ethnic groups reside permanently in the same region. Gelfand (1971, 1976) has made such a comparison for his Caucasian and African patients in Rhodesia. Diseases common or well-known in Europeans but rare in Africans include coronary thrombosis, diabetes mellitus in children, infant leukemia, and carcinoma of the breast. Endocrine disorders such as Cushing's syndrome, Addison's disease, and thyrotoxicosis are also in this category. Africans, on the other hand, were found to have considerable excess of liver cancer and Kaposi's sarcoma, essential thrombocytopenia, acute polyarteritis, tropical ulcer, and myositis. The two groups have very different ways of life, particularly with respect to nutrition and exposure to infectious, insect-borne and parasitic organisms. A comparison of these risk factors may provide working hypotheses for further investigation. The example of Burkitt's lymphoma comes immediately to mind. This highly malignant tumor of children was first described definitively by Burkitt (1958), who later showed that it is limited roughly to those parts of Africa in which the average temperature of the coolest months is at least 17.5°C (60°F) and average rainfall is greater than 508 mm (20 inches) (Burkitt and Wright, 1970). In some areas, such as Uganda, this particular tumor accounts for fully 50% of all childhood malignancies, and it has been found in Caucasian, Indian, and Lebanese children living in the endemic zone. Investigators have suggested the possibility that the tumor may be caused by a viral agent spread by an insect vector. Subsequent discovery that the same sort of tumor occurs in New Guinea and tropical South America under similar ecological conditions has greatly stimulated research efforts. It has been suggested that children whose reticuloendothelial system has been stressed, perhaps by malaria, may be particularly liable to develop lymphomas when infected with a certain viral agent. A herpeslike virus, which has been isolated from Burkitt's tumor patients, may be identical with that producing infectious mononucleosis in young adults in temperate areas. The growing web of associations enmeshes African children and American college students, viruses and vectors, climate and locality; and it demonstrates the complexity of relationships between man and nature.

Another example of a comparison between ethnic groups in the same area is illustrated in Figure 1-2, which shows the significant excess of hypertensive heart disease in American blacks when compared with American whites. Note that the left-hand scale is logarithmic. Hypertensive heart disease is present in 20.8% of the total adult black population and 8.2% of adult whites, but coronary heart disease, while less common in both groups, is slightly more prevalent among whites. Although these differences have been repeatedly confirmed, causal factors are still unknown. Hypotheses include genetics, diet, environmental stress, and effect of medical care.

Complementary to studies of different ethnic groups in the same area are observations upon a single ethnic group in different parts of the world. The Japanese in Japan, Hawaii, and mainland United States have been subjects of repeated investigations. Traditional Japanese culture and diet have generally been retained among Hawaiian Japanese to a greater degree than among those on the mainland. In Japan, mortality rates for diseases of the heart are low when compared with white Americans; but deaths from vascular lesions of the central nervous system (stroke) are more common. Death rates for both heart disease and stroke are intermediate among Hawaiian Japanese (Gordon, 1957). Gastric cancer is relatively common in Japan but rare among white Americans. Among Japanese immigrants incidence of gastric cancer is lower in Hawaii than

Figure 1-2

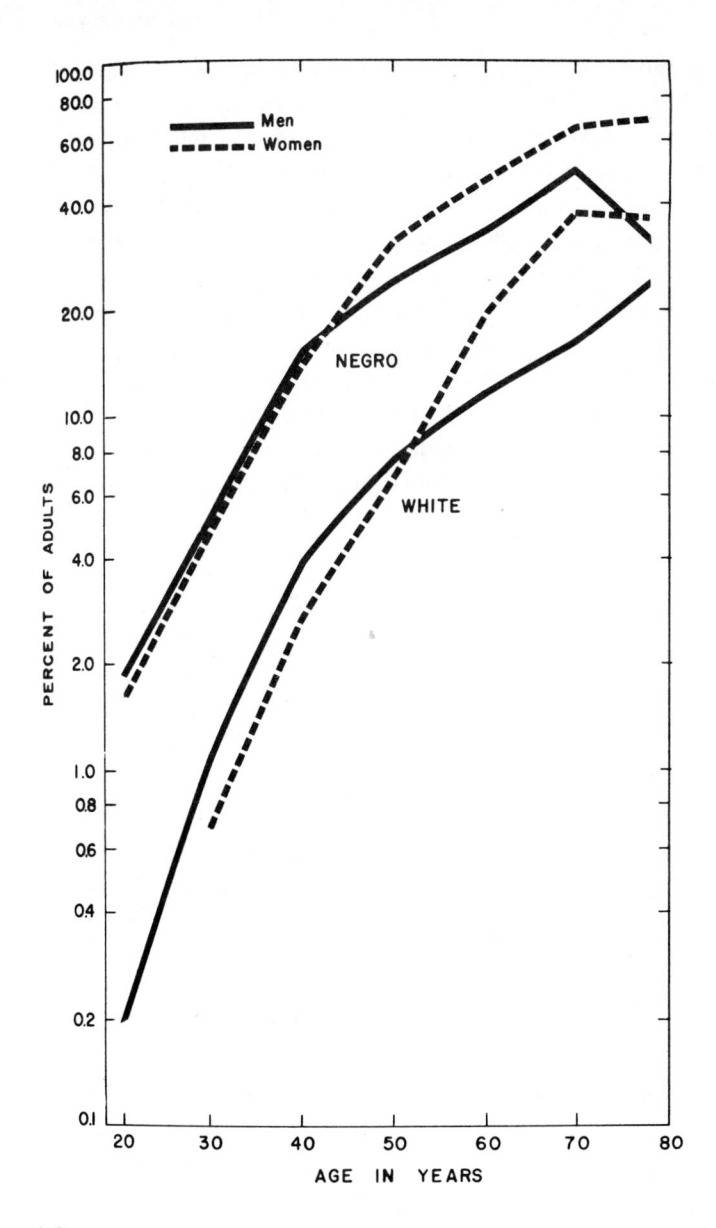

Prevalence of definite hypertensive disease among adults by age, race, and sex, U.S. 1960–62. SOURCE: Gordon and Devine, 1966.

in Japan, and lower still on the U.S. mainland. In American-born Japanese the incidence of gastric cancer is about the same as in other Americans (Haenszel and Kurihara, 1968). The adaptation with respect to colon cancer is similar, although opposite in direction (Fig. 1-3). It is likely that environmental conditions, perhaps food, are important in the genesis of this form of cancer and that a genetic predisposition among Japanese, if it does exist, is not expressed in the American milieu.

An example of a presumed ethnic predisposition that has been retained in a distant country is the relative insusceptibility of black Africans to infection with vivax malaria. Young and colleagues (1955) reported on experiments in which 104 Americans of African descent and 529 Americans of European descent were infected with the causative organism. Whereas 96.2% of the Caucasians developed the disease, only

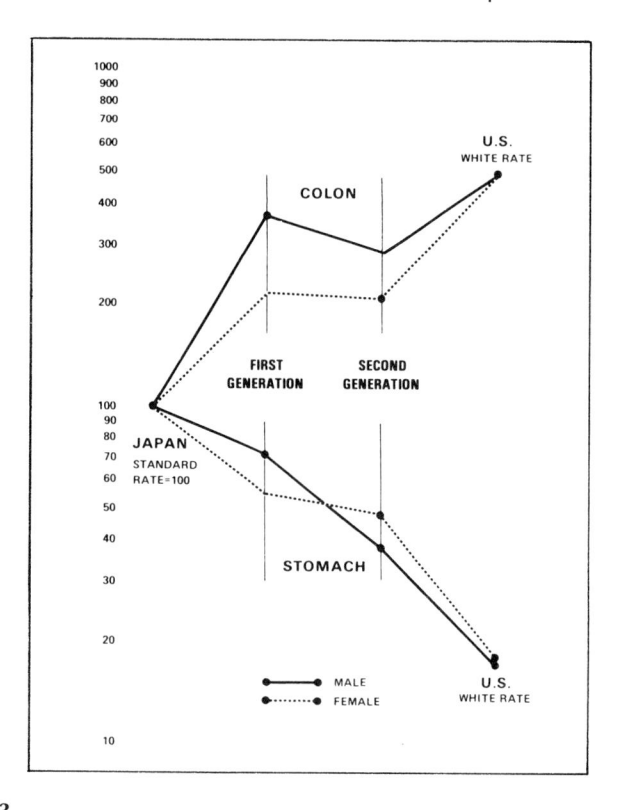

Figure 1-3

Mortality trends of Japanese migrants to the U.S. SOURCE: Gori and Peters, 1975; after data from Haenszel et al.

23.1% of the blacks showed evidence of infection. Twenty-one years later, Miller et al. (1976) reported a similar trial in which the presumed mechanism of susceptibility to vivax malaria was identified as a "Duffy determinant", a glycoprotein substance on the surface of human red blood cells. The genetically controlled absence of this substance, detectable as Duffy blood-group negative red cells, leads to resistance to parasite invasion. The Duffy-negative condition is common in Africa, affecting up to 100% of some populations, but usually rare elsewhere. Gelpi and King (1976) have shown in a small population within Saudi Arabia that 84% of persons with sickle-cell trait also were Duffy-negative. These people until recent years were exposed to both vivax and falciparum malaria, common in oases of eastern Arabia. It is proposed that the concurrence of these particular hemoglobin and cell-surface variants indicates the past introduction of these genes from black Africans and their maintenance through selection pressures exerted by two species of malaria.

Studies such as these are open to numerous interpretations and may raise more questions than they answer, but repeated observations in many areas over a span of years are helping to piece together the relative contributions of different factors to the genesis of many diseases.

Aspects of human biology not directly related to disease are also responding to changes in the heredity-environment complex. Consider, for example, human stature and rate of maturation. In the last 50 to 100 years children in developed countries have become substantially larger at all ages, and the average age at which growth stops has also declined. "At the turn of the century men reached their full height at around 20, whereas in Europe and America today they do so at 18 or 19" (Tanner, 1968). Although there has been a trend toward taller adult size, much of the increase in the size of children is apparently related to their earlier maturation. In girls, menarche (first menstrual period) is a well-defined event, and in a given population the distribution of ages at which it occurs follows the normal bell-shaped curve. Records from England, other European countries and parts of America were analyzed by Tanner (1968), who showed that age at menarche has declined by three to four months per decade over the past hundred years so that puberty is now attained, on average, $2\frac{1}{2}$ to $3\frac{1}{2}$ years earlier than a century ago. Although there is some genetic difference between certain populations, the reduction in age at menarche and the increase in stature are usually attributed to improved nutrition. In searching for the environmental factors responsible for "improved nutrition" we enter a morass. Is it fertilizers, tractors, food technology, marketing systems, parental income, changed habits, all of these, or something else?

Those who would duplicate the benefit of "improved nutrition" in those areas of the world that are underfed at present must grapple with a large number of potential ways to increase food quality and variety and availability. They must also ponder the effects of improved nutrition upon population growth. If the pattern described above will hold in developing countries, declining age at menarche may lead to lengthened reproductive life and a larger number of births per mother. Improved infant nutrition will lead to reduced mortality and still higher populations, at least in the short run, but many believe that the eventual effect of greater survival in childhood will be a lowering of birth rates and onset of the demographic transition (see Chapter 3).

Changing Environments

The surroundings in which human beings find themselves are clearly impermanent. The slow alternation of glacial and interglacial periods, imperceptible within the span of lifetimes, contrasts with the sudden earthquake or volcanic eruption, but each may have profound effects upon the health of involved populations. Most environmental changes of interest to us fall within an intermediate range, taking place over periods of years or centuries, and many of these have come about as a result of human activities.

Mention of environmental changes, particularly in the so-called developed countries, usually evokes images of factories discharging effluents, polluting air and water. Such factories certainly do exist and do affect health, but environmental change as considered here is far broader than this. At the simplest level, virtually every human activity results in some environmental change: picking a fruit, felling a tree, building a fire, killing a bear—all leave the immediate microenvironment slightly altered. In a large area, over many years, the accumulation of small events may result in profound changes. The desertification of much of northern India, for instance, is thought to have occurred by gradual destruction of the original forest in early historic times. Parts of North Africa, now desert, were wheat fields during Roman times. It seems reasonable to suppose that wherever and whenever a sufficient number of people has accumulated, significant changes in the environment have occurred.

The recent development of technology has given rise to an infinity of mechanical, chemical, and electrical devices that have made great changes in the environment of almost every human being. Automobiles, refrigerators, and computers are quite obviously inventions, and they have a impact upon health. But the industrial corporations producing these items are also inventions of man, as are the cities, governments, customs, religions, and myriad other less conspicuous gears whose turning moves the machinery of modern society. All of these are environmental factors that interact with each other and with the minds and bodies of human population and together exert a profound influence on health.

References

Ajello, L. 1956. The soil as a natural reservoir for human pathogenic fungi. Science 123: 876–878.
Astolfi, E. 1971. Estudio de arsénico en agua de consumo. Hidrarsenicismo crónico regional endémico. Prensa Medica Argentina 58: 1342–1343.
Aykroyd, W. R. 1970. Conquest of Deficiency Diseases; Achievements and Prospects. Geneva. World Health Organization Basic Studies Series No. 24. 98 p.
Belsey, M. A. 1973. The epidemiology of favism. Bulletin of the World Health Organization 48: 1–13.
Berg, A. 1973. The Nutrition Factor: Its Role in National Development. Washington. The Brookings Institution. 290 p.
Buck, A. A., T. T. Sasaki, and R. I. Anderson. 1968. Health and Disease in Four Peruvian Villages. Baltimore. Johns Hopkins Press. 142 p.
Burkitt, D. P. 1958. A sarcoma involving the jaws in African children. British Journal of Surgery 46: 218–223.
Burkitt, D. P. and D. H. Wright. 1970. Burkitt's Lymphoma. Edinburgh. Livingstone. 251 p.
Cavalli-Svorza, L. 1974. The genetics of human populations. Scientific American 231: 80–89.
Cruickshank, R. 1976. Streptococcal infections and sequelae. In: R. Cruickshank, K. L. Standard, and H. B. L. Russell, Eds. Epidemiology and Community Health in Warm Climate Countries. Edinburgh. Churchill Livingstone. pp. 50–56.
Eaton, R. D. P. 1968. Amebiasis in northern Saskatchewan: epidemiological considerations. Canadian Medical Association Journal 99: 706–711.
Edman, M. 1964. Nutrition and climate. In: S. Licht, Ed. Medical Climatology. New Haven. E. Licht. pp. 533–556.
Eisenbud, M. 1973. Environmental Radioactivity. 2d Ed. New York. Academic Press. 542 p.
Fierro-Benitez, R., W. Penafiel, L. J. deGroot, and I. Ramirez. 1969. Endemic goiter and endemic cretinism in the Andean region. New England Journal of Medicine 280: 296–302.

Folk, C. E., Jr. 1974. Textbook of Environmental Physiology. 2d Ed. Philadelphia. Lea & Febiger. 465 p.
Gelfand, M. 1971. The patterns of disease in Africa. Central African Journal of Medicine 17: 69-78.
Gelfand, M. 1976. The pattern of disease in Africa and the western way of life. Tropical Doctor 6: 173-179.
Gelpi, A. P. and M. C. King. 1976. Association of Duffy blood groups with the sickle cell trait. Human Genetics 32: 65-68.
Gelpi, A. P. and A. Mustafa. 1967. Seasonal pneumonitis with eosinophilia. A study of larval ascariasis in Saudi Arabs. American Journal of Tropical Medicine and Hygiene 16: 646-657.
Gordon, T. 1957. Mortality experience among the Japanese in the United States, Hawaii, and Japan. Public Health Reports 72: 543-553.
Gordon, T. and B. Devine. 1966. Hypertension and hypertensive disease in adults, U.S., 1960-62. U.S. Public Health Service Publication 1000, Series 11, No. 13. 62 p.
Gori, G. B. and J. A. Peters. 1975. Etiology and prevention of cancer. Preventive Medicine 4: 239-246.
Haenszel, W. and M. Kurihara. 1968. Studies of Japanese migrants. 1. Mortality from cancer and other diseases among Japanese in the United States. Journal of the National Cancer Institute 40: 43-68.
Hesse, B., W. C. Allee, and K. P. Schmidt. 1951. Ecological Animal Geography. 2d Ed. New York. John Wiley and Sons. 715 p.
Hoogstraal, H. 1961. Migrating birds and their ectoparasites in relation to disease. East African Medical Journal 38: 221-226.
Hopps, H. C. 1971. Geographic pathology and the medical implications of environmental geochemistry. In: H. L. Cannon and H. C. Hopps, Eds. Environmental Geochemistry in Health and Disease. Boulder, Colo. The Geological Society of America. pp. 1-11.
Houba, V. and D. S. Rowe. 1973. A comparison of African and European serum levels of immunoglobulin E. Bulletin of the World Health Organization 49: 539-545.
Hughes, C. C. and J. M. Hunter. 1970. Disease and "Development" in Africa. Social Science and Medicine 3: 443-493.
Hurtado, A. 1964. Animals in high altitudes: resident man. In: D. B. Dill, E. F. Adolph, and C. G. Wilber, Eds. Handbook of Physiology. 4. Adaptation to The Environment. Washington. American Physiological Society. pp. 843-860.
Jackson, D., J. J. Murray, and C. G. Fairpo. 1973. Lifelong benefits of fluoride in drinking water. British Dental Journal 134: 419-422.
Kelly, F. C. and W. W. Snedden. 1960. Prevalence and geographical distribution of endemic goitre. World Health Organization Monograph Series 44: 27-233.
Langer, P. 1960. History of goitre. World Health Organization Monograph Series 44: 9-25.
Lehmann, H. 1974. Haemoglobinopathies. In: A. W. Woodruff, Ed. Medicine in the Tropics. Edinburgh. Churchill Livingstone. pp. 465-503.

Lin, C-p and T-y Wu. 1974. Clinical analysis of 286 cases of pediatric high altitude heart disease. Chinese Medical Journal 1974: 99–100 (English abstract).

MacMahon, B. and T. F. Pugh. 1970. Epidemiology—Principles and Methods. Boston. Little, Brown & Co. 376 p.

Masironi, R., A. T. Miesch, M. D. Crawford, and E. I. Hamilton. 1973. Geochemical environments, trace elements, and cardiovascular diseases. Bulletin of the Pan American Health Organization 7: 53–64.

McClung, J. 1969. Effects of High Altitude on Human Birth; Observations on Mothers, Placentas, and the Newborn in Two Peruvian Populations. Cambridge, Mass. Harvard University Press. 150 p.

McGill, H. C., Jr., Ed. 1968. Geographic Pathology of Atherosclerosis. Laboratory Investigation 18: 463–654.

McKusick, V. A. 1973. Ethnic distribution of disease in non-Jews. Israel Journal of the Medical Sciences 9: 1375–1382.

Miller, L. H., S. J. Mason, D. F. Clyde, and M. H. McGinniss. 1976. The resistance factor to *Plasmodium vivax* in Blacks. New England Journal of Medicine 295: 302–304.

Mourant, A. E. 1973. Associations between hereditary blood factors and diseases. Bulletin of the World Health Organization 49: 93–101.

Pampana, E. 1963. A Textbook of Malaria Eradication. London. Oxford University Press. 508 p.

Peñaloza, D., F. Sime, and L. Ruiz. 1971. Cor pulmonale in chronic mountain sickness; present concepts of Monge's Disease. *In:* R. Porter and J. Knight, Eds. High Altitude Physiology: Cardiac and Respiratory Aspects. Edinburgh. Churchill Livingstone. pp. 41–52.

Pineo, C. S. and D. V. Subramanyam. 1975. Community Water Supply and Excreta Disposal Situation in the Developing Countries. World Health Organization Offset Publication 15. 41 p.

Poskitt, E. M. E. 1972. Seasonal variation in infection and malnutrition at a rural paediatric clinic in Uganda. Transactions of the Royal Society of Tropical Medicine and Hygiene 66: 931–936.

Price, E. W. 1976. The association of endemic elephantiasis of the lower legs in East Africa with soil derived from volcanic rocks. Transactions of the Royal Society of Tropical Medicine and Hygiene 70: 288–295.

Sandstead, H. H., A. S. Prasad, A. R. Schulert, Z. Farid, A. Miale, Jr., S. Bassilly, and W. J. Darby. 1967. Human zinc deficiency, endocrine manifestations and response to treatment. American Journal of Clinical Nutrition 20: 422–442.

Shaper, A. G. 1974. Cardiovascular diseases. *In:* A. W. Woodruff, Ed. Medicine in the Tropics. Edinburgh. Churchill Livingstone. pp. 553–578.

Singh, A., R. Dass, S. S. Hayreh, and S. S. Jolly. 1962. Skeletal changes in endemic fluorosis. Journal of Bone and Joint Surgery 44B: 806–815.

Stallones, R. A. 1971. Environment, Ecology and Epidemiology. Pan American Health Organization Scientific Publication No. 231. 15 p.

Tanner, J. M. 1968. Earlier maturation in man. Scientific American 218: 21–27.

Teotia, M., S. P. Teotia, and K. B. Kunwar. 1971. Endemic skeletal fluorosis. Archives of Diseases of Childhood 46: 686–691.

Tromp, S. C. 1963. Medical Biometeorology: Weather, Climate and the Living Organism. Amsterdam. Elsevier Publishing Co. 991 p.

Waldmann, E. 1973. Seasonal variation in malnutrition in Africa. Transactions of the Royal Society of Tropical Medicine and Hygiene 67: 431.

Wood, C. S. 1974. Preferential feeding of *Anopheles gambiae* mosquitoes on human subjects of blood group O: A relationship between the ABO polymorphism and malaria vectors. Human Biology 46: 385–404.

World Health Organization. 1967. Joint FAO/WHO Expert Committee on Zoonoses. Third Report. Technical Report Series, No. 378. 127 p.

World Health Organization. 1969. International work in cardiovascular diseases. Part 3. Research (continued). WHO Chronicle 23: 477–485.

World Health Organization. 1974. Ecology and Control of Rodents of Public Health Importance. Technical Report Series, No. 553. 42 p.

Young, M. D., D. E. Eyles, R. W. Burgess, and G. M. Jeffery. 1955. Experimental testing of the immunity of Negroes to *Plasmodium vivax*. Journal of Parasitology 41: 315–318.

THE PAST   2.

The preceding chapter dealt with some health consequences of the many interactions between man and environment. We will now consider some historical trends that have influenced the present picture of human health. Every shift of population, every political change, war, and invention has in some way left its mark, but only a general overview can be given here.

ANCIENT MAN

The recent discoveries of stone tools and skeletal remains of early hominids approximately 2 million years old in the Olduvai Gorge of East Africa have greatly extended the known prehistory of manlike primates. Fossil hominids more than a million years old have also been found in northern Africa and in Asia, and northern European remains approach that age. *Homo erectus,* considered by some ancestral to our own species (*H. sapiens*), is thought to have radiated from China and Java westward to Europe and Africa about 100,000 to 400,000 years ago (Davis, 1974). *H. sapiens* probably evolved during the middle to late Pleistocene (250,000 to 100,000 BC) In the absence of evidence we may imagine life during this period in the words of Thomas Hobbes's *Leviathan* (1651) "no arts; no letters; no society; and which is worst of all, continual fear and danger of violent death; and the life of man, solitary, poor, nasty, brutish, and short." Nevertheless, the many cave paintings of Spain and France done more recently in upper Paleolithic times (10,000 to 30,000 years ago) are evidence of substantial cultural development. Sigerist (1951), in his monumental though uncompleted history of medicine, mentions traces of medical lore in Neolithic times, which began perhaps ten to twelve thousand years ago. During this period agriculture and animal husbandry had their beginnings, and a variety of tools was used to build huts, clear forests, and make baskets and pottery.

Paleopathology Study of ancient remains shows that health problems of early man were, in some respects, not very different from those we know today. Most of the evidence for ancient diseases is found in bones, but careful sifting through the earth beneath some remains has yielded ova of intestinal parasites, and in some cases human feces thousands of year old have been preserved well enough for identification of these worm eggs. Mummies found in Egypt, China, and elsewhere have been rich sources of medical information and have shown that schistosomiasis, arteriosclerosis, emphysema, silicosis and anthracosis are long-standing maladies of man (Wells, 1964). Sigerist (1951) cites a study of 500 skulls of aristocrats from the Old Kingdom of Egypt in which tartar formation, dental caries, and alveolar abscesses were no less common than in modern Europeans; by contrast, the teeth of persons from the poorer classes of that era, accustomed to a coarse and uncooked diet, were in much better condition. Disturbances in development such as dwarfism and clubfoot are demonstrated in early remains, and osteomyelitis, gout, spondylitis, and tuberculosis all register their presence in ancient bones. Rickets occurred in neolithic bones in Denmark, but, as may be expected, has not been recorded from tropical areas. Gallstones and bladderstones have remained in place in some prehistoric burials. Of the many infectious diseases little is known but there seems no reason to doubt their presence.

In the hunting-gathering stage of human development the small size of social groups and low degree of contact among them would probably have limited epidemics. The number of new susceptible people available in such bands was probably not enough to maintain the infective agent once an immunity-producing disease had run its course. Afflictions such as head and body lice, pinworms, yaws, and malaria most likely evolved along with man from their primate ancestors; vector-borne and zoonotic diseases must have resulted in a great deal of ill health among early human groups exposed to them.

The establishment of agricultural settlements brought new problems, which have been reviewed by Polgar (1964). These include the increasing intensity of contaminative diseases spread via human feces, which would have accumulated to a greater degree around fixed abodes than near temporary nomadic camps. In addition, environmental alterations associated with agriculture, and particularly the keeping of herds, may have provided harbors or breeding sites for rodent and insect carriers of disease.

Health hazards associated with the development of settlements have not been limited to ancient times. There have been analogous situations down through the millenia. In the decades following the Russian Revolution in 1917, for example, outbreaks of severe disease occurred among road builders, woodcutters, and settlers in new communities being developed in the taiga and steppe regions. Many persons died, and others were permanently paralyzed. The dramatic nature of these outbreaks stimulated investigation and led to the discovery of tick-borne encephalitis, spirochetosis, relapsing fever, and other diseases in these remote, formerly uninhabited regions. These diseases had several common elements: association with particular habitats or even specific locations, animal reservoirs, and often, arthropod vectors. Outbreaks among humans resulted from intrusion into natural disease cycles occurring in the local fauna, particularly rodents, around whose burrows the agents and vectors were concentrated. The highly localized infective site was likened by Pavlovsky (n.d.) to a nest (in Latin, *nidus*) of disease, and the ideas of nidality and of "landscape epidemiology" followed. Pioneering development in new areas, for instance in the Brazilian Amazon, results in similar disease outbreaks to the present day.

Ancient Medical Care Not surprisingly, very little is known about the care of the sick and injured in prehistoric times. It is likely that herbs, incantations, and bonesetting were employed, and obstetrical practices of some sort were probably developed. In many regions, including Europe and the Pacific, trephining of the skull was practiced, a surgical procedure that reached its peak of perfection in the mountains of Peru. These daring operations in which a hole was cut through the skull may have been undertaken for ritual purposes or for treatment of epilepsy or some other disorder. The frequently successful outcome of trephining is attested to by the hundreds of skulls found healing neatly with the growth of new bone into the periphery of the aperture. The procedure itself has been described imaginatively by Selzer (1975):

There he squats, his back braced against a tree trunk, the patient's head firmly held between his knees. He selects a sharp-edged stone or fleam and makes an incision in the scalp, then bores into and through the bone. Such a stone, if expertly used, can penetrate the human skull in five minutes. He exchanges the dull stone for a new sharp one and bores another hole adjacent to the first, and so on until a complete circle of holes is made. These holes are joined and the disk of bone is lifted out... What a glorious enterprise was his! Alone, beneath the open sky, no team of consultants, assistants, and nurses milling about... Only his crafty hands, sharp stones, and compassion for his injured tribesman. One thrills at his performance.

EARLY HISTORICAL TIMES

The development of civilizations with urban commercial and ceremonial centers surrounded by agricultural lands marked an enormous turning point in human history. Populations became concentrated in such numbers that water supply and sanitation became critically important. Engineering works such as reservoirs and water distribution systems were built, for instance, by Aztecs, Mayas, and Incas in the Western Hemisphere; by the peoples of the eastern Mediterranean; by the Khmers, Aryans, and Chinese. Sometimes existing lakes were incorporated into the systems. Custom, ritual, and perhaps political sanction must have developed regarding the use of water for domestic and agricultural purposes. Waterborne diseases such as cholera, typhoid fever, and leptospirosis may have occurred in early epidemics wherever the proper microorganisms and sufficient population coexisted. Mosquito breeding sites and, in some areas, snail habitats created by those developments undoubtedly led to endemization of malaria, yellow fever, and schistosomiasis where conditions were favorable. As populations grew, sewage and waste disposal became more pressing problems. Urban dwellers became vulnerable to food shortages as artisan, priest, and trader depended for their nutrition upon the labor of others, and all were subject to the vagaries of weather as well as to insects and to other natural hazards.

In short, the basic ecological situations that still govern the welfare of much of contemporary mankind were established, in various regions, from about the fifth millenium BC to the first millenium AD.

Travels of Man in Antiquity

Three types of human movements should be distinguished. The first, and probably oldest, is the cyclical or irregular travel of a small group or band in a circumscribed area, perhaps following the seasons and availability of fruit and game. Hunter-gatherer groups must have moved in such orbits. The second is actual geographic migration from one area to another, with establishment of permanent residence in the new locality. Planned or unintentional ocean voyages have carried individuals or groups to distant shores. Thor Heyerdahl demonstrated this on the Kon-Tiki expedition, in which he and his companions drifted 3,700 miles from Peru to the island of Raroia in Polynesia. The island peoples of the Pacific must have had skills in sailing and navigation. Persons from Malaya, Sumatra, and Java migrated to Madagascar in ancient times, and the most remote piece of land on earth, Easter Island, was settled by the fourth century BC. Continual, slow extension of range overland resulted in the occupancy of North and South America by emigrants from Asia about 20,000 years ago, and other continental areas were being colonized in the same general time period. The number of humans on earth in ancient times is a matter of speculation. Coale (1974) hazards an educated guess of eight million at the dawn of agriculture, about 8000 BC.

The third kind of human travel falls under the very general rubric of "visiting", or movement from one place to another with the intention of returning. Invader or marauders raiding adjacent or distant groups seized slaves, wives, cattle, or goods. Establishment of permanent settlements was followed by roads or tracks between them, and by the time of the Bronze Age in Europe, for instance, trails had been established from the Atlantic to the Caspian and from Scandinavia to Italy. Trading followed or accompanied raiding, and early commerce gradually developed.

Records of travels and voyages are available from early classical times onwards, although some may be questionable. Phoenecian navigators reached Spain and Britain, and may have circumnavigated Africa about 600 BC; Carthaginians had commerce with West Africa (Guinea?) in the following century. By Greek and Roman times travel was well established, and even elephants from India were well known in Italy in the third and fourth centuries BC. Three ancient "silk roads" linked China, India, and Rome, and an alternate overland route passed from China through Yunnan and Burma to India. In the time of the emperor Trajan (AD 98–117) the Roman Empire extended from Scotland to the Sahara and from the Atlantic to the Persian Gulf, but goods of Mediterranean origin found their way to more remote places. Phoenecian beads have been discovered in Sarawak, on the island of Borneo, and Roman beads in Southern Malaya (Hoeppli, 1959). Articles originating in China have been unearthed in excavations at Zimbabwe in constructions dating from about the ninth century AD, a result of commerce existing a thousand years ago between the interior of Africa and trading settlements on the southeastern coast of the continent.

"The world," said Siegfried (1965), "is infinitely more permeable than one would believe." Since the earliest days, articles of booty or commerce, along with genes, infectious agents, and ideas have been distributed within and between human populations. Concepts relating to the body, to maintenance of health, and to avoidance or cure of disease were disseminated along the paths of human movements. Charms, amulets, herbs, and drugs were items of trade and exchange, and some early travels were undertaken specifically for purposes of medical learning. For example, a Chinese scholar traveled to Baghdad about AD 400, learned Arabic, and copied the works of Galen; later Arab scholars in turn collected writings on Indian, Chinese, Persian, Greek, and Roman medicine (Hoeppli, 1959). If we are to understand present-day cultural concepts and attitudes, or the distribution of certain genetic factors in populations, attention must be paid to their historical development.

GREECE AND ROME

An abundance of writings and artifacts from the Mediterranean classical periods has survived to modern times, and there is no lack of description and commentary upon medical practice at that time. It is clear that the Greek tradition did not spring fully formed from the pen of Hippocrates, but developed as an accretion and elaboration of previous ideas. From the Minoans came ideas of hygiene, healing temples, and the association with serpents still seen today in the caduceus, symbol of medicine. Egypt contributed its pharmaceutical lore and surgical techniques; Mesopotamia (present-day Iraq and Iran), different drugs and basic organization of medical practice. From all these sources were blended magical and mystical ideas. Later contributions, particularly from Sicily, brought the concept of four elements and their balance, the idea of *pneuma* or vital spirit, and rudiments of dissection. Persian and Indian elements were also incorporated into the Greek medical lore of around 300 BC (Singer and Underwood, 1962).

An essential part of Greek thinking was the early idea of balance of the four basic elements: fire, water, air, and earth. To each of these elements there was later associated one of the four bodily humors: blood, black bile, yellow bile, and phlegm, respectively, with behavioral characteristics assigned to persons according to their predominant humor. Those strong in the blood-fire combination were sanguine—fat, with hot blood, and prone to laughter. Excess of black bile produced a melancholy disposition—peevish, depressed, and passive, while yellow bile made people choleric—violent and fierce. Phlegmatic persons, slow and plodding, made up the last of the four primary categories (Wain, 1970). These terms still retain some descriptive utility and remain in common usage even though the underlying associations have long since been discarded. The basic idea of bodily humors, with illness ascribed to their imbalance, is a recurrent theme in many philosophic systems, not only in India and China but throughout the world, as will be discussed in Chapter 4.

A strong rational element existed in Greek medical thought, wherein clear descriptions of diseases such as tuberculosis, malaria, epilepsy, and puerperal fever were recorded. Signs and symptoms were carefully observed and reasonable prognoses were made as to the outcome of episodes of illness. Many medicinal plants were known, collected, used, and recorded. The importance of hygiene, sport, good diet, and clean water were recognized, and individual and social well-being were emphasized. Yet despite the superb natural history of Aristotle, Greek medicine was deficient in practical knowledge of anatomy and physiology, failings that were to play a role in European medicine for well over a millenium.

The aqueducts, baths, and public conveniences of Rome are too well known to require description here, but the state of medical knowledge can be briefly mentioned. The hard lot of workers and slaves gave rise to studies of occupational diseases. Martial wrote on sulfur workers, Juvenal on blacksmiths, and Lucretius on gold miners. Around AD 30, Celsus compiled current knowledge in his treatise *De Re Medica*, preceding by a century the writings of Galen, which were to form the basis for European medical practice for the following 1,500 years. The Romans, like the Greeks some four hundred years earlier, suffered from lack of good anatomical and, especially, physiological observations. Galen had himself examined a human skeleton and done dissections of animals, but anatomical study of human remains was generally uncommon even though Celsus had noted that "criminals were procured from prison by royal permission, and dissected alive."

The actual practice of medicine in Roman times was carried out in large part by public physicians (*archiatri*) employed by the state, who were sent to towns and institutions to provide care for the poor. These men also engaged in private consultation for paying patients in a pattern familiar today in many countries. The Justinian Code near the end of the Roman Empire (AD 533) reminded these public officers that it was their duty "to choose to do honest service for the poorest rather than be disgracefully subservient to the rich" (Leff and Leff, 1957). Some physicians had private practices, and some were salaried employees of the gladiators, baths, the courts, or other organizations. Although medical knowledge was scant, the needs of the military and the gladiators stimulated a substantial surgical practice, and many different instruments such as scalpels, forceps and syringes (some of Egyptian or Babylonian origin) were described by Celsus. In the ruins of Pompeii hundreds of such instruments have been found, some of which, such as vaginal specula, barely differ from those to be seen in modern practice.

Finally, public health measures and hospitals in Roman times may be mentioned, for the famous Roman legal and administrative systems served well in this regard. Control over the baths and aqueducts, the sanitation and maintenance of streets, and the wholesomeness of food and marketplaces was placed in the hands of public officials in a system that functioned until the decay of the empire about AD 400 to 500. Military hospitals were built all over the empire, and institutions (*valetudinaria*) originally intended for care of sick and aged slaves were in laters years made available to the general poor.

NON-MEDITERRANEAN MEDICINE

Indigenous ideas about the body, the maintenance of health, and the cure of disease must have developed wherever human civilization flourished. Of the Aztec, Maya, Inca, Khmer, and other high cultures not a great deal is known, and their influence upon other and succeeding peoples has been limited. Two major systems of medical thought should, however, be mentioned because of their antiquity, extent, and importance. These are the Indian and the Chinese.

Traditional Indian Medicine and Surgery

Earliest Indian medical writings date from the second millenium BC, when the so-called Vedic practice consisted largely of charms and magical practices for control of demons. From about 800 BC to AD 1000 Brahmanistic medicine predominated and several large technical treatises have survived from this period. Many conditions were described in such detail that they are recognizable today as tuberculosis, cancer, diabetes, leprosy, smallpox, or other diseases. The practice of physicians was well described, with ample warnings against quacks who, failing to obtain a cure, blame the patient for disobeying directions. Healers should direct full attention towards curing the patient and under no circumstances cause him harm; the patient should be treated as if he were the physician's own son. Diagnoses were made by listening to the sounds of the breath and entrails; observing color of the eyes, tongue, and skin; feeling the pulse and even tasting the urine for the characteristic sweetness of diabetes. A careful history was taken including the patient's origin and travel, diet, duration of disease, etc. Early prognosis was important because the clever physician did not wish to risk his reputation by treating an incurable patient (Jolly, 1951).

For curing and healing purposes hundreds of drugs were known, based primarily upon herbs. Specific remedies were prescribed for fevers, cough, diarrhea, abscesses, and other common maladies. Among the hundreds of medicinal plants known was the snakeroot, *Rauwolfia serpentina,* a source of "pacifying remedies" whose active principle of reserpine is still in use as a tranquilizer and hypotensive agent. Opium, introduced later from Arabia, was used especially as a cure for diarrhea, an application widely employed today in tincture of paregoric, an opium derivative. Drugs were classified by taste (sour, sweet, salt, pungent, bitter, astringent), power (hot or cold) and elemental properties (vacuum, wind, fire, water, and earth). They were given by mouth or enema, as drops in the eye, nose or ear; by inhalation or as sneezing powders; as suppositories; or applied to the body in poultices and ointments. Steam and sweat baths were used, as were cupping and bleeding. Certain drugs were burned and the smoke inhaled through pipes. Mineral-based medicines used mercury, arsenic, sulfur, and antimony.

Surgical operations were classified under eight headings: excision, incision, scarification, puncturing, probing, extraction, drainage, and suturing; and cauterization was also practiced. Patients were anesthetized with wine in order not to faint or feel the knife so sharply. A wide variety of procedures was undertaken, including laparotomy, removal of bladderstones, repair of fistulas, caesarian section, and even removal of cataracts and other ophthalmic maneuvers. More than one hundred different surgical instruments were in use.

Great stress was placed upon diet, hygiene, and mental preparation of both physician and patient, and all foods were endowed with mystical properties.

A pervasive theme of Ayurvedic medicine is the triad of wind, bile, and phlegm. Diseases arise from derangement of the balance among these three entities and may be treated with substances having opposite qualities in order to neutralize excesses. There are also seven basic elements of the body: chyle, blood, flesh, fat, bone, marrow, and sperm. Increase or decrease of these elements leads to the whole variety of diseases. A large and complex body of commentary has naturally developed over the centuries, but basic principles of ayurveda remain today as they were developed thousands of years ago. Many of the themes of Indian theory and practice sound familiar to students of early European medicine, and it is certain that there was considerable transfer of knowledge. Alexander the Great employed Indian physicians in his armies, and other contacts have already been mentioned.

Traditional Chinese Medicine

The bases of Chinese medical doctrine have once more come into prominence in both China and the West. In the People's Republic of China (P.R.C.) the conscious efforts to merge traditional and western practices have caused a great resurgence of interest in such modalities as herbal drugs and acupuncture and have led to the reprinting, often for the first time in many centuries, of medical texts from early dynastic times. Europe and America are currently passing through the latest of many cycles of fascination with the world's oldest and largest sustained cultural system.

The lendings and borrowings between Chinese and other traditions, including the Indian, have undoubtedly gone on for millenia, yet the Chinese early developed a highly distinctive system of medical and health lore. Its basis dates back at least to the time of Fu Hsi, an extraordinary personage who about 3322 BC "taught his people how to keep domestic animals, how to fish, how to cook, and how to get married. He also invented musical instruments and needles of nine different shapes. The needles were made of stone and used, in many instances, for the treatment of diseases" (Li, 1974).

Writers on classical Chinese medicine of the "great tradition" (as opposed to rustic folk remedies) invariably relate concepts of the body to those referring to the universe in general: "The basic idea behind these may be seen as a homeostatic concept of health and disease related to the cosmological ideas of Han philosphers. Just as equilibrium, or harmony, within an endless cycle of fluctuating changes is the basic principle of the natural order and of human society, so man (the microcosm of the universe) is healthy when his basic life forces are in harmony and unhealthy when the harmony is disturbed" (Crozier, 1972).

The Chinese concept of *ch'i* or life essence represents an abstraction unrelated to the anatomy of the body or to scientific physiology. It is the function, the essence, that is important. Born of chaos, ch'i gives rise to *yin* and *yang,* whose relative amounts and proportions help determine health and disease and many other things besides. Yin forces represent night, dark, cold, negative, passive, female, and are inherent in solid organs of the body; yang forces represent day, light, warm, positive, male, and inhere in hollow organs. The yin/yang couplet is but one part of the eight rubrics, the others specified by Agren (1975) as coldness/hotness, fullness/emptiness, and exteriority/interiority. Energetic balances in all of these must be properly maintained, and this is done by careful observance of outside forces, activities, and diet, each separate item of which may have a specific disequilibriating effect. Because of the unity of all nature, there is no sharp distinction made between food and medicines, although certain concentrated items, often powdered, ashed, or extracted, may provide the essence of one or another force.

As early as 2700 BC Shen-Nung (mentioned in Chapter 1 in connection with goiter) published a book listing 365 kinds of medicines—46 from minerals, 67 from animals, and 252 from plants. Many of these, and the thousands of other natural products in the Chinese traditional pharmacopeia, are empirical remedies containing specific active ingredients. Other aspects of classical Chinese medicine, including the 12 meridians of the body bearing 132 acupuncture points, and certain organs such as the "triple warmer," are more difficult to interpret, but they have a firm position in a coherent and adaptive system of medicine.

In comparison with the medical tradition of India, the Chinese system has often been viewed as embodying a poor morphologic sense and little or no knowledge of surgery. The traditional Chinese ignorance of anatomy may be explained by the enormous importance attached in classical times to the functional and symbolic aspects of health. "Chinese medicine," said Porkert (1975), "for almost three millenia, had been fostered and brought to maturity by what, for want of a better term, we may call Taoist consciousness, implying a vivid yet serene awareness of all cosmic phenomena including the diverse functions of the human personality."

Traditional Practices in Other Cultures

There are of course a great many traditions in all parts of the world, developed in harmony with local religious thought. As shrewd observers with finely developed powers of perception and deduction, native peoples in Africa, Asia and the Americas long ago discovered many practical and useful substances—along with much that, to our eyes, is of little value. LaBarre (1942) has emphasized the need for open-mindedness:

As scientists we cannot afford the luxury of an ethnocentric snobbery which assumes a priori that primitive cultures have nothing whatsoever to contribute to civilization. Our civilization is in fact a compendium of such borrowings, and it is a demonstrable error to believe that contacts of "higher" and "lower" cultures show benefits flowing exclusively in one direction. Indeed, a good case could probably be made that in the long run it is the "higher" culture which benefits the more through being enriched, while the "lower" culture not uncommonly disappears entirely as a result of the contact.

By way of demonstration of this point, Vogel (1970) has shown that more than 200 indigenous drugs used by American Indians have been official in various editions of the Pharmacopeia of the United States or in the National Formulary. North American Indians knew laxative, diuretic, emetic, and antipyretic drugs and were familiar with the use of foxglove (digitalis) as a heart stimulant. South American Indians developed the use of cocaine, cinchona (quinine), curare, ipecac (emetine), and numerous other drugs. The Aztecs, Mayas, and other Middle American groups made use of a wide variety of substances including tobacco, which has not been without influence in the course of later world developments.

THE MIDDLE AGES IN EUROPE

With the decline of the Roman Empire in the fifth century AD, Europe passed into a millenium of scientific somnolence, but several developments relevant to international health may be described. Knowledge, including medical knowledge, passed into the hands of the Catholic Church, and such of the Greek and Roman writings as were preserved in the West survived in the monasteries of Europe. Galen continued as primary authority during this time and little of value was added to his writings. Especially in the earlier part of the long decline the Byzantine Eastern Church, in Constantinople, surpassed the European Church in preserving and copying classical texts, and it was here that exchange continued with cultures to the east.

In the ninth century a medical school was founded in Salerno, near Naples, where during the next few hundred years Arabian, Byzantine, and Jewish scholars came to translate their texts and later brought new medical writings to Europe. Here was written the *Regimen Sanitatis Salernitarium,* a series of aphorisms on hygiene and healthful living which became immensely popular. With the invention of printing in the fifteenth century these jingles were translated into all known western languages and enjoyed the widest distribution of any book of the time with the exception of the Bible (Wain, 1970).

The crowded cities of medieval Europe, far below Greek and Roman standards in water supply, sanitation, personal hygiene, and enlightenment, were excellent candidates for epidemic diseases, and it may be said that the Middle Ages were bracketed by two great outbreaks of plague. The first pandemic, also known as the Plague of Justinian, struck in AD 542 and decimated the known world from Asia to Ireland, but the great Black Death of the fourteenth century is known as the most destructive epidemic in the history of mankind. Starting from wild rodents in the plains of Central Asia, the plague reached the Black Sea in 1346, spreading within a year to Cyprus, Italy, and Constaninople and by 1348 to the British Isles and all over the then known world. The entire social, economic, agricultural, and ecclesiastical structure of Europe was shaken to its foundations. Europe alone lost perhaps 25 million people, and through the Middle East, India, and China similar devastation resulted in the deaths of additional tens of millions. Physicians had no conception of the cause of the disease, ascribing it to a conjunction of the planets or to other cosmic and divine causes. Scapegoats were sought and many blamed the Jews, as a result of which this group suffered greatly.

Despite ignorance of its true cause, recognition of the contagious nature of plague led to the earliest attempts at international disease control. In the belief that plague was introduced by ships, the port of Venice in 1348 adopted a forty-day detention period for entering vessels, soon copied by Genoa, Marseilles, and other major ports. This period of *quarantine* (from the Italian word for forty) although ineffective in stopping plague, established a concept that was to be used frequently in succeeding centuries.

Plague was not the only great epidemic disease of the Middle Ages. Smallpox, diphtheria, measles, influenza, tuberculosis, scabies, erysipelas, anthrax, and trachoma were also rife (Rosen, 1958). Mass hysteria in the climate of superstition and ignorance led to outbreaks of dancing mania. Ergotism, arising from fungal contamination of rye, killed or crippled large numbers of people in dozens of epidemics between the ninth and fifteenth centuries. It is possible that leprosy, present in Europe for centuries, became epidemic in the thirteenth and fourteenth centuries, moving Voltaire to say that of all things gained in the crusades, leprosy was the only thing that Europe kept. After the Black Death, which carried off numerous inhabitants of leprosaria, the disease was never again important in Europe. The causative bacillus, however, was not eradicated and cases continued to occur. In 1868, in a leprosarium near Bergen, the Norwegian investigator Gerhard Hansen discovered *Mycobacterium leprae,* a finding that resulted in the modern term of Hansen's disease as the preferred designation for leprosy.

It was during the Middle Ages that hospitals became established in

Europe. Stimulated in part by ideas of contagion, these institutions were at the time the only places specialized for care of the sick. Religious orders dedicated to charity and healing were chartered in this period, partly to meet the needs of returning Crusaders. Some institutions such as St. Bartholemew's and St. Thomas's in London, founded in 1123 and 1215 respectively, are still functioning today. From about the thirteenth century, secular hospitals were founded in many municipalities, but these were staffed largely by monks and nuns.

Little by little, concepts of cleanliness and sanitation took hold in Europe's cities, and through public awareness and legislation urban centers began to approach the hygienic level of the Roman Empire a thousand years before. The great epidemics must have left in their wake renewed interest in preserving health. Town after town began to control the cleaning of streets, disposal of dead animals, and pollution of streams. Bathing became popular and the printing press brought enlightenment to the popular mind. The stage was being set for the Renaissance.

THE PERIOD OF EUROPEAN COLONIAL EXPANSION

During the Middle Ages in Europe, classical scientific and medical knowledge was retained by the Arabs, who established learned settlements in Spain, Portugal, and Sicily. Much of European medieval thought was expended on the rivalry with Islam, and although the Crusades had by and large failed, the contacts with the Moslem world opened new vistas to European eyes. Commodities of high value, mostly from the East, were in great demand, but the traditional routes of passage for such goods went through the Mediterranean and the Italian city-states. Partly as a continuation of the Christian-Moslem rivalry, partly for riches and adventure, and partly because of increasing abilities in navigation and seamanship, Western Europeans embarked in the early fifteenth century on a series of conquests by sea. The Iberian countries were early entrants, and Portugal, by virtue of its maritime traditions, large fleet, and well-established coastal trade, was first.

Beginning in 1415, the Portuguese attacked Moslem settlements in nearby North Africa, and instead of plundering and retreating, established permanent garrisons. In some ways the early fifteenth-century voyages may be considered extensions of the Crusades. The influence of Islam had expanded rapidly during the preceding few centuries—to the Balkan States, western Asia, Egypt, east Africa, India, and the East Indies, and the opportunity to spread Christianity was a powerful stimulus to the conquistadores of Portugal and Spain. Final success in the long struggle for eradication of the Moorish Kingdom of Granada coincided with the arrival of Columbus in the Caribbean in the year 1492. The excitement generated by discoveries of islands in the western Atlantic, thought to be a gateway to China, can only be imagined. The writings of men such as Bernal Diaz about the civilizations of the New World, rapidly disseminated by the recently developed but already widespread printing presses, fired the imagination, and the booty of gold and precious objects stimulated baser emotions.

The Portuguese arrived in India in 1498 and loaded the first of many cargoes of spices for the return voyage to Lisbon, thus challenging Italy for this trade; the English and Dutch in the seventeenth century finally ended the Mediterranean dominance and extended European influence to the farthest corners of the world. The colonial period thus begun lasted essentially until the 1950s and 1960s, with very few colonies remaining, in a legal sense, beyond 1970.

The period of exploration and colonization has had extremely important effects upon international health. Consider the "fatal impact" of early European ships upon the natives of the South Pacific. The *Dolphin,* under Captain Wallis, arrived in Matavi Bay, Tahiti, in 1697, and the exhausted sailors, long at sea, found to their delight that "the girls were prepared to make love at any time for the most trifling gifts; most of all they preferred ordinary carpenter's nails which they seemed to value as the Europeans value gold. There had been a commotion aboard the *Dolphin* when it was discovered that the sailors were not only withdrawing nails from the ship's planks but had even filched the nails from which their hammocks were suspended so that most of them were sleeping on the deck" (Moorehead, 1966). By 1769, Captain James Cook noted that within a few weeks of going ashore in Tahiti, a third of his crew were ill with venereal disease, which he felt "may in time spread itself over all the islands in the South Seas to the eternal reproach of those who first brought it among them." Later, in the same vein, "we debauch their morals already prone to vice and we introduce among them wants and perhaps diseases which they never before knew and which serve only to disturb that happy tranquillity they and their forefathers had enjoyed. If any one denies the truth of this assertion let him tell what the natives of the whole extent of America have gained by the commerce they had had with Europeans" (quoted by Moorehead, 1966). Destruction of the fragile cultures of the South Seas was accomplished within a few years, sometimes just months, after the first landfall by Europeans and their introduction of rum, gunpowder, and disease. Although still a matter of controversy, some investigators believe that syphilis itself may have been introduced to Europe by early Iberian explorers who acquired it in the Western Hemisphere. Thus, as in ancient times, genes and diseases continued to follow the trade routes of man.

In other parts of the world, destruction of aboriginal cultures and peoples was even less subtle. It is commonly believed, for example, that the first footfall of Columbus in the New World was on San Salvador (Watling's Island) in the Bahamas group, an archipelago from which the entire native population was quickly carried off to slavery and death on nearby Cuba and Hispaniola. From those larger islands, and indeed from all the Antilles the native Arawaks had essentially disappeared by the year 1600. Similar scenarios were then in progress, or were soon to occur, in many other parts of the Western Hemisphere.

The fatal impact was to prove two-edged, and European adventurers and settlers were often cruelly treated by the many endemic diseases to which they had scant resistance. Nowhere was this more true than in west Africa, the "White Man's Grave." The Portuguese had established slaving stations along the coast as early as the fifteenth century, but the small disease-ridden outposts did not develop into colonial settlements. Dysentery and malaria were rampant. Many European attempts at colonization were decimated by disease. Similar events occurred in the New World. Of ten thousand French colonists who landed in Guiana in 1765, eight thousand were dead within a few months, and the colony failed to develop despite the fact that France sent more persons there than to Canada (Gourou, 1966).

Mungo Park, the English botanist and explorer, entered the Gambia on his second reconnaissance expedition in May 1805. A few months later he was to write to Lord Camden:

Your lordship will recollect that I always spoke of the rainy season with horror, as being extremely fatal to Europeans; and our journey from the Gambia to the Niger will furnish a melancholy proof of it. We had not contact with the natives, nor was any one of us killed by wild animals or any other accidents; and yet I am sorry to say that of forty-four Europeans who left the Gambia in perfect health five only are at the present present alive—viz., three soldiers (one deranged in his mind), Lieutenant Maclyn and myself (quoted by Scott, 1939).

Shortly thereafter Park himself and the last few stragglers were drowned in an accident. Of the original 44 Europeans, 35 had died of malaria, 3 of dysentery, 1 of epilepsy, and 5 of drowning. James Tuckey's expedition to the Congo, July-September 1816 was scarcely more fortunate—in just 2½ months 21 of the original 44 Europeans died of malaria. In the Niger expedition of 1832, 32 of 41 Europeans died of fever. The extreme susceptibility of Caucasians vis-à-vis Africans was illustrated in the Niger expedition of 1841, which carried 145 Europeans and 158 Africans. Not a single one of the latter died of fever, whereas only 15 Europeans failed to become ill and 42 died of malaria (Gelfand, 1964).

The Slave Trade

The hope of obtaining quick riches in West Africa apparently outweighed the fear of sickness and death in many European minds. Gold from the Gold Coast, ivory from the Ivory Coast,—to say nothing of palm oil and, above all, slaves—provided the stimulus for frequent expeditions to the coasts of Africa.

Slavery was, of course, not a new phenomenon, having been common in antiquity. The early African slave trade went to north Africa and Europe, but with the discovery of America and the "unsuitability" of its natives for plantation labor, by far the greatest number of West African slaves made the dismal passage across the Atlantic. The total number captured has been estimated at some 11 million, of whom some 9.6 million were landed in North or South America or the Caribbean region (Curtin, 1968).

The slave trade was a source of enormous profit for those who invested in it, including (it is said) Queen Elizabeth I of England. By the middle of the eighteenth century, the city of Liverpool alone had 87 ships engaged in transport of slaves from west Africa to the Caribbean and southern United States. Scott (1939) has related the comments of Lovett Cameron in these terms:

He observed at one time a gang of fifty-two women tied together in three lots; some had children in their arms, others were far advanced in pregnancy, and all were laden. They were covered with weals and scars. To obtain these fifty-two women, at least ten villages had been destroyed, each with a population of one to two hundred, or about 1500 in all ... In chained gangs the unfortunate slaves are driven by the lash from the interior to the barracoons on the beach; there the sea-air, insufficient diet and dread of their approaching fate, produce the most fatal diseases; dysentery and fever release them from their sufferings.... On a short march, of six hundred slaves intended for the *Emma Lincoln* one hundred and twenty-five expired on the road. The mortality on these rapid marches is seldom less than twenty per cent.

Much has been written (e.g., by Hoeppli, 1969) about diseases brought to the Western Hemisphere through the slave trade. Numerous cases of African trypanosomiasis (sleeping sickness) were imported but transmission did not occur in the New World where tsetse flies or other suitable vectors were lacking. The situation is not so clear with respect to malaria, some authorities considering it probable that this disease antedated Columbus in the Western Hemisphere, others attributing its introduction to the slave trade. Dysentery, both amebic and bacillary, almost certainly was present in Africa and was introduced or reintroduced by slaves to the New World.

Several helminth parasites were probably introduced with the slave trade. The hookworm *Necator americanus* probably came in with African slaves, whereas *Ancylostoma duodenale* may have been introduced by the Spaniards or Portuguese themselves. Schistosomiasis due to *Schistosoma mansoni* was almost certainly a legacy of the slave trade, since it has been known in Africa for a very long time. Another form of the disease, that caused by *S. haematobium,* was also introduced to the Americas but did not become established for want of a suitable snail host. The filarial worm *Wuchereria bancrofti,* a causative agent of elephantiasis, was endemic in the region of Charleston, South Carolina from some time before 1808 until about 1920 (Savitt, 1977). This mosquito-transmitted parasite of man was probably introduced to the Charleston area from Barbados in the West Indies, which in turn had had the filaria brought to it from Africa through the slave trade. The peculiar ecological conditions in the Charleston area, together with its close commercial ties to the West Indies during the colonial period, led to conditions ideal for the introduction and maintenance of the filarial parasite.

Europe and the Tropical World

Some effects of European intervention in the tropics have been thoughtfully described by Gourou (1966). Among the first of these was the cross-diffusion of cultivated plants among the continents in the tropics, which previously were separate. Rice, bananas, yams, taro, and sugar from Asia; coffee and oil palm from Africa; maize, cassava, peanuts, tomatoes, papayas, pineapples, and potatoes from the New World have all become generally distributed and form common articles of diet throughout the world. European tastes for some of these products and needs for others stimulated development of estates or plantations in tropical areas, and the need for labor was met either by the importation of slaves or large-scale hiring of contract workers. A good example of the latter is in the rubber estates of Malaya.

The rubber tree (*Hevea brasiliensis*) is native to the rain forests of South America. Some seedlings, smuggled out of Brazil and grown in London hothouses, served as the basis of commercial plantings of natural rubber trees in several countries of the British Empire in the late nineteenth century. Conditions on the Malayan peninsula were close to ideal for this tree, and the development of motor transport and other industrial uses for rubber generated an enormous demand for latex. Large numbers of persons who spoke Tamil were brought from the Madras region of southeastern India. Almost immediately severe health problems were encountered on the rubber estates, particularly with regard to malaria. Sandosham (1959) has described the situation at that time, quoting from a contemporary report by a Mr. Carey: "Between the years 1892 and 1898 were on an average fifty Tamil women upon the check-roll each year. Yet in the whole period no living child was born. Several women became pregnant, but only in one case did the child become quick, and even in this case the woman eventually had a miscarriage. The estate was so riddled with malaria that the coolies were all miserably anemic and lacking in strength and the estate had eventually to be abandoned."

Quinine The severity of malaria in many parts of the world and the enormous impediment that it places in the way of economic development has put this disease in a special category at least since the time of Hippocrates. The recognition, in the early 1600s, of a cure for malaria can be considered a milestone in human history. This substance is quinine, an alkaloid occurring in the bark of *Cinchona officinalis,* a tree native to the forests of Peru. By the middle of the seventeenth century the fame of "Jesuit Bark" or *"lignum febrium"* had spread throughout Europe, where it rapidly gained favor as a specific for agues and fevers. Before the seventeenth century was over, cinchona had even been used by French Jesuits to cure Emperor Sheng-tsu (K'ang Hsi) of an attack of "tertian ague" in Peking, receiving in turn "great reward from the Emperor" (Scott, 1939).

The great demand for cinchona bark resulted in the virtual destruction of the trees in Peru, Bolivia, and Ecuador. Growing wild in the forests, they were searched out and killed by bark collectors without regard to the future. Several attempts at estate cultivation of the trees met with indifferent success until the Dutch were successful in establishing plantations in Java. Careful selection, grafting, and cultivation resulted in growth of high quality trees, rich in quinine, so that the Dutch had a virtual monopoly of quinine production up to the Second World War. The Japanese occupation of the East Indies added an additional incentive to the development of synthetic antimalarials, and the use of natural quinine has declined greatly in recent decades. With the discovery in South America and southeast Asia of strains of malaria parasites resistant to chloroquine and other synthetic drugs, however, natural quinine has enjoyed a small resurgence.

Sleeping Sickness One further example may be cited here of the pervasive importance of disease as an inhibitor of economic development, and this is the case of trypanosomiasis in Africa. Several forms of sleeping sickness have existed in Africa for many centuries; mention has already been made of this disease in connection with the slave trade. Presence of the trypanosomes, transmitted by biting tsetse flies, has prevented in introduction of large animals for food, labor, or transportation in many areas of the continent. Nash (1960) suggested that numerous attempts must have been made to introduce ox-drawn carts or ploughs into endemic areas because contacts have existed for centuries with areas to the north where these are in use, but "the tsetse dictated that the economy of the African should be based on the hoe and the head-load." The horses of Islamic travelers from the north, transport animals of the Portuguese in east Africa, and livestock of farmers moving northward from the Cape all fell victim to nagana, the animal version of African sleeping sickness. Pictures of early European travelers in Africa usually show long lines of porters, each carrying a box or bale on his head as safari meanders through the bush. One may have wondered why the conquistadores in Latin America or early European travelers in India or east Asia are not depicted in this way. The reason, of course, is that their animals survived to carry the burdens. Domestic animals are used for much more than power and transport—the meat and milk provided by cattle are major sources of protein, still greatly deficient in tropical Africa, and hides and wool are important items of commerce.

It seems certain that the commercial and agricultural activities of Europeans have been instrumental in spreading trypanosomiasis to areas beyond its "original" distribution. Until late in the last century sleeping sickness was not recorded in east Africa. Its introduction by the Stanley expedition from the Congo area to the east African lake region resulted in an enormous outbreak among residents of Uganda from about 1900 to 1908. In Busoga, on the north shore of Lake Victoria, the government tried to estimate the severity of sleeping sickness and "instructed the local chiefs to report to headquarters and to carry with them a twig to represent the death of each individual they thought died of sleeping sickness within their chiefdoms. A solemn procession of chiefs came to headquarters on the first day and the twigs numbered eleven thousand" (McKelvey, 1973). In fact, the toll along the fertile lakeshore of Uganda exceeded 200,000 people.

Panama Unfamiliar diseases encountered by Europeans abroad were of crucial imporance to empire builders. The threats to colonizers, to labor forces, and to resident populations have already been mentioned, but disease was also a potent inhibitor of construction projects and other commercial ventures. The Panama Canal is perhaps the most compelling example. After eight years of effort, 300 million dollars in expenditure, and almost 20,000 deaths from malaria and yellow fever, the Compagnie Universelle du Canal Interocéanique de Panama went bankrupt and abandoned its efforts in 1888. Almost no planning or funds had been allocated by the company for hygiene and sanitation; indeed, at the start of the French effort, the cause and means of transmission of the two great diseases that killed their canal had not yet become known. The successful completion of the Panama Canal by the Americans was accomplished in the years 1906 to 1914. In the interim between the French and American attempts, mosquito transmission of both malaria (by *Anopheles*) and of yellow fever (by *Aedes*) had been proven.

To understand the events in Panama, we must turn to Havana where, from 1881 onwards Carlos Finlay had been proclaiming that yellow fever was transmitted only by the bite of a mosquito (see Table 8-11). An American Yellow Fever Commission, headed by Walter Reed, fully confirmed Finlay's observation and announced at the Pan American Medical Congress in Havana in 1901 that the mosquito *Stegomyia fasciata* (now called *Aedes aegypti*) is the sole vector of yellow fever. William C. Gorgas, in charge of sanitation in Havana since 1898, established a series of ordinances that resulted, within a few years, in a dramatic decline in yellow fever prevalence within the city. These rules included the abolition, or protection by screening, of all collection of domestic water likely to breed mosquitoes; the daily inspection of houses and yards by an army of sanitarians; the imposition of a stiff fine on property owners found to have mosquito larvae on their premises; and the reporting and isolation within mosquito-proof screening of every suspected case of yellow fever.

In 1904 when the United States took over the Canal Zone, Gorgas was appointed to head the medical department of what was probably the most fever-ridden place on earth. By 1905 more than 4,000 men were employed in mosquito extermination alone. Two brigades were formed: the *Stegomyia* brigade to work primarily around houses and settlements, and the *Anopheles* brigade to clear jungles, drain and oil swamps, and work to reduce the recently-confirmed vector of malaria. Piped water supplies were constructed to eliminate the barrels that had formerly produced clouds of mosquitoes. Houses were screened and bed-nets provided to the canal workers. Quinine was issued both as a prophylactic against malaria and as a cure, and persons with fevers were isolated behind screening. As the engineers blasted and dredged, the war waged against *Aedes* and *Anopheles* by the sanitarians gradually brought yellow fever and malaria under control and marked a high point in the history of applied epidemiology in international health.

The Mixing Pot

The few examples cited here can do no more than hint at the multitude of health-related effects resulting from the worldwide activities of Europeans since the fifteenth century. Very significant demographic changes have occurred. Massive colonization from Europe has changed the character of populations most dramatically in North America, Australia, New Zealand, South Africa, and parts of Latin America where present-day inhabitants are overwhelmingly European in orgin. Substantial admixtures of Europeans with preexisting peoples are to be seen throughout much of the Western Hemisphere. In addition to the forcible transportation of millions of Africans to the Western Hemisphere, other peoples have been moved about the world to meet the needs of European-controlled agriculture. The East Indian populations in Fiji, Guyana, Surinam, Trinidad, and Malaya come especially to mind.

The establishment of colonial governments resulted in the inevitable introduction of the cultures and social institutions of the ruling country. Languages and legal systems were transported intact, often predominating over those formerly present, more frequently establishing parallel paths, each to be used by certain groups or on particular occasions. The same is largely true of medicine, both from the viewpoint of concepts of causality and the treatment of diseases, and with respect to the forms of medical organization and practice.

PRELUDE TO THE PRESENT

The period from 1750 to the beginning of the twentieth century was characterized by a complex web of interlocking developments in technology and science and in social and political thought. The great impact of the industrial revolution reverberated throughout this period and continues to the present day. Advances in science and technology contributed to industrialization and in large part were stimulated by it. Revolutionary movements in France, North America, and elsewhere generated and disseminated ideas of the innate rights of man to political freedom, while paradoxically the largest colonial empires in history were being assembled. Between 1750 and 1900 the world's population doubled, from about 800 million to 1.7 billion, but more significantly the annual *rate* of population growth increased tenfold, from 0.56 to 5.4 per thousand (Coale, 1974). The world as we know it was forged during this period.

The Industrial Revolution in England

The term "industrial revolution" is now commonly used to denote the period from about 1750 to 1830 during which power-driven machinery was first employed in factories for mass production of articles of commerce. A constellation of basic social and economic changes of considerable significance to health accompanied the development of the factory system, which was itself made possible by the rapid advances in technology during the eighteenth century. The textile industry played the leading role in early industrialization in England, with the flying shuttle, spinning machines, and, above all, intricate powered looms making possible the production of enormous amounts of cotton cloth. Britain imported 3 million pounds of raw cotton in 1751, but this increased to more than 32 million pounds by 1789 (Hunter, 1975). Early textile machinery was operated by water power, limiting the placement of the mills, but after Watt's invention of the rotary steam engine in 1781, factories could be located at almost any site subject to supplies of labor, coal, and materials.

The requirement for factory workers produced a whole new category of specialized wage laborers derived largely from impoverished rural folk, apprentices, and destitute women and children. Many owners of these early factories displayed an indifference to the welfare of the workers comparable to the attitudes of their colleagues in the west African slave trade. "The entrepreneurs expressed a brazen confidence in their own rights and believed, as did the nobles before them, that property was sacred, that every man had a right to do with his own as he willed, and that poverty invariably was the result of laziness and incompetence" (Goerke and Stebbins, 1968). Orphans and destitute children were collected by labor agents and sent to the grimy industrial towns where they were often subjected to great cruelty. Safety devices were unheard of and small children, sometimes literally chained to the machines, toiled from dawn to dusk in dusty, noisy, unventilated workrooms. Many who fell asleep at their work paid with fingers, hands, or worse. Food was often insufficient in quality and quantity, and home life in the squalid houses that surrounded the factories offered pitifully few comforts.

The exploitation of women and children in Midlands factories was yet exceeded by conditions in the coal mines. The steam engines in factories and railroads, and the heating needs of urban centers required an ever greater supply of coal from the mines of South Wales, Cornwall, and elsewhere in the British Isles. The mines were primitive in their operation, often dark, rat-infested, ill-ventilated, with constant pumping required to prevent flooding. Many passages were only large enough for children, and both boys and girls from five years of age were employed in the underground pits where they labored for twelve hours or longer at a time. "Being cheaper than horses, children were harnessed with chains to heavy trucks of coal which they hauled like dogs on all fours. As the passages were often low and narrow, it was necessary to use very small children for this purpose" (Hunter, 1975).

Many people were outraged at these shocking conditions in factory and mine. A rising tide of humanitarianism and social concern was gaining momentum in England, on the Continent and in America. Wesleyan Methodism gained great influence in the industrial and mining towns of England about the middle of the eighteenth century. The writings of the French intellectual and social philosophers—Rousseau, Voltaire, and Diderot—of John Locke, and of the Americans Thomas Paine, Thomas Jefferson, and many others served to disseminate the concepts of perfectability of man, inalienable human rights, and the essential dignity of the person. Rosen (1958) has pointed out that ". . . the question of health serves as a focal point around which the doctrines of economic freedom and political liberalism can be seen in various stages of modification. This transformation did not occur simply because of the growth of humanitarian sentiment or of a social conscience. Legislation on health and sanitation resulted from a variety of forces within the social and economic order." Legislation in England to control abuses of the industrial revolution began with the Health and Morals of Apprentices Act of 1802, limiting the work of children in textile factories to 12 hours per day, but setting no lower age limit for employment. The Factory Act of 1833 finally set a minimum age of nine years for work in textile factories, limited the work day of children from 9 to 13 years old to 9 hours daily, and those from 13 to 16, to 12 hours. Certain other reforms, such as two hours of compulsory schooling each day, were instituted. The Mines and Collieries Act of 1842 set 10 years as the minimum age for boys to work underground and forbade the employment of women and girls within the pits, but it was not until 1874 that employment of children under 10 in factories was prohibited in England. The writings of William Blake (*Songs of Innocence*) in the eighteenth century, and of Dickens, Elizabeth Barrett Browning, and other social reformers in the nineteenth were influential in inducing these changes, which were instituted over the vigorous and continuous opposition of the leaders of the industries concerned.

The cities of England and of other industrializing nations grew enormously in the first half of the nineteenth century. Between 1800 and 1841 the population of London doubled, and that of Leeds almost tripled. Birmingham grew tenfold in fifty years, and the populations of towns such as Bradford and Oldham increased a hundred times. Birmingham, Manchester, and other cities had instituted cleanup campaigns in the 1760s, correcting centuries of decay by installation of paving, sewerage, and piped water, but these civic improvements were swamped by the rapid growth of population. As wage-workers came in from the countryside and Irish emigrant laborers flocked to the factory towns, housing was constructed as quickly and cheaply as possible. City planning was nonexistent and sanitation neglected. Neighborhood standpipes provided water of poor quality to numerous residences. The smoke from innumerable coal fires filled the air and blackened buildings and lungs alike. The lack of recreational facilities combined with general illiteracy and cheap alcohol from the colonies to produce the conditions immortalized in Hogarth's famous "Gin Lane" etchings. Despite improvements in agricultural production, nutrition was poor. Rickets became common in children rarely exposed to sunshine, and contagious diseases such as tuberculosis, diphtheria, and louse-borne typhus took a great toll. The first cholera pandemic to strike England and Western Europe took thousands of lives in the early 1830s, and quickly extended to North America via shipping. Occupational accidents were common, as were diseases arising from unrestricted use of lead, mercury, and phosphorus in industrial processes.

Sanitary Reform in England

The period from about 1830 marked the beginning of widespread and more or less coordinated efforts to alleviate many of these conditions. Brockington (1966) has categorized these developments in England under four principal movements. First, the aftermath of the cholera epidemic of 1831–33 saw the formation of more than 1,200 locally elected boards of health, which functioned mainly in the area of environmental hygiene and proposed to prevent future epidemics by early detection of cases, isolation, quarantine, and similar measures. The true cause of cholera was still unknown, but the relationship of that and other diseases to crowded and insanitary conditions had become clear. Secondly, the increase in wage dependency and altered socioeconomic conditions had placed intolerable burdens upon the parish-based relief mechanisms contained in the Elizabethan Poor Laws of 1601. A Royal Commission, appointed in 1832 to look into these matters, was eventually responsible for the Poor Laws of 1834. This legislation provided for a centralized Poor Law Commission with a medical officer and medical inspectors, and it acknowledged the need for some sort of generalized health services for the poor. Thirdly, the Factory Act of 1833, already mentioned, incorporated provision for enforcement inspectors in the field under the supervision of the Home Office. Increasing interest in industrial health problems was reflected in the publication in 1831 of Charles Thackrah's monograph, *The Effects of the Principal Arts, Trades and Professions, and of Civic States and Habits of Living, on Health and Longevity, with Suggestions for the Removal of many of the Agents which produce Disease and shorten the Duration of Life*. Lastly, the establishment of the Registrar General's Office and the division of the country into districts for registration of births, marriages, and deaths made possible the orderly accumulation of basic demographic data as a basis for further legislation and action.

Edwin Chadwick The gradual recognition of the overriding importance of sanitation in the maintenance of public health was crystallized in Edwin Chadwick's *Report . . . on an Inquiry into the Sanitary Condition of* *the Labouring Population of Great Britain* (1842), a fundamental contribution to the development of modern public health. Here Chadwick pointed out that the majority of children of the working classes died before their fifth birthday, and he showed how mortality varied between social and economic classes (see Table 3-5). He also made a key point about public health measures:

The great preventives, drainage, street and house cleansing by means of supplies of water and improved sewerage, and especially the introduction of cheaper and more efficient modes of removing all noxious refuse from the towns, are operations for which aid must be sought from the science of the Civil Engineer, not from the physician, who has done his work when he has pointed out the disease that results from the neglect of proper administrative measures, and has alleviated the sufferings of the victims.

Chadwick's report was based on an extensive survey and analysis of conditions in various parts of England, and it stimulated the appointment of a Royal Commission in 1843 charged with investigating sanitary conditions in the larger towns. The findings of this Commission, which surveyed 50 towns, eventually formed the basis of the Public Health Act of 1848 that established the General Board of Health and authorized the post of Medical Officer of Health to local boards. The first M.O.H. of London, John Simon, was imbued with the spirit of the environmental reformer and fully recognized the economic implications of ill health. He wrote that, "Sanitary neglect is mistaken parsimony. Fever and cholera are costly items to count against the cheapness of filthy residences and ditch-drawn drinking water: widowhood and orphanage make it expensive to sanction unventilated work places and needlessly fatal occupations...The physical strength of a nation is among the chief factors of national prosperity." Simon knew very well the cost of cholera; he had assumed his office the year before the great cholera epidemic of 1848, of which William Farr was to write:

If a foreign army had landed on the coast of England, seized all the seaports, sent detachments over the surrounding districts, ravaged the population through the summer, after having destroyed more than a thousand lives a day, for several days in succession, and in the year it held possession of the country, slain 53,293 men, women and children, the task of registering the dead would be inexpressibly painful; and the pain is not greatly diminished by the circumstance, that in the calamity to be described, the minister of destruction was a pestilence that spread over the face of the island, and found on so many cities quick poisonous matters ready at hand to destroy the inhabitants (quoted by Pollitzer, 1959).

The year 1849 also marked the publication of a slender pamphlet *On the Mode of Communication of Cholera* by John Snow, a work expanded and augmented in 1854 and destined to become one of the great classics of epidemiological reasoning. Although ignorant of the still-undiscovered world of microbiology, Snow correctly deduced the mode of transmission of cholera through contaminated drinking water. He showed how contaminated water drawn from the lower Thames, after passage through London, was far more likely to transmit cholera than was cleaner water taken from localities upstream. These developments, so briefly reviewed here, helped to build the foundations of modern public health practice.

Sanitary Reform in Other Countries

The appalling conditions in England at the turn of the eighteenth century were not unique to that country. Similar conditions led to similar efforts on the Continent wherever industrial centers developed. France occupied the premier position in social and political thought in the early nineteenth century, but did not adopt legislation limiting child labor until 1841. Seven years later, at the time of creation of the British General Board of Health, laws were also passed in Paris to establish a national public health advisory committee and a network of local public health councils. In Germany agitation for similar legislation was led largely by Rudolf Virchow and a small reformist group. The year 1848 was marked by revolution and political turmoil in Germany, and it was not until 1873 that a Reich Health Office was set up. In that year Max von Pettenkofer delivered his well-known orations on "The Value of Health to a City," in which he reiterated the necessity of sanitation and added observations on nutrition, housing, bathing, customs and habits, and political and social conditions. Pettenkofer showed that the crude mortality rate in London had fallen from 35 per thousand around 1750 to 22 per thousand in 1873 while the population had increased fivefold to more than three million. He compared available mortality data from cities around the world with his own Munich, where the death rate was 50% higher than that of contemporary London or Paris, and exemplified the growing mood towards social responsibility in these words:

In every large community there are always many people who have not the means to procure for themselves the things that are absolutely necessary to a healthy life. Those who have more than they need, must contribute to supply these wants, in their own interest. It is not a matter of indifference if, in a city, the dwellings of the poor become infested with typhoid and cholera but is a threat to the health of the richest people also. This is true for all contagious or communicable diseases. Whenever causes of disease cannot be removed or kept away from the individual, the citizens must stand together and accept taxation according to their ability. When a city provides good sewerage, good water supplies, good and clean streets, good institutions for food control, slaughter houses and other indispensable and vital necessities, it creates institutions from which all benefit, both rich and poor. The rich have to pay the bill and the poor cannot contribute anything; yet the rich draw considerable advantages from the fact that such institutions benefit the poor also. A city must consider itself a family, so to say. Care must be taken of everybody in the house, also of those who do not or cannot contribute toward its support (Pettenkofer, 1873).

A decade later the paternalistic German state under Otto von Bismarck was to undercut the growing power of the Social Democrats and to introduce a comprehensive scheme of social security legislation providing insurance for workers against the hazards of accident, sickness, and old age. The Sickness and Maternity Law (1883); the Work-Injury Law (1884); and the Old Age, Invalidity, and Death Law (1889) soon became models for similar legislation in every other country of Europe, and eventually throughout the world.

The cities of North America had the great advantage of relative newness, but by the middle of the nineteenth century the crush of immigration had rendered the larger urban centers of the east coast fully as noxious as their European counterparts. New York City, for instance, increased in population from about 75,000 in 1800 to more than half a million in 1850. Local boards of health had been established in some of the larger eastern cities before 1800 but these were ineffective in stemming the tide of disease. From early colonial times North America had been swept by epidemics of smallpox, yellow fever, typhoid, and typhus; and tuberculosis, malaria, and other communicable diseases were firmly entrenched. The cholera pandemics of 1831 and 1849 struck America with full force, the latter coming to California along with the gold fever of the '49ers.

Using Chadwick's 1842 report as a model, John Griscom in 1848 published *The Sanitary Condition of the Laboring Population of New York,* and Lemuel Shattuck in Boston wrote his *Report of the Sanitary Commission of Massachusetts* (1850). The gradual awakening of interest in such matters resulted in the National Quarantine Conventions of the late 1850s and, after the Civil War, a National Board of Health was established by Act of Congress in 1879.

A detailed history of the development of health and welfare services in various countries is beyond the scope of the present discussion, which is intended only to describe the thrust of thought and action that lies behind the present-day conditions discussed in later chapters.

The Modernization of Medicine

The nineteenth century in the Western countries opened on a technological upbeat: ingenious mechanical devices were transforming the pattern and quality of life in city and farm. Industrial processes, based on advances in engineering, chemistry, and physics, were flourishing. Agriculture was becoming more efficient and less labor-intensive. Large volumes of raw materials and consumer goods criss-crossed the world. A philosophical outlook of realism and pragmatism was becoming firmly established. However, rational understanding of health and disease had proceeded so slowly that as late as 1851 the most learned men of Europe, debating for six months at the First International Sanitary Conference, could not agree whether cholera was or was not contagious.

From such a shaky foundation, through a remarkably concerted achievement of the human intellect, a flood of discoveries poured form the world's laboratories in the latter half of the nineteenth century and established the cause and basic means of transmission of virtually every major bacterial and parasitic disease of man and domestic animals. Within the span of one human lifetime, from about 1840 to 1900, vague theories of miasma and divine displeasure gave way to experimentally based laboratory data regarding the cause of disease and its effects upon the body. Knowledge of physiology, nutrition, and many other aspects of medical science also advanced during this period. Repeated epidemics of cholera in Europe and continuing havoc from other communicable diseases were intense stimuli for investigators. The extreme intellectual ferment provoked by Darwin's theories provided a further incentive to biological studies after about 1860.

Although some important work on disease control had been done in the eighteenth century (for instance, Lind's demonstration of the prevention of scurvy and Jenner's work on cowpox vaccination), the rise of microbiology depended upon the chemical and technological underpinning provided by the industrial revolution. Refinements in microscope design produced the condensers and the objective lenses of the 1880s, which are remarkably similar to those in use today. The chemistry of dye manufacture, developed for the textile industry, was incorporated into histology and bacteriology. Little by little the basis of modern medical practice was hammered together.

In this chapter we have touched lightly upon a wide range of human conditions, attitudes, interactions, and developments over a span of millenia. It is a truism of historians that all of these have left their imprint upon the world as we find it today. But more than this—the hunter, farmer, city dweller, exploiter, humanitarian, and scientist are all still here, and so are the basic problems of health that mankind has encountered from the beginning. That is why the study of history has the same relevance for students of international health as does the study of embryology for students of medicine. It was William Faulkner who said that "History is not dead. It is not even past."

References

Agren, H. 1975. Patterns of tradition and modernization in contemporary Chinese medicine. *In:* A. Kleinman, P. Kunstadter, E. R. Alexander, and J. L. Gale, Eds. Medicine in Chinese Cultures. Washington. U.S. Department of Health, Education and Welfare Publication No. (NIH) 75-653. pp. 37-59.

Brockington, C. F. 1966. A Short History of Public Health. 2d Ed. London. Churchill. 240 p.

Chadwick, E. 1842. Report on the Sanitary Condition of the Labouring Population of Great Britain. Reprinted 1965. Edinburgh. Edinburgh University Press. 443 p.

Coale, A. J. 1974. The history of the human population. Scientific American 231: 40-51.

Crozier, R. C. 1972. Traditional medicine as a basis for Chinese medical practice. *In:* J. R. Quinn, Ed. Medicine and Public Health in the People's Republic of China. Washington. U.S. Department of Health, Education and Welfare Publication No. (NIH) 72-67. pp. 3-21.

Curtin, P. D. 1968. Epidemiology and the slave trade. Political Science Quarterly 83: 190-216.

Davis, K. 1974. The migrations of the human population. Scientific American 231: 92-105.

Gelfand, M. 1964. Rivers of Death in Africa. London. Oxford University Press. 100 p.

Goerke, L. S. and E. L. Stebbins. 1968. Mustard's Introduction to Public Health. 5th Ed. New York. Macmillan. 472 p.

Gourou, P. 1966. The Tropical World. 4th Ed. London. Longmans. 196 p.

Hobbes, T. 1651. Leviathan, or The Matter, Forme, and Power of a Commonwealth, Ecclesiasticall and Civil. Reprinted 1968. Baltimore. Penguin Books (Pelican Classics). 728 p.

Hoeppli, R. 1959. Parasites and Parasitic Diseases in Early Medicine and Science. Singapore. University of Malaya Press. 526 p.

Hoeppli, R. J. C. 1969. Parasitic Diseases in Africa and the Western Hemisphere: Early Documentation and Transmission by the Slave Trade. Acta Tropica, Supplement No. 10. 240 p.

Hunter, D. 1975. The Diseases of Occupations. 5th Ed. London. English Universities Press. 1225 p.

Jolly, J. 1951. Indian Medicine. Translated from the German by C. G. Kashikar. Poona. C. G. Kashikar Publisher. 238 p.

LaBarre, W. 1942. Folk medicine and folk science. Journal of American Folk-lore 55: 197–203.

Leff, S. and V. Leff. 1957. From Witchcraft to World Health. New York. Macmillan. 236 p.

Li, C-l. 1974. A brief outline of Chinese medical history with particular reference to acupuncture. Perspectives in Biology and Medicine 18: 132–143.

McKelvey, J. J., Jr. 1973. Man Against Tsetse. Ithaca, N.Y. Cornell University Press. 306 p.

Moorehead, A. 1966. The Fatal Impact. An Account of the Invasion of the South Pacific 1767–1840. New York. Harper & Row. 230 p.

Nash, T. A. M. 1960. A review of the African trypanosomiasis problem. Tropical Diseases Bulletin 57: 973–1003.

Pavlovsky, E. n.d. Natural Nidality of Transmissible Disease. Translated from the Russian by Y. Shirokov, Moscow. Peace Publishers, 249 p.

Pettenkofer, M. von. 1873. The Value of Health to a City. Translated from the German by H. E. Sigerist. Reprinted 1941. Baltimore. Johns Hopkins Press. 52 p.

Polgar, S. 1964. Evolution and the ills of mankind. In: S. Tax, Ed. Horizons of Anthropology. Chicago. Aldine Publishing Co. 288 p.

Pollitzer, R. 1959. Cholera. Geneva. World Health Organization. 1019 p.

Porkert, M. 1975. The dilemma of present-day interpretations of Chinese medicine. In: A. Kleinman, P. Kunstadter, E. R. Alexander, and J. L. Gale, Eds. Medicine in Chinese cultures. Washington. U.S. Department of Health, Education and Welfare Publication No. (NIH) 75-653. pp. 61–75.

Rosen, G. 1958. A History of Public Health. New York. M.D. Publications. 551 p.

Sandosham, A. A. 1959. Malariology. Singapore. University of Malaya Press. 327 p.

Savitt, T. L. 1977. Filariasis in the United States. Journal of the History of Medicine 32: 140–150.

Scott, H. H. 1939. A History of Tropical Medicine. Baltimore. Williams & Wilkins. 1165 p.

Selzer, R. 1975. Twelve spheres of influence, eight bodily forces, and good old yin and yang. Harper's Magazine. January: 40–44.

Siegfried, A. 1965. Germs and Ideas: Routes of Epidemics and Ideologies. Edinburgh. Oliver & Boyd. 98 p.

Sigerist, H. E. 1951. A Histroy of Medicine. Vol. I. Primitive and Archaic Medicine. New York. Oxford University Press. 564 p.

Singer, C. J. and E. A. Underwood. 1962. A Short History of Medicine. 2d Ed. New York. Oxford University Press. 854 p.
Vogel, V. J. 1970. American Indian Medicine. Norman. University of Oklahoma Press. 584 p.
Wain, A. 1970. A History of Preventive Medicine. Springfield, Ill. Thomas. 407 p.
Wells, C. 1964. Bones, Bodies and Disease: Evidence of Disease and Abnormality in Early Man. London. Thames & Hudson. 288 p.

DEVELOPMENT 3.

ECONOMIC DEVELOPMENT

Socioeconomic status is clearly a major determinant of health and disease in individuals and populations, but it is not so easy to define just what is meant by the term. Although "socioeconomic status" refers mostly to the amount of money or resources that people have, it deals with perceptions as well as pocketbooks.

Universal adoption of the phrase "economic development" has cast most thinking about socioeconomic status into monetary terms. However, the process of economic development involves changes in many aspects of individual, community, and national life, some of which are shown on Table 3-1. Because development varies from one country to another, the degree of change in each aspect also varies. Modernization is a never-ending process, and at any given time some countries or societies are further along certain paths than others. At the moment, most people will equate modernization with westernization, but as we have seen western culture has itself had powerful accretions from elsewhere. The present time probably presages another period of learning, as well as teaching, by the West.

The essential core of modernization lies in the continual expansion of knowledge, a process that occurs in creative and receptive minds. As new knowledge is incorporated into everyday life, there is generally increased receptivity to further change and an increase in the degree of differentiation and specialization of individuals and institutions.

We will consider here some overall relationships between development and health. Economic issues will be discussed again in Chapter 6 in relation to the policy decisions of health planners.

Political Viewpoints

Most people consider economic development a good thing insofar as it offers improved conditions of life to the majority of the population. But there are also critics. Some criticize development on ecological grounds; Boulding (1970), for instance, states that "economic development is the process by which the evil day is brought closer when everything will be gone." Others consider development programs to be expolitative. The economists Adelman and Morris (1973), for example, conclude that

Table 3-1. Some aspects of modernization and development important to health[a]

Agricultural productivity and diversification
Assurance of adequate seasonal food supply
Degree and rate of urbanization and provision of amenities
Demographic structure of the population
Development of infrastructure: power, roads, communications
Emancipation of women from childbearing and domestic labor
Environmental protection and pollution
Exploitation of natural resources
Extent of citizen political participation
Industrialization
National and per capita income and their distribution
Nature and availability of health and medical services
Nature, stability, and policies of government
Participation in international trade
Provision of safe water, sanitation, and sewage facilities
Rate of population growth
Shift from ceremonial to utilitarian goals
Spread of education and literacy

[a] In alphabetical order. No ranking is implied.

"hundreds of millions of desperately poor people throughout the world have been hurt rather than helped by economic development." In a more specifically political vein, many neo-Marxist commentators believe that development is not basically a process of evolution from "traditional" to "modern" (i.e., industrial) societies in which western countries try to produce facsimiles of themselves. The position of the present-day developing countries is not considered comparable to that of preindustrial Europe and America, as described in Chapter 2. Rather, it is argued, the industrialized countries, through the rapacity of colonialism and modern-day transnational corporations, have made and kept the poorer countries poor and then tried to blame them for their own poverty. In this view, faith in developing country bourgeoisies to engage in evolutionary "nation building" is misplaced. Since class formation is said to be an inevitable consequence of capitalism, revolutionary change will usually be necessary to bring about "true" national development. It is of interest to note that, despite the traditional conservatism of the medical profession, several influential radical leaders, such as the writer Frantz Fanon and the activist Che Guevara, were physicians.

We cannot enter the interminable debate on the relative merits of various political viewpoints. The important lesson for students of international health is that the competing doctrines, based on differing interpretations of the human situation in our diverse world, are concerned with strategies for maintaining or establishing entire social, political, and economic systems. All of these systems embrace policies regarding each of the elements listed in Table 3-1 that impinge on people's health. The confrontations between adherents of different doctrines form the stuff of our daily newspapers. Yet there are still those who view health problems as a thing apart, divorced from societal conditions, and somehow soluble by the application of more, or more sophisticated, technology.

Economic Differences Between Countries

We are all familiar with the long annual lists of Gross National Product (GNP) per capita in the countries of the world (Table 3-2) and assume that there is some unspecified but real relationship between the figures listed and the health status of the populations concerned.

Much has been written about the inequitable division of the world's material resources. Countries have been subjected to various classifications for purposes such as recording of aid flows, or for differentiation by specific standards. International organizations (discussed more fully in Chapter 8) have compiled many lists of developing countries. The most commonly used are those of the Development Assistance Committee (DAC) of the Organization for Economic Cooperation and Development; the United Nations (UN), the World Bank (International Bank for Reconstruction and Development—IBRD), and the International Monetary Fund. These lists are revised from time to time. The United Nations has published two lists of less developed countries (LDCs) in need of special aid. The Most Seriously Affected (MSA) countries are distinguished by low per capita income (usually under $200) and sharp deterioration of current account balances owing to the 1973 oil price rise and subsequent recession. These countries show modest prospects for economic growth. By April 1975, 42 countries were on the MSA list. The other list, that of least developed countries (LLDCs), includes 28 nations with a per capita GNP of $100 or less and literacy of adults (over age 15) of 20% or less. The MSA and LLDC lists are provided in Table 3-3. Note that many countries appear on both.

The popular press shows increasing interest in the alignment of countries in economic groupings, an interest due in large part to the

Table 3-2. Per capita Gross National Product at Market Prices, 1974 (Countries with populations of one million or more. Rounded to nearest $10)

Country	Amount (US$)	Country	Amount (US$)
Switzerland	7,870	Venezuela	1,960
Sweden	7,240	Bulgaria[a,b]	1,780
United States	6,670	Trinidad and Tobago	1,700
Denmark	6,430	Portugal	1,630
Germany, Federal Republic of	6,260	Hong Kong	1,610
Canada	6,190	Argentina	1,520
Norway	5,860	Yugoslavia	1,310
Belgium	5,670	Iran	1,250
France	5,440	South Africa	1,210
Australia	5,330	Jamaica	1,190
Netherlands, The	5,250	Uruguay	1,190
Finland	4,700	Iraq	1,110
Libyan Arab Republic	4,440	Romania	1,100
Austria	4,410	Mexico[c]	1,090
New Zealand	4,310	Lebanon[d]	1,070
Japan	4,070		
German Democratic Republic[a,b]	3,590	Panama	1,000
United Kingdom	3,590	Brazil	920
Israel	3,460	Costa Rica	840
Czechoslovakia[a,b]	3,330	Chile	830
		China, Republic of	810
Saudi Arabia	2,830	Turkey	750
Italy	2,820	Peru	740
Poland[a,b]	2,510	Algeria	730
Spain	2,490	Angola	710
USSR[a,b]	2,380	Cuba[a,b]	710
Ireland	2,320	Malaysia	680
Singapore	2,240	Nicaragua	670
Puerto Rico	2,230	Dominican Republic	650
Hungary[a,b]	2,180	Tunisia[e]	650
Greece	2,090	Mongolia[a,b]	610

continued

Table 3-2.—Continued

Country	Amount (US$)	Country	Amount (US$)
Guatemala	580	Uganda	240
Syrian Arab Republic	560	Sudan[a]	230
Albania[a,b]	530	Yemen, People's Democratic Republic of[a,f]	220
Zambia	520	Central African Empire	210
Rhodesia	520	Kenya	200
Paraguay	510		
Colombia	500	Sierra Leone[g]	190
Ecuador	480	Madagascar	180
Korea, Republic of	480	Yemen Arab Republic[a]	180
Papua New Guinea	470	Indonesia	170
		Haiti	170
Congo, People's Republic of the	470		
Ivory Coast	460	Tanzania[h]	160
Jordan	430	Zaire	150
Morocco	430	Viet Nam, Socialist Republic of[a,b]	150
Ghana	430	India	140
		Lesotho[a]	140
El Salvador	410		
Liberia	390	Sri Lanka	130
Korea, Democratic People's Republic of[a,b]	390	Pakistan	130
		Malawi	130
Mozambique[a]	340	Benin, People's Republic of[a]	120
Honduras	340	Guinea	120
Senegal	330		
Philippines	330	Niger	120
Thailand	310	Afghanistan	110
China, People's Republic of[a,b]	300	Nepal	100
Mauritania	290	Ethiopia	100
		Chad	100
Nigeria	280		
Egypt, Arab Republic of	280	Bangladesh	100
Bolivia	280	Burma	100
Cameroon	250	Burundi[g]	90
Togo	250	Somalia[g]	90

continued

Country	Amount (US$)
Upper Volta	90
Rwanda[g]	80
Mali	80
Cambodia[a,d]	70
Bhutan[g]	70
Lao People's Democratic Republic[a,d]	70

[a] Estimates of GNP per capita are tentative.
[b] For estimation of GNP per capita, consult source.
[c] Estimate of GNP per capita does not reflect the significant devaluation of the peso in August 1976.
[d] GNP per capita estimated on the 1972–74 base period.
[e] GNP per capita growth rate relates to 1961–74.
[f] GNP per capita growth rate relates to 1969–74.
[g] GNP per capita growth rate relates to 1964–74.
[h] Mainland Tanzania.
Source: World Bank, 1976.

development of international affinity groups by members of the United Nations and its agencies. In the 1970s large international conferences in Stockholm (Environment), Bucharest (Population), Rome (Food), Mexico (Women), Vancouver (Human Settlements), Nairobi (Trade and Development IV and Desertification), New York (Sea Law), and elsewhere have been forums for the display of differences between rich and poor nations and have focused world interest on problems of economic development.

At the higher levels of economic development, the GNP figures can provide a valid base for comparing countries, but the numbers may be misleading for developing nations, since many people live outside the cash economy. Rural residents in particular, as subsistence farmers, may grow much of their own food and conduct many transactions by barter. Moreover, differences in the organization of societies and corresponding social and political relationships render the GNP less useful than it might appear. The prime example to be cited in this respect is the People's Republic of China (P.R.C.). While its per capita GNP (as estimated by the World Bank) may be no greater than that of some very poor countries of Africa or Asia, its levels of public and individual health, by all reliable

Table 3-3. United Nations lists of developing countries, 1975

Most seriously affected (MSA)		Least developed countries (LLDC)	
Afghanistan	Khmer Rep.	Afghanistan	Lesotho
Bangladesh	Laos	Bangladesh	Malawi
Benin	Lesotho	Benin	Maldives
Burma	Malagasy Rep.	Bhutan	Mali
Burundi	Mali	Botswana	Nepal
Cameroon	Mauritania	Burundi	Niger
Cape Verde Islands	Mozambique	Central African Rep.	Rwanda
Central African Rep.	Niger	Chad	Somalia
Chad	Pakistan	Democratic Yemen	Sudan
Egypt	Rwanda	Ethiopia	Tanzania
El Salvador	Senegal	Gambia	Uganda
Ethiopia	Sierra Leone	Guinea	Upper Volta
Ghana	Somalia	Haiti	Western Samoa
Guinea	Sri Lanka	Laos	Yemen Arab Rep.
Guinea-Bissau	Sudan		
Guyana	Tanzania		
Haiti	Uganda		
Honduras	Upper Volta		
India	Western Samoa		
Ivory Coast	Yemen, Arab Rep.		
Kenya	Yemen, P.D. Rep.		

Source: Development Coordination Committee, 1976.

indicators, are typical of countries with much higher per capita product, reflecting the activities of a highly motivated and disciplined population. Here, and perhaps in a few other countries, strong central planning, coupled with relentless public education and frequent mass campaigns, have reportedly achieved results obtained elsewhere only by great public and private monetary expenditures. Such social and political realities, in the P.R.C. and elsewhere, are not revealed in the stark figures appearing in the GNP tables.

Distribution of Incomes Within Countries

The ratio of relatively poor to relatively rich persons in the world as a whole is about 3 or 4 to 1, but within most developing countries the discrepancy is far greater (Table 3-4). While it is true that simplistic di-

Table 3-4. Approximate distribution of national income to the poorest 60% and the wealthiest 5% of the population of various countries, recent years

Country	Poorest 60%	Wealthiest 5%
Argentina	30%	29%
Benin (Dahomey)	30	32
Bolivia	27	36
Brazil	23	38
Burma	36	28
Chad	35	23
Chile	27	23
Colombia	16	40
Costa Rica	25	35
El Salvador	24	33
Gabon	15	47
Greece	34	23
India	36	20
Iraq	16	34
Ivory Coast	30	29
Jamaica	19	31
Lebanon	23	34
Libya	2	46
Malagasy	23	37
Mexico	22	29
Morocco	22	21
Niger	35	23
Nigeria	23	38
Panama	28	35
Peru	17	48
Philippines	25	28
Senegal	20	36
Sierra Leone	19	34
South Africa	16	39
Sri Lanka	27	18
Sudan	29	17
Surinam	37	15
Taiwan	29	24
Tanzania	29	43
Trinidad and Tobago	19	27
Tunisia	21	22
Venezuela	30	23
Zambia	27	38

Source: Adapted from Adelman and Morris, 1973.

visions into "poor" and "rich" obscure many social complexities, it is also true that most developing countries are characterized by sharply dualistic structures associated with political and economic domination by elite groups. This phenomenon is certainly not new. The earliest records of Egypt and China, histories from ancient Cambodia and Indonesia, and the chronicles of the Conquistadores in Mexico and Peru, all attest to equivalent, or even greater, social inequalities in many times and places. In nineteenth-century England Benjamin Disraeli, observing a similar dichotomy, suggested that Queen Victoria actually reigned over "two nations; between whom there is no intercourse and no sympathy; who are as ignorant of each other's habits, thoughts and feelings, as if they were dwellers in different zones, or inhabitants of different planets; who are formed by a different breeding, are fed by a different food, are ordered by different manners, and are not governed by the same laws . . . the rich and the poor" (Disraeli, 1845). This description might well apply today to many of the countries listed in Table 3-4.

There is one great difference between the pharoahs, mandarins, Khmer kings, and Aztec rulers and the world's contemporary ruling elites: the culture that has in the past few centuries been spread to every part of the earth by colonialism, commerce, and communication. It is now possible, indeed commonplace, for strangers from different continents to attend the same conference or business meeting, dressed alike in suit and tie or in the latest Paris fashion, drinking the same highballs and eating the same cuisine, exchanging the same political gossip and laughing at the same jokes. They may be graduates of the same universities or employees of the same multinational corporation or international agency; or they may be senior officials of their government, professional society, or bank. The ruling elites, whether they are traditional, are descendants of immigrants, or are expatriates, share many elements of a common culture that ignores national borders and ties its members together in a web of loyalties and affiliations.

Some sociologists have discerned a corresponding "culture of poverty" that "transcends regional, rural-urban and national differences and shows remarkable cross-national similarities. . ." (Lewis, 1968). In contrast to the transnational elite culture, the common elements in the culture of poverty have probably arisen independently in different areas, as common adaptations to the same basic socioeconomic problems. Especially among the urban poor, however, specific elements such as films, popular music, and many consumer goods may be identical in

Table 3-5. Deaths by social class, London, 1840

Class	Proportion of deaths from epidemics to total deaths of each class (%)	Proportion of deaths of children under 1 year to births in that year	Proportion of deaths of children under 10 years to total deaths of each class (%)	Mean age of death of all who died—men, women and children	Mean age of all who died above age 21 years
Gentry, professional persons, and their families	6.5	1 to 10	24.7	44	61
Tradesmen, shopkeepers, and their families	20.5	1 to 6	52.4	23	50
Wage classes, artisans, laborers, and their families	22.2	1 to 4	54.5	22	49

Source: Hanlon, John J. 1974. Public Health Administration and Practice, 6th Ed., St. Louis, The C. V. Mosby Co.; modified from Chadwick as quoted by Richardson, B. W.: The health of Nations, a Review of the Works of Edwin Chadwick London, 1887, Longmans, Green & Co., Vol. II, p. 80.

Table 3-6. Infant mortality per thousand live births, Great Britain, various years

Years	All classes	Social class[a]				
		I	II	III	IV	V
1921	79.1	38.4	55.5	76.8	89.4	97.0
1930–32	61.6	32.7	45.0	57.6	66.8	77.1
1949–53	29.5	18.7	21.6	28.6	33.8	40.8
1964–65	17.5	12.7		17.2	20.8	

[a]See text for specification of classes.
Source: Logan and Lambert, 1975.

Accra, Rio, and Bangkok, thus leading again to a certain commonality of experience and outlook.

Intermediate in international acculturation are the so-called middle classes: businessmen, civil servants, teachers, junior professionals, and others who share a common background of moderate education, limited wealth, and strong ambition for upward mobility, especially for their children. This middle group is dominant in industrialized countries. In some of the developing countries, particularly in Latin America, the middle class is increasing in numbers. The middle class is sometimes defined to a great extent by ethnic as well as by economic groups, for instance, the Chinese in parts of southeast Asia and, until recently, the Indians in east Africa.

The point of this discussion of socioeconomic status groupings is that the life experiences of each are reflected in its health, sickness, and mortality. There is nothing new about this, either: Edwin Chadwick published careful records, made in the London of Disraeli's time, to show how these characteristics varied with social class (Table 3-5). Note that for the highest social class (Gentry, professional persons, and their families), the infant mortality rate was 100 per thousand live births and mean life expectancy was 44 years—both figures characteristic of very poor countries today.

The British Registrar General has for some time classified occupations (not persons) in five official social classes, depending upon their general standing within the community (Hobson, 1975). These are:

I. Professional, etc., occupations (e.g., law, medicine, the Church)

II. Intermediate occupations (e.g., employers, managers, farmers)
III. Skilled occupations (e.g., fitters, clerks, engine drivers)
IV. Partly skilled occupations (e.g., machine minders)
V. Unskilled occupations (e.g., labourers, kitchen hands)

It is interesting to compare recent infant mortality rates in Britain (Table 3-6) with those of 1840, with respect to the actual values given, and their distribution by social class. The inverse relationship between socioeconomic status and mortality is maintained at all ages, and presumably in all countries. Table 3-7 illustrates this relationship among adult white males in the United States. Note that not all specific causes of death follow this pattern; some (such as breast cancer in females) show entirely the opposite trend.

Relationship of Economic Development to Health

It seems clear that modernization and development are here to stay, are spreading (sometimes hesitatingly and imperfectly) throughout the world,

Table 3-7. Mortality ratios by cause of death and education, white males ages 45 to 64, United States, 1960

Cause of death	Less than 8 years	Elementary 8 years	High school 1 to 4 years	College 1 or more years
ALL CAUSES[a]	115	106	97	77
Tuberculosis	184	119	80	21
Cancer, total	109	112	94	83
of lung, bronchus	118	114	95	61
(of breast)[b]	87	98	103	111[b]
Diabetes mellitus	103	80	124	71
Cerebrovascular disease	117	102	90	92
Arteriosclerotic heart disease	101	101	107	81
Influenza and pneumonia	163	106	76	63
Cirrhosis of the liver	96	108	101	94
Accidents, total	145	116	92	64
motor vehicle	129	118	96	70
Suicide	125	128	89	72

[a] Overall index for all causes, and each cause, = 100.
[b] White females, ages 45 to 64.
Source: Adapted from Kitagawa and Hauser, 1968.

and have complex interrelationships with health. To untangle some of these, one may look first at the single parameter of life expectancy. The infant mortality rates described above provide a hint. Lowe (1975) has gone further in examining death rates and expectation of life at birth, particularly in the United Kingdom. In the eighteenth century only half the population survived to their 15th birthday. A century later half survived to 40, and half the children born in 1973 can expect to see their 70th birthday (Table 3-8). Expectation of life at birth is often considered the best single indicator of the health status of a population because, unlike the crude mortality rate, it is independent of population age structure.

Even though average per capita income or GNP figures alone do not specify the different factors that affect health, it is generally true that improved socioeconomic conditions are reflected in higher expectation of life at birth. Figure 3-1 and Table 3-8 show this trend over time for several countries; Table 3-9 presents a current cross-sectional view of the

Table 3-8. The change in expectation of life in the Western world since the seventeenth century

	Number surviving out of 1,000 live-born males		
Age	End of 17th century[a]	Middle of 19th century[b]	Today (1973)[b]
0	1,000	1,000	1,000
5	582	724	978
10	531	690	976
15	505	673	974
20	481	652	972
30	426	595	960
40	356	532	948
50	275	456	909
60	191	356	803
70	110	223	575
80		80	246

[a]Halley's life table from Breslau data.
[b]English life tables.
Source: Lowe, 1975.

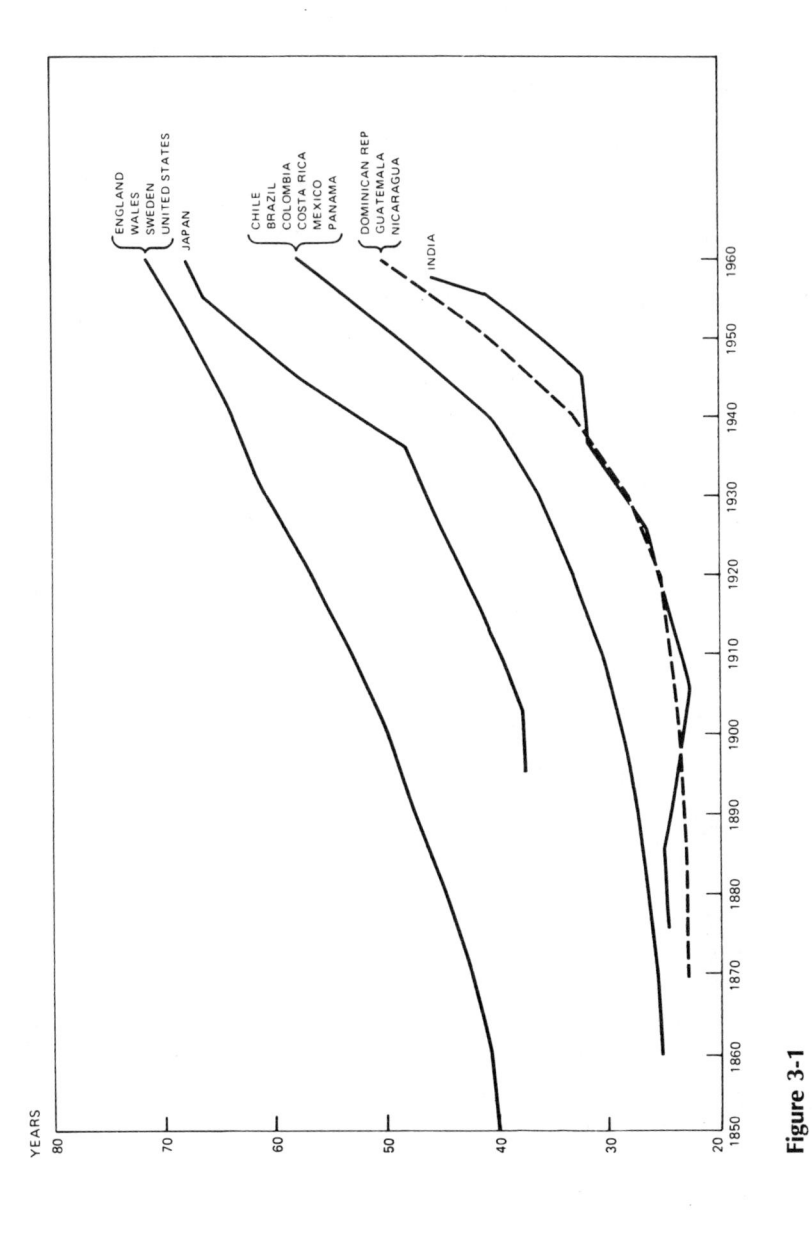

Figure 3-1
Trends in life expectancy in selected countries. SOURCE: World Bank, 1975.

Table 3-9. Per capita gross national product and expectation of life at birth for 59 countries of the world, mid-1960s

Per capita gross national product (in US $)	Expectation of life at birth							
	Less than 40 years	40–44	45–49	50–54	55–59	60–64	65–69	Over 70	Total
Less than 200	2	3	2	4	–	1	–	–	12
200–399	3	1	3	3	3	–	1	–	14
400–599	–	–	–	1	–	3	1	–	5
600–999	–	–	–	1	2	2	4	–	9
1,000–1,999	–	–	–	–	–	–	6	1	7
2,000 and more	–	–	–	–	–	–	8	4	12
TOTAL	5	4	5	9	5	6	20	5	59

Source: United Nations, 1974.

same relationship and confirms the correlation. The extensive studies of McGranahan et al. (1970) may shed some light on the ways in which present-day GNP differentials are associated with health-related statistics. Table 3-10 shows, for 115 countries, calculated correlation coefficients between two commonly accepted indicators of health status and 13 selected indicators of development. Note that infant mortality correlates most strongly with electrification, education, and employment in agriculture, while expectation of life at birth correlates best with these factors and, especially, with adult literacy. These numbers do not imply specific cause and effect relationship.

The dramatic improvements in expectation of life can be attributed mostly to reductions in mortality in infancy and childhood. Given survival to middle age, the expectation of further life has also improved over time, but not so much as in the very young. According to Table 3-8 the chance of surviving from age 50 to 60 was .69 at the end of the seventeenth century, .78 in the mid-nineteenth, and is about .88 today. The chance of surviving from birth to age 5 was .58, .72, and .98 respectively, an increase of 69% for the five-year interval, compared with 27% for the

Table 3-10. Correlation coefficients between infant mortality rate and expectation of life at birth with selected indicators of development, 115 countries, around 1960

Indicator	Infant mortality rate	Expectation of life at birth
No. of inhabitants per physician	.76	−.69
No. of inhabitants per hospital bed	.40	−.56
Calories consumed per person per day	−.70	.76
Animal protein eaten per person per day	−.73	.79
% of adult population literate	−.74	.90
% of ages 5–19 in prim. or sec. school	−.79	.84
% of dwellings with piped water	−.70	.69
% of dwellings with electricity	−.81	.88
Daily newspaper circulation per capita	−.75	.77
% of adult males in agriculture	.79	−.85
Steel consumption, kg per capita	−.68	.68
Energy consumption, kg coal equiv./cap.	−.61	.63
Gross national product per capita	−.70	.73

Source: Adapted from McGranahan et al., 1970.

ten-year interval from 50 to 60 in roughly two centuries. Of course, these figures are only general approximations and, however credible they appear, should not be taken too literally.

Virtually all commentators ascribe the great decline in childhood mortality in countries that were developing during the eighteenth and nineteenth centuries to improved nutrition, water supply, excreta disposal, and housing; legislation to control employment of women and children; and public health services in the broad sense. McKeown and Lowe (1974), for instance, show as a case in point the reduction in childhood mortality from measles in England and Wales from 1850 to 1970 (Fig. 3-2). One conceivable explanation for this trend might be that the measles virus spontaneously became less virulent during this period. That this probably has not happened is demonstrated in west Africa, where measles today, caused by the same virus that is found in England, produces a very high mortality in young children. The drop in childhood mortality from measles in England is not an isolated case; similar declines have occurred in scarlet fever, and the same sort of picture can be shown for diptheria, whooping cough, and the other infectious "childhood" diseases. The long-term trend in tuberculosis mortality is especially striking (Fig. 3-3). All of these declines have accompanied improvements in nutrition and living conditions, and they began before there was scientific knowledge of the causative agents, mode of transmission, prevention by immunization, or means of chemotherapy.

There are on the other hand some diseases, including communicable diseases of childhood, for which sanitary measures and improvements in nutrition have had no beneficial effect. An example of such a disease is rubella. As Krugman (1977) has shown (Fig. 3-4), a substantial and permanent reduction in rubella incidence in some areas arose only after the introduction of an attenuated rubella vaccine, developed "after many long years of scientific endeavor in basic virology." Indeed, it is widely believed that the prevalence of some diseases, such as paralytic poliomyelitis, has actually been fostered by improvements in standards of living. In this view, infection with poliovirus in early infancy will induce antibody formation and immunity, with relatively less likelihood of paralysis than a first infection in a susceptible older person. Where sanitary conditions are very good, many people are not exposed to the virus very early in life, do not develop the resulting immunity, and are therefore more severely affected by an encounter later on. The development and widespread use of killed and live poliovirus vaccines has been the critical

DEVELOPMENT

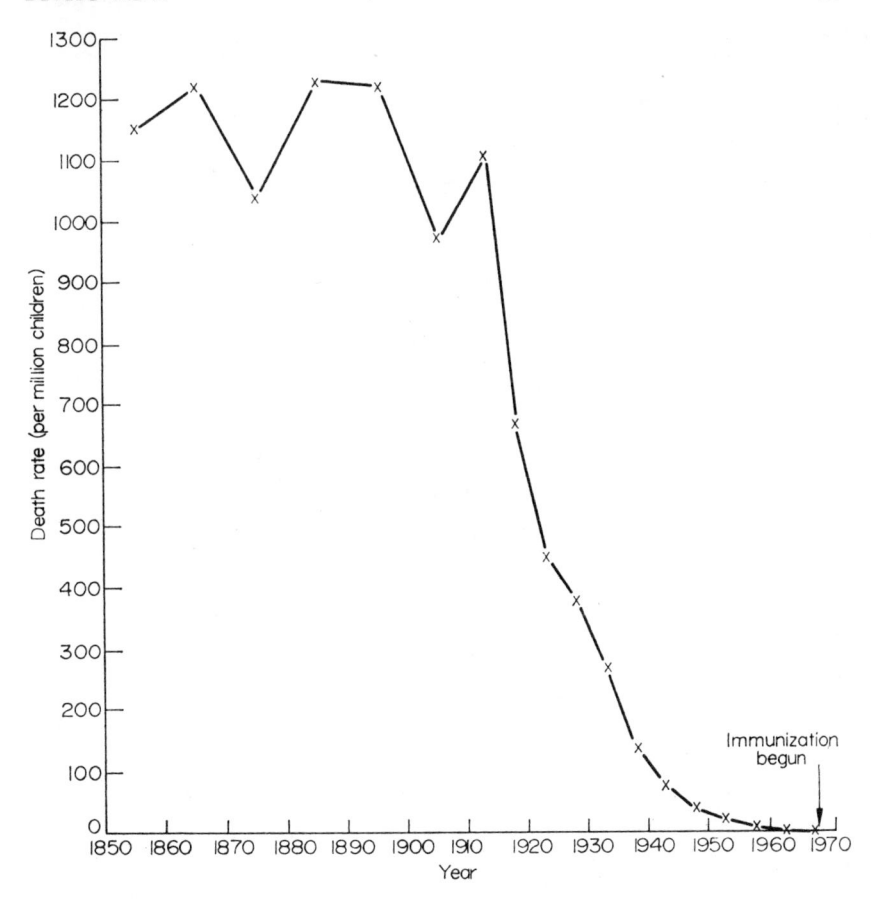

Figure 3-2
Mean annual death rate for measles of children under 15, England and Wales, 1850–1970. SOURCE: McKeown and Lowe, 1974.

factor in the sharp reduction in cases of paralytic poliomyelitis in recent decades.

Present trends toward greater life expectancy in twentieth-century developing countries are in general climbing at a much greater rate than those experienced in the past by the now-industrialized countries (Fig. 3-1). In Sri Lanka, for example, crude mortality dropped from 22.4 per thousand in 1930 to 9.7 in 1958, and in the same interval infant mortality declined from 175 to 64.5 per thousand live births (Griffith et al., 1971).

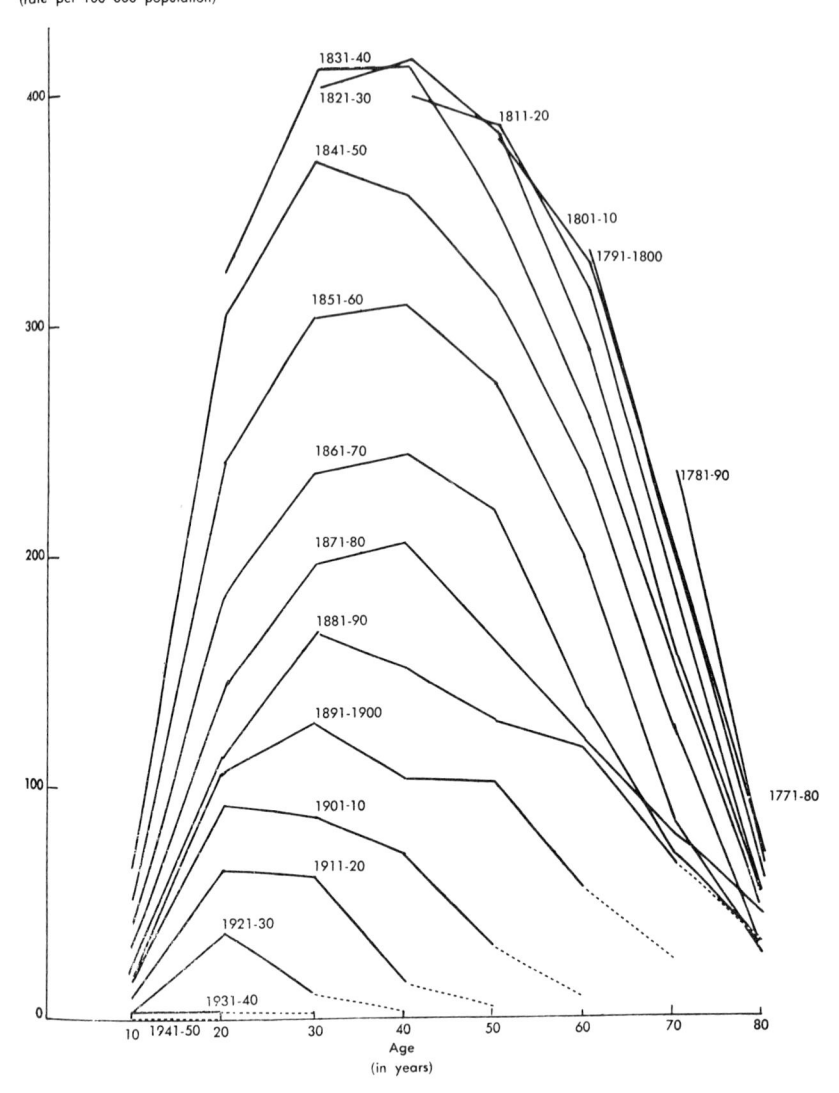

Figure 3-3

Age-specific mortality from respiratory TB, male generations, England and Wales, 1851–1959. Each curve represents a group of generations, the respective years of birth being shown above the curves. The rates have been computed by ten-year age groups. SOURCE: United Nations, 1963.

DEVELOPMENT 97

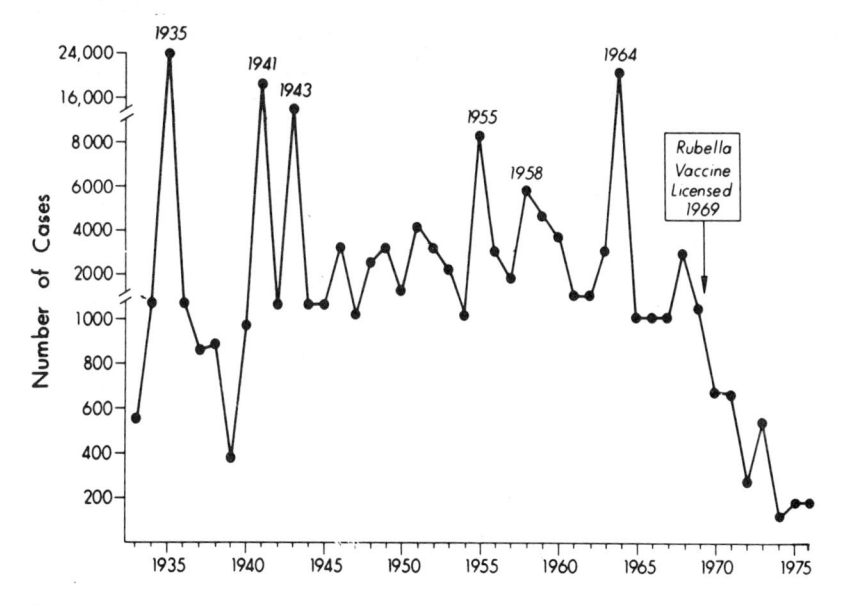

Figure 3-4

Reported cases of rubella in New York City, 1933–1977. SOURCE: Krugman, 1977.

For less developed regions as a whole, a gain of eight years in expectation of life at birth was achieved between the mid-1950s and mid-1970s so that on average the difference between developed and developing countries is now about 21 years, and the gap continues to narrow.

The World Health Organization, in analyzing this relationship, has observed that:

It appears plausible to assume that a certain take off in development is a prerequisite to rapidly falling mortality. A government structure conducive to socioeconomic development, progress in education, road communications, and an administrative infrastructure, even rudimentary, seem to play an important role in the initial stage. Once the process of decline is under way, public health measures, supported and coordinated in many cases at international level, become increasingly important and the decline takes place with such rapidity that improvements in levels of living are outdistanced. However, it seems that an expectancy of life at birth of 55–60 years constitutes a point beyond which the social, political, and economic factors again become increasingly operative. (WHO, 1974)

If the three-stage pattern described by the WHO is generally applicable, then health measures per se, such as immunization, are most effective in reducing mortality in the middle stage, in which most people in developing countries find themselves today. Because reductions in the mortality column inevitably appear as increases in the population column, it is a simple matter for some critics to accuse health professionals of responsibility for "the population explosion." In fact, the problem of population growth is by no means so clearcut. Let us look at the world population situation in its most general outline.

THE HUMAN POPULATION

The population of the world in the mid-1970s has reached 4,000 million people, and is expanding at about 2% annually (80 million per year or more than 9,000 per hour). The number of analysts and commentators upon this growth seems to increase at a rate even greater, and readers can select from a spectrum of predictions ranging from extremely optimistic to utterly gloomy. While the effects of population growth upon human health in the next decades are a matter for speculation, the importance of human numbers to an understanding of world health problems is not in doubt.

The number of people on earth increased rather slowly, perhaps at 0.1% annually, from earliest times until the late seventeenth century, when Europe and her colonies began to show a rapid rise. The elements that determine population growth are complex, and the whole story is not revealed by a simple comparison of crude birth and death rates. It is unmistakably true, however, that a birth rate of 40 per thousand in a year, with 38 deaths per thousand in the same year in the same population, will result in an increase of 2 per thousand, or 0.2%. Holding births constant, a reduction in deaths to 20 will yield a 2% increase, and further reduction to 10 will yield 3%. Just such a trend has occurred with rapid and significant reductions in mortality in some parts of the world, unaccompanied by equivalent declines in natality, resulting in the situation shown in Table 3-11. Any capital amount increasing a fixed percentage, x, when compounded annually, will double in about $70/x$ years. Therefore a 2% growth rate will result in a doubling in 35 years and a 3% rate in less than 24, situations that now exist in various parts of the world. Mortality is now very low in the so-called developed countries and expectation of life at birth for both sexes is 70 years or more. Even if death rates do fall somewhat more, their effect upon population growth in these countries will be negligible because the probability of survival through the normal span of fertility is already very high.

Table 3-11. Population, crude birth and death rates, and annual rate of increase, world and selected areas, 1965–1975

Region	Population[a]	Birth rate[b]	Death rate[b]	Annual increase %
World	3,967	32	13	1.9
Europe[c]	473	16	10	0.6
U.S.S.R.	255	18	8	1.0
North America	237	17	9	1.0
Australia & New Zealand	16.8	19	9	1.9
Japan	111	18	7	1.2
Africa	401	47	20	2.7
Latin America	324	38	9	2.7
Central America	79	43	9	3.2
South Asia	1,250	42	17	2.6
East Asia[d]	56	31	9	2.2
China	839	28	10	1.7

[a]1975.
[b]Per thousand population.
[c]Excluding the U.S.S.R.
[d]Excluding Japan and China.
Source: Adapted from United Nations, 1976.

World Food Supply

Starting from the current base, the present rate of growth or something close to it will almost inevitably bring the world over the 8,000 million mark early in the twenty-first century. Many commentators find this prospect menacing. Predictions of imminent starvation for large segments of mankind have now been popular for some time, but according to statistics of the Food and Agriculture Organization the per capita food production in the world has increased by about 24% since the 1930s (Table 3-12), and in the developing countries recent years have witnessed an improvement in the overall situation (Fig. 3-5). The situation is not entirely sanguine, however, for many specific areas, such as the Sahel region of Africa, have experienced large shortfalls in food supply. Moreover, just because food is produced does not assure that it is distributed equitably either demographically or geographically nor that it is of the most suitable types. Nutritionists do not agree on the optimal or minimal intake of calories, total protein, or animal protein per capita under different condi-

Table 3-12. Trends in per capita food production for major areas and regions of the world, 1934–1938 to 1971

	Index numbers (1934–1938 = 100)								Average annual rate of growth, 1959–1961 to 1969–1971 (percentage)
	1934–1938	1965	1966	1967	1968	1969	1970	1971	
WORLD[a]	100	116	119	122	123	121	122	124	0.6
More developed regions	100	139	147	150	154	150	152	158	1.5
Western Europe	100	146	156	159	164	160	165	168	1.7
Eastern Europe and U.S.S.R.	100								
North America	100	121	124	127	127	124	122	133	0.7
Oceania	100	100	114	102	122	114	111	113	1.4
Developing regions[a]	100	104	103	106	107	107	108	107	0.3
Africa	100	99	98	102	100	99	99	102	—
Far East[a]	100	99	98	100	104	105	107	105	0.4
Near East	100	121	122	124	124	123	120	121	0.2
Latin America	100	102	100	103	101	102	103	100	0.3

[a]Excluding China.
Source: Estimates provided by the Food and Agriculture Organization of the United Nations. United Nations, 1973.

Figure 3-5

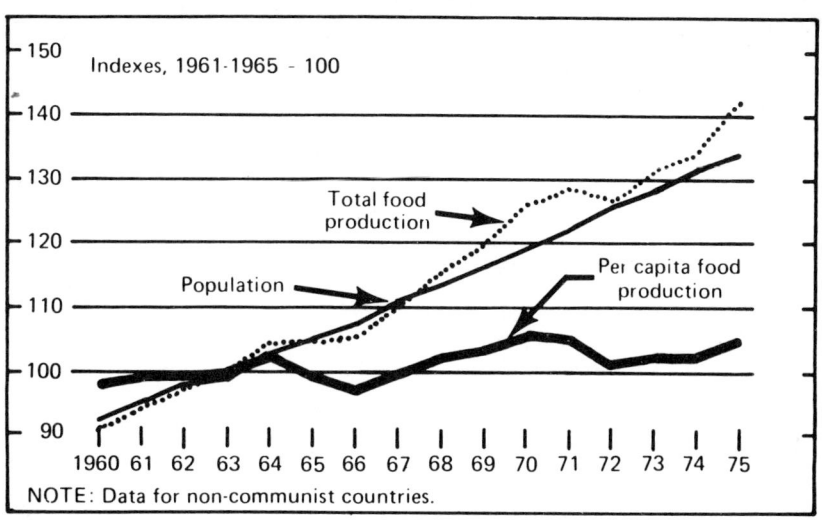

Food and population in developing countries, 1960–75. SOURCE: U.S. Agency for International Development. 1976.

tions. The situation is complicated by the quality of individual food items, their combination into characteristic menus, and an infinity of practices regarding food preparation and consumption. Loss of growing or stored food to rodents and insects may be very high. Seasonal factors, as we have already seen, may be important, both in respect to availability of nutrients and human activity cycles. In recent years nevertheless, it seems that the supply of calories in relation to requirements has been less than adequate in most developing countries with the exception of Latin America where there may be an overall excess of a few percent. Even here, however, there are many areas with severe deficiencies. The world's per capita protein supply has changed very little during the lifetime of most persons now living. The FAO has estimated an increase of a few percent per capita in some developing areas and in Latin America, and a drop of a few percent in other developing regions from about the mid-1930s to the mid-1960s. The type of protein produced and consumed varies greatly from one region to another, and decisions about what to grow and what to eat have far-reaching consequences. Figure 3-6 shows the almost 30-fold range in protein production per acre depending upon the food product. But it cannot be assumed that for any given acre, each of the 15 alternative foods listed is an equally useful option, nor that

Figure 3-6

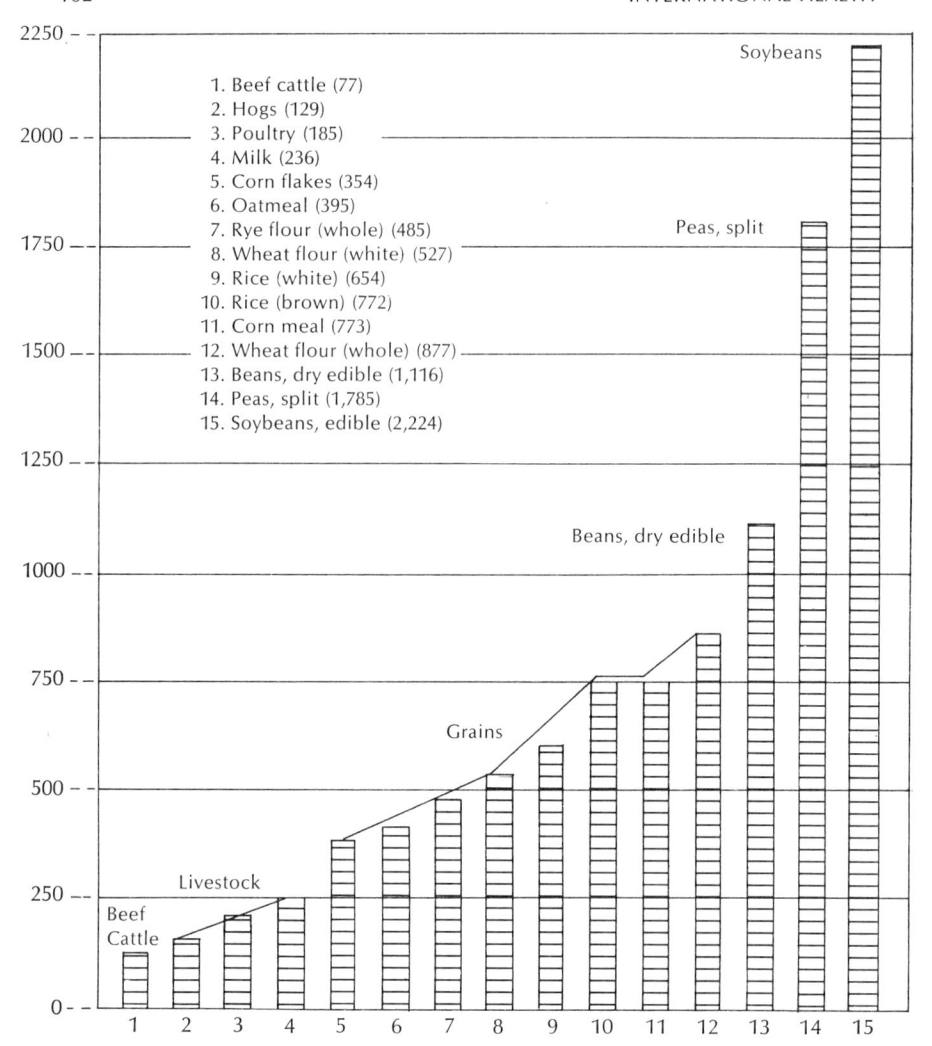

Number of days of protein requirement (by a moderately active man) produced by one acre, yielding selected food products. SOURCE: Bean, 1966.

1. Beef cattle (77)
2. Hogs (129)
3. Poultry (185)
4. Milk (236)
5. Corn flakes (354)
6. Oatmeal (395)
7. Rye flour (whole) (485)
8. Wheat flour (white) (527)
9. Rice (white) (654)
10. Rice (brown) (772)
11. Corn meal (773)
12. Wheat flour (whole) (877)
13. Beans, dry edible (1,116)
14. Peas, split (1,785)
15. Soybeans, edible (2,224)

the different proteins and other constituents of these crops are nutritionally equivalent. In addition, problems associated with production, storage, distribution, marketing, preparation, and consumption of these different foods vary greatly from one region to another. It would be a great mistake to conclude from Figure 3-6 that the world can solve its protein problems simply by growing more soybeans.

Environment and Resources

Man's use of the environment has generally been profligate. In many regions of the world soils have been eroded and depleted, forests denuded, and oceans and lakes used as sinks for wastes. Yet never before has there been a claim on the environment of such magnitude as exists today, and this will certainly accelerate in coming years. The unprecedented population growth is coupled in some areas with rising incomes and consequently increased per capita demand for all sorts of goods, a demand that agriculture, industry, and technology combine to promote as well as to meet. As a result, natural systems are everywhere strained. For the first time there seems to some a real possibility that the earth's stabilizing mechanisms may be permanently damaged by the drain, and by the wastes, of production and consumption. Needed increases in agricultural production will, for example, be accompanied by much higher total levels of environmental pollution from fertilizers and pesticides.

There is also growing concern that the supply of specific resources may become exhausted in coming decades. It is often said that the United States, with 6% of the world's population, consumes some 30% to 40% of its resources. It is therefore impossible even with today's population for the entire world to live at American standards. The energy consumption of one American is equivalent to that of 2.7 Frenchmen, 7 Yugoslavs, 64 Indians, 178 Nigerians, 443 Haitians, or 854 residents of Nepal (Table 3-13). Utilization of printing and writing paper, a telling measure of national development, shows the same discrepancies as does the consumption of energy (Table 3-14). Even if the world had a stable population, far-reaching realignments would be necessary in order to meet the growing demand for greater equity in the opportunity to share in its resources.

Population and Health

To many readers of this book the preceding comments will certainly sound familiar, perhaps hackneyed. Problems of food supply, consumption of resources, production of pollution, extension of services and amenities, and political and social stresses are considered by many social prognosticators to be essentially insoluble, and the apocalyptic view holds that disaster is inevitable. While this may or may not be true, we can

Table 3-13. Energy consumption per capita, kg of coal equivalent, selected areas, 1975[a]

WORLD	2,028		
Africa	393	Asia	545
Algeria	754	Bangladesh	28
Congo	209	China	693
Egypt	405	Dem. Kampuchea[c]	16
Ghana	182	Hong Kong	1,119
Kenya	174	India	221
Libya	1,299	Indonesia	178
Mali	25	Japan	3,622
Nigeria	90	Nepal	10
Rwanda	14	Philippines	326
South Africa[b]	2,953	Singapore	2,151
Tanzania	70	Thailand	284
Upper Volta	20		
Zaire	78		
		North America	10,888
		Canada	9,880
		United States	10,999
Middle East	1,055	Central America	1,174
Iran	1,353	Costa Rica	544
Israel	2,806	Cuba	1,157
		Guatemala	237
Jordan	408	Haiti	30
Lebanon	928	Mexico	1,221
Qatar	35,328	Panama	865
Turkey	630	Canal Zone	14,150
Yemen	49	Puerto Rico	3,203
South America	813	Oceania	4,782
Argentina	1,754	Australia	6,485
Brazil	670	New Zealand	3,111
Paraguay	153	Papua New Guinea	278
Surinam	2,063		

Europe	4,023
Belgium	5,584
France	3,944
Germany, Dem. Rep.	6,835
Germany, Fed. Rep.	5,345
Greece	2,090
Ireland	3,097
Italy	3,012
Luxembourg	15,504
Portugal	983
Sweden	6,178
United Kingdom	5,265
U.S.S.R.	5,546
Yugoslavia	1,930

[a]estimated
[b]including data for Botswana, Lesotho, Swaziland, and Namibia
[c]formerly Cambodia
Source: Adapted from United Nations, 1977.

attempt to describe here the role of population growth both as a determinant and a consequence of health and disease.

As mentioned, the primary immediate cause for the population surge of the last 200 years has been a reduction in mortality, particularly in younger age groups. Greater survival of children will alter the age structure of a population, giving it progressively more reproductive capability. If this is combined with the reduction of age at menarche as described in Chapter 1, and with social customs permitting marriage and/or childbearing at relatively early ages, a population boom is readily foreseeable. Improved health also increases fertility by reducing the effects of illnesses such as venereal disease, malaria, and toxoplasmosis that may cause significant fetal wastage and by lengthening the mother's (and the father's!) reproductive span. These effects also result from improving nutrition as well as by preventing or treating disease. Improved health may also extend the period of a mother's lactation and thus strengthen an infant's chances of survival. Another factor enhancing the infant survival rate may be the substantial reduction in fertility that nursing mothers experience.

High fertility of itself bears certain consequences for health. The risks of perinatal, infant, and child mortality, high with first births, decline with the second, third, and fourth, but thereafter these risks increase. Where birth intervals are short (less than a year), fetal, infant, and child-

Table 3-14. Paper consumption, kg per capita, selected areas, 1975

Area	Newsprint	Other printing and writing paper
WORLD	6.0	8.5
Developed countries	18.4	26.1
Developing countries	1.0	1.4
North America	43.4	54.0
Europe	13.0	24.7
Oceania	28.7	14.4
U.S.S.R.	4.4	4.8
Latin America	3.5	4.1
Asia	1.7	2.5
Africa	0.8	1.0

Source: Adapted from United Nations Educational, Scientific, and Cultural Organization, 1976.

hood mortality are all high. Generally, it has been found that the height and weight of children and the quality of maternal care are inversely related to family size. Large families may also be detrimental to the health of the harried mothers, as the risk of maternal mortality rises sharply after the third birth.

Populations having high birth rates and moderate to low death rates will be comparatively young. In developing countries today a median age in the late teens contrasts sharply with a median in the 30s in industrialized nations. In Europe, 10% to 12% of the total population may exceed 65 years, about four times the proportion in Africa or Asia. Therefore, diseases characteristic of advanced age (especially cardiovascular and malignant) have a far greater impact per 1,000 inhabitants in Europe. The entire spectrum of disease distribution is strongly related to the age distribution of particular populations, discussed further in chapter 5.

Control of Human Population Growth

We have seen that the two major determinants of human numbers are birth rates and death rates, and that the latter have fallen sharply in most parts of the world. If the goal is decreased population growth, there are two ways to achieve this: The first is to increase mortality, an option not at present widely advocated in public. The second is to reduce natality. There are many ideas about how this may best be accomplished. Some experts, looking at the historical record of the present-day developed countries, have placed emphasis upon the theory of demographic transition.

Demographic transition theorists have found that sharp declines in mortality have been followed, after some lag, by reduction in fertility. In the ideal situation, a "high stationary" stage with equally high birth and death rates gives way through an "expanding" stage of sustained birth and falling death rates to a "low stationary" stage, in which both rates are low and balanced. The transition may even be followed by a "declining" stage where mortality, however low, may still surpass natality. It has become commonplace to believe that economic development is the engine by which Europe, North America, and Australia have been pulled through this transition; that couples with money in their pockets, assured of the survival of two or three children, will opt for consumer goods and better living standards instead of larger families.

The realities of the situation are far more complex. Teitelbaum (1975), while supporting the generality of transition theory, has pointed out many exceptions within the European record of the past few centuries. More importantly, he and other authors have questioned the basic similarity between nineteenth-century Europe and the twentieth-century LDCs, and thus the relevance of one experience to the other. Nevertheless, it does appear plausible that without improvement in the standard of living, fertility declines are unlikely to occur except by coercion or disaster.

The decade 1965-74 did in fact see a reduction in the world's gross birth rate from 34 to 30 per thousand, with a corresponding minor decline in the rate of natural increase. If it were possible to reduce the number of children per family to 2 by 1990, then the world's population would increase by only 58% in 50 years rather than by 100% in 30 years (Table 3-15). One means by which it is hoped that such a fertility decline may be hastened is through "family planning."

Freedman and Berelson (1976) define family planning programs as:

organized programs—mainly governmental in sponsorship, support, and administration, but often involving private efforts (family planning associations) and occasionally commercial ones—designed to provide the information, supplies, and services of (modern) means of fertility control to those interested. Such programs frequently have a persuasional component as well, advocating the small-family norm, but that element is not strong. Usually the programs more or less accept existing levels of motivation and seek to meet the existing "need" by minimizing

Table 3-15. World population growth, 1970 to 2020, under two assumptions

	Number of inhabitants ($\times 10^9$)					
	Assumption 1[a]			Assumption 2[b]		
Year	LDCs[c]	MDCs[d]	Total	LDCs[c]	MDCs[d]	Total
1970	2.52	1.08	3.60	2.52	1.08	3.60
1980	3.23	1.17	4.40	3.14	1.16	4.30
1990	4.32	1.28	5.60	3.46	1.24	4.70
2000	5.82	1.38	7.20	3.91	1.29	5.20
2010	8.02	1.48	9.50	4.19	1.31	5.50
2020	11.12	1.58	12.70	4.40	1.30	5.70

[a]If the number of children per family remain at the 1970-75 level.
[b]If the number of children per family is reduced to 2 by 1990.
[c]Less developed countries.
[d]More developed countries.
Source: Adapted from U.S. Agency for International Development, 1976.

the cost of fertility control not only monetarily but personally, by legitimizing the idea and providing services through trusted sources.

The primary methods of fertility control provided by family planning programs are oral contraceptives, intrauterine devices, condoms, sterilization, and abortion. The actual role of such programs in the recently recorded decline in world birth rates is very difficult to estimate. In some small areas, such as Singapore, Jamaica, South Korea, Hong Kong, and Taiwan, the programs have gained wide acceptance; in other regions, particularly Africa, they have had little or no appreciable effect. A number of countries consider themselves underpopulated and have shown no interest in population limitation. By 1973, only 32 of 117 LDCs had official policies to reduce population growth rates, but these included some 75% of the inhabitants of the developing world (Freedman and Berelson, 1976). The largest such country is, of course, China, where fertility decline has been very substantial, particularly in the cities. However, it is not clear just what proportion of this reduction can be attributed to "family planning" per se within the larger context of Chinese goals and society since the revolution.

The consequences of rising human numbers have been so thoroughly discussed elsewhere that further comment here would be superfluous, but one other aspect of population does merit examination from the standpoint of international health. That is the distribution of people within countries.

THE RUSH TO THE CITIES

National statistics for persons per square kilometer range from about 1 in Libya or Mauritania to almost 4,500 in Singapore. Almost everywhere there is a strong tendency towards greater clumping of populations, so that the proportion of people living in urban areas is increasing at a rate faster than the underlying national population growth. The definition of "urban area" varies with reporting country; international comparisons are therefore difficult. The United Nations Statistics Office uses five main types of criteria in its urban classification: administrative area, population size, local government area, urban characteristics, and predominant economic activity. Many demographers feel that, at least on cultural grounds, the total population of industrialized countries should be considered "urban."

Urban-rural differences in mortality have been exhaustively analyzed by Federici et al. (1976). Historically, urban death rates substantially exceeded those in the countryside, at least in Europe. John Graunt demonstrated this in England in the late seventeenth century. The difference there became more acute with the industrial revolution and consequent bad living conditions in cities and towns. Prior to about 1900, urban mortality was also higher than rural in Prussia, Finland, Sweden, France, and the United States. In the present century the difference in urban-rural mortality has vanished in these countries owing to changes in society and better general standards of living, particularly improvements in sanitation and hygiene. Differences in specific causes of death tend to be small, but in general cancer rates are higher in urban areas, especially in males, and most particularly in the case of lung cancer. Whether this relative increase is a result of breathing city air, or cigarette smoking, or better diagnosis and reporting, is not known. Tuberculosis deaths have also tended to be higher in urban areas.

Cassel (1971) has found that in the United States death rates (for all causes) were higher in urban areas before 1950, but by 1960 the situation had reversed and since then the ratio of rural to urban deaths has steadily increased. Throughout the world, there is a decline in the proportion of persons dependent for livelihood on agriculture and an increase of de-

Table 3-16. Total population, urban population, and percentage urban in total population, in major areas and regions of the world, 1950 and 1970

	Total population (millions)	
Area or region	1950	1970
WORLD TOTAL	2,505.9	3,621.0
More developed regions*	857.3	1,084.2
Less developed regions	1,648.6	2,536.8
Africa	219.2	351.7
Eastern Africa	62.7	99.8
Middle Africa	26.1	40.2
Northern Africa	51.2	86.0
Southern Africa	8.9	14.2
Western Africa	64.9	101.5
Latin America	164.1	284.2
Caribbean	16.9	25.6
Middle America	35.8	67.0
Temperate South America*	25.5	36.4
Tropical South America	85.9	155.3
Northern America*	166.1	226.4
East Asia	673.5	926.2
East Asia without Japan	589.8	821.9
Japan*[a]	83.6	104.3
South Asia	698.4	1,111.3
Europe*	392.0	459.0
Eastern Europe	86.5	102.9
Northern Europe	72.5	80.3
Southern Europe	108.6	127.7
Western Europe	122.4	148.1
Oceania	12.6	19.4
Australia and New Zealand*	10.1	15.4
Melanesia	1.8	2.8
Micronesia and Polynesia	0.7	1.3
Soviet Union*	180.1	242.8

Urban population (millions)		Percent urban	
1950	1970	1950	1970
691.5	1,315.2	27.6	36.3
435.7	692.8	50.8	63.9
255.9	622.5	15.5	24.5
28.4	74.7	12.9	21.2
3.2	10.4	5.0	10.5
1.6	6.8	6.0	16.9
12.0	30.9	23.5	35.9
5.4	10.0	37.8	41.2
6.2	16.6	9.5	16.3
67.1	161.0	40.9	56.7
5.6	11.3	32.9	44.0
14.2	36.0	39.5	53.7
16.0	28.1	62.8	77.4
31.4	85.7	36.5	55.2
105.7	167.9	63.6	74.2
99.1	245.7	14.7	26.5
69.6	190.1	11.8	23.1
29.5	55.5	35.3	53.2
108.2	230.9	15.5	20.8
204.0	284.1	52.1	61.9
37.3	54.7	43.2	53.2
51.3	59.3	70.8	73.9
38.1	59.4	35.1	46.5
77.4	110.7	63.2	74.7
8.1	13.6	64.8	74.7
8.0	12.9	78.7	84.2
0.0	0.3	2.0	10.2
0.1	0.3	20.6	27.6
70.9	137.3	39.4	56.6

*The regions marked with an asterisk are those considered as "more developed."
[a]Urban population is that of "densely inhabited districts."
Source: Adapted from United Nations, 1974a.

pendence on industry and services. In industrialized areas (North America, Europe, U.S.S.R.) there is continuing absolute decline of agricultural population; in developing countries total population growth is so great that agricultural populations are still increasing, but at a far slower pace than the growth of industrial urban areas.

A dramatic illustration of rapid urbanization is given in Table 3-16. In 1950 just over one quarter of humanity lived in urban areas. By 1970 the proportion exceeded one third. It has been estimated (Davis, 1965) that by 1990 more than half of all humans will be living in cities of 100,000 or more. Not only are more people living in cities, but cities are growing larger. Table 3-17 shows that the number of cities of over one million more than doubled between 1950 and 1970, and that the propor-

Table 3-17. Number of cities having at least one million inhabitants, population of these cities and percentage of urban population contained in "million-cities," world and eight major areas, 1950 and 1970

Area	Number of "million-cities" 1950	Number of "million-cities" 1970	Population of "million-cities" (millions) 1950	Population of "million-cities" (millions) 1970	Percentage of urban population in "million-cities" 1950	Percentage of urban population in "million-cities" 1970
WORLD TOTAL	75	162	173.9	416.2	25	31
More developed regions	51	83	126.2	223.5	29	32
Less developed regions	24	79	47.6	192.8	19	29
Africa	2	8	3.4	15.6	11	20
Latin America	6	16	15.3	52.9	23	33
Northern America	14	27	38.1	71.2	36	42
East Asia	13	36	31.4	100.9	31	37
South Asia	8	27	15.0	63.1	13	26
Europe	28	36	60.2	86.3	29	30
Oceania	2	2	3.0	5.1	38	39
Soviet Union	2	10	7.5	21.1	10	15

Source: United Nations, 1974a.

DEVELOPMENT 113

tion of urban residents living in "million-cities" in 1970 was almost identical in more and less developed regions. The trend towards rapid growth of cities in developing countries continues to be strong, and United Nations predictions for urban growth (Table 3-18) show that within the next generation many of the largest cities will be in developing

Table 3-18. Populations of selected urban areas, 1950–2000 (in millions)

Country	1950	Average annual rate of growth (%)	1975	Average annual rate of growth (%)	2000
Developing countries					
Mexico City	2.9	5.4	10.9	4.4	31.5
Buenos Aires	4.5	2.9	9.3	1.5	13.7
São Paulo	2.5	5.7	9.9	3.9	26.0
Rio de Janeiro	2.9	4.4	8.3	3.4	19.3
Bogotá	0.7	6.5	3.4	4.2	9.5
Cairo	2.4	4.3	6.9	3.6	16.9
Seoul	1.0	8.3	7.3	3.8	18.7
Manila	1.5	4.4	4.4	4.3	12.8
Kinshasa	0.2	9.7	2.0	5.6	7.8
Lagos	0.3	8.1	2.1	6.2	9.4
Shanghai	5.8	2.8	11.5	2.6	22.1
Peking	2.2	5.8	8.9	3.7	22.0
Jakarta	1.6	5.1	5.6	4.7	17.8
Calcutta	4.5	2.4	8.1	3.7	20.4
Bombay	2.9	3.7	7.1	4.2	19.8
Karachi	1.0	6.2	4.5	5.4	16.6
Developed Countries					
New York	12.3	1.3	17.0	1.3	22.2
London	10.2	0.2	10.7	0.7	12.7
Paris	5.4	2.1	9.2	1.2	12.4
Tokyo	6.7	3.9	17.5	2.0	28.7
Novosibirsk	0.6	2.9	1.3	1.8	2.0
Moscow	4.8	1.8	7.6	1.4	10.8

Source: Adapted from Orihuela, 1976.

countries. Recall that a growth rate of 4% leads to doubling in 17.5 years; of 5%, in about 14 years; and of 6% in just under 12 years! Urban growth in many countries is characterized by great concentration in one or a few large metropolitan areas. Table 3-19 illustrates the phenomenon for the cities of Latin America; other regions, including many more developed countries, are similar. The importance of the mega-cities is emphasized if it is realized that in 1975, 73 of 104 developing *countries* had total populations of under 10 million (Table 3-20).

Cities are growing by becoming larger rather than more intensely populated. In fact, the average population density in major cities is said to have declined by more than half since 1900 (Doxiadis, 1967).

In developing countries there has typically been a growth of squatter settlements in less desirable parts of the cities, especially around the

Table 3-19. Percent of national population in the single largest city, Latin America, about 1970

Country	City	Percentage
Argentina	Buenos Aires	39.0
Bolivia	La Paz	12.6
Brazil	São Paulo	8.9
Chile	Santiago	27.3
Colombia	Bogotá	11.8
Costa Rica	San José	25.6
Cuba	Havana	19.6
Dominican Republic	Santo Domingo	15.0
Ecuador	Guayaquil	13.1
El Salvador	San Salvador	10.7
Guatemala	Guatemala	14.8
Haiti	Port-au-Prince	8.2
Honduras	Tegucigalpa	10.3
Mexico	Mexico City	17.7
Nicaragua	Managua	17.5
Panama	Panama City	30.0
Paraguay	Asunción	18.7
Peru	Lima-Callao	18.4
Uruguay	Montevideo	46.7
Venezuela	Caracas	20.6
AVERAGE		19.325

Source: Adapted from Portes and Walton, 1976.

Table 3-20. Number of developing countries, by population size, 1975

Population size (millions)	No. of countries	Cum. no. of countries	Total pop/group	Cum. % of population
under 1	24	24	10	.5
1–5	35	59	100	5.9
5–10	14	73	100	11.3
10–15	8	81	109	17.2
15–25	8	89	177	26.8
25–50	8	97	267	41.3
50–100	4	101	263	55.6
over 100	3	104	818	100.0
TOTAL			1,844	

SOURCE: Adapted from Development Coordination Committee, 1976.

urban margins. Sometimes referred to as "septic fringes" because of their poor or nonexistent sanitary facilities, these areas are known locally as *barrios* or *barriadas* in Spanish-speaking Latin America, *favelas* in Brazil, *bidonvilles* in North Africa, *bustees* in South Asia, shantytowns, locations, and by many other names. These communities are home to hundreds of millions. Ross (1973) has estimated that 20% to 50% of the nominal population in most cities in developing countries are squatters, and representatives at the United Nations Conference on Habitat in Vancouver (June, 1976) have placed the figure at up to two-thirds in some. Worldwide, squatter settlements are growing at an annual rate of 12% (Hill, 1976), six times the rate for the world population as a whole.

Urbanization is a manifestation of changing societies in which the relationships of individuals, families, and communities are enmeshed. These relationships and the values of all persons, except those in the most remote regions, are touched and altered.

Fendall (1963) and Ross (1973), among others, have listed some of the factors that induce people to leave rural areas and migrate to cities. Subsistence in the countryside may be impossible because of overfarmed land diminishing in productivity or excessive division into small plots by distribution to many heirs. Rural laborers may be displaced by technological innovation, or changes in world commodity prices may lead to economic reversals. Wars, revolution, political agitation, ethnic or religious persecution, rural boredom, social ferment, weakening of traditions, and natural disaster all have had roles to play in the urban trend.

The great attractions of city life are the amenities so often lacking in rural areas: a stable and adequate wage structure; public services such as health centers, water, and electricity; social interactions; shopping; entertainment; and perhaps above all, schools and the opportunities for education and advancement of children. Actuality rarely lives up to hope and expectation since most migrants find themselves stuck in a life of poverty and bare subsistence. Yet it is very likely that the migrants, in the great majority, arrive with a realistic view of life in the city. Many had come to live for a limited time, before returning with their families; all have heard stories from friends or relatives who have preceded them on the urban trek. They stay for a variety of reasons but mostly because conditions in the city, however poor, are still better than those from which they fled.

Health problems encountered by migrants to cities are many. Psychological and emotional stress is often extreme. In places, such as southern Africa, where adult males come in large numbers as wage laborers, alcoholism, violent trauma, and sexually transmitted diseases are common. The breakdown of extended family life, important in many societies, causes severe strains. Where village life had been self-sufficient, traditional, and hierarchical, city life is based upon cash exchange. Everything must be bought and paid for. Women may not be able to have a garden vegetable plot or keep a goat for milk for the children. The clock becomes a dominant factor where jobs are concerned.

In many ways, migration to the city is like emigration to a foreign country. New divisions of labor develop within nuclear families as both parents, and often the children, adopt what are essentially foreign ways of life. Where regional or tribal dialects are common, as in Africa, India, Indonesia, and parts of Latin America, language may be a great problem, often accompanied by racial or ethnic discrimination. Lack of education and ignorance of town ways makes life difficult and exposes migrants to ridicule and victimization.

In addition, employers may consider it to be in their interest to maintain instability of migrant workers. Zigas et al. (1972) have described how some employers in New Guinea towns intentionally maintain a shifting labor force in order to avoid providing family housing, pensions, or unemployment pay, and to discourage growth of labor unions. Nevertheless, social consciousness and community organization may be strong in squatter localities, easing the problems of dislocation.

If psychological conditions in urban squatter settlements are poor, the physical environment is at least equally hazardous. The squalor has been remarked upon by many. Lie et al. (1966) worked in an urban slum several square kilometers in size in Jakarta, Indonesia. The following description of their study area is reminiscent of the account by Friedrich Engels of the slums of Manchester in 1844, and might have been written about any of a hundred cities of Asia, Africa, or Latin America.

The survey was conducted in a crowded slum with an average population of 12,000 per km^2 ... The soil consists of thick clay, and the small houses, most of which are made of bamboo or wood with earthern floors and roofs of palm leaves, are usually crowded together. An average house contains one or two small sleeping rooms, a kitchen and an open veranda. There are no roads in this area; foot-paths with open earthen drains on each side form the only connexion between the houses. There is no electricity or piped water supply. Water is obtained from wells or bought from water sellers and is usually grossly polluted ... Insanitary outdoor latrines are built here and there for common use; most consist of a hole in the ground, usually unprotected from rain and open to flies. Others are built on stilts above a canal that runs along the border of the area. Water to wash the hands after defaecation is rarely available in these latrines. Children usually defaecate in the open drains along the footpaths, and fresh faecal deposits are frequent within or on the edge of the drains. Garbage usually is left in a hole in the ground, where it is burnt from time to time, or is thrown into the canal. In the rainy monsoon the area is sometimes flooded. People of a low socioeconomic class live here, mainly new settlers who have come to Djakarta from the rural areas to earn wages. The population is therefore transient. Malnutrition and kwashiorkor are often noted among the infants.

It is little wonder that the 66 infants who could be followed over the full two-year period of the Jakarta study experienced 409 diarrheal episodes, an average of more than six per infant. There were 30 recorded deaths among the 156 infants who started the study despite the fact that 60 infants (some of whom may also have died) moved out of the area before the study ended.

In an extensive report on patterns of childhood mortality in the Americas, Puffer and Serrano (1973) also found that "in families without water and toilet facilities high proportions of the deaths occurred in the age periods when unfavorable environmental conditions combined with susceptibility to infectious agents result in high death rates." Table 3-21 confirms that only a minority of low-income urban dwellers have acess to adequate water supply or sewage disposal.

In the more mature areas of cities in developing countries, and in

Table 3-21. Estimates of access to water supply and sewerage[a], 78 countries, recent years

	Per capita income in 1970 (US$)			
	Less than $100	$101 to $150	$151 to $450	Greater than $450
Number of countries	15	17	34	12
Percentage of population with access to water supply				
Rural, with reasonable access	13	8[b]	28	32
Urban, with public standpost	24	31	21	17
Urban, with pipe to house	21	36	58	63
Percentage of population with access to sewage disposal				
Rural, adequate	7	12	26	n/a
Urban, other disposal methods[c]	54	67	40	n/a
Urban, sewage system	6	14	24	n/a

[a] These estimates were obtained by calculating the population-weighted average of reported coverage within the group of countries. The definitions of coverage and of urban and rural are those developed by the individual countries and hence are not comparable. Furthermore, no attempt has been made to evaluate the quality of these statistics at the country level. The values reported in this table should therefore be interpreted only as crude "order of magnitude" indicators.
[b] This value is dominated by India and Pakistan which report 5% and 3% coverage, respectively.
[c] Buckets, pit privies and septic tanks not connected to public sewer system.
Source: World Bank, 1975.

temperate zone cities in general, most urban dwellers live in circumstances far better than those described. Where environmental conditions are of a high standard, most of the contaminative diseases retreat to relative insignificance. Nevertheless, considerable variations in health status, as measured for instance by infant mortality, can occur between cities and even within single urban areas in industrialized countries. In Boston, Massachusetts, and 25 adjacent towns, Donabedian et al. (1965) reported a fivefold difference in perinatal mortality rates between the areas of highest and lowest socioeconomic status, with sharp geographical localization of the zones of highest mortality showing the combined effects of housing, sanitation, nutrition, and medical care. In Melbourne, Australia, infectious disease rates were found to be three times as high in areas of poor housing than in more affluent neighborhoods (Burt, 1945). In industrialized countries, particularly the United States, a trend towards suburbanization has left city centers as commercial zones, virtually uninhabited at night and on weekends. Inner city neighborhoods, often old, decrepit, and bereft of their original inhabitants, have become slums.

As expected, relocation of slum families to better housing results in reduction of fecally transmitted infection, by reason of better water and sanitary facilities and of less opportunity for reinfection. In children moved from slums to new flats in Singapore, infection rates with soil-transmitted helminths dropped greatly (Kleevens, 1966) and similar reductions have often been found in corresponding situations elsewhere.

Despite the many hazards the evidence suggests that at present overall mortality is lower in the cities of LDCs than in the countryside. Figures are difficult to obtain and marginally reliable, but such statistics as are available from Egypt, Senegal, Brazil, India, and elsewhere substantiate this conclusion.

Though the large towns of developing countries show many of the negative characteristics that belonged to urban areas of western countries in the nineteenth century, they nevertheless enjoy public health services, a concentration of doctors and the most recent discoveries of medical science, which were unthought of a century ago and are lacking in most of the rural areas.... But it is not impossible that, in the future, if the massive influx into the town continues these towns may find themselves unprepared from the health and hygiene point of view to cope with the increased needs; so that the direction of the difference between urban and rural death rates might reverse once again. (Federici et al., 1975)

DEVELOPMENT AND ENVIRONMENT

The goals of industrial development where there is now little, or growth where some already exists, are high on the priority lists of all national planners. As applied technology of all sorts spreads rapidly around the world, it is impossible to evaluate the eventual social benefits or detriments. But insofar as human health and welfare are concerned, we can look at some of the consequences.

The world has gone through several rounds of dispersal of technology. Early Chinese development of printing, gunpowder, and the magnet, as Francis Bacon said, "changed the whole face and state of things in the world." In one sense, little has altered since the third century—communication, military power, and mobility through travel are still prime targets of technological development.

The industrial revolution began in Europe some two centuries ago, and was itself preceded by a preparatory evolutionary development. The early groundwork included growth of the merchant, craftsman, and worker groups in European cities; establishment of market economies with wealth based on commerce and productivity (rather than land); expansion of trade links for obtaining raw materials and distributing manufactured products. At the same time, the flowering of scientific knowledge, from astronomy to physics and chemistry, provided a firm foundation for the rapid expansion of technologic methods and, most importantly, a built-in mechanism for sustained continually refined diversification. The closely interwoven associations between scientific, economic, political, and social forces have controlled the growth and shape not only of the western industrialized world but to a great extent that of the less developed countries as well.

Recent decades, particularly since the end of the Second World War, have seen a sharp rise in industrialization in LDCs, spurred by their desire to attain as large a measure of self-sufficiency in as short a time as possible. National planners, working in concert with representatives of international development banking and lending agencies, the governments of industrialized nations, and transnational corporations, have acquired selected units of western technology for their countries. Capital investments have been made not only in extractive, manufacturing, and agricultural industries, but also in military hardware, airlines, radio and television broadcasting networks, hospitals, medical schools, and other complex elements of western society.

There are many problems inherent in these acquisitions, aside from the difficulties of paying for them in times of world inflation and depressed prices for some primary goods. The general absence in LDCs of the broad interlocking underpinning for self-sustaining technologic advance increases their dependence upon foreign providers, and the more technology that is absorbed, the greater will be this dependence as obsolescence takes its inevitable toll. The same lack of generalized modern infrastructure results in increased disequilibrium and internal tension between the small educated segment of society capable of handling new technologies, and the larger traditionally oriented groups that will be affected by them.

The question of the appropriateness of particular types of industrial development projects has been dealt with by numerous authors. The point has often been made, for instance by Schumacher (1973), that capital-intensive industries based on high technology, with many automatic control devices but few workers, are inappropriate to the needs of LDCs. In this context, such industries have been compared to organ grafts, to be rejected by the body into which they are transplanted. The rapidly increasing populations of the developing world require jobs, in large numbers, for socially useful goals. The dysfunctional effects of unemployment upon individual and family health are an important problem to be faced by national planners everywhere.

At another level, development projects may have serious adverse effects upon the health of workers and populations. The entire range of industrial occupational hazards can occur even in well-regulated plants. Workers in small or marginal industry, more common in the developing world, appear especially susceptible to accident and disease. El Batawi (1975) has reviewed the situation in industrializing societies, pointing out the inadequacy of knowledge of occupational health problems. Nevertheless, some specific hazards are well-known. Poisoning by toxic substances, including respiratory irritants and heavy metal salts, is widespread especially in foundries and battery manufacturing plants. Inhalation of dusts and fibers, as in the cotton and flax, stonecutting, or mining industries, is a frequent sources of respiratory allergy, asthma, chronic bronchitis, and other conditions. Carcinogenic substances are often poorly controlled.

Of all industries in LDCs, agriculture is still basic, and it is the one with the longest history of industrialization. Estate plantations were introduced on a large scale by colonial powers to provide raw materials for their expanding industry and trade: sugar, tea, coffee, rubber, palm oil, pineapples, and other agricultural products were grown, picked, processed, shipped, and used in many tropical areas. The need for workers resulted in large-scale migrations, voluntary or enforced, as with southern Indians to the Malay peninsula or west Africans to the Western Hemisphere—populations that not only brought pathogens with them (Chapter 2) but were often susceptible to the new diseases they encountered. Agricultural work still carries a high risk of infectious, parasitic, and zoonotic disease and often involves particular hazards such as insect-, tick-, or snakebite. Accidental injuries from falls or from cutting tools or machinery are always a danger. Long working days, poor nutrition, boredom, and fatigue are closely associated with accidents. More recently, the risk of poisoning from fertilizers, herbicides, and pesticides has become significant in many areas. In Guatemala, for example, a report from the cotton-growing area around Tiquisate (Riding, 1977) states that excessive aerial spraying of pesticides in that region has resulted in heavy environmental pollution, thousands of human poisoning cases, and "numerous unreported deaths." The political potential of such situations is high: guerrillas of the "Guatemalan Army of the Poor" were reported to have attacked and destroyed 22 crop-duster aircraft owned by the cotton planters.

Industrialization and its consequences are certainly not entirely harmful to health, despite the problems just described. For many persons the opportunity to earn regular wages provides a route to a much higher standard of living. In a study done in a mining area in Sierra Leone, for example, Mills (1967) found that the better housing, environmental sanitation, wages, and medical care in the town resulted in improved nutritional status and lower prevalence of vector-borne disease in industrialized urban dwellers compared to residents of nearby villages.

The environmental deficiencies so often found in LDCs prompted the Secretary-General of the United Nations to clarify the problem to the U.N. Conference on the Human Environment in Stockholm in June 1972.

The solution to the environmental problems of poor societies is to be found in the process of development itself: development is a cure for most of these problems, rather than their cause. Only the process of development can remove many of the factors which at present endanger not merely the quality of life but threaten life itself in many parts of the world.... While development is a necessary precondition for overcoming many of the environmental problems of poor societies, this is not to say that such problems could be automatically and spontaneously resolved, by the mere acceleration of economic growth. There is, on the contrary, ample evidence to suggest that certain patterns of economic growth could bring in their wake not the solution but the aggravation of acute social and environmental problems.

All sorts of industrialization, including agricultural, can have unfavorable effects upon the environment. It has been pointed out by Miller (1973) and others that indiscriminate cutting of forests on some Caribbean islands for the cultivation of sugar cane and other crops has resulted in total deforestation. Resulting soil erosion and run-off reduced soil productivity, which in turn limited available food and lowered the quality of nutrition. In addition, the loss of shade trees has increased ground temperature and sun penetration, which in some areas has fostered breeding of malaria vectors and other mosquitoes.

One type of development that has received considerable attention in recent years is the large engineering project intended to provide an infrastructural basis for further exploitation, commerce, and industrialization. Health problems encountered in opening the Soviet *taiga* were discussed on pages 46–47 in the previous chapter. In Liberia and Nigeria new road networks have resulted in extension of sleeping sickness due to *Trypanosoma gambiense*. Tsetse flies concentrate wherever a road is intersected by a stream or river, extending local foci for transmission of the disease (Hughes and Hunter, 1970). In Brazil, opening of a new trans-Amazon highway has unavoidably brought workers and settlers into contact with new disease agents. Within the first two years after completion of sections of the road, 20,000 people had been settled (Pinheiro et al., 1974). A new disease syndrome called the hemorrhagic syndrome of Altamira, fatal in seven of the first 55 known cases, was encountered and raised fears of distribution along the new road.

Dams and Health

Of all large-scale environmental engineering programs, major dams have had the most dramatic effects upon health. Where the physiographic conditions permit and rainfall is abundant, impoundments provide large amounts of cheap, useful electric power. In addition, the dams serve for flood control and controlled distribution of water to irrigation networks on the downstream side. Upstream from the dam, the large impoundment of water can be used for fish production and recreation. This seems the best of all possible worlds, and there is little wonder that in the past few decades many large dams have been built in developing areas, especially in Africa.

The Akosombo Dam across the Volta River in Ghana was constructed in 1961–64 primarily to provide electric power for an enormous aluminum smelting plant that opened in 1967. The small fishing village of Tema on the coast downstream from the dam was converted through construction of a new harbor and the smelting plant to a city of 100,000 by 1972 (Joubert, 1972). Above the dam lies Lake Volta with a surface area of 8,200 square kilometers. Although this area is only 3.6% that of Ghana, the shape of the lake is such that about one-third of the country is relatively near its 6,400 km of shoreline. Derban (1975) and Obeng (1975) have both discussed in detail this lake and its attendant health problems.

The filling of Lake Volta destroyed 739 villages, home to 14,657 households and about 80,000 persons, mostly subsistence farmers. Some 15% of the displaced persons chose to resettle themselves elsewhere, leaving 67,500 people to be moved to 52 resettlement sites around the margins of the new lake. The Volta River Authority attempted to provide places for dwellings, work, and recreation, with houses, offices, schools, playgrounds, markets, water supplies, streets, latrines and farms.

The resettlements, according to Derban (1975) were "bleak and featureless with no familiar market days for buying, selling and social contact. The settlers had exchanged a place of comfort for a place of insecurity." Communal latrines soon ceased to function; sewage collection and disposal systems broke down. Water supplies ceased in some settlement areas as pumps and pipes broke down, and conditions for spread of waterborne disease became ideal.

In addition to the inadequately planned and implemented resettlement schemes, the lake itself posed a severe health problem to surrounding residents. Schistosomiasis is a disease of man caused by parasitic worms transmitted through certain snails. Prevalence in school children in some localities increased from 5% before the dam was built to 90% a few years after formation of the lake. The changed ecological conditions around the lake margin fostered breeding not only of the *Bulinus* snails that transmit urinary schistosomiasis, but of newly introduced *Biomphalaria* snails, intermediate hosts for the worms causing the more dangerous intestinal form of the disease.

While the formation of the Volta Lake has greatly increased schistosomiasis transmission sites, it appears that the prevalance of some other diseases has been reduced. Small blackflies of the genus *Simulium* transmit the *Onchocerca* worms responsible for producing river blindness in vast areas of west Africa. These flies require fast-flowing water in stream rapids in order to breed, and the rising waters of Volta Lake above the dam flooded out the mainstream breeding sites. However, rapids in the stream below the dam, and in tributary rivers flowing into the lake, continue to produce blackflies. Flooding of the land adjacent to the old Volta River bed has also reduced breeding of the tsetse flies that transmit the Gambian form of African sleeping sickness.

Some other diseases, such as malaria, which has been hyperendemic in Ghana for generations, continue much as before. However, the thousands of kilometers of new lake shoreline offer numerous places suitable for breeding of the anopheline mosquitoes that transmit malaria and of the mosquito vectors of filariasis and various arboviruses.

Massive dams have been constructed on other great rivers of Africa: Kariba, on the Zambezi, between Rhodesia and Zambia; Kainji, on the Niger in Nigeria; the Aswan High Dam on the Nile in Egypt, with Lake Nasser extending southward into Sudan. For each of these, tens of thousands of people have been relocated, with numerous attendant problems. Both Kariba and Aswan have resulted in massive increases of schistosomiasis incidence, and the same may occur at Kainji. Large dams have recently been built, or are under construction or being designed for the following countries: Angola, Brazil, Cambodia, China, Colombia, Congo, Ghana, India, Iran, Ivory Coast, Mozambique, Nigeria, Pakistan, Rhodesia, Senegal, Surinam, Thailand, Turkey, Uganda, and Venezuela. Health aspects of these great irrigation works must be considered no less carefully than power, irrigation, flood control, and water supply.

It is not only in developing countries that dams have been associated with disease outbreaks. Construction of the great series of hydroelectric installations on rivers in the south-central and southeastern United States often had similar effects. The Hales Bar Dam on the Tennessee River (1912), the Lay Dam on the Coosa in 1914 and Gantt Reservoir on the Conecuh in 1923 (both in Alabama) and the Santee-Cooper project in South Carolina as late as 1943 were associated with rapid buildups of local populations of *Anopheles quadrimaculatus* and subsequent epidemics of malaria (U.S. Public Health Service and Tennessee Valley Authority, 1947).

Environmental Pollution

Pollution is difficult to define, but the term describes at the minimum substances in the environment detrimental to the quality of human or other life. One would not usually say, for example, that high natural concentrations of fluorides or arsenic in subsurface waters constitute pollution. Yet the same concentrations of the same elements, resulting from human activities such as mining, well drilling, industry, or impoundment of waters must be so considered. It is important to recognize that environmental pollution is not a recent development and is not restricted to industrialized societies. The great majority of harm to human health arising from pollution probably occurs in the developing countries where fecal contamination of soil and water is the most important environmental health hazard.

The disposal of human wastes has always been a thorny problem, becoming most acute in cities. Travelers often remarked upon the fragrance of early European towns. In the late thirteenth century, for example, London Bridge had 138 houses on it, providing a ready means of waste disposal for the fortunate residents. Not so lucky were the passengers of open boats plying the river, who knew well the risks of "shooting the bridge" (Wright, 1960). Five hundred years later the Thames was still foul, although substantial cleansing of the river has occurred in recent decades.

Until the introduction of the automobile, the many horses in the world's cities littered the streets with great volumes of manure, attracting flies and causing severe disposal problems. The fact of pollution is universal, only the details varying with time and place; with economic progress simple fecal pollution is replaced by the waste products of machine and factory.

Some may say that contamination by human and animal wastes is not "real" pollution—that chemicals in air and water are hallmarks of modern societies. Here again, reality is not so simple. Cleary and Blackburn (1968) have demonstrated high levels of aldehydes and carbon monoxide in native huts in the highlands of New Guinea, and in the same area Master (1974) has shown that because of long exposure to smoky hut fires, 78% of examined persons over 40 years old had obstructive or restrictive pulmonary disease. Diseases of the pulmonary tree, attributable to smoke air pollution, may be the most important causes of morbidity and mortality in the New Guinea highlands. That this situation is not unique to New Guinea was shown by Sofoluwe (1968), who found high levels of carbon monoxide, nitrogen, and sulfur dioxides and aromatic hydrocarbons in dwellings around Lagos, Nigeria. This extreme smoke pollution was correlated with high rates of bronchiolitis and bronchopneumonia in exposed infants. It appears that fires in dwelling places, whether for warmth, cooking, or insect repellancy, have since earliest times induced pulmonary symptoms in man. Not only in remote caves and huts, but in the cities of Europe smoke pollution has been an ever-present companion. A smoke abatement law was passed by the British Parliament in 1273, and in 1307 a commission was appointed in London to investigate the burning of coal and to punish offenders "with great fines and upon the second offence to demolish their furnaces." The pioneer demographer John Graunt in 1662 attributed the shorter life of Londoners to "smoaks, stinks, and close air." With the advent of the industrial revolution, forests of chimneys and stacks emitted smoke and products of inefficient combustion as well as chlorine, ammonia, and methane into the air of nineteenth-century Europe. It is likely that the early decades of the present century marked the high point of smoke pollution, at least in London, with gradual improvement of air quality since that time despite several acute episodes of air pollution, notably in 1952 and 1962. Chronic air quality problems plague many areas on all continents. As the number of large cities increases especially in LDCs, the situation is bound to deteriorate unless drastic action is taken.

GOVERNMENTS

In considering the factors that determine health and disease, we must look briefly at government, in general, in its roles as agent and controller of modernization and development.

Despite drawbacks, some of which have been discussed, modernization and development have generally been beneficial for health. The relatively early phases of this process in particular are characterized by rapid declines in infant and childhood mortality and increase in expectation of life at birth. The policies of those in power are important factors in determining the form of modernization and development and the consequent benefits or detriments to segments of the population. In the early industrial revolution, the investment decisions of the private sector led to excesses harmful to the health and welfare of many people and eventually to the need for government regulation, a need that still exists today. Private corporations make economic decisions for the basic purpose of maximizing financial returns on investments. Governments must not only invest their own funds wisely for efficient development but must also make political and social decisions that benefit the well-being of their citizens.

The world today is fragmented into numerous national entities. The four most populous, China, India, the Soviet Union, and the United States, account for 45% of the world's population; the addition of Indonesia, Brazil, and Japan brings this to well over half. The remainder live in some 140 or more sovereign nations of widely varying size, character, and stability. The period from about 1945 to 1975 saw many former colonies gain independence to become countries characterized not only by low incomes, but in many cases by boundaries drawn up decades ago in the capitals of Europe without regard to topography, ethnic composition of the people, or future economic viability. Their governments, which are often inexperienced, unsure, and unstable, are sometimes in the hands of a small proportion of the population concerned about the perpetuation of its own privileges. Without a secure economic base and lacking the organizational skills of concerted modernization and development, many countries can remain in this uncoordinated and unproductive phase for generations. In addition to the movement of money outwards for foreign profit, there is often excessive expenditure of those funds that are available to governments for prestigious public buildings and monuments. Altogether, the governments of developing countries devote as much public revenue to military programs as to education and health care combined—and in many cases much more (Sivard, 1976). The reasons for this unfortunate preoccupation with armaments are complex, but the consequences for public health are distressingly apparent.

The specific functions of governments as providers of health and medical care services will be examined in Chapters 6 and 7.

References

Adelman, I. and C. T. Morris. 1973. Economic Growth and Social Equity in Developing Countries. Stanford. Stanford University Press. 257 p.

Bean, L. H. 1966. Closing the world's nutritional gap - with animal or vegetable protein? WHO/FAO/UNICEF Protein Advisory Group News Bulletin No. 6: 20–31.

Boulding, K. E. 1970. Fun and games with the gross national product—the role of misleading indicators in social policy. In: H. W. Helfrich, Jr., Ed. The Environmental Crisis. New Haven. Yale University Press. pp. 156–170.

Burt, W. O. 1945. Poverty, housing and health. Medical Journal of Australia 2: 167–173.

Cassel, J. 1971. Health consequences of population density and crowding. In: National Academy of Sciences. Rapid Population Growth: Consequences and Implications. Baltimore. Johns Hopkins University Press. pp. 462–478.

Cleary, G. J. and C. R. B. Blackburn. 1968. Air pollution in native huts in the highlands of New Guinea. Archives of Environmental Health 17: 785–794.

Davis, K. 1965. The urbanization of the human population. Scientific American 213: 41–53.

Derban, L. K. A. 1975. Some environmental health problems associated with industrial development in Ghana. In: Ciba Foundation Symposium 32 (new series). Health and Industrial Growth. Amsterdam. Associated Scientific Publishers. pp. 49–71.

Development Coordination Committee. 1976. Development Issues. U.S. Actions Affecting the Development of Low-Income Countries. Washington, D.C. Agency for International Development. 164 p.

Disraeli, B. 1845. Sybil, or The Two Nations. Reprinted 1939. London. Oxford University Press. 431 p.

Donabedian, A., L. S. Rosenfeld and E. M. Southern. 1965. Infant mortality and socioeconomic status in a metropolitan community. Public Health Reports 80: 1083–1094.

Doxiadis, C. A. 1967. The inhuman city. In: G. Wolstenholme and M. O'Connor,

Eds. Health of Mankind. Ciba Foundation 100th Symposium. Boston. Little, Brown. pp. 178–193.
El Batawi, M. A. 1975. Health of working populations in industrializing societies. In: Ciba Foundation Symposium 32 (new series). Health and Industrial Growth. Amsterdam. Associated Scientific Publishers. pp. 141–156.
Federici, N., A. de Sarno Prignano, P. Pasquali, G. Cariani and M. Natale. 1976. Urban-rural differences in mortality, 1950–1970. World Health Statistics Report 29: 249–378.
Fendall, N. R. E. 1963. Public health and urbanization in Africa. Public Health Reports 78: 569–584.
Freedman, R. and B. Berelson. 1976. The record of family planning programs. Studies in Family Planning 7: 1–40.
Griffith, D. H. S., D. V. Ramana and H. Mashoal. 1971. Contribution of health to development. International Journal of Health Services 1: 253–270.
Hanlon, J. J. 1974. Principles of Public Health Administration. 6th Ed. St. Louis. C. V. Mosby. 748 p.
Hill, G. 1976. View of world's shanty towns less grim. New York Times, June 9.
Hobson, W., Ed. 1975. The Theory and Practice of Public Health. London. Oxford University Press. 685 p.
Hughes, C. C. and J. M. Hunter. 1970. Disease and "Development" in Africa. Social Science and Medicine 3: 443–493.
Joubert, C. 1972. Ghana—The VALCO medical service. In: J. P. Hughes, Ed. Health Care for Remote Areas. Oakland, California. Kaiser Foundation International. pp. 73–76.
Kitagawa, E. M. and P. M. Hauser. 1968. Education differentials in mortality by cause of death: United States, 1960. Demography 5: 335–339.
Kleevens, J. W. L. 1966. Re-housing and infections by soil transmitted helminths in Singapore. Singapore Medical Journal 7: 12–29.
Krugman, S. 1977. Present status of measles and rubella immunization in the United States: A medical progress report. Journal of Pediatrics 90: 1–12.
Lewis, O. 1968. A Study of Slum Culture. New York. Random House. 240 p.
Lie, K. J., B. Rukmono, Sri Oemijati, K. Sahab, K. W. Newlen, T. H. Sie and R. W. Talogo. 1966. Diarrhoea among infants in a crowded area of Djakarta, Indonesia. Bulletin of the World Health Organization 34: 197–210.
Logan, W. P. D. and P. M. Lambert. 1975. Vital statistics. In: W. Hobson, Ed. The Theory and Practice of Public Health. 4th Ed. London. Oxford University Press. pp. 8–28.
Lowe, C. R. 1975. Health needs and health services: a question of priorities. Central African Journal of Medicine 21: 229–235.
Master, K. M. 1974. Air pollution in New Guinea. Journal of the American Medical Association 228: 1653–1655.
Journal of Public Health 64 (Suppl.): 11–16.
McGranahan, D. V., C. Richard-Proust, N. V. Sovani and M. Subramaniam. 1970. Contents and Measurement of Socio-economic Development: an Empirical Inquiry. Geneva. United Nations Institute for Social Development. Report no. 70.10. 162 p.

McKeown, T. and C. R. Lowe, Eds. 1974. An Introduction to Social Medicine. 2nd Ed. Oxford. Blackwell Scientific. 356 p.

Miller, M. J. 1973. Industrialization, ecology and health in the tropics. Canadian Journal of Public Health 64 (Suppl.): 11-16.

Mills, A. R. 1967. The effect of urbanization on health in a mining area of Sierra Leone. Transactions of the Royal Society of Tropical Medicine and Hygiene 61: 114-130.

Obeng, L. E. 1975. Health problems of the Volta Lake ecosystem. *In:* N. F. Stanley and M. P. Alpers, Eds. Man Made Lakes and Human Health. London. Academic Press. pp. 221-230.

Orihuela, L. A. 1976. Where the streetlamps stop. World Health, May: 22-27.

Pinheiro, F. P., G. Bensabath, D. Costa, Jr., O. M. Maroja, Z. C. Lins and A. Andrade. 1974. Haemorrhagic syndrome of Altamira. Lancet 1(7859): 639-642.

Portes, A. and J. Walton. 1976. Urban Latin America. Austin. University of Texas Press. 217 p.

Puffer, R. R. and C. V. Serrano. 1973. Patterns of Mortality in Childhood. Washington. Pan American Health Organization Scientific Publication 262. 470 p.

Riding, A. 1977. Free use of pesticides in Guatemala takes a deadly toll. New York Times. Nov. 9.

Ross, M. H. 1973. The Political Integration of Urban Squatters. Evanston. Northwestern University Press. 228 p.

Schumacher, E. F. 1973. Small is Beautiful. New York. Harper and Row. 305 p.

Sivard, R. L. 1976. World Military and Social Expenditures 1976. Leesburg, Va. WMSE Publications. 32 p.

Sofoluwe, G. O. 1968. Smoke pollution in dwellings of infants with bronchopneumonia. Archives of Environmental Health 16: 670-672.

Teitelbaum, M. 1975. Relevance of demographic transition theory for developing countries. Science 188: 420-425.

United Nations. 1963. The situation and recent trends of mortality in the world. Population Bulletin of the United Nations 6: 3-145.

United Nations. 1973. The Determinants and Consequences of Population Trends. New Summary of Findings on Interaction of Demographic, Economic and Social Affairs. United Nations Department of Economic and Social Affairs. Population Studies No. 50. 661 p.

United Nations. 1974. Health trends and prospects in relation to population and development. World Population Conference, Bucharest, August 1974. Conference Background Paper 26. 51 p. mimeo.

United Nations. 1974a. Demographic trends in the world and its major regions, 1950-1970. World Population Conference, Bucharest, August 1974. Conference Background Paper 14. 35 p. mimeo.

United Nations. 1976. Demographic Yearbook 1975. New York. United Nations. 1118 p.

United Nations. 1977. Statistical Yearbook 1976. New York. United Nations. 909 p.

United Nations Educational, Scientific and Cultural Organization. 1976. Statistical Yearbook 1975. Paris. Unesco Press. 767 p.

U.S. Agency for International Development. 1976. Population Program Assistance. Annual Report 1975. Washington. Agency for International Development. Bureau for Population and Humanitarian Assistance Office of Population. 187 p.

U.S. Public Health Service and Tennessee Valley Authority, Health and Safety Department. 1947. Malaria Conrol on Impounded Water. Washington. U.S. Government Printing Office. 422 p.

World Bank. 1975. Health. Sector Policy Paper. Washington, D.C. World Bank. 83 p.

World Bank. 1976. World Bank Atlas. Washington, D.C. World Bank. 28 p.

World Health Organization. 1974. Health trends and prospects 1950-2000. World Health Statistics Report 27: 670-706.

Wright, L. 1960. Clean and Decent. New York. Viking Press. 282 p.

Zigas, V., J. van Delden and R. Rodrigue. 1972. New Guinea: Studies relating the medical and behavioral sciences. Part I. Urbanization, culture and disease. Social Science and Medicine 6: 681-687.

CULTURE 4.

In previous chapters our concern has focused upon *diseases*—such as goiter, schistosomiasis, or cancer of the lung—and the conditions that bring them about. Here we must look at *illnesses* and sick people. The distinction is far from trivial. Diseases are often dealt with in the medical literature as if they were independent entities, like species of animals or plants. The ecology of malaria is thereby not so different from the ecology of the long-eared fruit bat or the meadowlark. Effects of nutrition, temperature, substrate relations, susceptibility to this or that agent are all measurable parameters. Even epidemiologists, in many ways the most ecumenical of medical scientists, share this outlook.

Epidemiology may be defined as the study of the distribution of a disease or a physiological condition in human populations and of the factors that influence this distribution. The epidemiologist is interested in the occurrence of disease by time, place, and persons. He tries to determine whether there has been an increase or decrease of the disease over the years; whether one geographical area has a higher frequency of this disease than another; and whether the characteristics of persons with a particular disease or condition distinguish them from those without it. (Lilienfeld, 1976)

ILLNESSES

Illnesses occur in individual people, who are thereby transformed from healthy to sick. Being sick is a socially recognized state, carrying with it certain specific drawbacks, obligations, and privileges, depending upon the circumstances. A person may be perceived by himself, his family, or others to have signs of an abnormality, by which an illness is commonly recognized and named. For instance, he may have "a fever," or "diarrhea." The physician or healer diagnoses or assigns the illness to a more general, objective category of disease, by which it is related to a predictable chain of events embracing causality and prognosis (Table 4-1). Patients, of course, are concerned with the illness as a whole, which is their experience of the disease. The shift from consideration of disease to illness is no less than a shift from biological to social science. Most practitioners of modern scientific medicine are unprepared by training and orientation to deal with the social sciences, nor, perhaps, even to acknowledge the validity of anthropological or sociological approaches

Table 4-1. Some underlying causes to which human health problems are attributed

---

Accidental trauma
Acute poisoning or envenomation (mushroom, snake)
Allergy and immunological peculiarities
Bad habits (e.g., intemperance, masturbation, smoking)
Capricious acts of deities
Chronic poisoning (occupational exposure, pollution)
Congenital defects
Endocrine malfunction
Exposure to the elements
Failure to observe ritual or breaking of taboos
Genetic or chromosomal abnormalities
Imbalance of bodily forces or humors
Infections, including parasites
Intentional trauma (warfare, assault)
Mental or emotional stress
Nutritional deficiency or excess
Positions of the stars and planets
Pregnancy, labor, and childbirth
Senility
Witchcraft, evil eye, and spells

Any combination, including none, of the above

---

to health problems. Nevertheless, in the field of international health, these disciplines offer many insights.

The Importance of Culture

The most important aspect in this discussion of illness around the world is recognition of the central role played by culture. Numerous authors have attempted definitions of this term—for our purposes that of Paul (1955) can serve well. "Broadly speaking, culture is a group's design for living, a shared set of socially transmitted assumptions about the nature of the physical and social world, the goals of life, and the appropriate means of achieving them."

It is essential at the outset to agree that not only do "they" have a culture but we do too. For a characterization of western culture, Oswald Spengler's *Decline of the West* (published 1926–1928) provided a broad and useful, if somewhat metaphysical, overview. In Spengler's interpretation, each of the world's great cultures has had its unique "soul" or pattern of experience and creation, which is inherent in its art, religion, administration, commerce, thought, and behavior. Western culture is characterized as "Faustian"; its central tendency is a yearning for infinity, probing the limits of time, space, materials, and thought. This yearning is perhaps best expressed in the towering cathedrals built after about the year 900, in the mathematics that permitted their construction, in the music that was played within them, in the sermons of everlasting life delivered there, and in the worldwide commerce that supported the entire enterprise. Science, technology, government, social and family relations all fall within the same design for living. Although there is much room for variation within this western culture, it does provide a rough guide for comparison.

In the United States particularly there has developed a strong emphasis on continued mastery over the environment, achieved through rationalism, science, and technology. Individualism is stressed, initiative is rewarded, and above all achievement is the focus of evaluation. The poor boy or immigrant who "made it" is a folk hero; ascribed status through heredity is uncommon. Constant growth in knowledge, efficiency, and wealth is seen as both a virtue and an elusive goal. To strive for this growth (a yearning for infinity?) requires a willingness to probe, to analyze, to criticize, to adopt new methods, and to discard old ones. There is an assumption that given enough knowledge (and resulting technology), diseases can be "conquered" and life prolonged. The search for knowledge and efficiency results in complex organizations and a high degree of differentiation. There are corporation lawyers and tax lawyers, labor lawyers and public interest lawyers, malpractice lawyers, divorce lawyers, and a hundred other kinds. There are the metallurgists and engineers and astronomers and computer programmers who have sent rockets to Mars to search for other life in the solar system. Spengler would smile knowingly.

Traditional Societies

By way of contrast, in many traditional societies the overall emphasis of life is not to challenge nature but to harmonize with it; not to struggle for "achievement" but to acquiesce; not to thrust forward the individual, but to function within prescribed roles as members of an integrated society. For example, Malay culture has been described in these terms:

The world itself is perceived as in many ways incomprehensible, consisting of often conflicting facts. But somehow there is harmony in a live and let live sense. People too are different, and they are expected to be. Yet they must learn to live harmoniously. And by harmonious is meant *gentle:* one's actions must be such that they do not cause hurt or embarrassment... Conversation is low-keyed... The content of conversation too is mild. One expresses an opinion very tentatively in Malay company. No one will contradict... (The village chief) is not expected to display qualities of leadership—no one is. Nor is he expected to influence opinion, even less, action—no one is... To act aggressively is embarrassing. (Wolff, 1965)

Halfway around the world, Gelfand (1971) has examined the Shona society in rural Zimbabwe (Rhodesia) where wealth was seen as a social disorder and a deliberate effort was made to

ensure that everyone was equal in material benefits and that the family lineages or segments of the clan shared their possessions equally. If man is allowed to become acquisitive, jealousies and fighting result. Progress was sacrificed for the good of the group as opposed to the interests of the individual. At all costs peace was maintained within the group and tensions reduced to a minimum... Sharing was the rule.... Every man was able to live on a piece of land sufficient for his needs, and so each was limited in the wealth he could acquire. He could not accumulate and become wealthy in the Western sense... The Shona frowned upon change and what the modern world knows as progress.

In words remarkably reminiscent of the description of traditional Chinese medical thought in Chapter 2, Chilivumbo (1974) summarized the thought system of residents of rural Malawi, "in which all aspects of life are knitted, connected, no separation exists, all aspects of life are subsumed under one cosmos, only one philosophy covers nature, man, human relations, domestic, social and medical issues; such is the nature of 'rural society'." Also in Africa, Barker (1973) commented that "high infant death rates create attitudes which appear to us deplorably fatalistic. Mothers take with them to childbed a sense of the expendability of at least a portion of their brood, nor are they often disappointed."

Culture and Illness

Here we will explore the relationships between culture in general and notions of health, illness, and disease. Then we can see how these ideas are reflected in human behavior, an essential but often neglected element in international health studies.

Points of cultural variation with respect to health involve ideas about nosology, etiology, and therapy; or, more simply, the kinds of illnesses, how and why they occur, and what can be done about them. The official roster of scientifically recognized syndromes is the "International Statistical Classification of Diseases, Injuries and Causes of Death," revised every 10 years by the World Health Organization (WHO), and described more fully in Chapter 5. The fact of decennial revision indicates that recognized types of diseases are continually changing as scientific knowledge increases and information becomes available. Moreover, social and cultural factors influence the categorization of diseases, even in the developed countries. Two instructive examples may be given from recent events in the United States. The first is alcoholism, now generally regarded as a disease, and the second is homosexuality, which has now been declared by the psychiatric profession *not* to be a disease.

These two examples are of interest in that both represent what is often termed "deviant behavior." The extent of socially permissible deviance varies from one culture and time to another. The sociologist Talcott Parsons, among others, has examined the concept of definition of illness in terms of cultural expectations, especially the relation of the problem of health and illness to the whole range of categories of deviant behavior. In the complex, highly differentiated western societies, distinctions may be made between (1) deviance from commitment to accepted norms ("crime" or "illegality"); (2) deviance from accepted values ("sin" or "immorality"); and (3) deviance from the capacity to perform expected tasks and roles, if this deviance is involuntary (illness). The question of individual intention and responsibility is crucial. Obedience to institutionalized normative patterns (rules and laws) and adherence to cultural values are considered voluntary decisions for which a normal person can be held responsible. On the other hand,

> It has been long one of the criteria of illness that the sick person "couldn't help it." Even though he may have become ill or disabled through some sort of carelessness or negligence, he cannot legitimately be expected to get well simply by deciding to be well... Some kind of underlying reorganizing process has to take place, biological or 'mental', which can be guided or controlled in various ways, but cannot simply be eliminated by an "act of will." In this sense the state of illness is involuntary. (Parsons, 1972)

Concepts of illness vary widely between peoples. The spectrum of health status is divided in different ways in different cultures, as is the visible light spectrum. Languages, which are basic tools and extensions of culture, reflect the varying types of diseases known, just as they do the varying numbers of discrete colors recognized. It must be emphasized that there is no one true nosology any more than there is one true religion, one correct language, or one perfect form of music. The manifestations of an illness are generally viewed as an extension of its causation so that in most cultures the ideas of *etiology* and *diagnosis* are inseparable.

In many parts of the world, illness, catastrophe, accident, death and all sorts of unusual happenings are attributed to the intentional actions of malicious agencies. Disease is viewed as punishment inflicted by god(s) as chastisement for crime, impiety, negligence, or breach of taboos (Coury, 1967). With respect to causation of an illness the usual question is *"Who* sent it?" and not *"how* did it happen?" In his rural practice in Bomvanaland (South Africa), Jansen (1973) observed that "the ultimate intention of any occurrence must be sought out and it is by the process of divination that the spiritual forces behind a calamity can be determined." He found the native society "anxiety-loaded" because of the continuous fear of hidden powers that disturb peaceful life, of the sudden wrath of forefathers, or of action by malevolent spirits.

The apparent arbitrariness of illness and death, often in poor countries striking hardest at innocent children, must be accounted for in a way that is reasonable and consistent with the system of beliefs built up by observation of nature. In traditional, pervasively religious cultures that honor few of the "Faustian" values of power, progress, and material gain, where instead harmony, resignation, and fatalism endure, reality resides in the world of the spirt, and it is here that the most important questions are asked and answered.

All cultures have searched for "factors" that control distribution and severity of different diseases in the population. In Europe and the United States, there were repeated devastating epidemics of cholera in the nineteenth century. Before the era of bacteriology, the cause of this disease was the subject of much debate in America, where prevailing opinion held the epidemics to be "a scourge, a rod in the hand of God," and a remedy to save a once-favored nation from atheism and sin. Rosenberg (1962) points out that in 1832 the disease was so strongly held to be a divine punishment that "whenever any person of substance died of cholera, it was an immediate cause of consternation, a consternation invariably allayed by reports that this ordinarily praiseworthy individual had some secret vice or else had indulged in some unwonted excess." It must not be assumed that these views are no longer widely held in the United States. In a poll taken in 1973 by the Center for Policy Research, 48% of

Americans questioned believed in the existence of Satan (Wood, 1975), and a Harris Poll in April 1974 revealed that one-third of adult Americans believe that people can be possessed by "the devil." Entire churches with millions of adherents base their doctrines upon the supernatural origins of illness and healing. A minister can preach, and be widely believed, that "the causes of the diseases are all listed in the Bible.... A person is stricken with Parkinson's disease... after he or she has let others dominate his or her life. By developing greater free will, and with intensive prayer and the prayer of others... victims of that disease have been repeatedly cured" (Voakes, 1975).

In her analysis of the folk medical beliefs held in the United States "among lower-class blacks who have been socialized in the South or maintain kin ties to the South," Snow (1974) described a customary classification of happenings as "natural" or "unnatural." The former have to do with the world as God intended and allow predictability in daily life; the latter upset the plan intended by God and at worst represent the forces of evil and machinations of the Devil. Unnatural events are unpredictable, and therefore beyond the abilities of ordinary mortals to control. The belief is often expressed that everything has its opposite: a death for every birth, an antidote for every poison, and a cure for every illness. Illnesses, also classified as natural and unnatural, represent disharmony and conflict in some area of the individual's life and are associated with environmental hazards, divine punishment, and impaired social relationships. Evil influence and witchcraft are commonly cited as causes of many illnesses.

Another large ethnic group in the United States is the Mexican-American, whose health beliefs have been studied by various investigators (e.g., Clark, 1970; Martinez and Martin, 1966). Soul loss, wizardry, and the actions of malicious spirits figure prominently as causes and manifestation of illness. These beliefs are often retained after several generations of residence outside Mexico.

A great deal of money, effort, and computer time is expended in the United States and other developed countries in the continuing search for "risk factors" in certain severe illnesses. These investigations have led many epidemiologists to conclude that, even in our own context, much disease is the result of inappropriate personal behavior. The primary difference between "our scientific" and "their primitive" explanations of causality seems to lie within the concept of statistical reasoning. Those cultures and individuals unable or unwilling to acknowledge that the world is governed by the laws of probability are therefore restricted to explanations involving purposeful intent. From that perspective, it is logical to seek out the source of harm, where it be enemies, gods, or spirits. Not everyone would agree with Cole Porter that "It was just one of those things."

In addition to pervasive supernatural forces, many people throughout the world ascribe the causation of illnesses to disruptions in certain balances of vital forces. The European Hippocratic tradition (Chapter 2) holds that the four humors—blood, phlegm, yellow bile, and black bile—should be in proper balance. Excesses of one or another results in a person being sanguine, phlegmatic, choleric, or melancholic (i.e., in a bad humor), expressions that have become part of our language, if not of our conscious thought.

The balance of hot-cold, of "heaty" and "cooling" foods, is considered of great importance in many parts of the world. Possibly the idea of heaty and cooling foods originated with the Chinese concept of *yin* and *yang* forces and the need to maintain proper balance in order to strengthen the body's vital energy (*ch'i*). Regardless of their actual temperature or spiciness, some foods are thought to heat or excite the body, others to calm it. Persons with fevers should avoid heaty foods; those with weakness or needing stimulation should avoid cooling foods. Whereas the notion is well established in Asia, Latin America, and parts of Europe and Africa, there appears to be little agreement, even locally, about which foods belong precisely in which category (Anderson and Anderson, 1975). Chili peppers are commonly and understandably regarded as "hot" but so is beer in most of Mexico. White beans are considered very "hot," red beans "cold," and pinto beans, as expected, intermediate (Clark, 1970). Maintenance of proper health requires knowledge of the inherent, inapparent food properties and proper selection of a balanced diet. In Iran, Assar and Jakšić (1975) have shown that the concept of balance between "hot" and "cold" is highly developed and commonly invoked in everyday life, and in their view it derives from the teachings of the physician and philospher Avicenna (980–1037) about the genesis of disease.

The idea of universal opposites is pervasive in many societies and, as in the example of yin and yang, transcends concepts of health and body as a guiding principle for many aspects of everday life. Contradiction is inherent in all things; right includes some wrong, and wrong includes some right. Bearing this in mind, it may be easier to interpret the conditional or unenthusiastic acceptance of "obviously" beneficial innovations by many groups of intended recipients.

What is considered normal in one place may be thought pathogenic elsewhere, and vice versa. Yap (1951) has reviewed mental diseases peculiar to certain cultures, including Europe in the Middle Ages where waves of mass hysteria characterized by dancing manias swept through the population. The Indonesian-Malay *amok* (a word borrowed by English) signifies an acute burst of violence in an otherwise placid society, behavior "accepted by the community, and indeed expected of the individual who is placed for some reason or another in an intolerably embarrassing or shameful situation" (Yap, 1951). A condition known as *koro* or *su yang,* which recurs from time to time among the Chinese population of Singapore, is characterized by the conviction that the penis is shrinking and withdrawing into the body. Stringent measures are often adopted to prevent this from occurring, and men afflicted with the obsession may appear at the General Hospital with a flatiron or other heavy object tied tightly to their penis. In California, Guarnaschelli et al. (1972) have described a fatal case of *caida de mollera* in a two-month-old Mexican-American boy. This condition, well-known in parts of Spain and America, is thought to result when the part of an infant's head directly beneath the anterior fontanelle "drops down," perhaps as a result of pulling the nipple too strongly out of the child's mouth. Vigorous maneuvers are considered necessary to restore the "fallen fontanelle" lest the infant be prevented from eating properly. In the case reported the child was held by the ankles and his head partially immersed in boiling water—a desperate attempt by his grandmother to cure a condition that she perceived as grave, but which elsewhere in the world is considered perfectly normal.

Every culture is liable to carry forward beliefs regarding health, disease, and the causes of illness that may be deemed quaint, bizarre, or grotesque by foreign observers. Sometimes rituals or practices undertaken for quite different purposes have severe effects upon what we consider to be "health." The most extreme example in this regard probably is the custom of foot-binding in China (Chew, 1973). From the tenth century until about 1920, millions of girls suffered the culturally sanctioned infliction of severe pain and deformation as their toes were slowly crushed by tight bandages in an attempt to produce the idealized three-inch "lotus foot," a prized symbol of eroticism for the men but a festering, crippling lifelong infirmity for the women. Attempts made over the years to stop the practice were fruitless and the popularity of food-binding was such that even Manchu girls started to imitate Chinese girls in the custom.

BELIEF, BEHAVIOR, AND HEALTH

Alexander Pope, among others, believed that the proper study of mankind is man. The observation and comparison of human behavior and its consequences have delighted and infuriated people from the earliest days. They are perhaps humanity's chief occupation, or most reliable diversion.

It is considered improper these days to "stereotype" groups of people on ethnic or cultural grounds, particularly when this is done in a pejorative sense. Individual personalities certainly vary widely in all societies: some are more outgoing, some more taciturn, some more inquisitive in Madras or Tegucigalpa or Stockholm. Nevertheless, the long period of human childhood and dependency is used everywhere for learned socialization, for absorption of and indoctrination into the prevailing value structure. "The individual," observed Frank (1948), "except when uniquely endowed, cannot escape from his culture and the peculiar climate of opinion of his age; he is immersed in it, like the fish in water, and is unaware of the surrounding medium." While modified by idiosyncrasy, the broad, primary features of outlook and demeanor are so molded by social forces that certain generalizations or predictions can be made with some confidence.

Discussing health education programs, Mead (1961) has emphasized the need for a "careful knowledge of the culturally determined character structure of a given people—which often involves a knowledge of local region, class, and occupation and ethnic origin, religion and even politics as well." Mead points to the ways that people feel about the body—whether it is the root of evil, the temple of the spirit of God, a prison for the soul, or coterminous with identity. The associated beliefs in individual afterlife in heaven, reincarnation on earth, or focus on the present life strongly influence attitudes, such as those towards the death of an infant. "Whether an individual is the keeper of his own safety and dignity," says Mead, "or relies on his kin or his tribe, or the members of his profession to protect him will be a factor in whether a people are willing to assume responsibility for social programs, where complete participation is necessary if anyone is to be safe."

It is evident that behavior, both individual and group, affects and often determines health; conversely, health affects or determines behavior. The form and force of these influences vary from one human group to another.

Instances of gross behavioral effects upon health are legion but perhaps too obvious to be instructive. Belligerence in war or in everyday life (Table 4-2) can have sudden and dramatic results. There is risk of a traumatic fall from climbing a coconut tree, skydiving, or hang-gliding. Mainlining of heroin can result in severe illness. So can ingestion of hallucinogenic toxic fungi in shamanistic rituals. Yet most effects of behavior on health occur as more subtle, peripheral consequences of everyday activities. Few persons are truly aware of the health consequences of these daily activities, and even fewer know how to do anything about them.

Societal Attitudes

Travelers inevitably make, and are made the objects of, comparisons of culturally determined behavior (Fieg and Blair, 1975). Foreign visitors to the United States are struck by the "pace of life," the emphasis on time, efficiency, and precision. An Indonesian may ask "Did you enjoy the football game?" An American answers with the score, number of first downs, yards gained, and pass completions. An Ethiopian in the U.S. is struck by the paperwork, the computerization, the student enrollment numbers, the social security numbers, the form 1099, the W-2 form, the credit cards. The visitor from Manila, where stop signs are ignored and red lights unheeded, is astounded that her American host comes to a complete stop at a rural intersection with no car in sight for a mile in any direction. Almost all non-Europeans find it hard to believe that a nine o'clock meeting starts exactly at 9:00.

The American attitude towards work and schooling is often different from that in the visitor's home country. A Japanese may consider the American's loyalty to his profession or occupation, rather than to his employer, puzzling. The Latin American is amazed that wealthy Americans will do manual work in the garden, on the car, or even help in the kitchen. Upper-class visitors from developing countries often feel that taxi drivers, salespeople, waitresses, and hotel clerks are insufficiently humble, and find it extraordinary that even rich kids take such "demeaning" jobs during the summer. These, in return, do not like being spoken to as if they were servants. In a similar vein, the Iranian student, accustomed to standing when a teacher enters the classroom, may find the informality and lack of social distance between American students and faculty a sign of unbearable disorganization.

It is in the realm of more personal relations that many cultural

Table 4.2. Age-adjusted mortality from homicide per 100,000 by sex and age, selected countries, 1968

Country	Males Total	Males 15–24	Males 25–44	Males 45–64	Females Total	Females 15–24	Females 25–44	Females 45–64
United States								
White	6.6	7.8	10.5	7.4	2.0	2.2	2.9	2.0
Nonwhite	68.6	77.3	126.4	69.7	13.6	16.1	24.9	11.3
Total	13.4	16.7	23.1	13.2	3.4	4.0	5.6	2.9
Canada	2.2	1.8	3.7	2.2	1.3	1.5	1.9	1.4
Netherlands & Scandinavia	0.6	0.4	0.7	0.8	0.5	0.4	0.4	0.6
England & Wales	0.8	0.8	0.8	0.7	0.7	0.7	0.7	0.5
France	0.9	0.6	1.3	1.1	0.6	0.6	0.8	0.4
Japan	1.8	1.6	2.4	1.4	1.0	0.7	0.8	0.7

Source: Adapted from Metropolitan Life Insurance Company, 1972.

distinctions emerge. Public displays of affection, such as holding hands between teen-aged boys and girls, are shocking in some societies. On the other hand, in Pakistan, the U.S.S.R., Ethiopia, and some other countries it is common for two boys or young men to stroll hand-in-hand as a sign of friendship. Dating, courtship, and marriage are conducted under very different rules in different cultures. The rearing of children has many variants, often studied by anthropologists. While Americans try to encourage independence from an early age, an Egyptian might view a small child's sleeping in his own room as callous rejection by the parents. Privacy is looked upon in various ways. Many people from the Middle East and Mediterranean areas, for instance, feel free to drop in and visit, or be visited, with a casualness not always appreciated elsewhere. Visitors from bustling tropical cities are struck by the emptiness of streets in American residential areas, particularly in the suburbs.

Attitudes towards women and old persons vary greatly. In many societies women are expected to be submissive and dependent. The complex division of responsibilities between the sexes makes it at least undignified and perhaps humiliating for a man in West Africa, or much of the Caribbean or Latin America, to go marketing or profess to know anything about cooking. The famous Latin *machismo,* while an oversimplification, is real and widespread. Grandparents in most countries remain with their families. In most Oriental and African traditions the seniority of age confers authority and engenders respect; persons even of mature years would not consider contradicting their parents or acting without their advice and support.

The catalogue of cultural and behavioral diversity is endless, and these examples are only a meager sampling. How are they to be invested with meaning insofar as health is concerned?

Individual Behavior

Where economic conditions permit life free from the constant threat of subnutrition and contaminative diseases, health and illness are to a considerable extent determined by individual behavior. This should not imply that most people purposefully do things that are bad for them; on the contrary, good health and long life are universal goals. But the glass raised in toast to those very goals at many weddings paradoxically may contain the seed of their negation. It is a common notion (the law of opposites?) that many of the things we enjoy are also a little bit harmful—

"All life's pleasures are either fattening or immoral." To which one may add: or atherogenic or carcinogenic.

Although we are most interested in an international perspective, the difficulty of getting suitable comparative data on "way of life" and behavioral characteristics of people in different countries is enormous. Some studies in the United States can therefore be cited as examples. The relationship between "good" living habits and health has been explored in some detail by Belloc and Breslow (1972). In Alameda County, California, a questionnaire was answered by almost 7,000 adults on certain of their personal habits: cigarette smoking, alcohol consumption, regularity of meals, hours of sleep, weight in relation to height, physical activity, and eating between meals. Highly significant correlations were seen between the number of "good" practices observed and the state of health. In a later follow-up study in the same population, Belloc (1973) related the health practices to mortality, showing that the average expectation of life in males reporting six to seven "good" practices was over 11 years greater than in those reporting fewer than four; in females the difference was seven years. Other studies have confirmed that the risk of death increases with obesity and rises dramatically for cigarette smokers (Table 4-3).

Much evidence indicates that ischemic heart disease and other

Table 4-3. Age-standardized death rates per 100,000 population, by cigarette smoking status, sex, and ten-year age-groups, United States, 1966–68

Smoking status	Total 35–84	35–44	45–54	55–64	65–74	75–84
All men	1,974	412	991	2,423	5,066	10,491
Current smoker	2,516	523	1,243	2,960	6,705	13,443
Never smoked	1,482	249	628	1,768	3,795	9,418
All women	1,122	239	528	1,100	2,869	7,478
Current smoker	1,693	295	665	1,521	4,268	13,533
Never smoked	957	178	400	856	2,579	6,933

Source: Adapted from Health United States 1975, 1976.

atherosclerotic diseases arise primarily as a result of life-style. Every year about a million persons in the United States alone experience either a myocardial infarction or sudden cardiac death, and most other industrial countries (with the notable exception of Japan and France) are reporting high levels of death due to ischemic heart disease (Table 4-4). (For

Table 4-4. Reported deaths[a] due to ischemic heart disease (ICD No. A83)[b] per 100,000 population, selected countries, recent years[c]

Country	Year	Total	Male	Female
Sweden	1974	371	436	307
Scotland	1973	363	426	305
United States	1973	326	379	276
Denmark	1973	325	384	268
England and Wales	1973	309	364	256
Norway	1973	269	341	199
Finland	1973	254	330	184
Australia	1973	251	300	202
Austria	1974	250	263	239
Canada	1973	229	278	179
Israel	1973	216	256	176
Germany Fed. Rep. of	1973	197	233	163
Uruguay	1973	172	199	146
Italy	1973	150	166	135
Puerto Rico	1973	118	136	100
France	1973	88	102	74
Greece	1973	79	103	56
Spain	1973	67	82	53
Panama	1973	42	43	42
Japan	1973	39	45	34
Colombia	1972	38	43	32
Hong Kong	1974	30	30	30
Mexico	1973	21	24	18
Philippines	1973	21	25	17
Egypt	1972	19	27	10
El Salvador	1973	9	11	8
Thailand	1973	0.3	0.4	0.2

[a]Rounded to nearest whole number.
[b]1965 (8th) revision.
[c]See also Table 5-11.
Source: Adapted from World Health Organization, 1976.

further interpretation of this table, consult Chapter 5, where it appears again as Table 5-11). Of the three risk factors listed in Table 4-5, cigarette smoking is clearly a consciously chosen behavior trait; serum cholesterol level is usually related to the richness of diet, subject to control and selection; and hypertension is associated to some degree with salt intake, weight, and perhaps stress.

Dietary customs vary greatly between cultural groups. In east Finland, men may obtain 22% of their calories from saturated fatty acids, while Japanese men obtain just 3% from that source (Keys, 1970). The relationship between serum cholesterol level and five-year incidence rate of coronary heart disease in 13 localities is shown in Figure 4-1; the correlation coefficient for these parameters is .81. Additional risk factors for atherosclerosis that are commonly recognized include obesity, sedentary living (lack of exercise), and psycho-social tensions, all of which reflect cultural and behavioral characteristics.

A dramatic example of the effects of life-style on levels of health comes from a natural experiment involving the populations of two adjacent states in the western United States, Utah and Nevada. "Utah is inhabited primarily by Mormons, whose influence is strong throughout the state. Devout Mormons do not use tobacco or alcohol and in general lead stable, quiet lives. Nevada, on the other hand, is a state with high

Table 4-5. Age-standardized incidence of a major coronary event or death, per thousand men, by cigarette-smoking status, serum cholesterol level, and blood pressure, National Cooperative Pooling Project, United States, recent years[a]

Event	Number of risk factors			
	None	One	Two	Three
First major coronary event	20	48	90	171
Sudden death	7	13	30	42
Coronary heart disease death	13	23	44	82
Death from any cause	30	56	96	147

[a]Risk factors defined as: Cigarette smoking, any use; cholesterol, 250 mg/dl or more; blood pressure, diastolic, 90 mm Hg or more, all at entry to study. See source for details.
Source: Adapted from Inter-Society Commission, 1970.

Figure 4-1

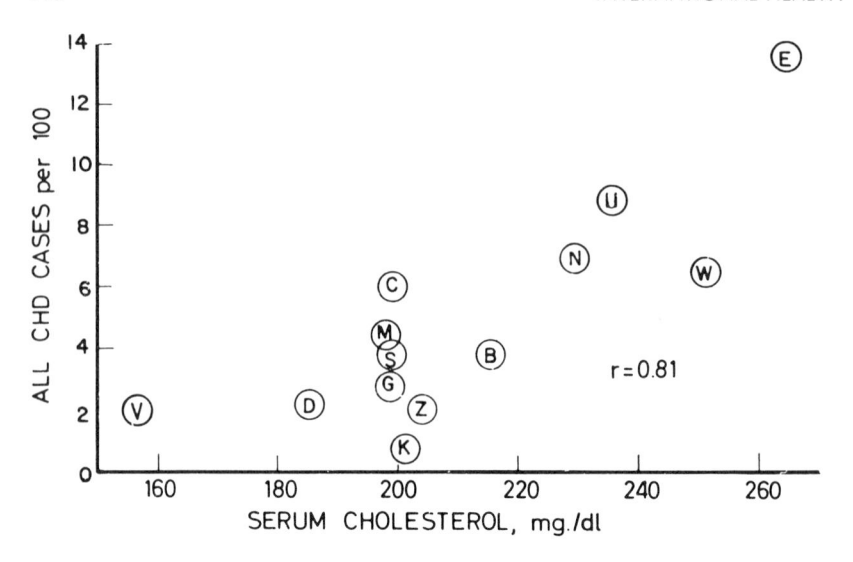

Age-standardized five-year incidence rate of coronary heart disease among men free at entry, plotted against median serum cholesterol concentration. SOURCE: Keys, 1970.

rates of cigarette and alcohol consumption and very high indexes of marital and geographic instability" (Fuchs, 1974). The adult mortality rate for all causes in Nevada is higher by about 40%–50% than in Utah, and for the most clearly alcohol- and tobacco-related diseases, liver cirrhosis and lung cancer, the differential is as high as 600%. Many studies have shown that Mormons, Seventh-Day Adventists, Jehovah's Witnesses, and members of other groups with similar moral tenets and subdued lifestyles have far lower rates of malignant diseases than do their indulgent neighbors.

Smoking and drinking may be manifestations of reactions to life stresses, which are likely to be more common among persons attuned to achievement than among those whose life runs at a more leisurely, placid pace, one better suited to acceptance than to challenge. This is not to say that harmful health effects associated with tobacco, for example, do not occur in developing countries. In parts of South and Southeast Asia many people chew tobacco, particularly those among the less educated groups, and oral and pharyngeal cancer are relatively common. In an extensive study-tour of these areas, Hirayama (1966) correlated the frequency of cancer of the buccal mucosa not only with the chewing of tobacco, but also with the intensity of exposure (Fig. 4-2).

In parts of south and southeast Asia and the Pacific, the custom of chewing betel is widespread. The "quid" is made of sliced areca nut, betel leaves, spices, lime, and sometimes tobacco in combinations that

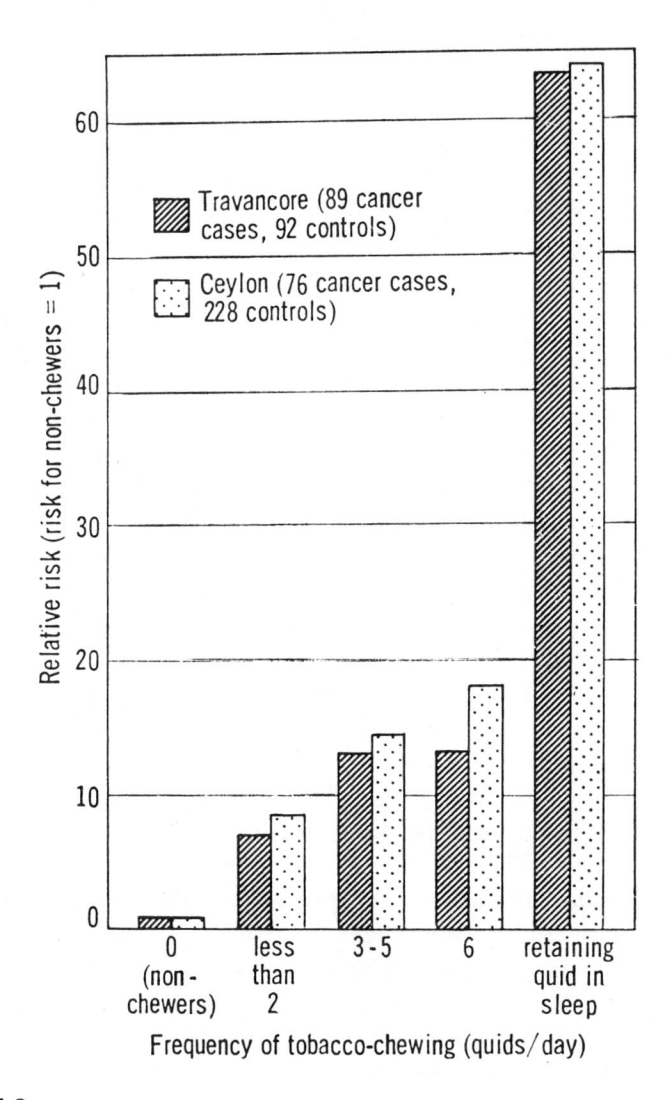

Figure 4-2

Relative risk of developing oral cancer according to frequency of tobacco-chewing, Travancore and Ceylon, 1964. SOURCE: Hirayama, 1966.

vary from place to place. Senewiratne and Uragoda (1973) studied betel chewing in Sri Lanka, finding the habit in about 29% of the Sinhalese, Tamils, and Moors, but in a much smaller proportion of the more westernized Burghers. Buccal carcinoma is the most common cancer in Sri Lanka, and cancer of the esophagus is also frequent, but both are very rare among the Burgher group. Among other ethnic groups, women were found to chew more, and more heavily, than men. Contrary to the situation in western countries, esophageal carcinoma was found to be more common among women than among men in Sri Lanka. Betel (and tobacco) chewing both appear to be declining with time and improved education, and tobacco smoking is increasing. It will be interesting to observe the relative rates of oral, pharyngeal, and bronchial carcinoma over the coming years.

Other types of malignancies appear to be associated with culturally influenced human behvior. Cancer of the uterine cervix has for over a century been known to be extremely rare in religious sisters and other chaste women, a finding repeatedly verified. On the other hand, women in prison populations in the United States and Canada were found to have four to six times as much cervical cancer as in the general population; and of a sample of London prostitutes in 1966, nearly 9% had uterine carcinoma in situ. (Kessler and Aurelian, 1975). The association of uterine cancers with age at first intercourse and number of sexual partners has been confirmed in many parts of the world. Precancerous changes in uterine epithelium are appearing more frequently, and at younger ages, as a manifestation of changed sexual behavior in countries such as Finland (Punnonen et al., 1974). The well-known spread of more conventional sexually transmitted diseases, particularly gonorrhea, in western populations hardly requires documentation.

A person's behavior pattern, largely learned, can affect his health even without the direct exposure to chemical or biological agents just mentioned. The effects of stress, while not yet well understood, are known to be mediated at least in part through changes in hormone levels. Animals, placed suddenly in dangerous situations, exhibit "fight or flight" reaction patterns characterized by release of adrenalin, localized vasoconstriction, and other rapid physiologic changes. Chronic or prolonged stress in animals may lead to longer-term adaptations such as arterial hypertension and adrenal hyperplasia. In man the roster of psychosomatic diseases is a long one.

A theory put forth by Friedman and Rosenman (1974) relates coronary heart disease to a cluster of behavioral traits termed by these authors "Type A," which is characterized by the following attributes: impatience; moving, walking, and eating rapidly; trying to do two things at once; feeling guilty when relaxing; having a sense of time urgency and no "spare" time; trying to do things faster; thinking of everything in numerical terms. Although there is controversy about the significance of these behavior traits with respect to heart disease, it is interesting that they reflect both the impression of Americans gained by foreign visitors and Spengler's picture of the Faustian drive.

In developing countries atherosclerotic lesions and coronary heart disease are comparatively far more rare than in many industrialized countries, even correcting for age distributions. The bimodal social structure in these countries tends to be extreme, and the typically small, wealthy leadership group is usually acculturated to an internationalized life-style. It is in this group that coronary artery disease is occurring with increasing frequency. The pathologist Zilton Andrade has, for example, reported (personal communication) from Salvador, Brazil, that "clinicians who attended wealthy-class patients usually state that they frequently diagnose cases of arteriosclerotic heart disease, a condition which is virtually unknown among poor-class patients dying at similar ages and who are necropsied at the University hospital."

Developing Countries

If the low-income populations of developing countries are relatively free from atherosclerosis, it should not be inferred that their lives are free from disease that is, at least in part, of their own making. Granted the severe limitations of low income, many groups fare far worse than they should because of culturally determined practices, particularly regarding diet. "The despotism of custom," said John Stuart Mill (1859), "is everywhere the standing hindrance to human advancement." It is impossible here to chronicle the many permutations of counterproductive food taboos, which fall most heavily upon those least able to tolerate them: children, pregnant woman, and lactating mothers. Berg (1973) has listed many of these inappropriate dietary restrictions. Fish may be withheld from children for fear it may make them ill (Peru, Indonesia, Malaysia). Eggs are linked with illness (India, Lebanon, Syria); mental retardation (east Africa); late speech development (Korea); and licentiousness (various countries). In Togo and elsewhere in west Africa eggs are kept from children on the grounds that they will come to expect luxuries and grow up to be thieves. In some tropical countries papya and similar fruits are thought to cause worms in children, who may develop xerophthalmia and suffer permanent blindness from the resultant avitaminosis A, an utterly needless tragedy when a papaya tree may be growing quite literally at the doorstep.

Increasing income, permitting greater expenditure for food, may actually lead to impoverishment rather than improvement in diet. In south Asia food preference may go from sorghum or millet to home-polished rice to commercially polished rice. Not only thiamine and other vitamins, but a good deal of protein may be lost by these changes. For reasons of prestige white corn has replaced yellow corn in parts of Latin America, with loss of methionine and vitamin A, or corn (maize) tortillas may be given up entirely in favor of white bread. In India, more costly but less nutritious substitutes may replace the abundant greens, fruits, and legumes. In virtually all countries the rapid spread of sweets, soft drinks, and other "junk" foods is well documented (Berg, 1973).

The "coca-colanization" of the world shows how rapid cultural changes can be. Consider automobiles. In Thailand prevailing tradition for centuries taught gentleness and elaborate politeness in personal dealings. However, the rules of traditional Thai culture did not develop within an environment that included automobiles. Ancient rules seem to be suspended when cars are involved, so that stepping off a curb in modern Bangkok is almost as life-threatening as facing the traffic in Rome or São Paulo. A combination of fatalism, adventurism (taught by Western movies?), inexperience, poor maintenance, poor roads, and contempt of authority has made road accidents a serious hazard in many developing countries, where the injury and fatality rate per vehicle mile far exceed that in industrialized countries with many times the number of cars per capita.

After long experience with automobile accidents a few countries have passed legislation requiring the installation of seat belts in all new vehicles. Public acceptance and use of these belts in the United States has been unenthusiastic. The cultural factors behind the decision not to use seat belts are apparently difficult to change in this case since intensive use of television messages has had no effect upon the proportion of persons using seat belts (Robertson et al., 1974). If exhortation does not succeed, at least in the short term, legislation may be more effective in changing behavior toward seat belts. The first laws for mandatory use of seat belts, enacted in the Australian state of Victoria in 1970, were followed by an immediate reduction of 15% to 20% in the number of deaths of adult car occupants. (For children under six years of age, not covered by the law, there was no reduction.) There was a sharp decrease in head and facial injuries to adults involved in frontal crashes. Compliance with the law among adults was 85%, but it was found that only 50% of drivers and a third of passengers involved in crashes were wearing belts (Trinca et al., 1975). The law-abiding persons, as could be expected, had fewer accidents.

Effects of Propaganda

Whereas propaganda for some purposes, such as the use of seat belts, may be ineffective in the short run, constant repetition of other health messages sometimes achieves a useful behavioral change. In Jamaica, a serious veno-occlusive disease of the liver can result from drinking tea made from the plant *Crotalaria fulva* which contains powerful alkaloids that produce pulmonary hypertension. Between 1935 and 1960 this disease was practically eliminated from the island through propaganda against drinking "bush tea" (Williams and Jelliffe, 1972). (In Afghanistan a similar disease results from eating bread contaminated with the seeds of a kind of *Heliotropium* flower.) In the United States the proportion of adult males who smoke cigarettes declined from 54% to 43% between 1955 and 1970, as a result of which coronary heart disease may have peaked and begun to decline in the middle-aged American men. Intensive publicity regarding the harmful effects of cigarette smoking may have played a part in this favorable trend. Not so encouraging, however, is the increase from 27% to 31% in the proportion of females who smoke cigarettes, an increase possibly responsible in part for a tripling of female lung cancer rates in the San Francisco, California, area between 1966 and 1976 (Palo Alto Times, 1977). Commercial advertising designed to appeal to the female market may be a powerful factor behind this increase. The portrayal of certain behaviors (such as smoking cigarettes) as glamorous, sophisticated, and attractive to the opposite sex is the stock-in-trade of the advertising industry everywhere. Straightening curly hair, curling straight hair, darkening light skin by tanning, lightening dark skin by bleaching are all examples of "needs" created or stimulated by advertising and readily met by the sponsor's product. Sometimes this desire for social acceptance has severe repercussions upon health. In Nairobi, an outbreak of nephrotic syndrome among sophisticated young African women was traced by Barr and colleagues (1972) to use of skin-lightening creams containing toxic compounds of mercury.

A final example of a widespread health-related behavioral change with many overtones is the great decline in breast-feeding that is occurring almost all over the world. Berg (1973) has indicated its extent: Chile (1949 to 1969), 95% to 6% at one year; Singapore, low income (1951 to 1971), 71% to 5% at three months; Philippines (1958 to 1968), down 31%; great reductions in breast-feeding in Mexico, Kenya, Colombia, and elsewhere. The replacement of the breast by the bottle is primarily an urban phenomenon in these countries. "Encroaching urbanization and modernization and new social values are significant influences. Breast-feeding is often viewed as an old-fashioned or backward custom and, by some, as a vulgar peasant practice ... In most developing countries, the greater the sophistication, the worse the lactation: the bottle has become a status symbol" (Berg, 1973). Ironically, just the opposite is happening among better-educated women in the United States, who have rediscovered breast-feeding along with "natural" childbirth in part as aspects of new feminist-oriented social forces and in part as a reaction against all the technology in their environment. No such trend to breast-feeding has yet occurred among less-educated American women, for whom the negative attitude of many doctors remains a powerful inhibiting factor (Brack, 1975). In some areas of the United States, women who breast-feed their infants in public are liable to arrest for "indecent exposure."

The consequences of the shift to bottle-feeding are many and severe among the urban poor of developing countries. Human milk, obviously, requires no preparation, and except for unusual conditions is clean and in most cases readily available. Cow's milk provides the infant with only about 85% of the nutritional value of mother's milk, and it lacks the protective factors passively transmitted from mother to child.

Properly prepared balanced infant formula can provide all needed nutrients for normal development of young infants, millions of whom have thrived on these products. The problem arises with poor and poorly educated parents for whom most of the requisites for proper formula preparation are absent: safe storage of the product; ability to read and follow directions; clean, uncontaminated water; and properly sterilized bottles and nipples of an appropriate design. The old soft-drink or medicine bottle with a cheap, shapeless rubber teat attached is a common sight in the urban slums of less developed countries. Containing highly diluted formula, sometimes mixed with rice water, cornstarch, or other low-cost extenders, almost always contaminated by coliform organisms in great number, these bottles are the primary vectors of diarrheal diseases that strike bottle-fed children many times more often than breast-fed children. The combination of malnutrition and infection results in greatly increased mortality among bottle-fed babies in such circumstances.

An unseen benefit of breast-feeding is the substantially reduced fertility of lactating women and consequently wider spacing of births in mothers who nurse their infants for extended periods.

Powdered cow's milk or infant formula based upon it is expensive. In Kampala, Williams and Jelliffe (1972) estimated sufficient milk for a three-month-old child would take up to one-third of a laborer' s wages. In the aggregate, the substitution of purchased milk or formula for breast milk represents an expenditure of hundreds of millions of dollars, a market that has not gone unnoticed by the dairy industries. Derrick Jelliffe, for many years a leader in the struggle to increase breast-feeding, has coined the term "commerciogenic malnutrition" to dramatize industry's role. Many authors (e.g., Muller, 1974, 1975; Bader, 1976) have pilloried the multinational corporations (together with much of the medical profession in developing countries) for their aggressive promotion of infant formula. In part as a reaction to such unfavorable publicity some of the larger international distributors of infant formulas have agreed to moderate many of their marketing practices.

Commercial advertisers often have substantial resources at their disposal and can raise the prospect of rapid gratification. Public health authorities and others who try to change customary behavior in order to achieve better health usually have a more difficult road before them. Foster (1962) has chronicled the difficulties encountered by health educators in traditional communities, citing numerous examples of cultural, social, and psychological barriers. While it is clear that pest control projects in Buddhist countries are incompatible with prevailing religious belief, it may not be so evident that classes for expectant mothers in Chile are inconsistent with local ideas of pride and dignity. When the classes were changed to "club meetings" and held in homes rather than in schools, they were perceived as social events and women attended readily. Paul (1955) has collected an instructive series of case histories of public health projects that have encountered culturally based resistance in a variety of settings. Of these, Wellin's account of water boiling in a Peruvian village is perhaps the best known and illustrates some frustrations of cross-cultural health education. In a village of 200 families, only 15 housewives boiled their drinking water for hygienic reasons. The local health department, noting the high incidence of water-borne diseases, sent a health worker to the village to try to convince more housewives to boil their families' drinking water. After two years of effort, with the occasional support of a visiting physician, the health worker was able to influence only 11 housewives to boil drinking water. Many people resisted this change in habits, in part because boiled water was considered as suitable only for sickly people, in part because of reluctance to abandon traditions. In a similar vein, Northrop (1959) has shown how purification of water was resisted by Mexican villagers because water, as the creative source of life, was considered sacred; natural water therefore cannot be bad, and tampering with it is viewed as sacrilege.

It is not only villagers in remote areas who may object to adoption of what appear to the western scientist as innocuous and obviously beneficial practices. In a modern industrial plant in Singapore, Phoon (1975) asked some workers to wear a cartridge respirator for protection from toxic fumes. He was "surprised to hear a refusal, not because of discomfort, but because it looks like a pig's snout!"

Resistance to vaccination is widespread, for a variety of reasons. Public health authorities have launched many campaigns against measles, one of the most highly fatal diseases of young children in west Africa. In some areas, the "jet injectors" were viewed with terror, and residents made elaborate plans to avoid vaccination, sometimes rehearsing for weeks to escape from the roving public health teams (Imperato, 1975). The tragic aftermath of such an incident in the village of Sossobee, in the Bambara-speaking region of Mali has been described in these words:

The chief who sat next to me on a straw mat said that one hundred and twenty-eight children had died in a month's time, almost half of those who had contracted measles. The epidemic began several weeks after a small girl from a neighboring village arrived in Sossobee with measles, but the chief and the elders did not draw any connection between the first case and the subsequent epidemic. For them the epidemic was a manifestation of God's will, the result of an evil wind which had blown in from the swamps and plains of the delta and penetrated the skins of their children. It wasn't long before scores of children were ill with coughs, running eyes and fever and shortly thereafter rashes came out. The people of Sossobee like all the Bambara attempted to bring out the rash as quickly as possible in their children because they have over the years made the empirical observation that once the rash appears the prodromal symptoms disappear. The children were given honey by mouth and had their skins rubbed with honey, monkey feces and dirt from termite hills so that the rash would come out. Because of the tremendous concern for the rash to appear, children were not washed with water and were kept in the dark interior of their huts until the illness was over. The children were given purges of tamarind juice in order to drive the illness out of the interior of the body and into the skin.

Although the sick children were dehydrated from their high fevers and from being kept in the hot unventilated huts, their parents refused to give them anything to drink for fear of impeding the development of the rash. They diminished their food intake, prohibited them from eating meat and put honey, goat's milk, tamarind juice and peanut flour solution in their eyes in the hope of preventing blinding corneal ulcers. Parents abstained from sexual relations because they believed that it worsens measles in their children. The people of Sossobee firmly believed that all of the practices and treatments they employed were for the benefit of their sick children and could not understand that sick children with high fevers needed protein and fluids, that serious eye infections with permanent damage resulted for the ophthalmic preparations they used, that purges were nefarious and solutions rubbed on the skin the cause of serious dermatitis. What was undertaken with the finest of intentions was in reality a major cause of the high morbidity and mortality associated with the epidemic. (Imperato, 1975)

Beneficial Practices   It must not be inferred from this discussion that all or even a majority of health-related behavioral practices among traditional peoples are harmful. As Read (1948) has observed:

Before modern medical science and modern education touched the [illiterate] people, they had their own ways of dealing with life and its problems, whether in food shortages, infant feeding, or minor ailments. An old woman in a village in Central Africa once told me, "You Europeans think that you have everything to teach. You tell us we eat the wrong food, treat our babies the wrong way, give our sick people the wrong medicine; you are always telling us we are wrong. Yet, if we had always done the wrong things, we should all be dead. And you see we are not."

SICKNESS

An earlier shift in emphasis from disease to illness turned this discussion towards social science. Now a focus on *sick*ness brings us into the more specialized realm of medical sociology. From the viewpoint of medical anthropology, culture refers to ways of perceiving and organizing ideas about health and illness as modified by the traditions of a society. The concerns of the medical sociologist, by contrast, are with the relationships of individuals, the interactions between them, and their place within the context of a society's institutional structures.

The recognition by a person himself or by another (e.g., the parents of an infant) that there is something wrong, requiring some sort of treatment, is the point of departure for the present discussion. The symptoms or signs perceived, the interpretation of their seriousness, the decision of whether to do something alone or to seek help—and what help, if any, to seek—are determined by cultural, individual, and situational factors. As a result of this process, a person may or may not become a patient, possibly entering the "health care system." It is usually at this stage that the conventional western medical practitioner begins to take an interest in the particular complaint at hand. However, it must be emphasized that the entire decisional sequence is of great importance to the practice of medicine. It is widely accepted that a person may have a disease (be "ill") without knowing it or acting "sick." A person who knows himself to be ill but does not act sick is a stoic; one who acts sick but is not really ill is a malingerer.

To decide whther or not a person is sick is often highly situational. Infection with the parasitic worm *Schistosoma haematobium* commonly produces an admixture of blood in the urine. This sign, which would prompt most Europeans or Americans to see a physician, is considered perfectly normal in some areas in which urinary schistosomiasis is endemic. Small children with swollen bellies characteristic of severe malnutrition may be viewed with pride as good and fat by uneducated mothers. On the other hand, a plump but healthy middle-aged housewife may decide to seek medical help for reduction of weight that she perceives as excessive only after her husband has taken an interest in a younger woman. Standards of normality and tolerability of any particular type of perceived deviation vary from one person and community to another and also from one time to another. In periods of social stress, as in wartime, many persons may decide to tolerate aches and pains that otherwise would have been brought to a physician; the personal sacrifice may be viewed as a contribution to the joint war effort.

In an earlier section it was pointed out that the roster of diseases recognized in one culture will not be the same as that in another. There are also differences in the perception of symptoms. The severity of pain, for instance, is at least partially determined by culturally conditioned expectations, particularly evident during childbirth (Melzack, 1961). Zborowski (1952) showed in New York that patients of Jewish and Italian descent, despite a substantial cultural experience in common, tended to respond to pain in an emotional way, others were more "objective," and some, particularly Irish, denied the presence of pain. The significance of pain also varied: Italian patients often sought simple relief while Jewish patients frequently requested interpretation and prognostication. The Cornell Medical Index, a questionnaire with 195 items about past symptom responses, was administered by Croog (1961) to several thousand recruits of the United States Army. Men of bilateral Italian or Jewish descent recorded about 40% more symptom responses than men of Irish, British, or German descent; similar differences are to be expected among all cultural groups. Zola (1966) cites evidence that up to 90% of apparently healthy adults have some physical aberration or clinical disorder and that "neither the type of disorder, nor the seriousness of objective medical standards, differentiated those who felt sick from those who did not."

The Sick Role

The interaction of doctor and patient is not an unstructured event. Each participant has a particular role to play, in the view of sociologists. Even if the two individuals have not previously met, they have learned to expect certain things and to act in certain ways provided they are similarly acculturated. Even so, the layman and the specialist may have very different understandings of a particular episode of illness. The patient may find it rewarding to enter into the *sick role,* a special socially institutionalized situation elaborated in detail by Parsons (1951, 1972). In this view the patient's incapacity is held to be beyond his own power to overcome by an act of will. He can therefore not be "held responsible" for his incapacity, and being sick exempts him to some extent from normal role and task obligations. However, the sick person must recognize that he should want and try to get well and to work with others to this end; he and his family should seek competent help and cooperate with attempts to help him get well. The particular rights and obligations associated with being sick vary greatly from one culture to another, with age, sex, and status.

Since illness is recognized as an acceptable cause for withdrawing from certain role obligations, social responsibilities, and expectations, persons may be drawn to the patient role in order to obtain secondary advantages, to make claims on others for care and attention, and to provide an acceptable reason for social failure. Thus invididuals may be motivated to adopt the 'sick role' ... and others may be anxious to accord people the status of sickness in order to avoid embarrassment and social difficulties. The interpenetration between medical and other social institutions is quite complex, and often these relationships are not fully appreciated. (Mechanic, 1972)

Seeking Help A person's decision to seek professional assistance may follow a reasoning process (largely intuitive) like the one charted in Table 4-6. It must be noted once more that many problems considered within their province by scientific physicians are not perceived as such by many others. Numberless are the bowls of chicken soup prepared by persons who answer "yes" to 6a, or 6b.

Table 4-7 lists some of the types of therapeutic practitioners who are available and sought out under various circumstances. Some characteristics of the mode of practice are described by the rubrics used. There are many others.

Data on actual rates of utilization of available medical services are hard to find for industrialized countries, and nonexistent elsewhere. In the few surveys done, it has been found that a great deal of perceived minor illness is not brought to medical attention. LeRiche and Stiver (1959), following the extensive Canadian sickness survey, studied medical utilization rates among members of a prepaid medical plan. They concluded, "It would appear that physicians in the plan see about one common cold in 15, one case of influenza in 10, and the same proportion of acute pharyngitis and tonsillitis as reported by the patient." White et al. (1961) found that in the United States and the United Kingdom each thousand adults 16 years and over experienced about 750 episodes of illness per month, of which about 250 were brought to a physician. Two-thirds of all

Table 4-6. Stages in the decision to seek treatment

1. Is there a problem?
2. Do I know what it is?
3. Is it harmful?
4. Is it likely to
    a. improve by itself?
    b. stay the same?
    c. deteriorate?
5. Is it remediable at all?
6. Can it be alleviated by
    a. myself
    b. family or friend?
    c. a professional?
    d. a God?
7. Could it be made worse by trying to alleviate it
    a. by myself?
    b. by family or friend?
    c. by a professional?
8. Will it cost a lot for treatment by
    a. myself?
    b. family or friend?
    c. professional?
    d. a God?
9. Will the cost be in
    a. money?
    b. time?
    c. pain?
    d. embarrassment?
10. Is the probable benefit worth the probable cost?

Table 4-7. The varieties of therapeutic practitioners

Axis of classification	Three examples
Ethnic	Chinese, Yoruba, Chicano
National	British, Nigerian, Yugoslavian
Historical	Modern, traditional, ancient
Geographical	Western, Caribbean, Asian
Clientele	Affluent, geriatric, immigrant
Social sanction	Consensus, state license, board certification
Occupational	Physician, priest, curandero
Mode of therapy	Herbal, surgical, faith healing
Official approbation	Orthodox, unconventional, quack
Rationale	Scientific, religious, supernatural
Clinical specialization	Psychiatry, pediatrics, soul loss
Professional commitment	Amateur, part-time, full-time
Sharing of practice	Solo, team, institutional
Expected payment	Gratitude, social obligation, money
Venue of treatment	Client's home, healer's place, hospital
Source of payment	Client, special group, government
Tradition	Ayurvedic, Moorish, Greco-Roman
Objective	Diagnosis, cure, prognostication
Recruitment	Hereditary, miraculous, education & schooling

Source: Based in part on Kunstadter, 1975.

recognized illness in those groups, therefore, was treated by the individual, the family, or not at all.

Many visits to physicians do not result in the cure or treatment of illness. A large porportion are for technical reasons such as insurance examinations and certification for absence from school or work. Routine periodic checkups (whose usefulness for asymptomatic adults has been seriously questioned) take up much physician time in the United States and elsewhere. Reassurance of patients about one or another worry, often concealed, occupies most of the rest. In this cateogry may be placed the practice of "esthetic surgery," perhaps best developed in the local cultures of southern California and Rio de Janeiro where physical appearance is highly prized. About 20,000 plastic surgery procedures are done annually in Rio, where it is said to be "a safe bet that just about any Brazilian woman past 40 and active in upper-class social functions has undergone some form of esthetic surgery" (Kandell, 1976). The leading surgeons are considered social superstars, have become millionaires, and tend to see themselves more as artists than as doctors. While face-lifts, breast rejuvenations, and abdomen slimmings occupy the dreams of society matrons and the talents of 500 surgeons in Copacabana and Ipanema, children suffer from malnutrition and chronic diarrhea in the crowded favelas a few blocks away. Here, as in the case of Chinese bound feet, predominant cultural values prescribe a situation, viewed as normal by its participants, and elsewhere considered bizarre. All societies have practices that may be subject to criticism on similar grounds.

The Clinical Encounter A physician who is raised and educated in one culture may find it difficult or impossible to deal with patients from another culture (and vice versa) except on the most simple mechanistic level. This is true not only with "foreign" doctors or patients, but within almost all countries as well. In developing countries in particular, physicians are generally drawn from the affluent segment of society. These doctors, even if seen by an outsider as being of the same ethnic group as their poorer compatriots, may be far away from them in their conceptualization of illness. Some patients may be more concerned with preservation or restoration of social status or of prestige, some with capacity of earning or accomplishment, others with appearance. These worries are often not enunciated; a specific or vague physical complaint may conceal an underlying emotional problem which is difficult for the person to express directly. The physician may interpret this as malingering. The patient, who seeks validation of his illness and legitimization of his sick role, accuses the physician of lack of sympathy. The physician may expect strict compliance with his instructions, for example, medication in the proper dosage to be taken at the proper intervals. The patient may expect immediate results from the drug; if he obtains rapid relief (or if he does not), he may see no need to continue. A medically sound request for a follow-up visit may be seen by the patient as a needless waste of money.

In western medical practice, particularly in the United States, the clinical encounter sometimes has overtones of confrontation, in which the physician is "challenged" to perform to the patient's expectations by implicit threat of legal action for malpractice, to which the physician responds by the excesses of defensive medicine, adding to the patient's expense and detracting from innovative (or minimal) treatment. This problem can perhaps be interpreted as emergence of patient and physician subcultures, with divergent goals and values.

In most traditional communities, by contrast, the patient and healer may be culturally more closely integrated, sharing the same values and outlook and often joining with family and friends to undertake the healing process. The curandero, bomoh, shaman, herbalist, or even the local pharmacist or barefoot doctor, while lacking in technical sophistication, generally speak the same cultural language as the patient.

Sickness, Illness, and Societal Goals

Early recognition of illness, or potential illness, in the absence of sickness is a major goal of preventive medicine. The mobile x-ray unit, the "Pap" smear, the multiphasic health examination, the PKU test for newborns, and other screening techniques are all designed to accelerate the process of becoming a patient. Much attention has also been devoted in industrialized countries to reinforcing the decision to seek professional help, and quickly, as in the case of chest pain or suspicion of a "warning sign" of cancer. An important social role of the "health care system" is the minimization of real illness, which is highly disruptive of invididual and group functioning. In this respect, the spartan man with severe chest pains who decides to "let it go" and do nothing is more important in the long run than his excitable neighbor who appears for an electrocardiogram with minimal indications. The social cost of incapacitating illness and premature death is so high that a certain proportion of false alarms is readily acceptable provided the true cases are also identified. Detection of an illness in its early stages permits some medical intervention, at least in theory, to keep it from becoming (more) disruptive and expensive. This process of arresting an existing condition is known as *secondary prevention*. But the social system may have an equal, or greater, interest in *primary prevention*—that is, keeping an illness from developing at all, as by vaccination, genetic counseling, water purification, ritual ceremony, observance of taboo, wearing of amulets or symbols, or other means. A comprehensive "health care" system must therefore be concerned with the nonpatient as well as with the patient.

References

Anderson, E. N. and M. L. Anderson. 1975. Folk dietetics in two Chinese communities, and its implications for the study of Chinese medicine. *In:* A. Kleinman, P. Kunstadter, E. R. Alexander, and J. L. Gale, Eds. Medicine in Chinese Cultures. Washington. U.S. Department of Health, Education and Welfare Publication No. (NIH) 75-653. pp. 143–175.

Assar, M. and Ž. Jakšić. 1975. A health services development project in Iran. *In:* K. W. Newell, Ed. Health By the People. Geneva. World Health Organization. pp. 112–127.

Bader, M. B. 1976. Breast-feeding: the role of multinational corporations in Latin America. International Journal of Health Services 6: 609–626.

Barker, E. A. 1973. Traditional African views on health and disease. Central African Journal of Medicine 19: 80–82.

Barr, R. D., P. H. Rees, P. E. Cordy, A. Kungu, B. A. Woodger, and H. M. Cameron. 1972. Nephrotic syndrome in adult Africans in Nairobi. British Medical Journal, April 15: 131–134.

Belloc, N. B. 1973. Relationship of health practices and mortality. Preventive Medicine 2: 67–81.

Belloc, N. B. and L. Breslow. 1972. Relationship of physical health status and health practices. Preventive Medicine 1: 409–421.

Berg, A. 1973. The Nutrition Factor: Its Role in National Development. Washington. The Brookings Institution. 290 p.

Brack, D. C. 1975. Social forces, feminism, and breastfeeding. Nursing Outlook 23: 556–561.

Chew, M. B. 1973. Chinese bound foot. Radiography 39: 39–42.

Chilivumbo, A. B. 1974. The social basis of illness. Central African Journal of Medicine 20: 181–185.

Clark, M. 1970. Health in the Mexican-American Culture: A Community Study. 2nd Ed. Berkeley. University of California Press. 253 p.

Coury, C. 1967. The basic principles of medicine in the primitive mind. Medical History 11: 111–127.

Croog, S. H. 1961. Ethnic origins, educational level, and responses to a health questionnaire. Human Organization 20: 65–69.

Fieg, J. P. and J. G. Blair. 1975. There *Is* a Difference. Twelve Intercultural Perspectives. Washington, D.C. Meridian House International. 136 p.

Foster, G. M. 1962. Traditional Cultures and the Impact of Technological Change. New York. Harper & Row. 292 p.

Frank, L. K. 1948. Society as the Patient. New Brunswick, N.J. Rutgers University Press. 395 p.

Friedman, M. and R. H. Rosenman. 1974. Type A Behavior and Your Heart. New York. A. A. Knopf. 266 p.

Fuchs, V. 1974. Who Shall Live? New York. Basic Books. 168 p.

Gelfand, M. 1971. The patterns of disease in Africa. Central African Journal of Medicine 17: 69–78.

Guarnaschelli, J., J. Lee, and F. W. Pitts. 1972. "Fallen Fontanelle" (Caida de Mollera) A variant of the battered child syndrome. Journal of the American Medical Association 22: 1545–1546.

Health United States 1975. 1976. Rockville, Maryland, U.S. Department of Health, Education and Welfare Publication No. (HRA) 76-1232. 612 p.

Hirayama, T. 1966. An epidemiological study of oral and pharyngeal cancer in Central and Southeast Asia. Bulletin of the World Health Organization 34: 41–69.

Imperato, P. J. 1975. A Wind in Africa. St. Louis. W. H. Green. 363 p.

Inter-Society Commission for Heart Disease Resources. 1970. Primary prevention of the atherosclerotic diseases. Circulation 42: A53–A95.

Jansen, G. 1973. The Doctor-Patient Relationship in an African Tribal Society. Assen, Netherlands. Van Gorcum & Co. N.V. 224 p.

Kandell, J. 1976. In Brazil, the women boast about their plastic surgery. New York Times, March 9.
Kessler, I. I. and L. Aurelian. 1975. Uterine cervix. *In:* D. Schottenfeld, Ed. Cancer Epidemiology and Prevention. Springfield, Illinois. Charles C. Thomas. pp. 263–317.
Keys, A. 1970. XVII. The Diet. *In:* A. Keys, Ed. Coronary Heart Disease in Seven Countries. American Heart Association Monograph No. 29. Circulation 41 (Suppl. 1): 1162–1183.
Kunstadter, P. 1975. The comparative anthropological study of medical systems in society. *In:* A. Kleinman, P. Kunstadter, E. R. Alexander, and J. L. Gale, Eds. Medicine in Chinese Cultures. Washington. U.S. Department of Health, Education and Welfare Publication (NIH) 75-653. pp. 683–695.
LeRiche, W. H. and W. B. Stiver. 1959. Illness as seen by the patient and the physician. Canadian Journal of Public Health 50: 284–291.
Lilienfeld, A. M. 1976. Foundations of Epidemiology. New York. Oxford University Press. 283 p.
Martinez, C. and H. Martin. 1966. Folk diseases among urban Mexican-Americans. Journal of the Americal Medical Association 196: 161–164.
Mead, M. 1961. Determinants of health beliefs and behavior. III. Cultural determinants. American Journal of Public Health 51: 1552–1554.
Mechanic, D. 1972. Public Expectations and Health Care. New York. John Wiley and Sons. 314 p.
Melzack, R. 1961. The perception of pain. Scientific American 204: 41–49.
Metropolitan Life Insurance Company. 1972. Homicide-International Comparison.
Mill, J. S. 1859. On Liberty. Reprinted in 1956. Indianapolis. Bobbs-Merrill. 141 p.
Muller, M. 1974. Money, milk and marasmus. New Scientist 61: 530–533.
Muller, M. 1975. Milk, nutrition and the law. New Scientist 62:328–330.
Northrop, F. S. C. 1959. Cultural mentalities and medical science. *In:* I. Galdston, Ed. Medicine and Anthropology. New York. International Universities Press. 165 p.
Palo Alto Times. 1977. Lung cancer rates triple for women. Palo Alto, California. April 6.
Parsons, T. 1951. The Social System. Glencoe, Illinois. Free Press. 575 p.
Parsons, T. 1972. Definition of health and illness in the light of American values and social structure. *In:*E. G. Jaco, Ed. Patients, Physicians and Illness. 2nd Ed. New York. Free Press. pp. 107–127.
Paul, B. D., Ed. 1955. Health Culture and Community: Case Studies of Public Reactions to Health Programs. New York. Russell Sage Foundation. 493 p.
Phoon, W. O. 1975. (discussion) *In:* K. Elliott and J. Knight, Eds. Ciba Foundation Symposium 32 (new series). Health and Industrial Growth. Amsterdam. Associated Scientific Publishers. p. 232.
Punnonen, R., M. Grönroos, and R. Peltonen. 1974. Increase of premalignant cervical lesions in teenagers. Lancet 2(7886): 949.
Read, M. 1948. Attitudes towards health and disease among pre-literate peoples. Health Education Journal 6: 166–172.
Robertson, L. S., A. B. Kelley, B. O'Neill, C. W. Wixon, R. S. Eiswirth, and W.

Haddon, Jr. 1974. A controlled study of the effect of television messages on safety belt use. American Journal of Public Health 64: 1071–1080.

Rosenberg, C. E. 1962. The Cholera Years. The United States in 1832, 1849, and 1866. Chicago. University of Chicago Press. 257 p.

Senewiratne, B. and C. G. Uragoda. 1973. Betel chewing in Ceylon. American Journal of Tropical Medicine and Hygiene 22: 418–422.

Snow, L. F. 1974. Folk medical beliefs and their implications for care of patients. A review based on studies among black Americans. Annals of Internal Medicine 81: 82–96.

Spengler, O. 1926–28. The Decline of the West. Trans. by C. F. Atkinson. New York. A. A. Knopf. Vol. I, 428 p.; Vol. 2, 507 p.

Trinca, G. W. and B. J. Dooley. 1975. The effects of mandatory seat belt wearing on the mortality and pattern of injury of car occupants involved in motor vehicle crashes in Victoria. Medical Journal of Australia 1: 675–678.

Voakes, P. 1975. Prayer seen way to cure diseases. Palo Alto Times, March 1.

White, K. L., T. F. Williams and B. G. Greenberg. 1961. The ecology of medical care. New England Journal of Medicine 265: 885–891.

Williams, C. D. and D. B. Jelliffe. 1972. Mother and Child Health. London. Oxford University Press. 164 p.

Wolff, R. J. 1965. Modern medicine and traditional culture: confrontation on the Malay Peninsula. Human Organization 24: 339–345.

Wood, J. T. 1975. New Standings. Harper's Magazine, January. p. 10.

World Health Organization. 1976. World Health Statistics Annual 1973–1976. Vol. I. Vital Statistics and Causes of Death. Geneva. World Health Organization. 839 p.

Yap, P. M. 1951. Mental diseases peculiar to certain cultures: a survey of comparative psychiatry. Journal of Mental Science 97: 313–327.

Zborowski, M. 1952. Cultural components in responses to pain. Journal of Social Issues 8: 16–30.

Zola, I. K. 1966. Culture and symptoms—an analysis of patients' presenting complaints. American Sociological Review 31: 615–630.

INFORMATION 5.

In 1690, William Petty's monograph entitled *Political Arithmetick* was published posthumously in London. This work, sometimes cited as the foundation of modern demography, dealt largely with populations, income distribution, employment, and similar matters rather than with health per se, but the words "political arithmetick" clearly express the sense of the present chapter.

The crucial and complex subject of statistical information often suffers from neglect by those whose chief motive is healing the sick, performing laboratory or clinical research, or providing expert technical advice and instruction. More significantly, the collection, dissemination, and utilization of health data are sometimes not considered matters of great urgency, even by persons charged with administration of health services. Data cost money, and as with most other things, the higher the quality, the greater the cost. In developing countries, where the need for preventive and curative services is acute and funds are perpetually inadequate, the amounts allocated for acquisition and flow of data must always fall short of requirements. Such is the arithmetick.

Now for the politics. Health is a highly public matter in all countries. A preoccupation with the nature, distribution, and cost of health services is found in socialist and capitalist countries, large and small, rich and poor. Pressures upon local and regional officials and upon ministries have been known to result in data of questionable reliability. Personal ambitions, coupled with promotion systems based on performance, may tempt administrators to overestimate the number of inoculations given or to minimize reported mortality or morbidity rates. Concern with international trade or with the tourist industry may prompt a government to describe cholera as gastroenteritis, and forthcoming elections may have strange effects upon all sorts of reported numbers. Such inaccuracies arising from human frailty need not be overemphasized, but must be kept in mind when reading and interpreting health-related data.

THE KINDS OF HEALTH-RELATED DATA

"Finagle's laws on information," as reported by Murnaghan (1974), provide a starting point for this discussion:

1. The information you have is not what you want.

2. The information you want is not what you need.
3. The information you need is not what you can obtain.

This recipe for frustration is an indication of the difficulties inherent in management of meaningful data. From the viewpoint of international health, the obvious questions are: What is it that we need to know? How can we find the data? Before these are considered, however, there is an underlying issue of great importance, namely, why this information is being sought.

Reasons for Seeking Health Statistics

Persons responsible for health services have always required information about the kinds, quantity, and distribution of illness to guide their planning and to evaluate the effectiveness of their services. During the past two decades great changes have taken place in the use of health data in many countries. These were discussed at an international conference in Copenhagen, where it was stressed that

The drive to secure a greater range of, and more precise, health statistical data arose not merely from an attempt to measure more comprehensively the disease prevalence in the population and the determinants of that prevalence but from new attitudes to the administration of health services. The adoption of insured schemes of health provision—whether public, private or tax provided—has stimulated a radical shift away from pragmatism ... to the planned utilization of resources designed to be adequate to match predicted need. This is an entirely new management situation calling for a much more positive and purposeful approach to health statistical services. (World Health Organization, 1974)

Planning and decision making in many countries are becoming more sophisticated as populations, costs, medical knowledge, and information processing techniques all advance. Weighing alternative strategies for maximum effectiveness (Chapter 6) has become a task for a new kind of specialist.

In addition to their prediction and evaluation functions, statistical data are gathered by health authorities for many other reasons. These data are also needed by other branches of government at municipal, provincial or state, and national levels. In most countries health-related legislation originates from a perception of need presumably based on realistic and reliable information. Legal requirements for detecting, reporting, and combatting locally important diseases; laws dealing with occupational and environmental hazards, with regulation of hospitals, and with training and licensing of professional personnel; and many similar subjects all clearly depend upon relevant data. In addition, compliance with existing laws and regulations must be monitored.

Health statistics derived from continuous monitoring can have an early warning function. Prompt detection of outbreaks can lead to knowledge of their cause and steps to minimize the hazard. New or newly recognized conditions can be discovered early. For example, a syndrome of eye, ear, and heart damage has been described in children whose mothers contracted rubella during pregnancy, and limb malformations in newborns have been related to maternal use of thalidomide. In both cases, monitoring was informal, and the first indications of these relationships arose not from the conventional government statistical system but from alert private practitioners (in Australia, and in Germany respectively). Both have resulted in worldwide awareness and control efforts. Many similar instances could be cited.

On an international level, each country needs to know about real and potential threats to the health of its citizens, particularly from imported communicable diseases. The danger of plague and especially of smallpox pandemics is now greatly reduced, but yellow fever, cholera, influenza, and other diseases still pose a hazard to many countries. The health problems likely to be encountered by nationals traveling abroad also require international collation and dissemination of data. Members of the World Health Organization (see Table 8-12) are obligated under the organization's constitution to provide certain information in the form of regular reports. They must also report annually on the action taken and progress achieved in improving the health of their people (Art. 61). Member states must communicate promptly to the WHO important laws, regulations, official reports, and statistics pertaining to health (Art. 63) and provide other statistical and epidemiological reports as determined by the World Health Assemblies (Art. 64). In addition, the International Health Regulations adopted by the twenty-second World Health Assembly in 1969 and in effect since 1971 specify certain obligations of health administrations. These requirements are complex and not easily summarized, but refer primarily to notification of cases or outbreaks of cholera, plague, smallpox, and yellow fever and of measures taken to prevent their spread.

Many people are interested in international compilations of vital and health statistics as a yardstick to compare their country with others. Statistics concerning the ratio of population to physicians, hospital beds, etc. are often cited by advocates of one or another viewpoint, both on national and regional levels. Such data, as well as evaluations of nutritional status and similar conditions linked to socioeconomic development, are often highly sensitive and laden with political overtones. Health is clearly an issue of great importance to every person and questions of policy cannot realistically be determined on scientific grounds alone. Epidemiologic findings associating cigarette smoking with lung cancer and heart disease, for example, have often been cited as arguments in favor of restrictive legislation. Proponents and opponents of smoking bans have sought and interpreted data to support their particular positions. The same is true of partisans on either side of more esoteric issues such as the construction of nuclear power plants or the conduct of recombinant DNA research. The overlapping of medical science and public policy leads to advances in both by stimulating research designed to provide definitive data in answer to pressing questions. Certain epidemiologic information is best obtained by worldwide, multinational, or cross-cultural analyses: detailed investigations in areas of high prevalence of specific diseases may lead to hypotheses about causation which, if confirmed elsewhere, can be translated into strategies for intervention.

It is not only official government agencies that require health-related data. Life insurance companies have a great interest in such information. Indeed, early work on mortally by demographic pioneers such as John Graunt and Edmund Halley were more useful to underwriters than to bureaucrats. The recent burgeoning of proprietary health insurance companies, particularly in the United States, makes the need for appropriate data on risks of illness much more acute. In fact, any person responsible for the administration of numbers of people, whether in industry, schools, the military, or elsewhere must have a certain amount of information on which to base projections of needed services, absenteeism, and other aspects of management.

Comparative information about the organization of health and medical care systems, mechanisms for their coordination and financial support, and ways in which they are utilized in other countries can provide valuable insights into the realm of human problem solving. The training of physicians and other members of health-care teams varies from one country to another, as does the use made of auxiliary personnel such as midwives or barefoot doctors. No nation is so omniscient that knowledge derived elsewhere can be safely ignored.

And finally there is another human characteristic that drives men and women to probe, to ask, to travel, to compare, to consider every scrap and nuance of information about the world and its contents, one that needs neither analysis nor justification, namely, curiosity.

What Constitutes Health Data?

An infinity of variables acts to influence the health of individuals and populations. The amount of rainfall can affect nutrition by altering agricultural production, and, by control of mosquito breeding, can influence subsequent malaria rates in endemic areas. In the United States, changes in speed limits play a part in determining deaths and injuries in automobile accidents. While granting that such variables have undoubted effects on health, their general nature and local significance do not qualify them as health statistics in the conventional sense. The basic categories of health-related statistics are:

1. *Data on the population.* The number of people and their attributes such as age, sex, ethnic origin, urbanization, geographic distribution, and similar fundamental characteristics.
2. *Vital statistics.* Live births; deaths (including fetal deaths) by sex, age, and cause; marriages and divorces. In some areas migrations (internal and external), adoptions, and related categories are also included.
3. *Health statistics.* Morbidity by type, severity, and outcome of illness or accident; data on notifiable diseases, on blindness, incapacity, etc. This category is not so clearly defined as the previous two and varies from one country to another.
4. *Statistics bearing upon health services.* Numbers and types of services available and their distribution of personnel and facilities; nature of the services and their utilization rates; organization of government and private health care systems; payment mechanisms and related information.

The compilation and issuance of these data on a continuing basis entails a great deal of effort and expense for all modern governments. The situation is made far more complex, however, by the need for comparability between countries and time periods. A high degree of international cooperation is required to assure that definitions, terminology, diagnostic techniques, certification practices, data-handling methods, and reporting schemes are sufficiently standardized for comparative purposes, but flexible enough to take into account the variety of circumstances throughout the world.

International health is largely an extension of public health. The methods and concerns of local and national health administrations, each concentrating upon a particular population, are observed, analyzed, collated, and to a degree integrated in a larger overview encompassing the entire world. The goals of workers at every level are nevertheless the same: improving the quality of life for people—for individual human beings. From a global viewpoint it is possible to compare activities and philosophies at different levels in the concentric progression of responsibilities extending from individuals through the series of communities of which each is a member. Table 5-1 considers, by analogy, some ways of looking at aspects of the health of individuals and of populations. It is included here primarily as a framework for interpreting the functions of health statistics. It may be noted that while all societies have traditions associated with healing and persons specialized for this function, relatively few have corresponding roles for persons dealing with collective or community ("public") health. The activities of traditional or folk healers such as bomohs or curanderos, although often very important, fall outside the realm of health data as generally constituted.

Table 5-1. Population as patient

Classification	Individual	Population
Health specialist is called	Doctor of medicine	Doctor of public health
	Internist, etc.	Epidemiologist
	Feldsher	Sanitarian
	Barefoot doctor (in part)	Barefoot doctor (in part)
	Traditional healer	
Emphasis generally	Curative	Preventive
Request for service	Usually personal	Usually governmental
Looks mostly at	Sick people	Sick and healthy people
Subject composed of	Cells, organs	Individuals, groups
	Nerves, hormones	Communications, laws
	Psyche, spirit	Traditions, culture
	Environment	Environment
Rapid health breakdown	Acute illness	Epidemic disease
Continuing health problem	Chronic illness	Endemic disease
Information collected	History	History
	Age, sex, weight	Vital statisics
	Physical examination	Surveys
	Health status	Health statistics
Treatment	Immunization, preventive measures	Immunization program, sanitation
	Therapy: drugs, ritual	Control program
	Education	Education
Follow-up	Observation	Observation
	Examination, tests	Surveys
Monitoring	Check-ups	Surveillance
Cost per person	Relatively high	Relatively low

DATA ON THE POPULATION: THE CENSUS

The basic demographic characteristics of a population literally underlie most vital and health statistics because they provide the denominators for the relevant rates and ratios (Table 5-2). Data on the population are usually obtained in two ways: by enumeration and by registration. Enumeration, when complete, is done by means of a population census, which in many countries in recent times has been repeated each decade. Registration "is the continuous, permanent, and compulsory recording of the occurrence and characteristics of vital events..." (United Nations, 1973).

It should be noted that neither enumeration nor registration is done for the primary purpose of providing vital and health statistics. Census data have been used for millenia for purposes of taxation and conscription. The birth of Christ is said to have occurred at Bethlehem because Mary and Joseph were travelling home to Judea to be counted in a census. At about the same time (AD 2) in China a census was ordered and data were recorded on more than 12 million households, including the heads of families and the name, age, and birthplace of more than 59.5 million people (Hookham, 1972). More recently, census data have been used for determining political representation, as required for instance by the constitution of the United States (1790), as well as for many other purposes. The effort and expense involved in a complete census is considerable. The total expenditure for the 1970 Census of Population and Housing in the United States was $221.6 million, or $1.06 per person enumerated (U.S. Bureau of the Census, 1976). Information on a variety of topics is usually collected. The United Nations recommends inclusion of questions on the following subjects: total population, sex, age, marital status, education characteristics, economic characteristics (occupation, etc.), place of birth, language, fertility, citizenship, and urban and rural populations.

The information obtained from enumeration and registration data permit the characterization of a population by a variety of classifiers, of which age, sex, and ethnic group are most often used. These figures serve as denominators for the age- and sex-specific mortality and morbidity rates defined on Table 5-2 and make possible more meaningful comparisons of the measures than can be obtained from crude (whole population) figures. As an illustration, the age and sex distributions of the populations of six countries are compared in Figure 5-1. Figure 5-2 and Table 5-3 summarize the distribution of total population in four functional age

Table 5-2. Commonly used vital and health statistics

Category	Meaning
A. Annual crude live birth rate (= "Birth rate")	$\dfrac{\text{Number of live births occurring in a defined population during a year}}{\text{Number in that population at midyear of the same year}} \times 1{,}000$
B. Annual crude death rate (= "Death rate", "mortality rate", "gross death rate")	$\dfrac{\text{Number of deaths occurring in a defined population during a year}}{\text{Number in that population at midyear of the same year}} \times 1{,}000$
C. Annual specific death rate 1. for age 2. for sex 3. for cause 4. for combination of these	$\dfrac{\text{Number of deaths at a specified age, of a specified sex, or cause occurring in a defined population during a year}}{\text{Number in that population of the specified age, or sex, or susceptible to die of the specified cause, at midyear of the same year}} \times 1{,}000$
D. Annual infant mortality rate	$\dfrac{\text{Number of deaths under one year of age occurring in a defined population during a year}}{\text{Number of live births occurring in that population during the same year}} \times 1{,}000$

E. Annual neonatal mortality rate

$$\frac{\text{Number of deaths under 28 days of age occurring in a defined population during a year}}{\text{Number of live births occurring in that population during the same year}} \times 1{,}000$$

F. Annual postneonatal mortality rate

$$\frac{\text{Number of deaths at ages 28 days to the end of the first year occurring in a defined population during a year}}{\text{Number of live births minus neonatal deaths occurring in that population in the same year}} \times 1{,}000$$

G. Annual fetal death rate (= "Stillbirth rate")

$$\frac{\text{Number of fetal deaths at 20 weeks[a] or more gestation occurring in a defined population during a year}}{\text{Number of live births plus fetal deaths of 20 or more weeks occurring in that population during the same year}} \times 1{,}000$$

H. Annual maternal mortality rate

$$\frac{\text{Number of deaths from puerperal[b] causes occurring in a defined population during a year}}{\text{Number of live births occurring in that same population during the same year}} \times 10{,}000$$

continued

Table 5-2.—Continued

Category	Meaning
I. Proportionate mortality	$$\frac{\text{Number of deaths in specific category occurring in a defined population during a year}}{\text{Total number of deaths occurring in that same population during the same year}} \times 100$$
J. Standardized mortality ratio (SMR) 　1. for age 　2. for occupation, ethnic group, social class, etc 　3. for sex 　4. for disease 　5. for combination	$$\frac{\text{Number of deaths in specific category occurring in a defined population during a year}}{\text{Number of deaths in the same specific category occurring in a selected defined comparison population during a year}} \times 100$$
K. Annual incidence for occurrence of a specified condition	$$\frac{\text{Number of new cases of the specified condition occurring in a defined population during a year}}{\text{Number in that population at midyear of the same year}} \times 100,000^{c}$$

L. Point prevalence of a specified condition $$\frac{\text{Number of cases of the specified condition existing in a defined population at a particular point in time}}{\text{Number in that population at the same point in time}} \times 100{,}000^c$$

M. Morbidity rate
   1. crude
   2. specific for age, sex, occupation, place, etc

   $$\frac{\text{Number of cases of specified disease occurring in specified categories during a year}}{\text{Average population in the category during the same year}} \times 1{,}000^c$$

---

[a] Varies somewhat in different jurisdictions.
[b] As listed in latest revision of the ICD.
[c] Multiplier varies depending on frequency.

Philippines

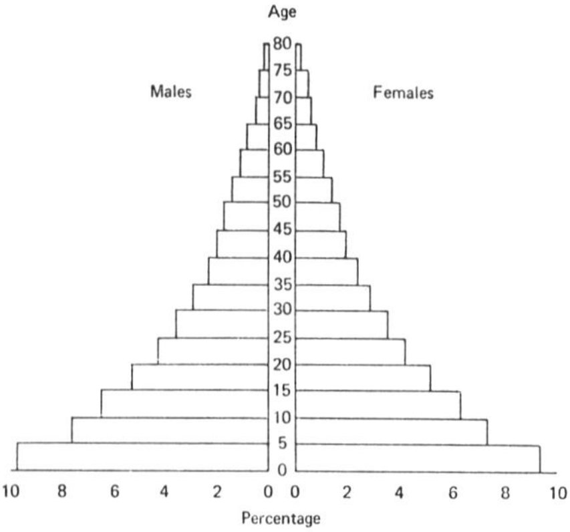

Mexico

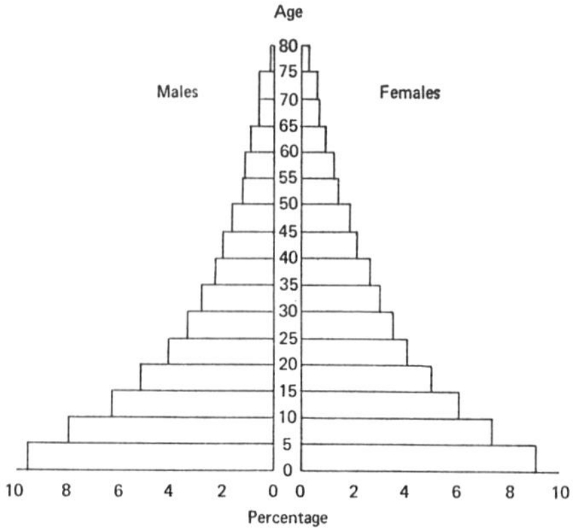

Singapore

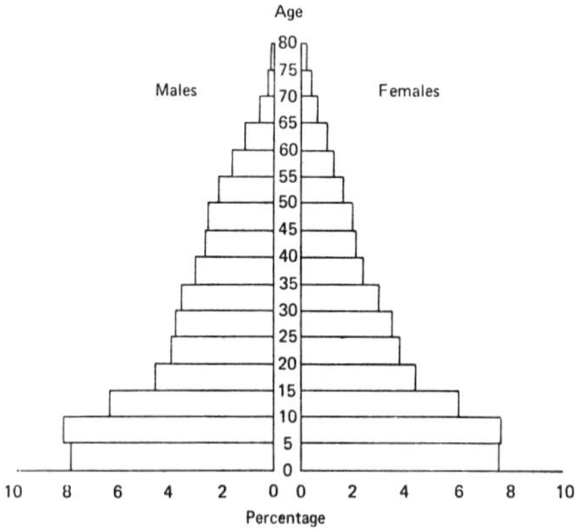

Japan

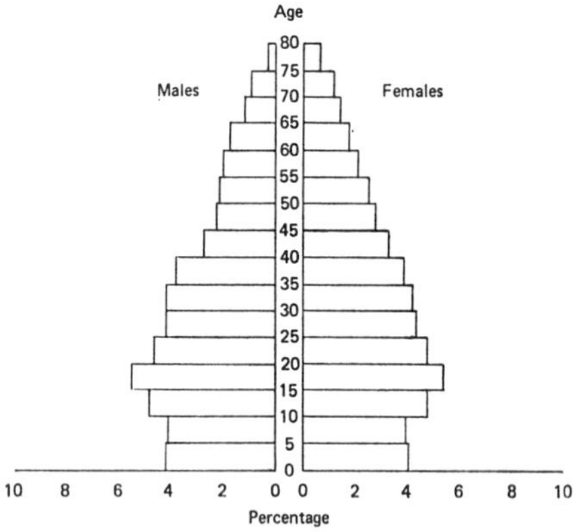

Sweden

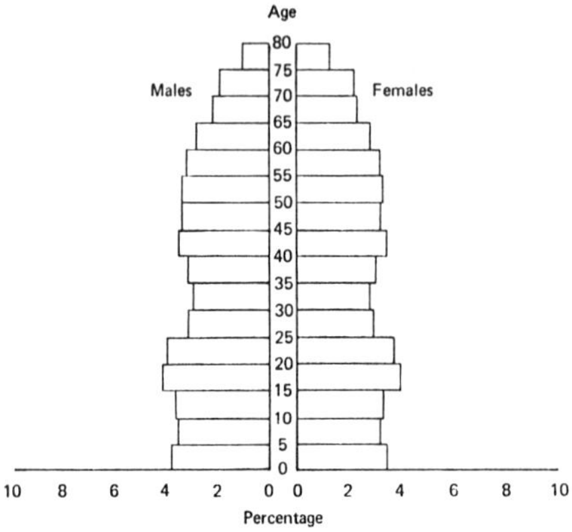

United Kingdom

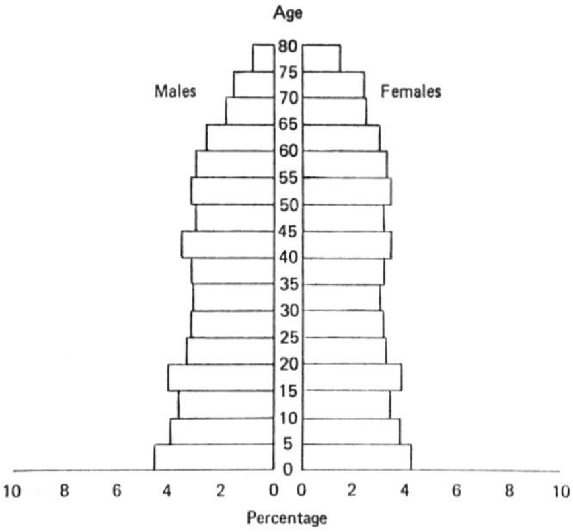

INFORMATION

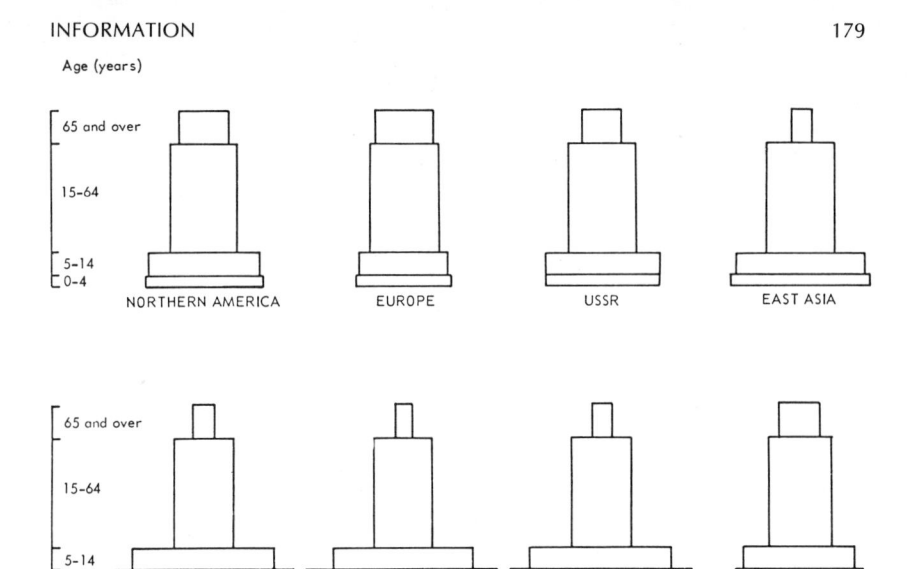

Figure 5-2

Percentage of total population in each of four functional age groups in eight major world areas, 1965. SOURCE: United Nations, 1971.

groups in eight world areas. The age groups are: preschool age (under 5); school age (5–14); working age (15–64); and advanced age (over 65) (United Nations, 1971).

Methodologically, it may appear that after a national census is decided upon, enumerators trained, and data processing materials prepared, the rest is a simple matter. In actuality, appraisal of completeness and accuracy of census data calls for careful checks and sophisticated techniques. Errors can infiltrate the raw data with great ease, and this is particularly true when questions are asked of poorly educated people who are unaware of the significance of the census and quite likely to be suspicious of its purpose. Coverage of large populations is never perfect, even under the best of circumstances. The 1960 census of the United States failed to enumerate about 3.5 million persons, or some 2% of the population! The 1970 U.S. Census received about 1,900 official com-

---

Figure 5-1

Age pyramids for populations of six countries, 1965. SOURCE: United Nations, 1973a.

Table 5-3. Percentage of total population in each of four functional age groups in eight major world areas, 1965

	World Area			
Age group	Northern America	Europe	USSR	East Asia
0–4	10.6	8.7	10.2	12.9
5–14	20.4	16.7	20.4	24.0
15–64	59.8	64.1	62.1	59.0
65+	9.2	10.4	7.4	4.1
	Latin America	Africa	South Asia	Oceania
0–4	16.5	17.7	16.9	11.8
5–14	26.0	25.8	26.1	21.0
15–64	53.8	53.7	54.0	59.9
65+	3.6	2.8	3.0	7.3

Source: United Nations, 1971.

plaints from communities, all alleging undercounts (which would reduce certain payments based on population). After many cross-checks, the Bureau of the Census agreed to increase official counts in 600 communities by an average of five persons per 10,000 originally enumerated (U.S. Bureau of the Census, 1976).

The question of age may be taken as an example of the uncertainty inherent in census taking. Errors arise from underenumeration of certain components of the population. Children, particularly babies, are often overlooked by respondents when asked about the number of people in their household. Many persons do not know their age and some may deliberately misstate the figure for one reason or another. Local customs in reckoning age also vary; some groups of Chinese, for instance, count a child's age at birth as 1 rather than 0 and state all ages as of the next rather than the last birthday. It is often considered more accurate to ask a person not for his current age, which changes, but for his year of birth, which is a constant more likely to be recalled correctly. Figure 5-3 shows the strong effect of number preference in one particular case, the 1945 census of Turkey, by rounding to terminal 5 or 0. Ages ending with 1, 4, 6, and 9

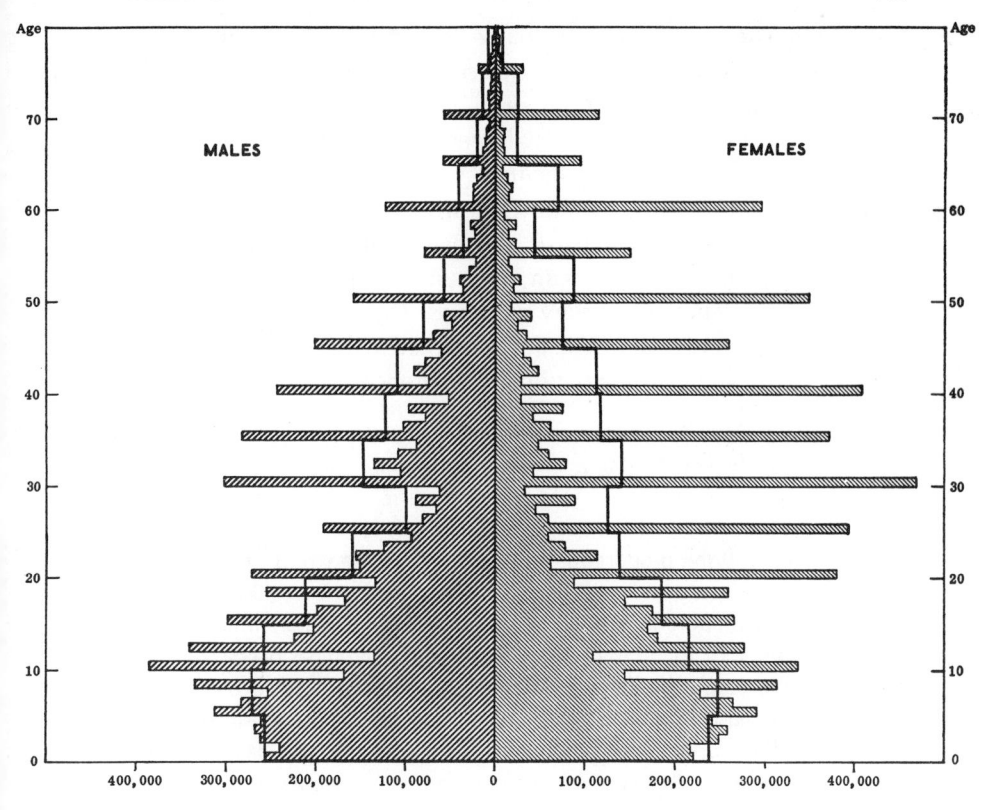

Figure 5-3

Population of Turkey, 1945, by sex, by single year of age, and five-year age groups, according to census. SOURCE: United Nations, 1955.

were in this census commonly stated to the nearest number divisible by 5, and even 2 and 8 were preferred to odd 3 and 7. Also "the forces of attraction of preferred final digits (or repulsion of disliked digits) are more marked in the case of females.... Evidently, the age statements of females are less accurate" (United Nations, 1955). Without attempting to test this claim beyond the borders of Turkey, we turn to other matters.

VITAL STATISTICS

Registration of vital events is usually done at a legally designated place near the occurrence of the event. Depending on local custom and national practice, this may be a police post, courthouse, municipal or district office, special civil registry office, or other locale. Compilation of records by administrative divisions (towns, municipalities, counties, provinces, or states), and by regions or geographic areas, provides a comprehensive national picture of vital events that is essential for planning and allocation of government services. Vital records have many personal and administrative uses, as shown in Table 5-4. Where an effective, inclusive registration system exists, the availability of good quality data is often taken for granted, but it is an unfortunate fact that civil registration is still lacking or deficient in many countries. The 1973 Copenhagen conference on vital and health statistics attempted to assess world progress in this field since the first International Conference some 20 years earlier:

In some areas of health statistics—for example, the statistics of health personnel and health establishments—there have been substantial improvements in the past 20 years but in the really basic field of vital statistics, achievement has been far from satisfactory.

Since 1950 the proportion of the estimate of the world's population that derives from total census enumeration has risen from just over 70% to rather less than 95%. The proportion depending on conjecture or undertermined methods has fallen from 5.9% to 2.8%. In Africa where information has been most lacking, the rise in the census-based proportion has been from 43% to 64%. The improvement in census has been much greater than that in data derived from vital registration. The proportion of the population for which reliable data of live births is available has generally improved but little; in the world as a whole from 28% to 35%; in Africa from 2% to 17%; but in Asia, the proportion has remained at 7%. Almost two-thirds of the world's population (four-fifths of the population of Africa and Asia) lack adequate birth registration. For death registration the picture is just as gloomy, and it is even worse for infant mortality. (World Health Organization, 1974)

The reasons for this unfortunate situation are many. Money is in short supply everywhere, and government services are often very thinly dispersed. In some areas there may be a lack of conviction by lower-level government officers about the value of collecting vital statistics. The absence of a clear administrative mandate is an impediment in some countries since responsibility for parts of this work may, for reasons of historical development, be divided among several government departments or ministries: health, finance, planning, census, social security, central statistical bureaus, or others. Trained, competent persons for this complex work are often unavailable. Because the need for constant, worldwide integration is, however, a help in many ways to the national officers concerned with vital records, the United Nations and World Health Or-

Table 5-4. Some uses of vital records

I. Personal Uses
   A. Birth Certificate
      1. Establishing date of birth
         Enter school, military or civil service
         Obtain work permit, marriage license, driver's license
         Qualify for voting, pension, retirement
         Determine insurance premiums, legal capacity
      2. Establishing place of birth
         Qualify for passport, voting, civil office
         Determine citizenship at birth
      3. Establishing family relationship
         Trace descent, prove legitimacy, birth order
         Prove legal dependency
         Qualify for insurance and inheritance benefits
   B. Marriage Certificate
      1. Qualifying for housing allocation, inheritance, pension, insurance, tax deductions
      2. Proving legal responsibility of spouse, legitimacy of offspring, citizenship by marriage
   C. Divorce Certificate
      Establishing right to remarry
   D. Death Certificate
      1. Establishing fact of death
         Claim, as heirs, pension, insurance, inheritance of deceased
      2. Establishing cause of death
         Determine insurance award
II. Administrative Uses
   A. Birth Records
      1. Providing basis for child health and immunization programs, education planning, etc.
      2. Evaluating family planning programs, prenatal clinics, etc.
      3. Contributing to intercensal estimate of population size
   B. Marriage Records
      1. Proving establishment of households for benefit programs
      2. Predicting population trends
      3. Basis for construction and allocation of housing, etc.
   C. Death Records
      1. Providing basis for cause-of-death analysis and specific prevention or control programs, particularly for infant and maternal mortality
      2. Clearing of files, e.g., electoral rolls, tax or military service registers, disease-case registers
      3. Contributing to intercensal estimate of population size

Source: Based in part on Swaroop, 1960; and on United Nations, 1973.

ganization, among others, have published detailed recommendations for methodology. The Expert Committee on Health Statistics of the WHO has over the years issued more than a dozen technical reports on various aspects of the problems involved.

Difficulties in obtaining data in developing countries include the isolation of rural populations or inaccessibility of registry offices, the lack of education and knowledge about the system, and the suspicion by the public that records may not be kept confidential or that they may be used by the government for taxation, enforced military service, or other purposes considered contrary to their interests. Squatters, illegal aliens, persons without identity cards, nomads having no fixed residence, and others may have strong disincentives towards registration. Fees (or bribes) may be demanded for the initial registration or for copies of certificates. A legal requirement for a death certificate before authorization of burial may work a hardship in remote areas and can be easily overlooked by a bereaved family. The very same vital events to be recorded—births, marriages, and deaths—are accompanied by an infinite variety of cultural and religious traditions in human societies. These customs and rituals, developed over centuries or millenia, may be incompatible with the local government's needs for vital statistics data. Among many peoples, for instance, dissection of the dead is considered abhorrent and rigidly proscribed, thus preventing autopsy to determine cause of death.

Many different kinds of difficulties can thus produce great variations in the quality of the data emanating from different countries. As a result, the United Nations attempts to obtain national estimates of the completeness and accuracy of vital statistics and assigns quality codes to the figures published in its demographic yearbooks. Data are considered "virtually complete" when stated coverage is at least 90%, "unreliable" where it is less, or given the symbol (. . .) where information on quality is lacking. On this basis only 46 of 220 countries and areas (including those with populations of 50 or more, not all U.N. members) qualified as having satisfactory codes in the mid-1960s (Table 5-5). The United States National Center for Health Statistics applies further criteria when using data to rank national indices—only self-governing countries of at least one million population are considered, and each data element entering into the health index must be quality-rated as "virtually complete." Under this more stringent definition only 41 countries qualified for comparison in ranking of infant mortality rates in the mid-1960s—the 46 satisfactory countries in Table 5-5 minus those five under 1 million popu-

Table 5-5. Countries with satisfactory vital statistics quality codes, by area and population size, mid-1960s

Area	Total countries or areas	Sovereign countries	Satisfactory quality codes	Less than 1	1-9	10-99	100 or more
TOTAL	220	143	46	5	22	17	2
Africa	59	42	0	0	0	0	0
America, North	37	15	9	1	5	2	1
America, South	15	11	1	0	0	1	0
Asia	44	38	5	0	2	3	0
Europe	36	32	27	3	14	10	0
Oceania	28	4	3	1	1	1	0
Union of Soviet Socialist Republics	1	1	1	0	0	0	1

Source: Adapted from Chase, 1972.

Table 5-6. Percentages of population for which specified mortality data are available through either civil registration or sample surveys: The world and each continent, computed on 1971 estimated population

	World	Europe	North America	Oceania	Africa	Asia	South America
General mortality							
1. Annual totals	78	100	98	89	72	68	51
2. Age and sex	47	100	98	85	34	22	51
3. Monthly totals	45	100	98	85	21	21	46
4. Cause	32	99	98	81	17	11	51
5. Cause and sex	32	96	98	81	17	11	51
6. Marital status, age and sex	28	100	80	79	10	9	42
7. Cause, age and sex	27	87	94	79	7	8	47
8. Cause and type of certification	17	89	29	16	0	2	33
9. Occupation and age	11	47	4	80	10	5	6

Urban/rural mortality							
10. Annual totals	19	38	91	15	15	8	16
11. Age and sex	8	37	0	15	4	5	—
12. Cause, age and sex	3	19	0	15	—	—	—
Infant mortality							
13. Annual totals	53	100	98	87	56	30	51
14. Monthly totals	38	100	97	82	13	11	46
15. Age and sex	33	100	98	84	26	12	43
Urban/rural infant mortality							
16. Annual totals	16	38	73	15	14	7	3
17. Age and sex	2	19	0	1	1	—	—

Source: United Nations, 1974.

lation (Chase, 1972). Tables 5-6 to 5-9 present further information on quality of vital statistics in various countries of the world.

It would seem that birth and death are both clear and unmistakable events, universally recognized and not needing a rigid definition for vital statistical purposes. But things are not so simple, especially where stillbirths and fetal deaths are concerned. It is important to distinguish whether a baby is alive at birth even if it dies moments later, not only for proper allocation and recording of the event (Table 5-2 D, E, G) but also for medical understanding. Until at least the late 1940s local practices varied widely from one country to another. "In Spain and some of its former South American colonies, a child had to survive 24 hours to be registered as a live birth. In others, including France, the case of a child born alive but dying before registration was counted as a stillbirth; and yet in others it was counted as a death, but not as a live birth. Such differences in classification might, in some cases, mean a reduction in the

Table 5-7. Estimated percentage of population for which mortality statistics are available by age, sex, and cause of death, for the world and major areas, around 1973

Areas WHO Regions[a]	Estimated total population (millions)	Estimated population of the countries for which mortality data are available in WHO	
		Number (millions)	Percentage
AREAS			
Africa	401	38	9.5
America	561	439	78.3
Asia (excl U.S.S.R.)	2,256	224	9.9
Europe (excl U.S.S.R.)	473	470	99.4
Oceania	21	17	81.0
U.S.S.R.	255	–	–
TOTAL	3,967	1,189	30.0

[a]See Figure 8-4.
Source: World Health Organization, 1976.

Table 5-8. Percentage of deaths for which the cause has been medically certified, selected countries, recent years

Country or area	Year	%	Country or area	Year	%
AFRICA			EUROPE		
Mauritius	1973	76.1	Austria	1970	100.0
			Czechoslovakia	1972	100.0
AMERICA			Finland	1972	99.8
			France	1967	96.9
Canada	1973	99.9	German Democratic Republic	1972	100.0
Chile	1971	83.4	Germany, Federal Republic of	1970	100.0
Colombia	1970	67.1	Greece	1973	94.7
Costa Rica	1972	75.0	Hungary	1973	100.0
Dominican Republic	1971	45.5	Iceland	1973	98.9
Ecuador	1973	47.8	Italy	1971	100.0
El Salvador	1973	37.1	Luxembourg	1973	100.0

continued

Table 5-8 *Continued*

Country or area	Year	%	Country or area	Year	%
Mexico	1973	77.0	Netherlands	1972	99.3
Panama	1973	62.4	Poland	1973	94.2
Peru	1970	57.0	Portugal	1973	97.7
Venezuela	1973	76.1	Spain	1968	100.0
			Switzerland	1972	100.0
			U.K.: England and Wales	1972	78.6
			U.K.: Northern Ireland	1973	84.1
ASIA			Yugoslavia	1972	62.3
Hong Kong	1966	95.1	OCEANIA		
Israel (total population)	1973	99.5			
Jordan	1972	55.6	Australia	1973	81.8
Philippines	1970	26.5	New Zealand	1969	99.7

Source: World Health Organization, 1976.

Table 5-9. Percentage of all deaths ascribed to symptoms and ill-defined conditions (ICD: A136[a] & A137[b]), selected countries, 1972, 73, or 74.

Country or area	Year	%	Country or area	Year	%
AFRICA			Singapore	1974	10.4
			Thailand	1973	52.9
Egypt	1972	21.8			
Mauritius	1974	18.5			
			EUROPE		
AMERICA					
			Austria	1974	1.7
Barbados	1973	4.5	Belgium	1972	8.4
Canada	1973	0.8	Bulgaria	1974	6.3
Chile	1973	8.2	Czechoslovakia	1973	1.2
Colombia	1972	10.1	Denmark	1973	2.0
Costa Rica	1973	7.6	Finland	1973	0.2
Dominican Republic	1973	38.7	France	1973	7.6
Ecuador	1972	19.9	Germany, Federal Republic of	1973	3.8
El Salvador	1973	32.4	Greece	1974	11.0
Guadeloupe	1974	17.6	Hungary	1974	0.1
Honduras	1973	30.2	Iceland	1974	1.5
Mexico	1973	12.4	Ireland	1972	1.7
Nicaragua	1973	27.3	Italy	1973	3.3
Panama	1973	17.8	Luxembourg	1974	4.8
Paraguay	1973	19.4	Netherlands	1974	3.9
Peru	1972	9.1	Norway	1973	5.2
Puerto Rico	1973	3.2	Poland	1973	8.5
Surinam	1973	12.5	Portugal	1974	15.9
Trinidad and Tobago	1973	4.0	Romania	1973	0.2
United States	1973	1.5	Spain	1973	6.0
Uruguay	1973	6.2	Sweden	1974	0.4
Venezuela	1973	22.0	Switzerland	1973	1.3
			U.K.: England and Wales	1973	0.6
			Northern Ireland	1973	0.6
ASIA			Scotland	1973	0.4
			Yugoslavia	1973	24.5
Hong Kong	1974	8.7			
Israel	1973	4.4			
Japan	1973	6.1	OCEANIA		
Jordan	1973	21.5			
Kuwait	1972	10.9	Australia	1973	0.9
Philippines	1973	11.4	New Zealand	1972	0.5

[a]Senility without mention of psychoses.
[b]Symptoms and other ill-defined conditions.
Source: World Health Organization, 1976.

general death-rate of the order of 1.2%" (Gear, 1959). In 1950 a special subcommittee of the WHO considered this problem and proposed rigid definitions for the various categories but 20 years later another WHO Expert Committee noted continuing difficulties and recommended review and revision of these definitions (World Health Organization, 1970).

The great recent increase in "therapeutic terminations of pregnancy" (abortions) accounts for much of the difficulty. Very early and patently nonviable fetuses may well show evidence of life, however transitory, and would qualify as live births under the conventional definition. In many countries the number of abortions performed is very significant when compared with the number of live births. Rigid application of the current definition, or variations in local interpretation and practice can result in large discrepancies in reported rates for live births and fetal, neonatal, and infant deaths. There is no need here to discuss these technicalities in great detail, but this sort of problem must be borne in mind when comparing infant mortality data from different countries and time periods.

Recent advances in medical techniques have enabled physicians to keep alive individuals with advanced illnesses or massive injuries who under other circumstances would undoubtedly succumb. The problem of defining the precise moment of death has been brought into prominence with the advent of organ transplantation, and is particularly troublesome in the case of heart donors. A recent court case in California in which the heart of a homicide victim was removed for transplantation illustrates the dilemma. Attorneys for the assailant argued that, since the victim's heart was still beating when taken for the transplant, death had been caused not by shooting but by removal of the heart. The transplant surgeon, testifying for the prosecution, stated that the victim was dead because his brain was dead and "the brain is the single criterion for death." The jury, instructed by the judge to consider the victim legally dead from brain damage inflicted by the bullet, returned a verdict against the defendant (San Francisco Chronicle, 1974). Situations of this type arising from technical advances in medical capability are likely to become more common in the future. Long-accepted definitions of death become ambiguous in the face of such unanticipated technical developments. While we presume that the removal of beating hearts or other functioning organs will never become common enough to make an impression on vital statistics rates, the principles involved force attention towards this problem and invite review and revision of the definition of death.

Mortality Statistics

In the middle of the seventeenth century a London cloth merchant, John Graunt, began a study of the *Bills of Mortality*—church parish registers of births and deaths. One may well wonder why this particular man, untrained in medicine or science, undertook such a curious hobby, but the indisputable result of Graunt's work, published in 1662, was to show that human life conforms to certain predictable statistical patterns. Graunt classified deaths by cause and found that these varied from place to place and from year to year. He described the age pattern of deaths and constructed a simple forerunner of the modern life table. It was Graunt who discovered the fact that the number of males born slightly but regularly exceeds the number of females. Since his time many others have undertaken similar studies so that the volume of information now available about the pattern and causes of human mortality is truly monumental.

In our time, mortality statistics must be considered in the first rank of measurements for international health studies.

Mortality statistics, because of their unambiguity, remain, where they are available, the most practical index of variations in the level of health of populations, and provide a basis for hypotheses concerning the determinants of variation, which may be tested by appropriate means. Their informativeness depends, first, upon their completeness and, secondly, on their analysis.

The advantage of mortality statistics over other statistics relating to health, however, is mainly that they exist on a much more widespread scale throughout the countries of the world. They help to define health problems, to monitor the efficacy of health programmes and to identify the emerging problems of the public health. (World Health Organization, 1970)

Despite the importance of mortality data, their quality is far from uniform, and deficiencies of completeness and accuracy are common, inaccuracy being a problem in both developed and developing countries. As of 1970, reliable national mortality statistics were available for only about 35% of the world's population (World Health Organization, 1970).

International Comparability The need for international comparability of cause-of-death data was recognized early, and was a prime subject of discussion at the earliest International Statistical Congresses, the first held in Brussels in 1853 and the second in Paris two years later. At the 1855 Congress, William Farr of England and Marc d'Espine of Switzerland proposed tabulations that were later merged into a single list of 139 causes applicable to all countries. That list, officially adopted by the Congress, has formed the basis for subsequent classifications. The subject continued to be of great interest and four revisions appeared within the nineteenth century. In 1900 the First International Conference for the Revision of the International Classification of Causes of Death was convened in Paris, and since then revisions have appeared at approximately ten year intervals. This work, now commonly called the International Classification of Diseases (ICD), was greatly modified at the sixth revision (1948), with the addition of coding rubrics for morbidity as well as for causes of death.

The eighth, a major revision, was adopted in 1965 and issued in 1967 for use throughout the world. Almost as soon as it appeared, work began on its revision. The twenty-ninth World Health Assembly (see Chapter 8) in May 1976 officially adopted the list of categories, the rules recommended by the Revision Conference for selection of a single cause in morbidity statistics, and adopted recommendations of the Conference

Table 5-10. Major categories in the International Statistical Classification of Diseases, Injuries, and Causes of Death (8th Revision)

		ICD Nos.
I	Infective and Parasitic Diseases	000–136
II	Neoplasms	140–239
III	Endocrine, Nutritional, and Metabolic Diseases	240–279
IV	Diseases of Blood and Blood-Forming Organs	280–289
V	Mental Disorders	290–315
VI	Diseases of the Nervous System and Sense Organs	320–389
VII	Diseases of the Circulatory System	390–458
VIII	Diseases of the Respiratory System	460–519
IX	Diseases of the Digestive System	520–577
X	Diseases of the Genito-Urinary System	580–629
XI	Complications of Pregnancy, Childbirth, and the Puerperium	630–678
XII	Diseases of the Skin and Subcutaneous Tissue	680–709
XIII	Diseases of the Musculoskeletal System and Connective Tissue	710–738
XIV	Congenital Anomalies	740–759
XV	Certain Causes of Perinatal Morbidity and Mortality	760–779
XVI	Symptoms and Ill-Defined Conditions	780–796
EXVII	Accidents, Poisonings, and Violence (External Cause)	E800–E999
NXVII	Accidents, Poisonings, and Violence (Nature of Injury)	N800–N999

Source: World Health Organization, 1967.

regarding statistics of perinatal and maternal mortality, with worldwide use of the ninth revision beginning officially on January 1, 1979.

The basic structure of the ICD is an outline in about eighteen major categories (see Table 5-10) of all the ills of mortal flesh, according to the doctrines of western medicine. These are divided into neat three-digit rubrics, usually with decimal subclassifications. The ninth revision provides for an optional fifth digit in some places (such as for the mode of diagnosis of tuberculosis), and also includes an independent four-digit coding system to classify histological varieties of neoplasms. In general, the ninth revision is rather conservative and incorporates few drastic changes from previous versions.

When a death occurs, a certificate (Fig. 5-4) should be completed by the certifier. Medical certification of cause of death is normally the responsibility of the attending physician, where there is one. In cases of sudden, violent, or suspicious death in developed countries a coroner or other medicolegal officer, who may not be a physician, could be the certifier. In many countries the certifier may be a midwife, nurse, policeman, village chief, teacher, or layman, whose name and credential

Cause of Death		Approximate interval between onset and death
I		
Disease or condition directly leading to death*	(a) .... due to (or as a consequence of)	....
Antecedent causes Morbid conditions, if any, giving rise to the above cause, stating the underlying condition last	(b) .... due to (or as a consequence of) (c)	....
II		
Other significant conditions contributing to the death, but not related to the disease or condition causing it	....	....
* This does not mean the mode of dying, e.g., heart failure, asthenia, etc. It means the disese, injury, or complication which caused death.		

Figure 5-4

International form of medical certificate of cause of death. SOURCE: World Health Organization, 1967.

Figure 5-5

General pattern of vital registration and statistics in the United States. SOURCE: National Center for Health Statistics, U.S. Public Health Service.

RESPONSIBLE PERSON OR AGENCY	BIRTH CERTIFICATE	DEATH CERTIFICATE	FETAL DEATH CERTIFICATE (Stillbirth)	RE-PORTING OFFICIALS	MARRIAGE RECORD	DIVORCE OR ANNULMENT RECORD
Physician, Other Professional Attendant, or Hospital Authority.	1. Completes entire certificate in consultation with parent(s). Physician's signature required. 2. Files certificate with local office of district in which birth occurred.	1. Completes medical certification and signs certificate. 2. Returns certificate to funeral director.	1. Completes or reviews medical items on certificate. 2. Certifies to the cause of fetal death and signs certificate. 3. Returns certificate to funeral director. 4. In absences of funeral director, files certificate.	Clerk of Local Government	1. Receives application for marriage license, and reviews application for completeness, accuracy, and compliance with law. 2. Issues marriage license, and records date. 3. Checks completeness of entries about the marriage ceremony. 4. Sends specified information regarding marriage to State Registrar.	
Funeral Director		1. Obtains personal facts about deceased. 2. Takes certificate to physician for medical certification. 3. Delivers completed certificate to local office of district where death occurred and obtains burial permit.	1. Obtains the facts about fetal death. 2. Takes certificate to physician for entry of causes of fetal death. 3. Delivers completed certificate to local office of district where delivery occurred and obtains burial permit.	Marriage Officiant	1. Checks the validity of the marriage license. 2. Performs the marriage ceremony. 3. Certifies to the facts of the marriage ceremony. 4. Returns the record to the license clerk within the legally prescribed time.	

Local Office (may be Local Registrar or City or County Health Department)	1. Verifies completeness and accuracy of certificate. 2. Makes copy, ledger entry, or index for local use. 3. Sends certificates to State Registrar.	1. Verifies completeness and accuracy of certificate. 2. Makes copy, ledger entry, or index for local use. 3. Issues burial permit to funeral director and verifies return of permit from cemetery attendant. 4. Sends certificates to State Registrar.	1. Provides form for report to plaintiff or attorney, or makes entries on such form from petition for decree. 2. Verifies entries on return form. 3. Enters information on final decree. 4. Sends completed report to State Registrar.
	City and county health departments use certificates in allocating medical and nursing services, followups on infectious diseases, planning programs, measuring effectiveness of services, and conducting research studies.	Clerk of Court	
		Attorney for Plaintiff	1. Enters personal characteristics of spouses. 2. Returns form to Clerk of Court.
State Registrar, Bureau of Vital Statistics	1. Queries incomplete or inconsistent information. 2. Maintains files for permanent reference and as the source of certified copies. 3. Develops vital statistics for use in planning, evaluating, and administering State and local health activities and for research studies. 4. Compiles health related statistics for State and civil divisions of State for use of the health department and other agencies and groups interested in the fields of medical science, public health, demography, and social welfare. 5. Prepares copies of birth, death, fetal death, marriage, and divorce certificates or records for transmission to the National Center for Health Statistics.		
Public Health Service National Center for Health Statistics	1. Prepares and publishes national statistics of births, deaths, fetal deaths, marriages, and divorces; and constructs the official U.S. life tables and related actuarial tables. 2. Conducts health and social-research studies based on vital records and on sampling surveys linked to records. 3. Conducts research and methodological studies in vital statistics methods including the technical, administrative, and legal aspects of vital records registration and administration. 4. Maintains a continuing technical assistance program to improve the quality and usefulness of vital statistics.		

NOTE.—In some States there is no central file for marriage and divorce records at the State level.

should appear on the forms actually used. The flow of information following completion of the death certificate varies among countries, but in general a centralized national statistical office eventually receives the individual records and collates the data for administrative purposes, sending summaries to Geneva for compilation by the WHO. The complex flow of vital statistics data in the United States is shown in Figure 5-5.

At one point in the system the three-digit code of the ICD is applied to the data by a coder or nosologist especially trained for this purpose. In the United States this is done at the state level; elsewhere usually at the national level. In some countries (e.g., the United States since 1968) multiple causes are tabulated but usually only the underlying cause of death is coded and it is this rubric under which the data finally appear in the World Health Statistics Annual and other publications.

The underlying cause is considered to be the disease or injury that initiated the train of events leading directly to death or the circumstances of the accident or violence which produced the fatal injury. Many problems arise with respect to accuracy of these statements, even in developed countries where most deaths are attended or certified by a physician. Questions of definition, correctness of diagnosis, proper selection of underlying cause, etc. are clearly involved. The capability of the certifying physician and presence of technical facilities (diagnostic laboratory support, pathology reports, autopsy) vary greatly and affect the reliability of certified cause of death. Errors can also occur in application of the rules, in coding, and in transcribing. Problems of international comparability of mortality data include all of the above, plus variations in language, terminology, and definition of disease; and local differences in medical practice and in rules for coding causes of death. In an effort to foster uniformity of diagnosis and terminology, the WHO publishes a series of small volumes with accompanying color transparencies of tissue sections as part of their project on the international histological classification of tumors. Similar publications are issued on standardized classification of atherosclerotic lesions, hypertension, and coronary heart disease. In developing countries generally the application of such criteria is distressingly rare, for reasons already mentioned. Moreover, deaths due to these specific causes are relatively few outside of the industrialized countries.

A concrete illustration of some of these problems is given in Table 5-11, reprinted from its previous incarnation as Table 4-4. When this information was first presented in Chapter 4, it is unlikely that many readers questioned its accuracy and validity. Now that we have been sensitized to some of the difficulties inherent in international comparisons of cause-specific mortality, the table may not appear quite so authoritative as before. Yet ischemic heart disease has been studied more than almost any other cause of death. Its victims are usually adult males whose death is most likely to be recorded. The manner of dying, often by heart attack, is relatively distinctive and dramatic. It may be expected that most of these numbers are fairly reliable in comparison with other cause-specific mortality data. Nevertheless, a questioning attitude based upon a knowledge of the many caveats mentioned is still highly recommended.

Further hindrance to the comparability of mortality statistics lies in the periodic changes in the ICD. At each revision, some categories are reassigned, resulting in sudden increases or decreases in the affected mortality rates and breaks in the comparability of statistics. In the United States, Percy et al. (1974) have shown how the adoption of the eighth revision of the ICD in 1968 was accompanied by dramatic changes in reported death rates for certain types of cancer. Secondary cancer of the thoracic organs showed a drop of 61.5% between 1967 and 1968, after average annual increases of about 15% from 1963 to 1967. Primary cancer of the lung, normally increasing at 5.7% annually rose at a 9.6% level in 1968, and then fell to a 4.1% increase the following year. Trends in cancer mortality have been studied for almost a century and are closely watched by many people searching, for instance, for clues to environmental effects. Changes in cause assignment or in coding rules make long-term studies much more difficult. It may be noted that a rules change in the sixth revision (1948) resulted in a sudden decline of approximately 50% in the number of deaths assigned to diabetes. Nevertheless, changes in the ICD are needed from time to time as advances in medical knowledge and diagnostic technology contribute to new ways to define and distinguish among the many known diseases and possible causes of death.

Age-Adjustment   We have seen (Figs. 5-1, 5-2; Table 5-3) that the age structure of different populations may be very dissimilar. The "average" African population, for instance, has twice the proportion of under-fives and about one-fourth as many over 65 as the "average" European population. It would be inappropriate and misleading to compare crude or cause-specific mortality rates between two such groups because their mortality experience can be expected to differ on the basis of age structure alone. In order to increase the validity of international comparisons, the crude death rate of one population is apportioned into a set of age-specific death rates (Table 5-5, B and C). These age-specific rates are then

Table 5-11. Reported deaths[*][a] due to ischemic heart disease (ICD No. A83)†[b] per 100,000 population[c], selected countries[d], recent years[e]

Country	Year	Total	Male	Female
Sweden	1974	371	436	307
Scotland	1973	364	426	305
United States	1973	326	379	276
Denmark	1973	325	384	268
England and Wales	1973	309	364	256
Norway	1973	269	341	199
Finland	1973	254	330	184
Australia	1973	251	300	202
Austria	1974	250	263	239
Canada	1973	229	278	179
Israel	1973	216	256	176
Germany, Fed. Rep. of	1973	197	233	163
Uruguay	1973	172	199	146
Italy	1973	150	166	135
Puerto Rico	1973	118	136	100
France	1973	88	102	74
Greece	1973	79	103	56
Spain	1973	67	82	53
Panama	1973	42	43	42
Japan	1973	39	45	34
Colombia	1972	38	43	32
Hong Kong	1974	30	30	30
Mexico	1973	21	24	18
Philippines[f]	1973	21	25	17
Egypt	1972	19	27	10
El Salvador[g]	1973	9	11	8
Thailand[h]	1973	0.3	0.4	0.2

*Rounded to nearest whole number.
†1965 (8th) revision.
Source: Adapted from World Health Organization, 1976[i]

[a]*Reported deaths* ... How many are reported? From where? Rural/urban?

[b]... *due to ischemic heart disease (ICD No. A83)* ... How valid are the diagnoses? How many autopsies are done to determine cause of death? How many deaths are medically certified?

[c]... *per 100,000 population* ... How good is the population estimate? Has there been a recent census? What is the age distribution of the population mentioned? Are the various national populations age-adjusted?

[d]... *selected countries* ... How are the countries selected? How do countries *not* get selected (i.e., have no data at all)?

applied to the proportionate age distribution of a second population (see Fig. 5-1). This process provides a picture of the mortality experience that population A would have had if it had the same age structure as population B; it also describes the mortality pattern if population B had the age-specific death rates of population A. In actual practice when many populations are compared, all are adjusted against a standard population, which may be real or a model generated for the purpose of the analysis. Often the standard population is a composite of all the populations being compared (Table 5-11, note c). Identical procedures may of course be used for age-adjustment of morbidity rates, as shown in Table 1-6. Various rates may be made more comparable between populations by adjusting for features other than age, such as educational attainment or economic status.

Infant Mortality

The infant mortality rate (Table 5-2, D) has often been cited as a sensitive indicator of the general standard of sanitary and socioeconomic conditions of a population. This interpretation, while valid, is overly simplistic, and we must probe further into methodological factors underlying reporting of these rates. Because claims of inheritance and of pension and insurance benefits are rarely involved, there is generally little incentive for reporting infant deaths. This is particularly so in areas of economic deprivation where one may expect these rates to be higher than elsewhere. Where births are seldom registered and medical attention is lacking, many infants who subsequently die go entirely unrecorded and are permanently lost to the statistical system. Special surveys may be done to estimate infant mortality, or questions about past pregnancies may appear

---

[e] *... recent years ...* What years? All for the same year? Are any trends lost by comparing different years?
[f] *Philippines* Only 26.5% of deaths were medically certified in 1970 (Table 5-8).
[g] *El Salvador* Only 37.1% of deaths were medically certified in 1973 (Table 5-8). Almost a third of deaths in the same year were ascribed to "Symptoms and other ill-defined conditions" (Table 5-9).
[h] *Thailand* More than half of all deaths in 1973 were ascribed to "Symptoms and other ill-defined conditions" (Table 5-9). The percentage of deaths medically certified is not known, but doubtless is low.
[i] How and why was this adapted? What was left out? What was added?

on census schedules. Women who have had many pregnancies may, on questioning years later, overlook or wish to forget some who have died, particularly when the loss occurred very early before the child was named and became part of the functioning family. Culture and tradition may act to make the subject of deceased infants and children unsuitable for discussion, especially with strangers. In some countries, registration of births and infant deaths covers not the whole country but only certain areas, which may change from time to time. Coverage may be better in urban than in rural areas.

The infant mortality rate differs from all other age-specific death rates in several important respects. First, the denominator of this particular rate is not the standing population in that age group but the number of live births occurring during the year. This is so because the pattern of deaths during subsequent years of life may be expected to be random over the course of the year (i.e., about one-twelfth of deaths from age 20 to 21, for example, would occur in each month). Infant deaths, however, are not uniformly distributed from birth to first birthday. This leads to the second special feature of the infant mortality rate—its division into neonatal and postneonatal mortality rates. In some cases further subdivision of the former is made: first-day deaths are those occurring between birth and 24 hours of age, early neonatal deaths from birth to seven days (168 hours), and late neonatal deaths those occurring from the eighth to the twenty-eighth day.

A major basis for these fine distinctions is the idea that early deaths tend to be due to immaturity or certain inherent congenital conditions or circumstances of birth that are relatively independent of the postnatal environment, while postneonatal deaths tend to result from deficiencies in nutrition and from infectious disease. If this is so, the ratio of neonatal to postneonatal deaths would provide a sensitive measure of unfavorable environmental conditions and would indicate the type of remedial action to be taken. Factors such as maternal nutrition and prenatal care are also significant. One difficulty with this type of analysis is that the quality of the statistics tends to vary inversely with the infant mortality rate; where this rate is high, the poor environmental conditions are grossly and painfully apparent.

A third feature of the infant mortality rate distinguishing it from other single-year age-specific death rates is that there does appear to be an irreducible lower limit that varies in place and time. This asymptote is determined in part by genetic and biologic factors and in part by environmental factors such as maternal prenatal nutrition, infection, and behavior, and available medical facilities. In the next chapter we will examine infant mortality rates once again, looking at this lower limit from the standpoint of economics and of public policy.

In addition to infant mortality, a great deal of attention has been given in recent years to the problem of *perinatal* deaths. The perinatal period extends from the gestational age at which the fetus or infant attains 1,000 grams in weight (or where this is unavailable, 35 cm crown-heel length, or 28 weeks of gestation) until the end of the seventh completed day of life. Many discussions at the Ninth ICD Revision Conference dealt with this issue, whose significance is shown by the observation that the number of lives lost in the perinatal period exceeds that for the subsequent 30 years of life. The main reason for concentrating on perinatal deaths as a special category is that this period is unique because the great majority of deaths occur through some unfavorable influence of the mother upon the fetus. Pathological processes in two separate people are involved, and they cannot be unraveled with conventional means of mortality reporting. A special certificate of perinatal death has therefore been introduced by the Ninth Revision Conference (and, as mentioned above, adopted by the World Health Assembly of the WHO) to include information about diseases and conditions in both fetus (or infant) and mother.

MEASURING HEALTH AND SICKNESS

Figures about sickness in populations are in many ways more germane to the needs of health analysts than are data on death. Swaroop (1960) quotes Charles Dickens in this regard: "It concerns a man more to know the risk of the fifty illnesses that may throw a man on his back than the possible date of the one death that must come. We must have a list of the killed and of the wounded too." Such a "list of the wounded" is useful in providing information on the following points:

1. How many people suffer from particular diseases—how often, and for how long
2. What demands these diseases place on the medical and public health resources, and what financial losses they cause
3. How fatal the different diseases are
4. To what extent people are prevented by these diseases from carrying on their normal activities

5. To what extent diseases are concentrated in particular groups of the population, e.g., according to age, sex, ethnic group, occupation, or place of residence
6. How far the above factors vary from time to time (variation according to season or from year to year)
7. What is the effect of medical care and health services on the control of disease incidence (Swaroop, 1960)

The same difficulties inherent in the collection, interpretation, and comparison of vital statistics are evident to a far greater degree when data on health status are being considered. While at least some of the elements underlying all vital statistics are mandated by law, no such compulsion exists for most of the information related to measures of health status. Problems of definition and assessment are far more complex in health and sickness data than in mortality statistics. In many infectious diseases there is a wide spectrum of clinical severity ranging from inapparent to extreme, and the overwhelming majority of infections never come to medical attention. It is indeed likely that most infections are undetected by the person harboring them, or cause only generalized and nonspecific symptoms. Serological surveys to determine the prevalence of antibodies to many viruses, for instance, do not necessarily correlate with the known distribution of these viral diseases in the same population. Moreover, people have many episodes of sickness during their lifetimes, and even in the most developed countries very few persons can document their own complete health history. One difficulty, of course, is knowing what to document or measure, that is, how to define health.

Definitions of Health

One of the great ironies and frustrations facing persons who deal with this subject is the absence of an acceptable definition of "health," either at an individual or a community level. This deficiency cannot be blamed on a lack of attempts. Many recent formulations have been reviewed by Goldsmith (1972), who faults them on all grounds of ambiguity and obstruseness. A definition of health found in a good modern dictionary: "1. the general condition of the body or mind with reference to soundness and vigor ... 2. soundness of body or mind; freedom from disease or ailment ..." (Random House, 1966) does not differ greatly from the ideal of Juvenal (ca. AD 60–140): *mens sana in corpore sano*. Most often quoted in recent years is the statement in the Preamble to the Constitution of the World Health Organization: "Health is a state of complete physical, mental and social well-being and not merely the absence of disease or infirmity"—an affirmation of belief and principle rather than a quantifiable technical definition. Wylie (1970) has distinguished two types of definitions of health—an asymptotic or open-ended concept, directed towards an ideal (such as the WHO statement) and an "elastic concept" in which health is viewed as an ability to withstand stresses of disease and is related to interaction with community and environment.

Each of us has an adequate mental compass that points towards "health" and indicates deviations, but none of us can specify exactly what we mean by it, any more than we can explain the magnetism in a real compass. And, in fact, a rigid rendering of the meaning of health is not essential for much good work to be done. Bates (1959) admitted this, only half in jest: "I worked for seventeen years for the International Health Division of the Rockefeller Foundation, which gave me considerable opportunity to talk about health. I never quite understood what the word meant, but lack of understanding, of course, rarely prevents people from talking. If it did, I suppose we would all become Trappists."

Even without a universal definition of health, some indicators of health status are desirable. A WHO study group described three groups of needed indicators:

1. Those associated with the health status of persons and populations in a given area (vital statistics, nutrition, etc.);
2. those related to physical environmental conditions having a more or less direct bearing on the health status of the area under review; and
3. those concerned with health services and activities directed to the improvement of health conditions (availability and use of hospitals, physicians and other health personnel). (World Health Organization, 1957)

The group also classified health indicators in terms of the unit of reference, whether a single individual ("the *micro*-approach") or family, household, community, population group or whole country ("the *macro*-approach"). These indicators would be useful in measuring levels of health of a community, in public health action, and making international comparisons.

A number of such indicators proposed in the interim have been extensively discussed by Goldsmith (1972), who voiced a caution about their validity: "The problem of measuring something, assuming it is health, and therefore calling it health, is not unusual with health status indicators." Nevertheless, there is a great deal of activity directed toward the development of an "index" of health status. Sullivan (1966) has reviewed some methodological problems in developing an overall index, particularly from interview data. A WHO group (World Health Organization, 1971) has grappled with the significance of indices, and a considerable portion of the first two volumes of the International Journal of Epidemiology (for 1972 and 1973) dealt with the construction and utilization of health status indices.

The reason for so much concern with overall indices of health status may be found in the resolution 27.55 of the Twenty-Seventh World Health Assembly, quoted earlier. As health services everywhere pass into an increasingly introspective phase, a simple and reliable index of conditions—a sort of "Gross Health Product" (GHP)—is a desideratum of agencies and planners. For the time being, however, the most direct way of estimating this GHP is to look at the level of ill health in a population.

Morbidity Statistics

Morbidity statistics are merely numerical representations of one kind or another dealing with the occurrence of ill health in a population. Ideally, this information should describe ill health by type (i.e., diagnosis), by severity and duration, by distribution in place and time, and by characteristics—age, sex, occupation, marital status, etc.—of the persons affected. In practice, data on these subjects áre partial at best, usually fragmentary, and often virtually nonexistent. There are two general categories of sources for morbidity data: the records routinely compiled and accumulated by various offices; and the special surveys made to obtain information on particular issues.

The continual reporting of disease occurrence in any country is limited to certain "reportable" or "notifiable" diseases for which it is mandatory that cases be brought to the attention of health authorities. Legislation to this effect began, in modern times, with Norway in 1860, followed by the Netherlands, Sweden, Switzerland, Italy, Great Britain, France, Uruguay, Japan, and Chile, all before 1900. The twentieth century has seen essentially all other countries adopt some form of compulsory notification within their borders. In most cases these laws refer to highly communicable diseases that pose an immediate threat to the community, but often specific cases of other types must be reported. Botulism, which may be caused by improperly processed canned foods, is such a disease: prompt notification may result in recall of affected production lots and thus avert additional cases. Other conditions requiring notification in certain countries include nutritional deficiency diseases (e.g., beriberi in New Zealand), snakebite, tetanus, and various malignancies. As conditions change, additional diseases may be added to the list—epilepsy may be a notifiable disease when a driver's license is involved; rubella became reportable after its association with birth defects was established. The large and diverse group of occupational diseases and work-related injuries is legally notifiable in many countries, in part for validation of compensation claims.

The variety of legislation governing notifiable diseases is very great. Some countries require immediate reporting of suspected cases, some only after laboratory confirmation; in some countries certain diseases must be notified only from schools, institutions, or resorts. Special regulations may require that cases or outbreaks of specified diseases in dairy farms be notified, and others may deal with nosocomial (hospital-acquired) infections. In some countries otherwise healthy carriers, particularly of typhoid organisms, must be reported and registered.

Persons legally responsible for notification may be physicians, school authorities, directors of laboratories in which positive diagnoses are made, or even heads of families. The completeness of reporting often leaves much to be desired. Whereas ominous diseases such as smallpox are unlikely to escape official detection in most countries, notification of the more common illnesses is frequently neglected by busy physicians despite the legal requirement to do so. Lossing (1955), for instance, estimated the following percentages of completeness of notification in his Canadian study: measles, 13.8%; whooping cough, 10.9%; chickenpox, 17.3%; mumps, 13.9%; and rubella, 17.1%. More recently, Marier (1977) has searched the discharge records of 11 hospitals in Washington, D.C. for cases of selected notifiable diseases and determined the percentage of each that were actually reported to the local health department as required by law. The rates found were: viral hepatitis, 11%; *H. influenzae* meningitis, 32%; salmonellosis, 42%; meningococcal meningitis, 50%; shigellosis, 62%; tuberculosis, 63%; total of all cases, 35%. In this study teaching hospitals reported 42% of cases and nonteaching hospitals only 20%. If such a small proportion of *hospitalized* cases of important communicable diseases is reported to the health department of a modern city such as Washington, one can only speculate about the state of knowledge of disease prevalence in the world in general.

The International Health Regulations (1969) define the diseases that are officially notifiable *by* health authorities (not *to* them) (World Health Organization, 1974a). These diseases, termed "subject to the regulations," are cholera (including cholera caused by the El Tor vibrio), plague, smallpox (including variola minor, or alastrim), and yellow fever. Notification in this case means a report by telegram or telex to the World Health Organization in Geneva within 24 hours of awareness of the first case of a disease subject to the regulations. Before these regulations became effective on January 1, 1971, the International Sanitary Regulations had been in effect for some 20 years. That agreement had required international reporting of the four diseases mentioned plus louse-borne relapsing fever and louse-borne typhus. The latter two, because of diminishing importance, have now been shifted to a new group of diseases "under surveillance," which includes in addition influenza, malaria, and poliomyelitis.

Another source of "continual data" on the occurrence of disease is hospital in-patient statistics which, when complete, can provide information about the following:

1. the geographical sources of patients;
2. the age and sex distribution of different diseases and durations of hospital stay;
3. the distribution of diagnoses;
4. the associations between different diseases;
5. the period between disease onset and hospital admission;
6. the distribution of patients according to different social and biological factors; and
7. the cost of hospital care. (World Health Organization, 1968)

Continual collection of limited types of sickness and disability records is also done by many other institutions and organizations. Among these are:

General clinics, health centers, hospital outpatient departments
Special clinics (e.g., venereal disease, drug addiction, maternal and child health)
School and factory dispensaries
Voluntary health agencies
Visiting nurses, midwives, etc.
Physicians and dentists in private practice
Military services and veterans hospitals
Workmen's compensation programs
Census bureaus
Police and traffic organizations for road accidents
Health insurance and life insurance companies
Business corporations, schools, military services, etc. (physical examination on entrance)
Registries (special registers)

The last category listed above has been reviewed by Weddell (1973), who described many different types of registers. Of special interest here are the disease-specific registers of which those for tumors are best known and most widely distributed. In many countries there are also special registers of blind and disabled, handicapped children, congenital defects, and diseases of specific local importance.

The quality and completeness of these records and the length of time that they are kept varies greatly, as does their accessibility to outsiders. In many cases the information is considered confidential or privileged. This may be true especially where individual patients are identified and where the information forms the basis of legal claims in accident or compensation situations. Annual reports with statistical summaries may be compiled on a local, district, state, or service basis and submitted to a central agency or ministry, which may be one of health, commerce and industry, social security, defense, etc., or to a central statistical office. A high degree of coordination between these agencies is seldom achieved, even in the most economically developed countries, because the information is collected differently and for different purposes, and it is compiled at different intervals. The problems of international comparability of such data are obvious, as are the frustrations that may beset a foreign scholar or expatriate expert who wishes to analyze them for an overview of the health situation in a particular country.

Special surveys are undertaken to estimate the scope of illness in a particular population at a particular time. General morbidity surveys of large populations are notably few in number. The Canadian Sickness Survey of 1950–51 is a well-known example. In that nationwide survey trained enumerators visited a sample of approximately 10,000 households distributed throughout the 10 provinces in metropolitan, small urban, and rural areas. An initial interview established particulars about the household, including income, housing, and environment. A special calendar was left at each household designed to help the informant keep a detailed day-to-day record of current sickness and expenditure on health care of each member of the household. Each month for the next year the enumerator visited the household to obtain the monthly diary. Participants reported "complaint," "disability," or "bed" days and included every deviation from their own concept of their "normal good health." The information thus obtained was extremely useful in extending knowledge of ill health far beyond the bounds of traditional health statistics (Fig. 5-6) (LeRiche and Milner, 1971).

In the United States, the National Health Survey Act of 1956 pro-

Traditional Health Statistics | **Sickness Survey**

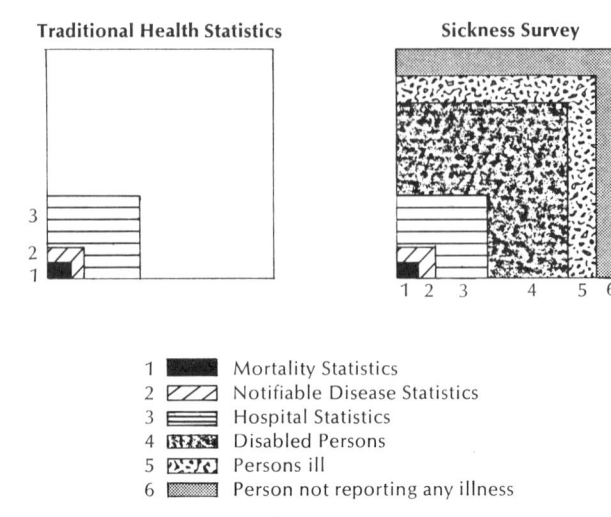

1 ▬ Mortality Statistics
2 ▨ Notifiable Disease Statistics
3 ▤ Hospital Statistics
4 ▦ Disabled Persons
5 ▩ Persons ill
6 ▨ Person not reporting any illness

Figure 5-6
Sick people of whom we know. SOURCE: LeRiche and Milner, 1971.

vided for the establishment and continuation of a long-term national health survey. Responsibility for development and conduct of the program is placed with the National Center for Health Statistics, a division of the Department of Health, Education and Welfare. The studies conducted are extensive and complex, based in part on sampling methods and including interview surveys, examination surveys, and data on health facilities and institutions. Findings of these surveys are published in hundreds of reports in many different series under the general heading of "Public Health Service Publication 1000."

Some other countries have undertaken large-scale sickness surveys. Finland, for instance, through its National Pensions Institute has since 1964 worked to describe morbidity and health services utilization on a national basis. Katz et al. (1973) have shown how large-scale surveys have changed in emphasis from earlier concern for bookkeeping to new community-centered social epidemiological studies. General estimates of community health levels at less than national scale have been undertaken widely, particularly in Europe and North America. Mention of the work of Chadwick, Pettenkofer, and others in the nineteenth century has been made in a previous chapter.

Far more common in recent years have been surveys designed to determine the prevalence of particular diseases. Often these are based on relatively simple and inexpensive diagnostic tests applicable to populations on a large scale. Parasitologic surveys of hookworm, for instance, use the method of stool examination for the characteristic worm ova, and schistosomiasis prevalence surveys are based on stool or urine examinations. Population surveys for malaria and filariasis utilize microscopic examination of blood films. Mass miniature radiography has been used widely for detection of active pulmonary tuberculosis. Trachoma, venereal disease, and nutritional deficiencies are examples of other specific health problems for which large population-based survey methods are commonly employed. In many cases only defined subgroups of populations are included in specific disease surveys, as with schoolchildren or persons exposed to particular occupational hazards. The distinction is not always clear between prevalence surveys, which demonstrate the existence of disease or infection (with or without symptoms), and screening programs, which have been undertaken in several countries for conditions such as diabetes, glaucoma, and sickle-cell trait. As surveys become more restricted in scope and size, their sponsoring organizations become more varied, health authorities have less control over content and methodology, and results become less comparable on an international basis. Medical schools, community agencies, specific disease-oriented voluntary associations, international aid organizations, missionary and other charitable groups, pharmaceutical companies planning drug trials, government research institutes, and others may all be engaged in surveys of one kind or another within a population, often without sufficient coordination. Results may appear in official reports, journal articles, or privately circulated documents.

An instructive example of the problems inherent in developing reliable morbidity data is provided by Ng (1976), who attempted to estimate the prevalence rate of blindness in Hong Kong. Although the 1961 census had enumerated only 856 blind persons, a 1963 estimate, based on unknown information, placed the number at 50,000, a figure later published in WHO comparative statistics. Based upon the 1963 population of Hong Kong, this estimate yielded a blindness prevalence rate of 1,392 per 100,000 population, quite high in comparison with other countries. The Social Welfare Department of Hong Kong, which maintains a register of blind persons, had on their books a total of 3,767 names at the end of March, 1963. By 1975, with a far larger population base, only 7,001 persons were listed on the register, yielding a blindness prevalence rate of about 160 per 100,000. Because of differences in definition of blindness in various countries, the Hong Kong figure, based on a rather strict interpretation, may need to be increased somewhat, as the author suggests: "perhaps, doubling it will produce a fair estimation and this is 320 per 100,000, putting the Hong Kong rate above U.K. and U.S.A., but below China and Sri Lanka."

The problems inherent in obtaining comparable morbidity statistics have led to many attempts at standardization. During the 1940s both the Medical Research Council of Great Britain and the U.S. Public Health Service issued classification manuals for specifying and coding disease. Within a few years the sixth revision (1948) of the ICD incorporated a morbidity classification that superseded both of these. The American Medical Association for many years issued a Standard Nomenclature of Diseases and Operations, which after 1961 was divided into separate disease- and procedure-nomenclatures, each of which has since gone through several editions. The latter, originating from a classification of surgical operations, has been expanded into a terminology for naming, coding, and reporting medical services. A variety of other taxonomies has been developed in response to particular needs, and their number is growing quickly. It is interesting to see how simple lists of causes of death have developed over the decades to cover nonfatal diseases, surgical procedures, nonsurgical procedures, and finally in the most recent versions laboratory, other diagnostic, prophylactic, therapeutic, and virtually all possible health-related procedures and measures.

STATISTICS ON HEALTH SERVICES

In the past, health services generally have been characterized by insufficient planning and coordination, by independent operation of their different elements, and by *ad hoc* responses to novel situations. Today, most countries view information about the working of their own health services as an indispensable part of their overall health statistics. With the increasing trend towards integrated, comprehensive programs, planners must have access to data about the characteristics of health establishments and personnel, about their activities, and about the costs involved. Nevertheless, while mortality statistics are in many places approaching a high standard and information on morbidity is improving, "few countries, if any, have sufficient data to describe their health services . . . It has been stated that the principal impediment to the reduction of ill-health at the present time is not the lack of medical knowledge about diseases but the problem of applying this knowledge, i.e., bringing it to bear upon the population's health needs in the most effective manner possible within the restraints imposed by economic, political, and other considerations" (World Health Organization, 1969).

In many ways, the functioning of health services is a more prominent issue in the minds of administrators, legislators, and the public than is the status of health itself. The availability and accessibility of physicians or hospital beds, the cost of medical care, and related items seem everywhere to be subjects of vigorous discussion, while the presence of disease may be tacitly considered inevitable. There is a common tendency to assign to physicians and hospitals primary responsibility for "health" and to neglect the myriad environmental and personal characteristics that actually determine the amount and severity of disease and disability in most communities. In considering the statistics on health services, it is thus essential to start with a clear understanding of just what a health service is supposed to do within a particular context, what its component parts should be, and how these relate to other elements within the society. We will examine these issues in some detail in the next two chapters.

The comparison of data on health services in different countries is far more difficult than similar studies of population, mortality, and morbidity statistics. Whereas human physiology is essentially the same everywhere, the organizational patterns of governments and societies are clearly very diverse. In countries where most aspects of life are regulated by a pervasive central authority, health facilities and personnel can be identified with relative clarity. Elsewhere, a variety of components forms a mosaic of health services characteristic for each area and time. Environmental, and to a considerable extent, preventive services generally fall within the province of governmental responsibility. Personal health services, especially those of a curative nature, are the most variable and include many kinds of establishments. Government-operated facilities range from university-based medical centers to district health subcenters staffed by auxiliary personnel on a part-time basis. Semiofficial providers of health services in many developing countries include governmentally sanctioned missionary or voluntary hospitals and clinics, often financed largely from abroad. Industrial establishments, plantations, and estates may have their own clinics and infirmaries. Private, nonprofit, member-financed facilities may be operated by trade unions or other groups. The private practice of medicine may take the form of individual physicians' offices or "surgeries," joint or group practices, clinics, or large proprietary hospitals. Ancillary services such as diagnostic laboratories may be incorporated into larger establishments or may be independent units. In many countries individual practitioners work for the government part-time in a clinical, teaching, or administrative capacity and also maintain their private practice for patients who pay as individuals. Pharmacists, midwives, medical assistants, dressers, and other paramedical personnel may be the only dispensers of advice and service, particularly in rural areas. The permutations are almost infinite, and the problem of coding or categorizing the forms of licensed provision of health services for purposes of international comparison is truly herculean. More difficult still is accounting for the activities of traditional healers, native practitioners, herbalists, and the other types of nonspecific health specialists found in all countries. The large aggregate amount of "informal" health care given in the home by family, neighbors, and friends must also be considered. To many people in the world, folk healers and family members provide the only form of medical care experienced throughout their lives.

Health services statistics deal not only with resources (facilities, personnel, financing) but also with their activities and utilization. There are very few standard methods for defining, specifying, and registering these events. Where social security or other health insurance schemes have established predetermined payment or compensation rates for certain procedures, these are categorized and coded for data-processing purposes. However, with the exception of some surgical operations, there has been little in the way of international standardization of preventive and curative activities. Immunizations by conventional methods using fixed doses of vaccine of uniform potency may come close to the ideal of a comparable procedure, but what is to be said of a "physical examination"? How are users and nonusers of services to be identified and characterized, and how are outcomes of treatment to be assessed? In some way each country must face questions of these kinds if it wants to evaluate the *effectiveness* of its health services. When *efficiency* (i.e., value for investment) is considered, these questions become even more pressing.

It should be mentioned that certain large-scale programs, international in origin and scope, have been planned in order to permit standardized recording of activities and outcomes. Perhaps the best example is the worldwide malaria eradication program in which field, laboratory, and clinical work as well as assessment procedures should follow carefully predetermined universal protocols. Programs of this type, however, represent only a small part of the activities of health services, and in some countries, they are organized and administered separately from the other activities of the health departments or ministries.

How much information is enough?

The main reasons for requiring health service statistics are:

1. to assist in the administration and coordination of health services in any particular community, region, or country;
2. to promote a basis for the short-term and long-term planning of health services, both locally and nationally;
3. to assess whether health services are accomplishing their objective (their effectiveness) and whether they are doing so in the best possible way (their efficiency);
4. to aid the study of particular problems of health and disease and their effect on the administration of health services, i.e., for research purposes; and
5. to provide background data that may be required from time to time by the health service agencies, by legislative bodies, and by members of the public. (World Health Organization, 1969)

In view of these functions, a question arises about the degree of accuracy and completeness of information needed for effective and efficient operation of health services. The collection of health statistics, including mortality, morbidity, and health services data, is itself an activity that requires planning, financing, and evaluation. Where budgets and personnel are limited, priorities must be assigned for allocation of funds; understandably, pressures will dictate that most expenditures go for direct service activities. Data gathering for planning and evaluation is vulnerable to criticism as an "administrative" rather than a "substantive" function of a health service, and funds for statistical purposes are likely to be kept to a minimum. This is acceptable, because all expenditures should be kept to a minimum, provided they are effectively and efficiently used. How much information is needed to make policy decisions about services for health care depends upon various factors, but at some point the kind and quality of information available—and the political pressures at work—will determine the practical outcome. The acquiring of good quality data is expensive, and the collecting and processing of an excess is wasteful both in money and staff time. What is needed is a strategy for arriving at sound conclusions based upon data that are neither too sketchy nor too costly; in other words, a way of applying techniques of decision analysis to the planning of health services. Methods for rational selection of best alternatives in the face of insufficient information have been developed by statisticians, economists, and business analysts, and should be applied to a variety of public policy areas, including health. These strategies can help to determine the amount of information needed for sound planning; if surveys and sampling methods are employed the number of cases needed can often be predetermined to minimize the exercise of exuberant empiricism. The techniques can help to secure the greatest good for the greatest number from limited resources.

Sampling and survey methods may also be used for continuous monitoring of activities (quality control), to evaluate effectiveness, to keep track of costs, and to determine when programs should be terminated. It is usually easier to launch a new project than to stop an old one that no longer serves the purpose for which it was designed.

The preceding discussion assumes that decisions are made in light rather than heat. Acquaintance with the daily newspaper should quickly dispel the notion that health services or any other significant human enterprises are designed, operated, and utilized on entirely rational grounds. Political considerations, pride, prejudice, and activities of special interest groups often influence the allocation of money and effort. In practice, health services are always skewed in their economic, geographic, and programmatic distributions. Their accessibility to various groups in the population is always unequal and the problems addressed are not necessarily equivalent to actual or perceived needs.

References

Bates, M. 1959. The ecology of health. *In:* I. Galdston, Ed. Medicine and Anthropology. New York. International Universities Press. pp. 56–77.

Chase, H. C. 1972. The position of the United States in international comparison of health status. American Journal of Public Health 62: 581–589.

Gear, H. S. 1959. International work in health statistics. 3. Securing international comparability. WHO Chronicle 13: 253–261.

Goldsmith, S. B. 1972. The status of health status indicators. Health Services Reports 87: 212–220.

Hookham, H. 1972. A Short History of China. New York. New American Library (Mentor Books). 381 p.

Katz, S., C. A. Akpom, J. A. Papsidero, and S. T. Weiss. 1973. Measuring the health status of populations. *In:* R. L. Berg, Ed. Health Status Indexes. Chicago. Hospital Research and Educational Trust. pp. 39–52.

LeRiche, W. H. and J. Milner. 1971. Epidemiology as Medical Ecology. London. Churchill Livingstone. 472 p.

Lossing, E. H. 1955. Reporting of notifiable diseases. Canadian Journal of Public Health 46: 444–448.

Marier, R. 1977. The reporting of communicable diseases. American Journal of Epidemiology 105: 587–590.

Murnaghan, J. 1974. Health-services information systems in the United States today. New England Journal of Medicine 209: 603–610.

National Center for Health Statistics. U.S. Public Health Service. 1975. Vital Statistics of the United States, 1970. Volume I—Natality. Department of Health, Education and Welfare Publication No. (HRA) 75-1100. Sections separately paginated.

Ng. T. K. W. 1976. Official statistics and blindness in Hong Kong. Southeast Asian Journal of Tropical Medicine and Public Health 7: 470–481.

Percy, C., L. Garfinkel, D. E. Krueger, and A. B. Dolman. 1974. Apparent changes in cancer mortality, 1968. A study of the effects of the introduction of the eighth revision International Classification of Diseases. Public Health Reports 89: 418–428.

Random House. 1966. The Random House Dictionary of the English Language. The Unabridged Edition. New York. Random House. 2059 p.

San Francisco Chronicle. 1974. Guilty verdict in transplant case. May 23.

Sullivan, D. F. 1966. Conceptual problems in developing an index of health. U. S. Public Health Service Publication 1000, Series 2, No. 17. 18 p.

Swaroop, S. 1960. Introduction to Health Statistics for the Use of Health Officers, Students, Public Health and Social Workers. Edinburgh. Livingstone. 343 p.

United Nations. 1955. Methods of Appraisal of Quality of Basic Data for Population Estimates. Population Studies No. 23. 67 p.

United Nations. 1971. A Concise Summary of the World Population Situation in 1970. Population Studies No. 48. 35 p.

United Nations. 1973. Principles and Recommendations for a Vital Statistics System. Statistical Papers, Series M, No. 19, Revision 1. 220 p.

United Nations. 1973a. The Determinants and Consequences of Population Trends. Vol. I. Department of Economic and Social Affairs. Population Studies No. 50. 661 p.

United Nations. 1974. The Availability of Demographic Statistics around the World. World Population Conference, Bucharest, August 1974. Conference Background Paper No. 27. 28 p. mimeo.

U.S. Bureau of the Census. 1976. 1970 Census of Population and Housing. Procedural History. Bureau of the Census Publication PHC(R)-1. 17 chapters, numbered separately.

Weddell, J. M. 1973. Registers and registries: a review. International Journal of Epidemiology 2: 221–228.

World Health Organization. 1957. Measurement of Levels of Health. Technical Report Series, No. 137. 29 p.

World Health Organization. 1967. International Classification of Diseases. Manual of the International Statistical Classification of Diseases, Injuries, and Causes of Death. 8th Rev. Vol. I. Geneva. World Health Organization. 478 p.

World Health Organization. 1968. Morbidity Statistics. Technical Report Series, No. 389. 29 p.

World Health Organization. 1969. Statistics of Health Services and their Activities. Technical Report Series, No. 429. 36 p.
World Health Organization. 1970. Programmes of Analysis of Mortality Trends and Levels. Technical Report Series, No. 440. 36 p.
World Health Organization. 1971. Statistical Indicators for the Planning and Evaluation of Public Health Programmes. Technical Report Series, No. 472. 40 p.
World Health Organization. 1974. New Approaches in Health Statistics. Technical Report Series No. 559. 40 p.
World Health Organization. 1974a. International Health Regulations (1969). 2nd Annotated Ed. Geneva. World Health Organization. 102 p.
World Health Organization. 1976. World Health Statistics Annual 1973-1976. Vol. I. Vital Statistics and Causes of Death. Geneva. World Health Organization. 839 p.
Wylie, C. M. 1970. The definition and measurement of health and disease. Public Health Reports 85: 100-104.

POLICY 6.

Health status has been defined, quantified, measured, coded, summarized, tabulated, compared, and evaluated in the preceding chapters. We now turn our attention to the complex subject of intervention.

It is commonly believed that formal efforts to improve health are channeled through so-called "health care delivery systems." These, in turn, are often thought to be more or less equivalent to the administration (if any) and financing of personal medical care by health professionals. In earlier chapters we have seen that a great range of factors affects health status; thus, it would be strange if the only element in society acting to improve the people's health were the "health care delivery system."

The present chapter will deal with the different sorts of things that can be done in an organized way to improve health, and why certain of these are, or should be, selected for use. The enunciation of *policy* leads, in principle, to the determination of *strategy*, which is carried out by *tactical operations*. We will examine here two aspects of health policy and strategy: identifying problems and specifying the means of attack. The following chapters will concentrate on tactics, comparing some existing national health services and discussing international efforts towards improvement of global health.

WHAT ARE THE PROBLEMS?

The cardinal law of economics, that resources are scarce relative to wants, is as true for health services as for other aspects of life. Regardless of political system or national income, no country possesses the personnel, facilities, material, knowledge, and resolution to resolve every health problem. But even if resources were unlimited and money grew on trees, someone would have to make decisions about what needs to be done, how to do it, and how to evaluate the outcome. Although it may seem peculiar that, after 219 pages we must once more ask, "What are the problems?," that is an unavoidable first step in the rational planning of any health service. The recognition of a problem depends upon the knowledge of its existence, and the establishment of some sort of acceptable limits for its impact upon the population.

For some years, governments have been asked by the WHO to indicate what they consider to be the major health problems in their own countries. Recent responses, summarized in Table 6-1, offer few surprises. Each entry on the list represents (1) an acknowledgment of the existence of the problem, (2) a judgment that it is considered unacceptable and, implicitly, (3) the notion that something can be done about it. Note the sharp cleavage in Table 6-1 between communicable diseases, listed by governments in developing countries and chronic diseases, specified in Europe, North America, Japan, Australia, and New Zealand. Special problems of individual countries are frequently described by their representatives to the Annual World Health Assembly of the WHO (see Chapter 8) and may be found in the verbatim records.

Many diseases, as we have seen, have declined or perhaps disappeared as side effects of general socioeconomic development. This should not be taken to indicate that health problems will all disappear by themselves in the pursuit of ever-higher GNPs, because the hydra-headed monster of disease keeps producing new forms and combinations as fast as the older ones can be put to rest. A particular disease may be important in a population, but hidden from health planners for a variety of reasons. Some have always been present but unrecognized until chance, genius, or scientific knowledge made them apparent. In 1941 the Australian

Table 6-1. Major health problems designated by governments, by world regions, mid to late 1960s

Region	Problems
I. Africa	Tuberculosis, malaria, leprosy, schistosomiasis, onchocerciasis, trachoma
Americas (except U.S.A. and Canada)	Tuberculosis, intestinal parasitosis, malnutrition, malaria, poliomyelitis, accidents
Asia (except Japan)	Tuberculosis, diarrheal diseases, malaria, intestinal parasitosis, respiratory infections, leprosy
II. Europe	Cardiovascular diseases, malignant neoplasms, environmental pollution, accidents, mental disease
U.S.A. and Canada	Cardiovascular diseases, malignant neoplasms, mental disease, bronchitis, kidney disease
Japan	Cardiovascular diseases, malignant neoplasms, tuberculosis, venereal disease, food handling
Australia and New Zealand	Cardiovascular diseases, malignant neoplasms, mental disease, accidents, environmental pollution

Source: Adapted from World Health Organization, 1974.

ophthalmologist Norman M. Gregg described in infants a new syndrome including cataract, deaf-mutism, and heart disease, and related it to an epidemic of rubella ("German measles") that had taken place some months previously. A check of historical records of similarly afflicted children, and of past rubella epidemics, confirmed the relationship. Amebic meningoencephalitis, mentioned in chapter 1, has been recognized as a clinical entity only in recent years. Retrospective examination of brain autopsy slides showed that the causative organisms had been overlooked for decades by competent pathologists unaware of their existence. A final example of a recently recognized "disease" is the genetically controlled deficiency in the enzyme glucose-6-phosphate dehydrogenase (G6PD), which was mentioned in regard to favism in the Middle East. This deficiency first came to light as a result of research on antimalarial drugs, when it was found that administration of the drug primaquine produced hemolytic anemia in certain individuals and not in others. All known diseases were of course "newly recognized" at some stage in history, and despite (or perhaps because of) advances in medical science, many others remain to be described.

Truly new diseases or syndromes are also seen with some frequency. Many of these are caused by viral or other agents spread from other animals to man; Lassa and Marburg fevers are noteworthy recent examples. In East Africa, Chikungunya virus when first found affected some 80% of the 200,000 members of the Makonde tribe in Tanzania (Lumsden, 1975). O-nyong-nyong disease appeared suddenly in 1959–60, also in East Africa, and eventually affected a million or more people (Barker, 1973). A few years earlier a severe hemorrhagic disease of children was described in Manila, Bangkok, Kuala Lumpur, Singapore, and other large southeast Asian cities. Seasonal epidemics of this disease, in some way related to dengue fever, have since killed thousands of young children in these areas (Jusatz, 1974). Mucocutaneous lymph node syndrome (MCLS) of unknown cause has appeared in Japan and elsewhere (including Hawaii) in recent years (Anon, 1974). Numerous other diseases will certainly be identified in years to come.

In addition to newly recognized and truly new natural health hazards, health planners always face the threat of unexpected outbreaks of well-known diseases. Perhaps the best-known example in recent years is the seventh cholera pandemic, which spread from Celebes to other parts of Asia in the early 1960s, then slowly westward, arriving with explosive force in West Africa in 1970 and 1971 when thousands died in many countries (see Chapter 8), and extending to Europe and

Oceania. A similar explosive pandemic had struck Central America a few years earlier, with extremely virulent and frequently fatal diarrheal disease. Here the organism responsible was a multiply drug-resistant strain of *Shigella* that produced an outbreak "the equal of which [had] not been seen anywhere in the world for 70 years" (Dupont et al., 1971). In this case also the organism spread by international travel to Mexico and to the United States where several secondary cases were reported.

All of the health problems just mentioned share, along with many others, the common feature that they were unanticipated by health planners. Definition of problems for the purpose of predictive planning obviously could not have taken them into account until their characteristics were known and assessed. But more commonly the informational block to planning lies in the lack of epidemiologic data about the routine and the familiar. In less-developed countries where basic demographic data are lacking the specifics of virtually all health problems are enclosed in a black box—this includes nondisease conditions such as antenatal and postnatal needs, and promotive health services in general. In all countries information is inadequate with respect to many of the silent threats to health that, while potentially serious, are present in the early asymptomatic form. Hypertension is an example, as are early diabetes, tuberculosis, and other conditions for which screening and secondary prevention programs may be set up.

A particularly difficult problem emerging forcefully in industrial countries is that of how to evaluate the eventual threat to health by the products and by-products of technology. Newly emergent "man-made maladies" are known to be legion, produced in part directly by pollution from industrial processes (Minamata disease in Japan, asbestos-induced mesothelioma), in part by consumer products (automobile accidents, childhood poisonings), in part by the stresses of modern life (divorce, perhaps carcinoma of the lung), and in part by the medical enterprise itself (adverse drug reactions, trauma from unneeded surgery). In terms of problem definition, the potential health hazards arising from technology, while anticipated in general, often can not be assessed in advance with any degree of specificity. The assessment process itself often requires development of still more technology. For example, determination of the carcinogenic potential of pesticides, solvents, food additives, and other chemicals is a long, expensive, and difficult process, but new tests involving mutagenesis in the bacterium *Salmonella typhimurium* show promise of providing fairly reliable answers relatively easily.

The case of nuclear power plants is instructive. Opponents of these installations cite as a chief argument against them the unknown risk of a potentially vast health threat in the event of accidental or deliberate malfunction. The direct hazard of radiation as well as the possibility of genetic damage to future generations has been vividly depicted. Faced with the choice of foregoing present consumption for the possible future benefit of eliminating an unknown risk, the public (at least in the U.S.A.) has consistently voted to take both the consumption and the risk, and health planners have followed suit.

What is acceptable?

Even if health planners knew every microbe and blood pressure within their jurisdiction, the problem would remain of what, if anything, to do about them. Beyond the technical capabilities of diagnostic science lies the value judgment of a population, expressed in its behavior, its vote, and (it is hoped) in the policies of its government. Values are expressed, in the context of health, in related decisions on acceptable risks and acceptable standards.

We have seen that the risk of the illness or death from plutonium radiation seems to be acceptable to the American public in view of alternative health risks (e.g., of air pollution from coal-burning power plants) and of immediate benefits (employment, electric power, and reduced dependence on imported oil). The underlying issue seems really to be an unwillingness to change an accustomed life-style. Virtually all Americans accept the risks of riding in an automobile. Somewhat fewer will ride in an airplane, or smoke cigarettes. Very few will drink strychnine, or handle rattlesnakes as do the members of some fundamentalist churches in West Virginia. Risks are not static. A man who would earlier have taken a chance on a liaison with a prostitute may think twice after reading about multiply drug-resistant gonococci. Fish lovers may switch to sardines when they hear of mercury contamination of tuna. Or they may not. Objective reality exists in the world, but the decision whether a problem exists, or a risk is worth taking, or a habit needs to be changed, is made only in the human mind.

The question of standards has troubled ethical thinkers since earliest days. What is good? What is moral, honest, proper, fair, acceptable? What is the value of life or of health? In an ancient dialogue in the style of Plato, Socrates is made to ponder health and riches:

Are not the healthy richer than the sick, since health is a possession more valuable than riches to the sick? Surely there is no one who would not prefer to be poor and well, rather than to have all the king of Persia's wealth and to be ill. And this proves that men set health above wealth, else they would never choose the one in preference to the other (Jowett, 1892).

A more modern observer has a different view:

Many people in the public health field greatly overestimate the value that the consumer places on health. The health literature frequently seems to read as if no price is too great to pay for good health, but the behavior of consumers indicates that they are often unwilling to pay even a small price. For example, surveys have shown that many people do not brush their teeth regularly, even when they believe that brushing would significantly reduce tooth decay and gum trouble. (Fuchs, 1966)

Who is right? The national expenditure on health services in the United States now exceeds $140 billion, suggesting that the relationship between wealth and health is more than platonic. Yet Scherp (1971) has shown that each 100 inductees into the U.S. Army required 600 dental fillings, 112 extractions, 40 bridges, 21 crowns, 18 partial, and 1 full dentures. Dental caries is the most prevalent and probably the most preventable disease of young people in North America. Score one for Fuchs.

The value of life itself is often difficult to define. Nowhere is this better exemplified than in attitudes toward abortion. Persons who supported the bombing of Vietnam may be repelled by the idea of therapeutic termination of pregnancy. In Latin America, illegal septic abortion and attempted abortion are major causes of hospital admission of women to obstetric wards, and they account for 34% of maternal deaths (Puffer and Griffith, 1967). In Japan, by contrast, abortions are freely available and have been a major factor in population control since the Second World War.

The value of one's own life may be thought to be infinite, but suicide and other self-destructive acts are not rare. Table 6-2 shows how the rate of suicide varies among countries. For many reasons (social stigma, insurance claims, etc.) suicides often are not reported as such on death certificates; thus these figures probably represent understatements.

Standards clearly vary from one community to another. What, for instance, is a tolerable or acceptable infant mortality rate (IMR)? For the world as a whole, infant mortality in 1965–69 was estimated at 120 per thousand live births, averaging 140 in the less developed and 27 in the more developed countries. Within Europe, Portugal in 1969 had an IMR of 56, and Sweden 12 (World Health Organization, 1974). Reaching a rate of, say, 26, would be considered a disaster in Sweden, normal in the

Table 6-2. Standardized suicide rates per 100,000, ages 15 and over, by sex, selected countries or areas, 1965–1969

Country or Area	Male	Female
Mexico	4.4	1.2
Greece	6.4	2.8
Italy	10.2	4.0
Israel	12.7	8.4
England and Wales	14.7	9.4
United States	23.0	8.4
Japan	24.7	18.4
Singapore	27.5	15.2
Denmark	31.8	17.0
Sweden	36.8	13.8
Czechoslovakia	45.2	16.5
Hungary	58.5	22.3
West Berlin	63.9	31.7

Source: Adapted from Ruzicka, 1976.

U.S.S.R., a cause for celebration in Portugal, and an impossible dream in Africa.

In some industrialized countries, sufficient data exist for more intricate analyses that can identify health problems which are perhaps not

Table 6-3. Years of life lost due to deaths at 1 to 70 years of age, by cause and sex, Canada, around 1971

Cause	Total years lost Males	Females
Motor vehicle accidents	154,000	59,000
Ischemic heart disease	157,000	36,000
All other accidents	136,000	43,000
Respiratory diseases and lung cancer	90,000	50,000
Suicide	51,000	18,000
TOTAL	588,000	206,000

Source: Adapted from Lalonde, 1974.

obvious at first glance. The Canadian Minister of National Health and Welfare, Marc Lalonde (1974), citing the greater death rate for males by most causes in Canada (Table 6-3), has concluded "there is no doubt that Canada has a male mortality problem of great significance." A problem has been identified, verbalized, and given official status.

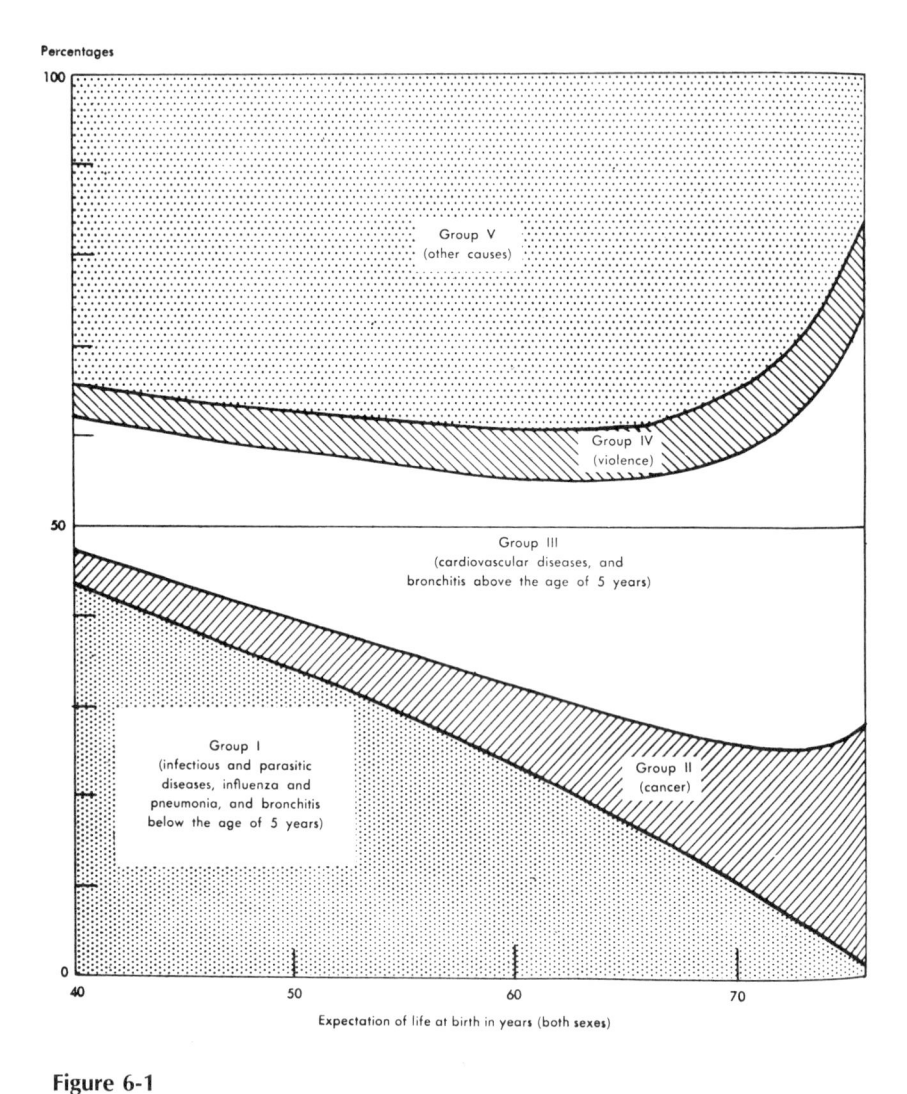

Figure 6-1

Distribution, in a standard population, of deaths (all ages and both sexes) by cause-of-death groups for different levels of expectation of life at birth ranging from 40 to 76 years. SOURCE: United Nations, 1963.

It seems hardly necessary to note that specified health problems vary not only by country but also by time in any given area. Figure 6-1 shows graphically how the mix of causes of death changes with changing expectation of life. Table 6-4 shows the occurrence of a similar shift, over time, in a single country, the United States. In 1900 the expectation of life at birth in the U.S. was 49.9 years, and in 1972 it was 71.1 (both sexes). The distribution of causes of death can be compared in Table 6-4 and Figure 6-1.

From the preceding discussion it may appear that a nation's pattern of health problems is inexorably linked with its socioeconomic development and that little can be done to alter an inevitable pattern of disease and premature death. Of course, this is not true, and fatalistic resignation in the matter is completely unwarranted. Even in poor coun-

Table 6-4. The 10 leading causes of death, by rank, rate per 100,000, and percentage of deaths, United States, 1972 and 1900

Cause	1972 Rank	1972 Rate	1972 %	1900 Rank	1900 Rate	1900 %
Diseases of the heart	1	361	38.3	4	137	8.0
Cancers	2	167	17.6	8	64	3.7
Cerebrovascular diseases	3	101	10.7	5	107	6.2
Accidents	4	55	5.8	7	72	4.2
Pneumonia and influenza	5	29	3.1	1	202	11.8
Diabetes mellitus	6	19	2.0			
Certain diseases of early infancy	7	16	1.7	9	63	3.6
Arteriosclerosis	8	16	1.7			
Cirrhosis of the liver	9	16	1.7			
Bronchitis, emphysema, asthmas	10	14	1.5			
Nephritis				6	81	4.7
Diphtheria				10	40	2.3
Diarrhea, enteritis				3	143	8.3
Tuberculosis				2	194	11.3
All other causes		149	15.8		615	35.9
ALL CAUSES		942	100.		1,719	100.

Source: Adapted from U.S. House of Representatives Committee on Ways and Means, Subcommittee on Health, 1975.

tries with a history of high rates of contaminative, infectious, parasitic, vector-borne, and nutritional disease and a correspondingly high infant and child mortality rate, morbidity and mortality can be quickly and inexpensively reduced to a degree that required generations or centuries in the present industrialized countries. The key elements are motivation and organization.

WHAT CAN BE DONE?

Legend has it that the god Zeus, angered at the theft of heavenly fire by Prometheus, decided to punish the human race. Accordingly, he gave the woman Pandora a box enclosing all human ills, which promptly escaped when she opened the box. Hope, also in the box, alone remained there. Our problem is how to get the largest possible number of ills back in the box, while releasing hope.

Although healers have treated patients for centuries, the modern health service is a relatively recent development. It is clearly more than the organized practice of clinical medicine on the one hand, or sanitary and environmental manipulation on the other. An ideally comprehensive health service not only bridges the two fields (for too long artificially separated) known as "medical care" and "public health," but meshes with many other sectors of daily life. A sociologist might view a health service as a means for promoting the effective performance of certain social roles. A politician may see it as a mechanism for distributing specific benefits among his constituents, and an economist would be interested in the allocation of resources to and within the service.

The stated goals of all health services are the protection, promotion, and restoration of the health of individuals within their jurisdiction, for optimal personal and social fulfillment. To these ends, health services may draw upon a large armamentarium of measures (some of which are shown in Table 6-5) whose translation into reality in different countries is accomplished through a great variety of administrative and financial arrangements. Chapter 7 will describe some of these, with emphasis on personal care.

To illustrate the integration of health services into a national government and society we can turn to the mythical nation of Ruritania. Some characteristics of this nation are listed in Table 6-6. The following discussion covers the major operational areas of the health sector in Ruritania.

Table 6-5. Some basic measures for protection, promotion, and restoration of health

Target	Measure	Example
Environment	Swamp drainage	Malaria
	Water supply	Typhoid
	Sanitation	Hookworm
Food	Meat inspection	Cysticercosis
	Pasteurization	Brucellosis
Animal reservoirs	Rodent destruction	Plague
	Casefinding, treatment (dogs)	Hydatid disease
Vectors	Insecticiding	Yellow fever
Susceptible persons	Education	Drug addiction
	Isolate from hazard	Industrial fumes
	Provide nutrients	Pellagra
	Drug prophylaxis	Malaria
	Convert to immune	Measles
	Monitor	Pregnancy
Cases, preclinical	Education	Alcoholism
	Screening, management	Hypertension
Cases, clinical	Casefinding, treatment	Gonorrhea
	Primary care	Mild illness
	Secondary care	Serious illnesses
	Tertiary care	Critical illnesses
	Rehabilitation	Coronary patients

1. *Central coordination.* The unit responsible for establishing policy and planning, general budgeting for official services, fighting for funds in the central government, and coordinating with other government ministries at central and provincial levels. Here also may be found linkages, through the Ministry of Foreign Affairs, with official intergovernmental organizations (Table 8-10), and to some extent with nongovernmental organizations (Table 8-3). Vital and health statistics are compiled at a national level by the Central Statistical Bureau of the Ministry of Planning and then shared with the Ministry of Health.
2. *Information and personnel.* A. *Research.* The purpose of biomedical research is to increase the productivity of health services. Accordingly, investigations are conducted into the functioning of health services—their efficiency and effectiveness—and the means of improving them. Applied biomedical research is carried out on the causes and treatment of particular diseases, the development of pharmaceuticals, the modes of rehabilitation,

Table 6-6. Some characteristics of the mythical Republic of Ruritania

Population: 14.5 million, 50% urban
  Median age: 19
  Crude birth rate: 24 per thousand per year
  Crude death rate: 11 per thousand per year
  Expectation of life at birth (both sexes): 68
Per capita income: US $ 1,000 equivalent annually
Chief industries: Agriculture, manufacturing, mining, fishing
Central government:
  Democratically elected Parliament. President, Prime Minister, and Ministers of Agriculture, Commerce and Industry, Defense, Education, Foreign Affairs, Health, Information, Justice, Labor, Planning, Public Works, and Welfare and Social Security.
Regional government:
  5 Provincial legislatures. 8 Municipal councils

etc. Basic research delves into more theoretical aspects of biological and social organization. Research may be done by government departments or may be funded by them. Private industry and charitable foundations also support work done in universities, institutes, and commercial laboratories. The total amount of research done is small, but it helps to keep scientifically oriented personnel from emigrating. The National Research Council of Ruritania, a private body, advises the government on matters of policy. B. *Personnel.* The recruiting, training, and licensing of physicians, dentists, nurses, sanitarians, midwives, auxiliaries, technicians, and the host of other health employees is included here. This is mostly a function of the central government of Ruritania, but some private proprietary or nonprofit institutions are also involved. Professional and other health workers through their societies and trade unions exert a strong influence upon their own regulation. The faculties of Medicine, Public Health, and Allied Health Sciences work closely with the research establishment and with the Ministry of Education.

3. *Provision of services to the community.* A. *Environmental protection and control.* These responsibilities include: monitoring and management of water supply standards, of sewage treatment, and of programs for clean air and water, with appropriate regulation of the private sector. They are performed jointly by Ministries of Health, Public Works, Commerce and Industry, and various local authorities, coordinating with each other and with private industry. Associated police functions involve the courts. B. *Community disease and hazard control.* i. *Regulation and inspection.* Meat and

food inspection; restaurant hygiene; checks on pharmaceuticals; port and foreign quarantine; and enforcement of building, health, and safety codes are common functions. Several ministries, plus municipal authorities, share responsibility in these areas. ii. *Health education and promotion.* The public is told of the dangers of smoking, the benefits of seat belts; and the importance of childhood nutrition and immunization through posters and radio messages prepared together with the Ministry of Information. Health education classes, compulsory in the Ruritanian school system, are prepared by cooperating health educators in the Ministry of Education. iii. *Screening programs.* In addition to the antituberculosis center, there are smaller programs to perform the Papanicolaou test for cervical cancer, blood pressure determinations for hypertension, eye tonometry to detect early glaucoma, and various biochemical tests on newborns. It is hoped that these can be expanded in the future. iv. *Communicable disease control.* There is a central laboratory in each province and a national central reference laboratory. Certain diseases of importance in Ruritania are subject to surveillance (e.g., malaria, tuberculosis). In the capital city there is a permanent venereal diseases clinic operated jointly by the municipality and the Ministry of Health. Medical students help to staff this clinic. Mass campaigns against specific diseases are mounted periodically, in cooperation with voluntary organizations such as the Anti-Tuberculosis Society. A special field unit works in rodent and vector control. v. *Control of injuries and special hazards.* The nuclear power plant of the Ministry of Public Works is monitored continuously for radiation leakage. Occupational risks to the Ruritanian labor force are evaluated by inspectors from the Ministry of Labor. Factories can be made to meet standards by the Ministry of Commerce and Industry, and the Ministry of Agriculture is concerned with pesticide exposures of workers in the fields. Labor unions and businessmen's organizations are also concerned with developments in these areas, each trying to advance its own interests. vi. *Family planning.* The government has embarked upon a family planning program in hopes of reducing population increase to 2% within 10 years (see Chapter 3). An operational unit has been set up with representatives from the Ministries of Health, Information, Planning, and Welfare and Social Security. The National Family Planning Association, with a grant from a large private overseas foundation, is carrying out a pilot study.

4. *Provision of services to individuals.* A. *Social and welfare services.* Emergency plans for civil defense and natural disasters are made by the Ministry of Defense and by officials in Public Works, Health, and Welfare through the Prime Minister's office. Long-term care of the mentally retarded, of the aged poor, and of orphans is administered jointly by Ministries of Health and of Welfare and Social Security, as are rehabilitation and services to the

blind. All are closely linked to private philanthropy and charitable organizations. B. *Personal medical care services.* i. *General population.* A network of primary health centers exists in the Ruritanian towns, with maternal and child health a prominent feature. Family planning auxiliaries are often based here, and immunizations and other preventive measures are done routinely. There are government hospitals in the cities, operated by the Ministry of Health. The capital and a few other cities have private hospitals, some physician-owned, some operated by religious and voluntary organizations. A teaching hospital at the University School of Medicine can provide all specialist services. Local cancer, diabetes, heart, and other citizen associations are involved in appropriate ways.

Persons desiring medical attention may consult physicians in private practice, almost all of whom are members of the Ruritanian Medical Association (RMA). In some areas practitioners of traditional Ruritanian folk medicine are kept busy.

ii. *Special segments of the population.* The military services and the prison system maintain their own medical staffs, clinics, and hospitals. Especially difficult cases are sent to the University Hospital. The government helps to provide medical care to merchant seamen and to the small nomadic aboriginal population. Certain categories of government employees and their dependents receive "free" medical services, as do old age pensioners. And the list goes on. . . .

WHAT SHOULD BE DONE?

It is evident from this fictionalized account that health services are extremely complex and pervade the institutions of society to such an extent that rigorous definition becomes very difficult. Indeed, activities in other sectors such as education, agriculture, and transportation may in some cases have more bearing upon health than health services themselves. We must nevertheless consider the specific needs of the health planner, who determines where money, effort, and time are best to be expended within that sector. Which programs are most effective and most deserving of support? That depends upon the situation: there are no simple solutions. In the best way possible, a course of action must be presented to the administrative authorities, whose ultimate decisions are based largely on political and economic pragmatism. Ideally, a plan to reach a particular societal goal should be made with knowledge of all the options available and the consequences of adopting each, or none. In the following sections we will explore briefly some of the analytic tools available to health planners.

Health as wealth

In the late seventeenth century, William Petty, estimating the value of a resident of England at between £69 and £90, decided that it was a good investment to take care of people's health. The sanitary reformer Chadwick, in his great 1842 report (see Chapter 2) estimated that ill health reduced national production by £14 million, at that time a great sum. As large factories developed in England and elsewhere, with workers becoming highly skilled in special tasks, managers became more and more aware of the monetary investment in the labor force. "The economist," said Chadwick in 1862, "for the advancement of his science may well treat the human being simply as an investment of capital, in productive force." Workers and their families were faced with destitution in the event of disability or death, becoming burdens to society. Recognizing that this was not only a social problem, Chadwick wrote in 1862, "When the sentimentalist and moralist fails, he will have as a last resource to call in the aid of the economist." At the same time, the great development of life insurance in the nineteenth century drew attention to the monetary value of human life. The stage was now set for the establishment, in Bismarck's Germany of 1883, of social paternalism, including health insurance for poor industrial workers and their families. Since that time, health, government, and economics have been inextricably tied together.

Political leaders often emphasize the importance of health. Eduardo Frei, a former President of Chile, said, "In the case of Latin America—I can speak knowledgeably only of this continent—the eradication of epidemic and endemic tropical diseases has a priority above any other kind of investment" (Frei, 1975). Other leaders are more cautious. Hector Acuña, Director of the Pan American Sanitary Bureau, has written:

With the increasing role of health planning on the one hand and economic development planning on the other, the need for better understanding of how the level of health influences the economy, and for quanitification of its effects, has received ever more attention. The true integration of health plans into national development plans requires more complete knowledge than we now have of the economic gains that may be possible through improving the condition of health. (Acuña, 1975)

Economists and social scientists interested in determining the precise economic value of health and illness on a national scale face a sea of uncertainty. Conly (1975) asks, "How much does ill health cost?" and answers herself: "The great bulk of the actual cost of illness remains submerged and unknown. The cost to society of even one specific disease affecting one specific segment of the population has yet to be quantitatively known. Most of the attempts to formulate such a cost have been speculative with little concrete basis."

Because a population is made up of individuals, it may be well to look first at the microeconomic level, to see the relationship between health and wealth for a person, and then try to generalize to the national level.

The monetary value of a life Economists and health planners may view each human being as possessing a certain monetary value. There is first of all a cost involved in pregnancy and childbirth—loss of productivity and earnings, consumption of special foods, prenatal care and delivery. In industrialized countries this cost may be very high. In poor countries there may be little cash investment in a pregnancy, but other costs may accrue, such as the value of the time spent by midwives and family. The cost of rearing children has been recognized as an investment at least since Chadwick's day. Once again, the expenditure on food, housing, clothing, education, medical care, and recreation varies from very little to a great deal. The death of a child represents the loss of all these expenditures as well as parental time devoted to the child that could have been otherwise gainfully used. In less developed countries where the economic base is already very low, and where half or more of all deaths may occur by age five, infant and child mortality represent a very great financial burden and an unproductive investment.

In addition to the costs of rearing and maintenance, a person's economic value can be described by his present and future earning power. When dealing with such calculations involving a long time span, economists always consider both the present and discounted monetary values. A certain amount of money has different values when obtained or spent at different times, and the process of discounting changes the future "stream" of earnings (or other benefits) into its present cash value. (Discounting, in a sense, represents the value of the funds if available for other uses.) Premature death, defined as death before retirement from productive work, results in the loss of all future earnings.

How are these abstractions to be translated into health policies and actions? The answer is not at all clear, but some observers have attempted to focus attention on this problem. Enke and Brown (1972), for example, have analyzed the economic values of individuals of different ages in developing countries (Fig. 6-2). They conclude that if the age element alone is considered, "preventing the death of a man of age 30 is ordinarily more worthwhile to his national economy than preventing the death of a young child of 5 years." A policy corollary of this finding might be that measures to prevent premature deaths under those circumstances should be concentrated upon adults of ages 20 to 45. Governments, doctors and families do not always agree, because of important noneconomic considerations. Although the authors acknowledge that their analysis illustrates a "dehumanized economic viewpoint," they argue for the establishment of "an explicit basis for allocating doctors' energies and clinics' resources that are financed by government. This criterion should be understandable and defensible." This analysis might be interpreted as suggesting relative neglect of young children where resources are severely limited. As we have seen (Table 5-3), however, in many developing areas the proportion of children under 15 exceeds 40% of the total population. Children under five may approach 20% of the total, and it is in this group that half of all deaths occur, deaths that are in large part readily and cheaply preventable. Morley (1973) has argued strongly for increasing attention to this segment of society:

In every country the most precious possessions of parents are their young children. We now have the technical knowledge and means needed to reduce the mortality among children by half.... In the past it was advantageous to parents and communities to have large numbers of children; today there is some realization that small families of healthy children, with opportunities for education, are

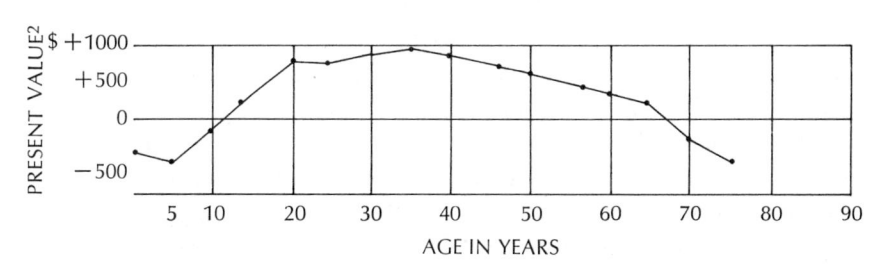

Figure 6-2

Economic value of an individual, by age, hypothetical developing country.[1]
SOURCE: Adapted after Enke and Brown, 1972.
[1]Labor force participation by age at rates believed typical of Southeast Asia, consumption and output weighted by age, expectation of life at birth = 43 years, national output = $150 per capita.
[2]Discounted at 15% per year compounded.

to be preferred.... At present, in most of the world, increasing attention is being given to the health of mothers and young children and considerably larger funds are being invested in their care. If a country is to make rapid strides in economic and other development, it may well be that this can be brought about only 20–30 years after services have been provided for the medical, nutritional and general care of small children, that is, when these well-cared-for children have become members of the adult society.

It is clear that policy decisions regarding the distribution of resources to health services for specific segments of the population must be linked to decisions about family planning, education, economic growth, and employment opportunities, and all of the other interlocking elements that comprise overall national planning in any country. All of these are aspects of investment in the future; all require a future-oriented pattern of thinking, which is not equally developed in all countries.

Health as an investment

Illness in sufficient degree results in loss of working time (disability) and in reduced effectiveness or productivity (debility), both leading to economic loss. In addition, money is often expended in medical care, drugs, special foods, or devices necessary to cope with an illness. Hence the cost of ill health has at least two aspects: losses from unrealized production and expenses for alleviation of the condition. Where the individual is not covered by any sort of social welfare scheme, these costs must be borne privately, usually within the family. It is the function of insurance (in the broad sense, private or public) to compensate for at least part of these losses. There is one more thing to consider here: the cost of pain and suffering. How is this to be determined? Usually it is not; even though it is generally acknowledged that pain and suffering are inevitable accompaniments of ill health, society does not know how to put a monetary value on them. Therefore these are not "reimbursable" except where the pain itself is the illness, and then a search is made for its "true cause." In courts of law, however, a monetary value is often assigned to a person's pain and suffering, provided that it resulted from the actions of *another* person who is found guilty of a tort.

Since ill health, disability, and premature death all incur individual and social costs, it is in the interests of society to minimize these. Health care in its preventive, curative, and rehabilitative aspects is directed towards this goal. Insofar as expenditures for health result in increased productivity and earnings, or reduce expenditures for later medical care, they are an *investment*. Insofar as such expenditures serve only to reduce anxiety, to eliminate trivial symptoms, or to enhance social status (e.g., by cosmetic surgery) they can be considered as *consumption*, equal to the purchase of any other commodity. The relationships between the investment and the consumption aspects of health expenditures have occupied many economists: how are improvements in the quality of life and the quality of people to be considered?

Mushkin (1962) has looked at the quality of people in relation to economic growth and has compared the investment in health with that in education. Both forms of investment increase an individual's productivity, effectiveness, and future labor product, and they also enhance his function as a consumer. Moreover, these investments are entwined. Better health improves the investment in education not only by reducing absences from school, and perhaps improving learning ability, but also by increasing the life span, thus providing a greater long-term return from schooling. On the other hand, good health depends in part on educational level, and some education programs train future health workers. Investments in both health and education have "external" benefits to the community at large. Whereas education improves only the quality of human capital, health expenditures can increase the quantity also. In both cases, participation of the individual is important. The preservation and restoration of health do not come from "being doctored" any more than learning comes from "being taught." It is evident that improvement in the quality of "human capital" through investment in health, or education, or in other ways (such as migration) can provide substantial returns to a society.

Cost-benefit analysis

Implicit in the investment aspect of health expenditure is the idea of a cost-benefit ratio. Those responsible for planning and financing health services projects usually want to know the return that they may expect from their investment. This is always difficult, and usually impossible to specify with accuracy. The business investor can usually tell just how much profit (or loss) has accrued to him from purchasing shares or new equipment and from figuring taxes, depreciation, and so on. Investments in health cannot furnish such exact figures primarily because benefits realized are largely in the form of *averted future costs:* the avoidance of losses from mortality, disability, debility, and medical expenses that otherwise would have occurred. The more costs can be averted, the greater is the cost-benefit ratio of the investment. Preventive measures that avert costs altogether therefore are often considered the best ways to spend health money. Of these, the most obvious measure is immunization.

Cost-benefit analyses of immunization programs have been favorite subjects of health economists because fairly specific data are often available. In the United States, Axnick et al. (1969) have described the economic benefits arising from immunization against measles. Before the licensing and introduction of measles vaccine in 1963, there were about 4 million cases per year, associated with 4,000 cases of measles encephalitis; of these about one-third led to mental retardation and about 400 died. From 1963 to 1968, use of the vaccine was credited with preventing 9.7 million acute cases at a saving of 32 million schooldays, 1.6 million workdays, and 555,000 hospital days. More importantly, 973 lives were saved and 3,244 cases of mental retardation prevented. In addition, over $423 million in costs were averted, at a cost per administered dose of about $3.

The prime example of a successful vaccination program is the worldwide campaign against smallpox. D. A. Henderson, formerly Director of the World Health Organization Smallpox Campaign, has pointed out that eradication of smallpox saves the world's governments more than one billion dollars annually. "With vaccination stopped, and with smallpox quarantine measures abolished, the United States alone will recoup in savings, in less than 2½ years, every penny which it has contributed to W.H.O. since it was founded 28 years ago" (quoted in Altman, 1976). This is, of course, in addition to the savings of lives and the prevention of blindness, disfigurement, and other effects of smallpox.

Grab and Cvjetanovic (1971) have produced a nomogram for rough determination of the cost-benefit balance point of immunization programs, useful in the case of cholera, typhoid, tetanus, or other bacterial diseases (where protection is often not so strong nor so long-lasting as with viral vaccines). To use the nomogram, the following data should be available: annual incidence of cases per 10,000 population; cost of treatment per case, by severity if possible; cost of immunization per individual per year; and effectiveness of the vaccine and duration of protection. Grab and Cvjetanovic use their method to reach the following conclusions (among others): In Dakar where the incidence of tetanus is high in the general population, but higher in newborns, a program to immunize pregnant mothers would be far more beneficial than immunizing the whole population. In Yugoslavia, where the incidence of typhoid is low and treatment costs high, the benefit of mass immunization is questionable, while in western Samoa this procedure is beneficial because the incidence is high and treatment costs are lower than in Yugoslavia.

Screening programs have also been analyzed from the cost-benefit viewpoint. Here the question is not *primary* prevention of disease, but the identification of early or inapparent cases already existing so that further pathology can be reduced and a clinical case avoided (i.e., *secondary* prevention). The cost of diagnosing a case is compared to the cost of *not* diagnosing a case. The Massachusetts Department of Public Health (1974) reported on screening of newborns for a battery of disorders including phenylketonuria, galactosemia, maple-syrup urine disease, and six other rare diseases, many of which lead to mental retardation and hospitalization. Considering specimen collection, testing, and treatment of detected individuals, the expenditure of $461,000 averted $825,000 in costs, yielding a saving to the state of $364,000.

Many cost-benefit analyses have been done on water works, including irrigation, hydroelectric, and other schemes. Pyatt and Rogers (1962) studied the money value of municipal water supply improvements in Puerto Rico, taking into account numerous factors including presumed mortality, morbidity, and debility benefits arising from averted deaths, work absences, and production decreases attributable to waterborne disease. Using appropriate discounting, these authors calculated an economic 'break even' point accruing about ten years after vigorous inception of a water supply program, and a long-term ratio of benefits to costs of about 2.5 to 1.

One field in which both costs and benefits are often indeterminable is research. Because of the spillover of knowledge it is impossible to assign the costs of research "on" a specific subject. Nevertheless, an attempt at cost-benefit analysis of polio research has been made by Weisbrod (1971). Considering the avoidance of 36,000 cases annually at $1,350 per case (1957 prices—an extremely low estimate today) and an application cost of $1 to $2 per person, Weisbrod estimated that the most likely rate of return on research expenditures is about 11% to 12% per year, without counting benefits outside the United States.

We cannot enter into a discussion of the enormous literature on costs and benefits of procedures in clinical medicine, including drug therapy and surgery (see Bunker *et al.*, 1977), except to point out that this is an area of active investigation and clashing opinions.

Cost-benefit analyses are useful only when both costs and benefits can be estimated fairly well, and when an appropriate technology exists to absorb the costs and produce the benefits. In the absence of a known way to achieve control, cost-benefit analysis is little more than wishful thinking. Moreover, the cost of a disease must be determined by some rational method. The presence of a disease in an area does not inevitably result in economic loss. Many people were surprised by an analysis of the economic impact of schistosomiasis on the island of St. Lucia in the West Indies. No evidence was found of excess mortality due to this disease, nor of reduced weekly labor productivity of workers having the infection. The academic performance of school children with schistosomiasis was equal to that of their uninfected classmates, and it was found that children who were passing schistosome eggs were absent *less* from school (Weisbrod et al., 1973). Undeniably, schistosomiasis is extremely important in Egypt, Brazil, and other countries where severe economic losses occur. In St. Lucia, if infection rates and intensities remain low, the allocation of large amounts of money for control of this disease may not be warranted.

Cost-benefit analyses suffer from several drawbacks that limit their usefulness as a guide to decisions on health policy. Many published analyses are retrospective, describing and perhaps justifying past programs, so that they become defensive tools of health planners. Moreover, as we have seen, costs and benefits can not really be quantified. In the example of metabolic screening of newborns, a positive cost-benefit ratio depends upon the prior existence of buildings and laboratories, the means of shipping specimens, and the total related infrastructure. How can this be accounted for in the calculations? The same screening program, using the same methods, in Chad or New Guinea would certainly not be cost-beneficial.

Another important consideration is given too little attention by health planners: Any procedure, however useful, has drawbacks and side effects. This introduces into the equation a third factor, risk. The costs averted by applying a procedure must be balanced against the risk averted by not doing it. Surgeons and physicians encounter this equation daily in dealing with individual patients, but public health planners do not often face the risk factor. The decision by the U.S. Public Health Service to terminate routine childhood smallpox vaccination was based upon an increasingly negative benefit-risk ratio. Vaccination carries a small but calculable risk (about 12.3 per million) of vaccinial encephalitis with possible permanent brain damage, and death may occur once per million vaccinations (Lane et al., 1969, 1970). As the world smallpox threat is declining and no known case had been brought into the U.S. since 1949, the risks of vaccination were finally judged greater than the

POLICY

Table 6-7. Deaths from respiratory tuberculosis in selected countries, per 100,000 population, 1947 and 1967

Country	Deaths per 100,000 population 1947	Deaths per 100,000 population 1967	Percentage decrease in death rate 1947–1967
Australia	27.5	2.1	92.4
Canada	36.8	3.0	91.8
Denmark	24.4	1.5[a]	93.9[b]
Ireland	95.3	7.3	92.3
Netherlands	26.2	1.1	95.8
Norway	46.1	3.2[a]	93.1[b]
United States	31.0	3.2	89.7

[a]For 1966.
[b]For 1947–1966.
Source: United Nations, 1973.

risk of introduction of smallpox in the absence of a vaccination program. In Britain, Bradney (1976) has described the extent of vaccine-induced damage to children. From whooping cough (pertussis) immunization alone, he reports 56 cases of brain damage from 1969 through 1974, a period in which 64 deaths were attributed to this cause. The total number of vaccine-damaged children in Britain was estimated at 500 to 1,000, although this is a matter of dispute. A second example of declining cost-benefit ratios is in mass miniature radiography for detection of tuberculosis. Recent decades have seen a rapid decline in tuberculosis cases and deaths (Table 6-7) in developed countries. The diminishing detection of new cases, the possibility of radiation-induced damage in some persons being screened, the inherent insensitivity of the procedure and the development of newer types of chemotherapy all combined to reverse the cost-benefit ratio of this screening procedure. Cost-benefit analysis is thus seen as a tool to terminate as well as to introduce health programs.

Cost-effectiveness analysis

Cost-benefit analysis, at home in the corporate boardroom, is a means for identifying maximum return on investment. Cost-beneficial programs should of course be promoted by health planners, but their investment decisions must also be based on a determination of social needs. The aim of health planning is the achievement of certain policy goals for improvement of the health of the population. Once these are determined (often by forces outside the health establishment), planners must find the best means to reach them—for this purpose the tool of cost-effectiveness analysis is sometimes proposed. In this type of analysis a decision is made as to the best way to spend a given sum in order to achieve a particular goal.

An illustration of the use of cost-effectiveness analysis is offered by Levin (1968), whose policy objective was (among other things) to reduce infant mortality while making maternal and child health services acceptable in "health-depressed" areas in the United States. Various programs were considered with respect to the number of infant lives likely to be saved per $10 million spent. Levin concluded that "a program to expand family planning services to reach an additional one-half million women... would be about five and a half times as cost-effective in reducing yearly infant deaths as a program to provide intensive-care units for high-risk newborn infants."

Cost-effectiveness analysis can sometimes guide policy decisions in very specific ways. Klarman, Francis, and Rosenthal (1968) attempted by this means to answer the question, "Under existing conditions of knowledge regarding the cost and end-results of treating patients with chronic renal disease, what is the best mix of center dialysis, home dialysis and kidney transplantation?" The basic parameters were these: in the United States each year there were about 6,000 deaths from end-stage renal disease, and only about 10% of these cases had received any of the stated treatments. A transplant at that time cost $13,000, dialysis $5,000 per year at home, and $14,000 per year at a center. No other treatment modalities were known, and chronic cases proceeded to death. No means of prevention were known.

An interesting aspect of this analysis is that a relative numerical value was given to the *quality* of life gained by two methods: a year of life after transplantation was equated with 1.2 years on dialysis (a notoriously depressing procedure). Considering all of the relevant aspects, including the demographic characteristics of patients and transplant failure rates, the authors concluded that transplantation was the more cost-effective alternative. Therefore research funds would be better invested in study of donor kidney preservation and similar details than in improved dialysis technology.

Most decisions in public policy must take account of a complex of societal factors in addition to cost-effectiveness alone. Consider two equally reliable methods of reading blood smears to determine the prevalence of malaria in a tropical developing country. A newly developed computer-based microscopic pattern recognition device, imported from an industrialized country, can read 500 smears daily. It costs $50,000 a year, including service contract, power supply, air-conditioned room, and personnel. Ten locally trained technicians can each read 50 smears a day, at a total cost of $50,000 annually, including laboratory supplies. There are advantages and drawbacks to each method, but basically the cost and work output of the machine and the men are equivalent. Which option should be selected? Many people think that under these circumstances the choice should be the more labor-intensive methodology, which provides a livelihood for ten families while supplying a product of acceptable standard within the resources of the country. This is one basis of appropriate, or intermediate, technology, a concept that has been gaining numerous adherents in recent years (primarily it may be noted, in the more developed countries).

HOW MUCH IS ENOUGH?

We have seen that some programs, such as routine childhood smallpox vaccination in the United States, reached a negative cost-benefit balance and were then terminated. It is often a more difficult matter to know when the societal goals of a program have been achieved so that money and effort can be devoted to other ends. For example, can the infant mortality rate ever become too low?

Before giving a categorical negative answer to this question, we must look at the causes, consequences, and control of infant mortality. As we saw in Chapter 4, deaths in the first year of life are classified by statisticians as neonatal or postneonatal deaths, depending on whether they occur in the first 28 days or in the remaining days of the year. Neonatal deaths are often caused by congenital anomalies, prematurity, and trauma at delivery. Postneonatal deaths more commonly occur in infants, healthy at birth, who are subject to malnutrition, infection, and poor environmental conditions. The ratios of neonatal to postneonatal, or of neonatal to total infant deaths are sometimes used to compare countries; those with a very high proportion of very early infant deaths are considered to have the best socioeconomic conditions. We have seen that socioeconomic development is often accompanied by a rapid decline in infant mortality, most of which is in the postneonatal period. In the process, expenditures attributable to health services in the broad sense are largely in the areas of promotion and prevention: water supply, sanitation, immunization, maternal care and education, and so on, which are low or very low on a per capita basis. In terms of added years of life, these expenditures in LDCs are highly cost-beneficial and cost-effective (Table 6-8).

In developed countries where infant mortality rates are already very low, a different picture is found, and early infant deaths predominate. Some further reductions in infant deaths may be achieved by improving prenatal care: better nutrition; education to reduce use of tobacco, alcohol, and other drugs; and careful maternal monitoring. Some may result from better delivery room techniques, but there is a residue of cases resulting from genetic defects or developmental anomalies whose rescue may require heroic medical effort. As clinical expertise and technology improve, an increasing proportion of such births becomes salvageable. Life support systems can maintain many infants, who formerly would have died, until they can manage on their own. Some may survive with handicaps, either correctable by surgery or requiring lengthy (or permanent) medical care. Some may pull through and develop normally, but these individuals may carry genes that will necessitate similar medical efforts 20 years later. Dependence upon medical technology, which is

Table 6-8. Infant mortality rates for selected developing countries or areas, per 1,000 live births, 1935–39 and 1960–64

Country	Average annual rates 1935–1939	Average annual rates 1960–1964	Percentage decline	Average decennial percentage decline
Ceylon	182	54[a]	70	28
China (Taiwan)	144	28	81	32
Costa Rica	144	73	49	20
El Salvador	125	70	44	18
Jamaica	127	48	62	25
Malaysia	149	58	61	24
Mauritius	151	61	60	24
Puerto Rico	123	45	63	25
Singapore	152	31	80	32
Trinidad and Tobago	104	41	60	24

[a]Four-year average.
Source: United Nations, 1973.

viewed by some as interfering with the selective processes of evolution, can be fostered. The struggle for ever-greater minimization of infant mortality also involves genetic counseling, fetal monitoring, amniocentesis, and therapeutic abortion, and such indirect steps as immunization against rubella. The remaining stubborn core of deaths becomes a subject of ever more complex research. Clearly, the cost per life saved now increases very rapidly, and some would argue that the average quality of saved lives also declines. Is there a point at which society is willing to accept a certain level of infant deaths in order to devote the resultant savings to other purposes? In other words, how do we handle the problem of *marginal benefits?*

Most expenditures in the health sector are not in the form of large amounts of money devoted to special new programs, but rather as some more to this or less to that existing service. Economists use the concept of margins as a fundamental tool in many fields—how much benefit will accrue from a given *additional* expenditure. This concept has been discussed for health expenditures by Fuchs, who points out the difference between the economist's, and the health professional's view of the "optimum" level of health:

For the health professional, the "optimum" level is the highest level technically attainable, regardless of the cost of reaching it. The economist is preoccupied with the *social optimum,* however, which he defines as the point at which the value of an additional increment of health exactly equals the cost of the resources required to obtain that increment. For instance, the first few days of hospital stay after major surgery might be extremely valuable for preventing complications and assisting recovery, but at some point the value of each additional day decreases. As soon as the value of an additional day falls below the cost of that day's care, according to the concept of social optimum, the patient should be discharged. (Fuchs, 1974)

On a global scale the reduction in infant mortality discussed above is paralleled by reductions in mortality at other ages also. Figure 6-3 shows a series of survivorship curves that span approximately the entire range of human population experience. The mortality experienced by India early in the present century lies near the maximum sustainable by a human population, even with high fertility. The mortality projections for Swedish females born in 1974 are the lowest for any human population. Per thousand live births, about the same number would survive to age 1 for Indian males in 1901–11, as to age 70 for Swedish females in 1974. (The mid-1970s world average survivorship curve approximates line 6.) It

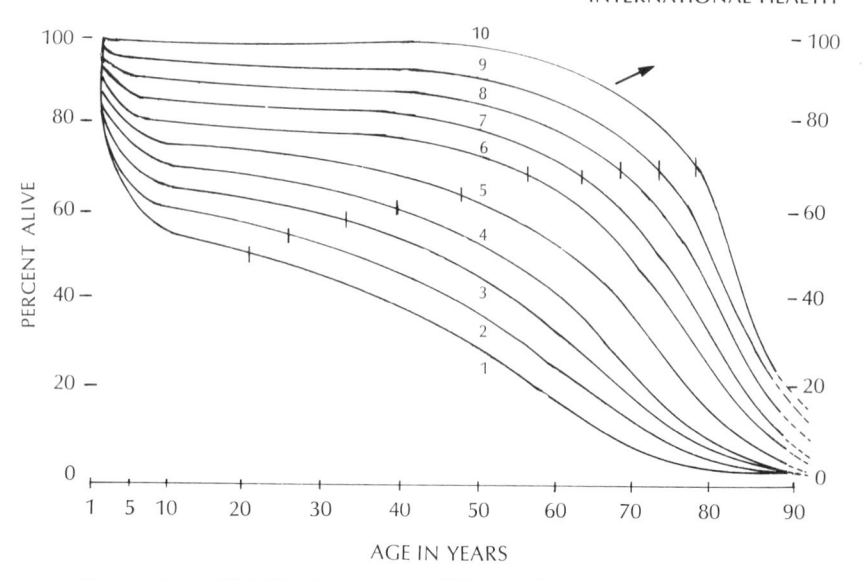

Figure 6-3

Survivorship curves, by age and sex, selected countries, 1861–1974. SOURCES: United Nations, 1955; Preston et al., 1972; World Health Organization, 1976. The small vertical bars on each line represent the expectation of life at birth.

1. India, Male, 1901-1911. (Expectation of life at birth, 22.59 years)
2. Guatemala, Male, 1921. (25.59 years)
3. Mexico, Male, 1930. (33.02 years)
4. England and Wales, Male, 1861. (40.47 years)
5. Guatemala, Male, 1964. (48.51 years)
6. England and Wales, Male, 1921. (55.94 years)
7. Venezuela, Male, 1964. (63.74 years)
8. Netherlands, Male, 1947-49. (69.40 years)
9. Sweden, Male, 1964. (75.93 years)
10. Sweden, Female, 1974. (78.10 years)

seems possible for any population eventually to approach or perhaps surpass line 10, moving the curve in the direction of the arrow. The policy question is: Where shall we set our goals, and how much are we willing to pay (i.e., what else are we willing to give up) to achieve them? The economic questions are: How much will it cost? How can sufficient money be obtained? And how should the expenditures be allocated?

Both the policy and the economic questions are clouded by uncertainty, in part because we do not know how much of the increases in life span (or reductions in mortality) illustrated in Figure 6-3 are due to general socioeconomic developments, to behavior patterns and ways of life, to the effects of health services, or to other factors. Within the health services sector, we do not know how much is attributable to each element. Despite the analyses detailed on the preceding pages, the alliance between economics and health may be more of a shotgun wedding than an undying romance. As Abel-Smith (1972) has observed:

> In this brave new world where emphasis is on quantitative planning, the health sector is often regarded as a backward, underdeveloped area. Indeed, there is a tendency for the economic planner to treat the health planner as a dunce, ignorant as he often is of econometrics and innocent of regression analysis.... It is because the doctor often suspects the economist of being incapable of thinking beyond economic criteria that the dialogue between [them] is so often unfruitful.

And, as if in confirmation, Hilleboe and colleagues (1972) have called into question the utility of the analytic method:

> One country, proceeding in an openly pragmatic fashion, may go on making value and fact judgements one after another. Another may base decisions on extensive, but inappropriate, data and analysis, or may systematically gather considerable data and then, in the last analysis, base decisions upon relatively unsupported judgements. The apparently scientific character of the most systematic methodologies for health planning has considerable appeal, yet their techniques for analysing social and political factors, which experience indicates are of critical importance, are substantially the same as those of pragmatic planners. It cannot be stated categorically that systematic planning is better than pragmatic planning.

Even though it is difficult to determine the best basis for making decisions in the health sector, we can ask whether most health services are doing a good job at their assigned tasks. Are health resources within countries utilized on a problem-solving basis, with different mixes of preventive, curative, promotive, and rehabilitative services? Which medical interventions are truly effective and specific? Can these be described so that the necessary skill and knowledge for their application can be assessed? Can a health care system be designed to carry out the tasks to reach the greatest proportion of persons at risk, as early as possible, at the least cost, and in an acceptable manner? These questions have been asked by the Director-General of the World Health Organization (Mahler, 1975) who observed that persons outside the health establishment might "even express astonishment at these questions because many fondly assume that their health services *are* designed to deal with problems; the interventions they pay for *are* known to be effective and appropriate; and the person who is responsible for the medical care they receive *is* the appropriate person in training and position for their needs. Such is not the case" (emphasis in original).

The Effectiveness of Medical Expenditures

Because all mortals are fallible, we should look for evidence to support this rather gloomy opinion, even though it comes from a leader in world health. One place to look is in the correlation between the amounts of money spent on health care and the level of health in various countries. For ten countries in Europe and North America, Table 6-9 lists the annual health expenditures per capita and the corresponding percentage of GNP devoted to health services in 1968–69, and it also ranks the same countries by several age- and sex-specific mortality rates. Even after allowing for differences in definition of health service expenditure, the correlation is poor. This general type of analysis led the participants in a WHO interregional seminar on Health Economics (World Health Organization, 1975) to conclude that "there is no predictable relationship between improved health on the one hand and the amount or cost of resources used in producing health services on the other. For instance, the indicators for one Latin American country show no improvement in health over the past decade in spite of a high and increasing ratio of physicians and hospital beds to population." As a general observation it seems that a given increment in health expenditure will yield benefits roughly in inverse proportion to the level of socioeconomic development of the beneficiary. In view of this apparent discrepancy we can ask whether in some countries health problems are simply more expensive than in others (which is possible), whether in some countries money is being spent unproductively (which is likely), and whether there are other societal goals being bought besides reduction of mortality and morbidity (which is probable).

In very poor countries where basic needs are unmet, money spent for promotive, protective, and primary care services results in relatively large and rapid improvements in health indicators and has significant external benefits (to the community at large). Poor people usually have inexpensive possessions, and this includes their illnesses. Hookworm, cholera, and amebiasis cost very little to get, compared with a sports-car accident, a transplant rejection, or even ischemic heart disease. Diseases cheaply acquired may also be relatively cheaply prevented. Although capital investments in water supply and sewerage systems are high, we have seen that their long useful life can make them very cost-beneficial to users from a health standpoint alone, not to mention the accompanying improvement in the standard of living. With advancing development and *per capita* income, most of the problems attributable to malnutrition, poor

Table 6-9. Rank order of health expenditure and of selected mortality rates, ten countries, around 1968–69

	Expenditures		Mortality rates[a]					
					Men		Women	
	Per capita amount	As % of GNP	Infant	Maternal	35–44	45–54	35–44	45–54
U.S.A.	1	1	7	5	9	9	10	10
Sweden	2	2	1	1	2	1	2	1
Netherlands	5	3	2	3	1	2	1	2
Fed. Rep. Germany	3	4	8	9	6	5	9	6
France	4	4	5	6	8	8	6	4
Austria	[b]	6	9	8	7	7	8	8
Italy	7	7	10	10	5	3	3	3
Finland	[b]	8	3	2	10	10	4	5
United Kingdom[c]	6	9	4	3	3	4	5	7
Rep. Ireland	8	[b]	6	7	4	6	7	9

[a]Lower number = lower rate.
[b]Unavailable.
[c]Expenditures given as "United Kingdom"; Mortality rates as "England and Wales."
Source: Adapted from Maxwell, 1974.

sanitation, and other manifestations of poverty decline and health dollars (or pesos or rupees) are increasingly spent to improve the quality, rather than the quanity, of life.

A key element in this discussion lies in the definition of medical care. An oversimplified analysis might look like this: There seems to be some central cluster of practices and procedures essential to maintaining or restoring good health—professional advice, laboratory testing, the prescribing and taking of medicines, surgery, and the like—whose application is highly cost-beneficial and cost-effective. This essential core is embedded within a far broader area replete with practices and procedures that are very similar in appearance but that cost more than their social value. These peripheral elements of medical care may be sought to relieve anxiety or uncertainty, or for a variety of purposes considered of value by the persons concerned, but they are not really essential for health.

If the total amount of expenditures now classified under "health care" or "medical care" somehow could be separated into essential and peripheral (i.e., truly necessary versus socially desirable), the apparent discrepancies in Table 6-9 might be substantially resolved. Considering this problem with reference to hysterectomy in the United States, Bunker, McPherson, and Henneman (1977) have concluded, "There are no data on what proportion of women, on the balance, are benefited by elective hysterectomy. While the benefits are unmeasured and uncertain, the costs are large. These costs are rarely paid by the patient. Society, if it is to pay the costs, must decide whether to allocate public funds for a procedure if it appears to be more of a convenience or luxury than a necessity." A similar statement might be made for many other medical procedures in the United States and, to an extent, in other developed countries. It is important, however, to recognize that money spent for medical care is not intentionally squandered by the patient, or intentionally expended for unproductive trivia. The vast majority of persons seek to obtain the best possible value in medical care as in other types of expenditures. Why, then, does the recognizable benefit derived from the medical care enterprise correlate so poorly with the costs involved? Why do different individuals and different countries buy different amounts of health for the same amount of money? Part of the answer lies in distinguishing central from peripheral aspects of medical care.

There are at least five interconnected factors. First, the "health market" uses money differently from the more familiar market of goods and services. For personal medical care in particular, the patient (i.e., the consumer) has very little control over how his or her money is spent. Whereas a television set or a theater ticket can be bought now or delayed with little consequence, an accident or illness may require medical care at any moment. Once the decision has been made by (or forced upon) a person to enter the medical system, someone else then decides upon further expenditures. Decisions about diagnostic tests, surgery, medicines, return visits and many other costly "purchases" are made not by the consumer but by the physician. Moreover, the choice of grade, size, quality, and cost per item, usually available to the consumer, is also absent. The consumer is not only essentially powerless to control expenditures but often ignorant of the need for the particular item in the first place. Most importantly, however, it is generally impossible after the money has been spent to tell whether the expenditure was necessary, useful, or even harmful. The dissatisfied customer in wealthier countries may try to find another physician, but he is likely to encounter much the same level of service. The medical profession, by dominating education and licensure, maintains not only uniformity of standards, but also control of prescriptions and use of facilities. In attempting to cure, or to satisfy the patient, the physician may not place first priority upon the cost of doing so. This general situation is found in many countries regardless of the form of government.

Second, the money spent or allocated by the physician is often third-party money, from an insurance company or a government program, to be described in detail in the next chapter. Hence, neither the patient nor the physician may have an incentive to save. In fact, both may have strong motivations for overusage: the patient because it "doesn't cost me anything," and the physician "to provide the maximum level of services." The policies of the impersonal third-party payer therefore become very important in controlling expenditures, and the forces that determine those policies assume a decisive position.

Third, varying amounts of money charged to health services may go to purposes having no health benefit. To name a few: useless, highly peripheral procedures ("placebo technology"), high incomes and profits, beautiful buildings, graft and corruption, error and inefficiency, inordinate bureaucracies, and premiums for malpractice insurance absorb substantial amounts of health expenditures in different countries.

Fourth, money is not the only resource to be considered. Where money is not limiting, time may be. Many people in the United States and elsewhere do not hesitate to pay money in exchange for convenience. The use of preprocessed food products, for instance, instead of preparation "from scratch" is justified on the basis of saved time. So is spending more money to have more doctors, rather than spending time waiting or traveling.

The final and most pervasive reason is that health services reflect the characteristics and values of the societies of which they are a part, and the use made of health resources is really determined by cultural and political factors rather than by rational allocation on any basis.

Table 6-10 shows the total number of years and years of working life that would be added in various circumstances if specific causes of death were eliminated. In the U.S. population of 1964, the number of working years per capita lost to cancer was equal to that lost to motor vehicle accidents, less than the number lost to other violence, and less than half the loss attributable to cardiovascular diseases. If investment priorities guided research needs, one might imagine that expenditures for control of these causes of death would be about in proportion to the economic losses caused. However in 1969, U.S. federal outlays for research on cancer were $170 million; heart and lung, $142 million; and mental health, $108 million. By 1974 the amounts were: cancer, $350 million; heart and lung, $234 million; mental health, $116 million. In that year, federally supported cancer research amounted to $1,019 per cancer death and cardiovascular disease research was $293 per cardiovascular death (National Planning Association, 1974). Automobile safety research expenditure was presumably very much less.

Note in Table 6-10 that elimination of all the listed causes of death for the U.S. population of 1964 would have added only 3.5 years to the length of the average working life but 23.7 years to the total expectation of life. For Chile 1964, corresponding figures are 4.1 and 15.8; for Guatemala, 5.2 and 16.5; for Sweden, 1.3 and 15.1, etc. The effect of these changes is of course not to lengthen the total life span but to change the shape of relevant survivorship curves of the type shown in Figure 6-3. Pulling the curve in the direction of the arrow will flatten the slope for the portion under 65 (thus increasing the mean working life) and raise the expectation of life at early ages. The total resource cost for proceeding from each curve on Figure 6-3 to the next becomes progressively greater, as *appropriate* expenditures on health come closer and closer to achieving attainable goals. The increase in appropriate resource costs may be compared to the decay of an isotope of a given half-life. A given investment of time (or expenditure) will see a certain reduction in activity (or mortality). A second identical investment will result in perhaps half the amount of reduction, a third investment in a quarter of the original effect,

Table 6-10. Added years of life[a], and of working life[a], if specific causes of death were eliminated, by sex, selected countries, various years, 1861 to 1964

Country	Year	Sex	Exp. of life[b]	Influenza, pneumonia, bronchitis	Diarrhea	Respiratory tuberculosis	Other infectious and parasitic diseases	Neoplasms	Cardio-vascular diseases	Motor vehicles	Other violence
England[c]	1861	M	40.5	3.5 *0.8*	1.5 *0.2*	3.4 *3.3*	5.2 *1.0*	0.2 *0.1*	1.9 *1.1*	0.0 *0.0*	1.4 *1.0*
Guatemala	1964	M	48.5	4.3 *1.0*	3.5 *0.6*	0.6 *0.4*	5.2 *1.4*	0.4 *0.2*	1.0 *0.4*	0.2 *0.2*	1.3 *1.0*
Chile	1964	M	55.8	3.6 *0.3*	1.2 —	1.0 *0.6*	1.1 *0.1*	1.8 *0.5*	4.4 *0.9*	0.2 *0.1*	2.5 *1.6*
U.S.A. (NonW)	1950	M	58.6	1.2 *0.2*	0.2 —	1.1 *0.7*	0.8 *0.3*	1.5 *0.5*	11.4 *2.2*	0.7 *0.5*	2.3 *1.4*
U.S.A. (Total)	1964	M	66.9	0.6 *0.1*	0.1 *0.1*	0.1 —	0.1 —	2.3 *0.6*	18.3 *1.4*	0.9 *0.6*	1.3 *0.7*
England[c]	1964	M	68.6	1.6 *0.2*	0.1 —	0.1 —	0.1 —	2.8 *0.7*	8.4 *1.0*	0.5 *0.3*	0.7 *0.3*
Japan	1964	F	73.0	0.6 *0.1*	0.3 —	0.3 *0.1*	0.2 —	2.2 *0.6*	6.1 *0.5*	0.2 *0.1*	0.7 *0.2*
Sweden	1964	F	75.9	0.5 —	0.1 —	— —	0.1 —	2.8 *0.6*	10.9 *0.3*	0.2 *0.1*	0.5 *0.2*

[a] Ages 15–65, given attainment of age 15 (in italics).
[b] Expectation of life at birth.
[c] And Wales.
Source: Adapted from data of Preston et al., 1972.

and so on in increasing diminution. While this analogy is imperfect, it does illustrate the kind of limits involved. The important question that any society must ask itself is: how much are we willing to spend for a given increment in the survivorship curve, and what is the quality of life in the years added?

FACING THE TOUGH ISSUES

Despite the great scientific advances of the past century, there exists all over the world a widespread dissatisfaction with the available health services. In the poorest countries, people are increasingly aware that their overwhelming problems are not foreordained. They see not only that the means for improvement are at hand, but that they can seize the major role in determining their own destinies. Julius Nyerere, president of Tanzania, has said that "change is inevitable in the modern world.... The only choice for any society is whether to change of its own volition, seeking its own chosen direction, or whether to be changed by choices and decisions made by others elsewhere." Better health is seen as both a goal and a manifestation of progress, and the current situation is clearly unacceptable. The wealthy countries are faced with skyrocketing expenses and waning confidence in their medical establishments. Everyone seems to need guidance in determining and implementing policies, but the principles for doing this seem too often to be just beyond reach.

One difficulty is that the range of health problems is as broad as the variety of national experiences. Declining mortality and increasing expectation of life are accompanied by a change in the causal pattern for illness and death in a population, usually characterized by growing detachment from the tyranny of microbes (Fig. 6-1). Health services then need to devote less attention to mass campaigns against infectious and parasitic disease and gross malnutrition. Emphasis can shift towards more personal services: diagnosis, validation, reassurance, alleviation, and cure. Unit costs increase, productivity declines. Most countries have areas or populations at disparate levels of development, requiring different, decentralized services, each capable of change in unpredictable directions. Politics, tradition, resources, and needs are everywhere different. Can any general guiding principles be found? Of course. We can, for instance, learn from critics about how *not* to do things. In recent years every aspect of medical care has come under scrutiny, but two general types of concerns are appearing to crystallize: the appropriateness of medical procedures, and the distribution of medical care.

The appropriateness of medical procedures

Technology In its most common and simplest form, the controversy over investment and return in health care centers on the costs and benefits of high technology. Shapiro and Wyman (1976) have provided a useful case study—"CAT fever," whose "predominant symptom appears as a feverish impulse to own, operate, exploit or write about... Computerized Axial Tomography." This is a technique for x-ray scanning of part or all of the body that produces cross-sectional images and can often replace such invasive techniques as pneumoencephalography. Brody (1976) reported that as of May of that year 19 manufacturers "were competing for the attention and dollars of diagnostic radiologists and medical institutions whose imaginations have been captured...." Each machine then cost $400,000 to $700,000 plus expenses of space and personnel, and technical developments promise rapid obsolescence and reduction in price. CAT is, of course, only a diagnostic tool, helping to define certain problems in people who are already patients. There is no foreseeable limit on the devices engineers can design or the amount of information that might possibly be of use to a physician. The question of marginal benefits has been asked so often about the products of high technology that the National Health Planning and Resources Development Act of 1974 (PL 93–641) of the U.S. Congress requires all states to regulate their proliferation by establishing "Certificate of Need" programs for hospitals.

Not only has expensive hardware been criticized as wasteful, but so have many other features of modern health care systems: the annual medical checkup, clinical laboratory tests, certain categories of surgery, intensive and coronary care units, the prescribing of drugs, and the deployment of highly trained medical personnel for routine duties. Many people question the economic or moral value of heroic efforts to postpone the inevitable death of terminally ill patients. A pioneering law has recently given residents of California the specific right to refuse, in advance, such treatment for themselves—surely a consequence of growing public awareness of questions of health policy.

If excessive and unneeded technology constitutes one horn of a dilemma, then insufficient application of appropriate technology represents the other. In an extended study of the interactions of science and technology with U.S. foreign policy, a congressional committee has recently reported that

> half of the world's people have no access to health care at all; millions die each year of readily preventable sicknesses. There is even some retrogression as the

effects of urban blight strike the slum poor in the midst of affluence. Against this dismal picture of underachievement must be seen a great and growing array of unused and underused technical capabilities for controlling disease and building health. The issue is how to advance world health through programs utilizing these capabilities supported by the combined efforts of diplomats, scientists, and the public. (U.S. House of Representatives, 1976)

Even the most sanctified of all health-related activities, medical research, has its detractors, often within the establishment. An unfortunate but deep cleavage exists between "basic" research which is pure and prestigious, and "applied" research, which is practical and somehow tainted. Basic research has historically been highly cost-beneficial, and future benefits of today's investigations are impossible to estimate. This does not mean, however, that expenditures for medical research, like any other expenditures, should not be evaluated against the best available standards. "The tremendous burst of public investment in medical research in the 1950s and 1960s was an expression of the people's faith in their miracle workers," said King (1974): "Unfortunately, that faith was largely misplaced. Encouraging society to 'expect a miracle' resulted first in rising expectations and more recently in increasing disenchantment."

Work on social or behavioral aspects of health has not achieved status or legitimacy in the view of many basic medical scientists, who are concerned with the "how" of disease processes (or with basic biology) rather than the "why" of illness. This is even true in many developing countries, where public health hazards are much more prominent.

Few countries, especially poor ones, have a national research policy. Some, such as China, have decided that efforts should be devoted first to the most common diseases and that research should include not only biological aspects but the means of motivating and mobilizing the public to combat illness and promote health.

Relevance Excessive costs for "the otherwise laudable pursuit of quality" (World Health Organization, 1975) are not just a phenomenon of the richer countries. Elaborate showpiece hospitals, with the latest medical instrumentation, have been built in Africa and Asia, frequently with foreign donor capital. Unfortunately, shortages of trained staffs and operating budgets have too often resulted in underutilization and rapid deterioration both of buildings and equipment. Nor have medical schools in developing countries been immune from criticism. Bryant (1969) writes:

The more advanced nations have exported philosophies of medical care and education of health personnel that have focused on high quality care of individual patients. The less developed countries have accepted these as standard, have been proud of their own capability to match them, and have been reluctant to deviate from them... Educators of health personnel in the more advanced countries have generally not appreciated the extent to which their educational systems do not fit the needs of the developing world... The failures of this philosophy have been serious and widespread.

Behrhorst (1975) has provided his own list of priorities that must be tackled aggressively "before health can supplant disease among the 2,000 million rural poor of the world...."

1. Social and economic injustice
2. Land tenure
3. Agricultural production and marketing
4. Population control
5. Malnutrition
6. Health training
7. Curative medicine

Can allegations about the irrelevance or counterproductiveness of certain medical procedures be evaluated, and can strategies be devised to correct deficiencies? One general methodology has been advocated by A. L. Cochrane (1972), who suggests a wider application of the randomized controlled trial (RCT), a technique which allocates subjects on a statistically randomized basis to one or another group to assess the value of some procedure or intervention. Randomized controlled trials have been used to evaluate the effectiveness and efficiency of many modalities in prevention, diagnosis, and treatment, particularly in determination of drug regimens. "The general scientific problem with which we are primarily concerned is that of testing a hypothesis that a certain treatment alters the natural history of a disease for the better" (Cochrane, 1972). It is certainly correct that the scientific method often calls for application of the RCT to pressing problems in the field of medical care, and of health services in general, but it is equally true that researchers who may wish to apply this basic decisional tool face many ethical and legal problems. How can a drug or procedure in need of evaluation be withheld from some patients? How should a potentially useful but untried new intervention be tested in man? Can certain procedures be done just as well by paraprofessionals as by physicians? These and many similar questions, often deceptively simple, are of crucial importance to the form and future of health care policies in many countries.

The distribution of medical care

The second main focus of criticism is concerned not with the outcomes of medical care, but with its *distribution*. Here our frame of reference shifts from economics to politics, and the basic text may be found in the preamble to the constitution of the World Health Organization: "The enjoyment of the highest attainable standard of health is one of the fundamental rights of every human being without distinction of race, religion, political belief, economic or social condition . . . Governments have a responsibility for the health of their peoples which can be fulfilled only by the provision of adequate health and social measures."

The basic failing of health services, according to their political critics, is that despite the fine phrases of the World Health Organization constitution, too many people cannot obtain an acceptable quantity and quality of health care. The left says that health care is a right, and therefore everyone is entitled to full and free medical services. The right says that there is no more justification for giving everyone free medical care than for giving free food or shoes. Curiously, both sides seem to agree that, insofar as medical care is concerned, more is better. Problems of effectiveness and efficiency, important to the technical side of health planning, have no relevance to the nub of the political issue: *control* over health resources.

Before exploring these questions further, we must mention one aspect of the "right to health" controversy that should be beyond question: the right *not* to have one's health damaged or destroyed, especially through purposeful, institutionalized violence by one's own government. Although virtually all governments on earth are signatories to the Universal Declaration of Human Rights (". . .No one shall be subjected to torture or to cruel, inhuman or degrading treatment or punishment. . ."), the sad truth is that dozens of countries resort to these means as a matter of national policy. Organizations such as Amnesty International and the United Nations Commission on Human Rights estimate that in the decade 1965–75 about 60 countries officially practiced torture for the primary purpose of repression of opposition. Clearly, where these crimes are carried out the government's commitment to its own perpetuation greatly exceeds any social concerns for the well-being of its citizenry, and any discussion of health services in these countries must recognize, *a priori*, the nature of those in power.

The "right" to health   Is health a "right?" If so, is there a corresponding right to medical care? A claim of right ordinarily "invokes entitlements;

POLICY

and when we speak of entitlements, we mean not those things which it would be nice for people to have, or which they would prefer to have, but which they must have, and which if they do not have they may demand, whether we like it or not." (Fried, 1976) Obviously each citizen cannot demand from society unlimited efforts to reverse the effects of advancing years or to undo every bodily defect. Fried puts forth the notion of "a decent minimum" to reflect some conception of what constitutes tolerable life in general. Even if the decent minimum could be specified, controversy would still flare over whose responsibility it is to achieve and maintain the minimum.

Perhaps health is like happiness as mentioned in the Declaration of Independence of the United States: It is not the thing itself that is an inalienable right, but rather its pursuit. While an individual may pursue happiness alone, however, it is unlikely that the highest attainable standard of health can be pursued without some outside help.

The amount of money and other resources available to the health sector (whether public or private) is everywhere limited, although in the richer countries the totals may be vast. In many poor countries government expenditures *per capita* are so small as to be almost negligible (Table 6-11). How are these resources, in the form of services, to be apportioned among the population? Let us answer: *equally.* Equality of distribution leads to a paradox. If the *amount of resources* per person is to be equally distributed, then the volume of services available to each will not be uniform unless the population is evenly dispersed with respect to access. If the *per capita volume* of services is equally distributed, then it will inevitably cost more to provide them to some than to others. Physical distance, social distance and many other factors serve to destabilize equality of distribution based either on expenditure or accessibility or services *per capita.* In poor countries the cost of providing services to a thinly dispersed rural population may be far more than that for town dwellers. In the Sahel region of West Africa, Imperato (1974) has described a program offering immunization, health education, and some basic medical care to nomadic and sedentary segments of the population in Mali, Mauritania, Senegal, Niger, and Upper Volta. In one campaign for both nomads (Bedouin Arabs and Tuaregs) and sedentary groups in the same topographic zone, it was found that operational costs in terms of man-hours and gasoline were about 11 times higher per recipient for the nomad then for those persons living in permanent settlements. In this case, mobile teams were sent to seek out the persons served, and the direct costs of doing so accrued to the health services; but even if fixed stations are established to offer health care, the cost of transportation,

Table 6-11. Health expenditures in developing countries, about 1971–73

Country	Health budget as percentage of national budget	Health budget as percentage of GNP	Government health expenditures per capita (US$)
Rwanda	8.7	0.8	0.45
Upper Volta[1]	4.8	0.7	0.56
Somalia	6.7	2.0*	1.40
Ethiopia	6.9	0.8	0.67
Burma	6.2	1.1	0.85
Malawi	6.1	0.8*	0.50
Sri Lanka	8.1	3.6*	3.76
Tanzania	6.3	1.5*	1.68
India	4.9	0.9	0.91
Haiti	13.7	0.7*	0.78
Uganda	9.6	1.7*	2.24
Togo	6.5	1.0*	1.51
Central African Republic	8.4	1.9*	2.81
Kenya	6.4	1.7	0.14
Bolivia	3.6	2.0*	3.74
Cameroon	7.8	1.0*	2.02
Liberia	7.4	1.4*	2.90
Sierra Leone	6.2	0.9*	1.95
Thailand	6.0	1.2	2.45
Egypt, Arab Republic of	8.4	1.8*	3.91
Viet-Nam, Republic of	2.3	0.4*	1.00
Philippines	5.4	0.5	1.06
Senegal	9.1	1.4*	3.49
Ghana	7.3	1.3	3.76
Jordan	9.5	2.8	10.10
Congo	6.1	1.8*	4.82
Paraguay	26.4	2.4	6.77
Mozambique	4.9	0.9*	2.47
Korea, Republic of	1.4	0.5	1.33
Syrian Arab Republic	2.6	0.7	2.03
Honduras	7.6	1.3	3.33
Ecuador	2.8	0.3	1.04
El Salvador	12.6	1.5	4.40
Turkey	21.4	2.6	8.21
Algeria	5.3	1.4	4.53
Colombia	10.4	0.6*	2.04
Angola	5.1	1.1*	3.95

Country	Health budget as percentage of national budget	Health budget as percentage of GNP	Government health expenditures per capita (US$)
Malaysia	6.7	2.5	7.18
Dominican Republic	8.6	1.4	7.71
Iran	2.5	0.6*	2.60
Brazil	1.4	0.2*	0.80
Lebanon	3.5	0.6*	3.80
Mexico	5.9	0.4*	2.64
Jamaica	10.0	2.7*	19.54
Yugoslavia	38.2	10.1*	73.75
Romania	5.7	2.5	18.56
South Africa	1.8	0.3*	2.61
Panama	16.7	2.2	16.70
Trinidad and Tobago	7.8	1.8	14.27
Venezuela	18.4	4.1*	43.18

*Calculated by dividing "per capita expenditure" figure in last column by estimates of per capita GNP for 1971, as published in World Bank Atlas, 1973.
[1]GNP extrapolated from 1958.
Source: World Bank, 1975.

lodging, and lost work may dissuade most potential users from obtaining the services offered. In the United States, North Dakota has the greatest density of community hospital beds in relation to its population, 6.4 per thousand people. Yet North Dakota has only 0.9 hospitals per thousand square miles, while Massachusetts has 25 (1973 figures; U.S. House of Representatives, 1975).

Let us then apportion health resources to individuals according to their medical need—that is, the state of their health. But here again we are caught in a dilemma. The greater the need, as in the case of gravely or terminally ill patients, the less may be the likelihood of recovery despite the consumption of substantial resources. It may appear unreasonable to devote to the already hopelessly ill an amount of effort and money that could permit many less serious illnesses to be treated before they progress to an intractable stage or that could be used for disease prevention.

The claim may therefore be made that health care resources should be distributed on the basis of optimal social value, to improve population-based health indicators and provide the greatest good for the greatest number. Once again we encounter difficulties. Just who is to receive the kidney transplant or be connected to the dialysis machine when the demand exceeds the supply, and who is to make the decisions? Which of two premature infants is to be placed in the one available incubator? The infant mortality rate will be the same either way.

Medical care is in fact often rationed by ability to pay. Since ancient times this has seemed to some unjust, and at least the very poorest in many societies have received services from private charities or public funds. Starting in the 1880s, governments in general have underwritten a larger and larger proportion of medical care expenses, often mixed with personal payments (see next chapter). In 1960 the medical historian Henry E. Sigerist wrote:

> One thing is certain, that the *laissez faire* system has failed in the distribution of medical care as it has failed in other fields. This is evidenced by the fact that even in the wealthiest countries large sections of the population remain without adequate medical care, and that billions are wasted through unnecessary illness. There is no escape ... Medical services must be organized. All health work must be planned. A highly differentiated organism cannot function unless all parts cooperate planfully. Competition must be replaced by cooperation. Rugged individualism under such a plan becomes anarchy. Organization is not identical with regimentation, as some conservatives would make us believe.

Many changes have occurred since 1960, not least of which is the gradual acceptance of some ideas that were considered radical extremism at the time Sigerist was writing. The following paragraph, from a 1975 policy paper of the World Bank, may be compared in its essentials with the statement of Sigerist.

> The private market cannot be expected to allocate to health either the amount or the composition of resources that is best from a social perspective. The most critical failure of the market derives from the inability of consumers of health services to choose rationally. This inability is in part a consequence of the extraordinary complexity of medical problems and the consumer's lack of experience as a patient. Market failure also results from the presence of externalities. For example, procedures which held the spread of communicable diseases yield benefits to entire communities and, therefore cannot be chosen properly by individuals acting in their own interest. The health care system possesses many of the characteristics of public utilities. Often the unit producing services (health station, clinic or hospital) must be large relative to the local service area so that effective competition is not possible. For these and other reasons, governments have found it necessary to intervene in the health sector.

Where, then, is the controversy? And who is the villain in the piece? If there exists a right to health, or to health care, there must be someone from whom its fulfillment may be demanded. Therefore an adversary relationship is implicit in the idea of health as a right, whose claiming is viewed by the left as a manifestation of class struggle. The practice of public health involves the political process and, according to Beauchamp (1976), the challenging of some powerful interests in society, which will not readily yield their influence.

Halfdan Mahler has said that by legislation, by training, by organization, and by the way in which health-related interventions are stated and restricted, there has been a progressive "mystification" of medical care, a "gross restriction in the information available and decisions to be made by people outside the health professions, and an unnecessary but inevitable dependency of the population upon the holders of these mysteries." He advocates a reversal of the trend that "is pushing medical action higher up the professional tree." In this view, it makes good social, economic, and professional sense to take the choice of intervention options nearer to the consumer whenever possible, with specific basic skills known in every household. In country after country among the LDCs, there are programs for grass-roots community action, including local training of health promoters and primary care workers, often patterned after the "barefoot doctors" of China (see Chapter 7). These programs will develop in harmony, one hopes, with the professionals now in leading positions in each country, not only in health but in other fields as integrated development proceeds.

The mood is such that if cooperation is not freely given, it will be demanded or circumvented. The militant statement of Ruderman (1972) might raise some eyebrows and then be dismissed as gratuitous complaining:

The sooner physicians accept the fact that they are the servants and not the masters, the sooner they will be able to learn how to live with the politicians—which involves giving a little in order to take a little—and participate more effectively in priority-setting. Having worked alongside physicians in many countries over the past 25 years, I for one feel that the size of the medical ego is itself one of the principal problems in the organization and administration of health services.

When the Director of the Pan American Health Organization says much the same in more diplomatic language, people are more likely to listen:

This needed coordination will not come about painlessly. All of the sectors—education, economics, health, etc.—are accustomed to choosing their own approaches and alternatives. The professions and the scientific disciplines are certain to resist any intrusion into their domains. But it is essential that this resistance be broken down (Acuña, 1975a).

The professional organizations have not, of course, been unaware of these world trends. The World Medical Association in 1963 adopted a document entitled "The Twelve Principles of Social Security and Medical Care," whose points are as follows:

i. The conditions of medical practice in any social security scheme shall be determined in consultation with the representatives of the professional organisations.

ii. Any social security scheme should allow the patient to consult the doctor of his choice, and the doctor to treat only patients of his choice, without the rights of either being affected in any way. The principle of free choice should be applied also in cases where medical treatment or a part of it is provided in treatment centres.

iii. Any system of social security should be open to all licensed doctors; neither the medical profession nor the individual doctor should be forced to take part if they do not so wish.

iv. The doctor should be free to practise his profession where he wishes and also to limit his practice to a given speciality in which he is qualified. The medical needs of the country concerned should be satisfied and the profession, wherever possible, should seek to orient young doctors towards the areas where they are most needed. In cases where these areas are less favourable than others, doctors who go there should be aided so that their equipment is satisfactory and their standard of living is in accordance with their professional responsibilities.

v. The profession should be adequately represented on all official bodies dealing with problems concerning health or disease.

vi. Professional secrecy must be observed by all those who collaborate at any stage of the patient's treatment or in the control thereof. This should be duly respected by authority.

vii. The moral, economic and professional independence of the doctor should be guaranteed.

viii. When the remuneration of medical services is not fixed by direct agreement between doctor and patient proper consideration should be taken of the great responsibility involved in the practice of medicine.

ix. The remuneration of medical services should take into consideration the services rendered and should not entirely be fixed according to the financial status of the paying authority or as a result of unilateral government decisions and should be acceptable to the agency which represents the medical profession.

x. Control in medical matters should be carried out by doctors only.

xi. In the higher interest of the patient there should be no restriction of the doctor's right to prescribe drugs or any other treatment deemed necessary.
xii. The doctor should have the opportunity of participating in any activity directed toward improving his knowledge and status in his professional life. (from Gilder, 1972)

More recently the World Medical Association has taken note of changes in public attitude and the increasing demand for medical care as a right. Its Secretary-General has written that, in view of this change in perspective worldwide, "The concern of organised medicine should be to achieve a reasonably smooth transition from the old to the new without sacrificing the quality of medical care, either from the human or the scientific point of view" (Gilder, 1972).

Change in health care systems, whether slow or fast, evolutionary or revolutionary, is inevitable. Certain general trends are appearing in the world that may be accepted a generation hence as the norm. These must be acknowledged and somehow incorporated in the mix of power and value conflicts, theoretical guidance, and institutional reality that is eventually translated into health policy:

1. *Health services are rapidly expanding the technical and social limits of their concerns.* In developed countries pervasive technology forces the evaluation of immediate and long-term effects of numerous potential hazards. Less developed countries recognize the retarding effect of illness upon national unity and development. Health services everywhere are becoming more closely integrated with other sectors of society and more comprehensive in: (a) the kinds of workers accepted into the system; (b) a change from medical care of the sick towards overall public and community health problems; and (c) shift from a purely biological to a biological-environmental-social approach, with renewed attention to the dignity of individuals.

2. *Health services are coming under increasing scrutiny.* Governments, nonhealth professionals, and the public are coming to demand results both in demonstrably better health and in more equitable access to care by the entire population as *quid pro quo* for their continued acceptance of the burgeoning costs of the health sector. Some of the most basic assumptions of health planners are being challenged or even contradicted. These include: (a) the primacy of health care systems centered upon hospitals; (b) the necessity for highly trained professionals to do many tasks; (c) the emphasis upon disease treatment and relative neglect of prevention; (d) the view of disease as a biomedical phenomenon only, with corresponding biotechnological responses to all health-related problems.

In the next chapter we will look more closely at the ways in which medical care systems actually function.

References

Abel-Smith, B. 1972. Health priorities in developing countries: the economist's contribution. International Journal of Health Services 2: 5–12.
Acuña, H. 1975. Foreword to Pan American Health Organization Scientific Publication 297 (see Conly, 1975).
Acuña, H. 1975a. Teaming up for health. Pan American Health 7(3/4): 4–5.
Altman, L. K. 1976. New viral epidemic viewed as contained. New York Times. Nov. 21.
Anon. 1974. Dangerous lymph node syndrome found in Hawaii. Journal of the American Medical Association 229: 1030.
Axnick, N. W., S. M. Shavell, and J. J. Witte. 1969. Benefits due to immunization against measles. Public Health Reports 84: 673–680.
Barker, D. J. P. 1973. Practical Epidemiology. London. Churchill Livingstone. 168 p.
Beauchamp, D. E. 1976. Public health as social justice. Inquiry 13: 3–14.
Behrhorst, C. 1975. The Chimaltenango development project in Guatemala. *In:* K. W. Newell, Ed. Health By the People. Geneva. World Health Organization. pp. 30–52.
Bradney, D. 1976. The vaccine damage campaign. New Scientist 70: 404–406.
Brody, J. E. 1976. Popular new x-ray unit could raise cost of care. New York Times. May 8.
Bryant, J. 1969. Health and the Developing World. Ithaca. Cornell University Press. 345 p.
Bunker, J. P., B. A. Barnes, and F. Mosteller, Eds. 1977. Costs, Risks, and Benefits of Surgery. New York. Oxford University Press. 401 p.
Bunker, J. P., K. McPherson, and P. L. Henneman. 1977. Elective hysterectomy. *In:* J. P. Bunker, B. A. Barnes, and F. Mosteller, Eds. Costs, Risks, and Benefits of Surgery. New York. Oxford University Press. pp. 262–276.
Chadwick, E. 1862. Quoted by Fein, R. 1964. Health programs and economic development. *In:* Department of Medical Care Organization, University of Michigan. Economics of Health and Medical Care. Proceedings of the Conference May 10–12, 1962. Ann Arbor. University of Michigan. pp. 271–281.
Cochrane, A. L. 1972. Effectiveness and Efficiency: Random Reflections on Health Services. London. Nuffield Provincial Hospitals Trust. 92 p.
Conly, G. N. 1975. The Impact of Malaria on Economic Development: A Case Study. Pan American Health Organization Scientific Publication 297. 117 p.
Dupont, H. I., M. M. Levine, R. B. Hornick, M. J. Snyder, J. B. Libonati, and S. B. Formal. 1971. Oral attenuated vaccines in the control of shigellosis. Pan American Health Organization Scientific Publication 226: 364–367.
Enke, S. and R. A. Brown. 1972. Economic worth of preventing death at different ages in developing countries. Journal of Biosocial Science 4: 299–306.

Frei, E. 1975. The political realities of health in a developing nation. Bulletin of the New York Academy of Medicine 51: 577–579.

Fried, C. 1976. Equality and rights in medical care. Hastings Center Reports 6: 29–34.

Fuchs, V. R. 1966. The contribution of health services to the American economy. Millbank Memorial Fund Quarterly 44(4 part 2): 65–101.

Fuchs, V. R. 1974. Who Shall Live? New York. Basic Books. 168 p.

Gilder, S. S. B. 1972. The World Medical Association and medical care. *In:* J. Fry and W. A. Farndale, Eds. International Medical Care. Wallingford, Pa. Washington Square East Publishers. pp. 316–325.

Grab, B. and B. Cvjetanović. 1971. Simple method for rough determination of the cost-benefit balance point of immunization programmes. Bulletin of the World Health Organization 45: 536–554.

Hilleboe, H., A. Barkhuus, and W. C. Thomas. 1972. Approaches to National Health Planning. Geneva. World Health Organization. 108 p.

Imperato, P. J. 1974. Nomads of the west African Sahel and the delivery of health services to them. Social Science and Medicine 8: 443–457.

Jowett, B. 1892. Eryxias. *In:* B. Jowett, Trans. The Dialogues of Plato. New York. Random House. (Reprint, 1937) Vol. 2. pp. 807–821.

Jusatz, H. J. 1974. Changes in the state of infectious diseases in south and southeast Asia. Journal of Biosocial Science 6: 269–276.

King, T. C. 1974. Environmental health: effluence, affluence, and influence. *In:* R. L. Kane, Ed. The Challenges of Community Medicine. New York. Springer Publishing Co. pp. 237–259.

Klarman, H. E., J. O. Francis, and G. D. Rosenthal. 1968. Cost-effectiveness analysis applied to the treatment of chronic renal disease. Medical Care 6: 48–54.

Lalonde, M. 1974. A New Perspective on the Health of Canadians. Ottawa. Information Canada. 76 p.

Lane, J. M. and J. D. Millar. 1969. Routine childhood vaccination against smallpox reconsidered. New England Journal of Medicine 281: 1220–1224.

Lane, J. M., F. L. Ruben, J. M. Neff, and J. D. Millar. 1970. Complications of smallpox vaccination, 1968: results of ten statewide surveys. Journal of Infectious Diseases 122: 303–309.

Levin, A. L. 1968. Cost-effectiveness in maternal and child health; implications for program planning and evaluation. New England Journal of Medicine 278: 1041–1047.

Lumsden, W. R. 1975. Impact of independence and nationalism on tropical medicine. Bulletin of the New York Academy of Medicine 51: 595–607.

Mahler, H. 1975. Health—a demystification of medical technology. Lancet II: 829–833.

Massachusetts Department of Public Health. 1974. Cost-benefit analysis of newborn screening for metabolic disorders. New England Journal of Medicine 291: 1414–1416.

Maxwell, R. J. 1974. Health Care: The Growing Dilemma. New York. McKinsey and Company, Inc. 75 p.

Morley, D. 1973. Paediatric Priorities in the Developing World. London. Butterworths. 470 p.

Mushkin, S. J. 1962. Health as an investment. Journal of Political Economy 70(Suppl.): 129–157.

National Planning Association. 1974. Chartbook of Federal Health Spending 1969–74. Washington. National Planning Association. Center for Health Policy Studies. 63 p.

Newell, K. W. 1975. Health by the people. *In:* K. W. Newell, Ed. Health By the People. Geneva. World Health Organization. pp. 191–202.

Preston, S. H., N. Keyfitz, and R. Schoen. 1972. Causes of Death. Life Tables for National Populations. New York. Seminar Press. 787 p.

Puffer, R. and G. W. Griffith. 1967. Patterns of Urban Mortality. Pan American Health Organization Scientific Publication 151. 353 p.

Pyatt, E. W. and P. P. Rogers. 1962. On estimating benefit-cost ratio for water supply investments. American Journal of Public Health 52: 1729–1742.

Ruderman, A. P. 1972. Letter to the editor. Prevent 1: 72.

Ruzicka, L. T. 1976. Suicide, 1950 to 1971. World Health Statistics Report 29: 396–413.

Scherp, H. W. 1971. Dental caries: prospects for prevention. Science 173: 1199–1205.

Shapiro, S. H. and S. M. Wyman. 1976. CAT fever. New England Journal of Medicine 294: 954–956.

Sigerist, H. E. 1960. On the Sociology of Medicine. Ed. by M. I. Roemer. New York. M. D. Publications. 397 p.

United Nations. 1955. Age and Sex Patterns of Mortality. Model Life-Tables for Under-Developed Countries. Department of Economic and Social Affairs. Population Studies No. 22. 38 p.

United Nations. 1963. The Situation and Recent Trends of Mortality in the World. Population Bulletin No. 6 (for 1962): 3–145.

United Nations. 1973. The Determinants and Consequences of Population Trends. Vol. I. Department of Economic and Social Affairs. Population Studies No. 50. 661 p.

U.S. House of Representatives. 1975. Committee on Ways and Means. Subcommittee on Health. Basic Charts on Health Care. WMCP 94-48. Washington. U.S. Government Printing Office. 67 p.

U.S. House of Representatives. 1976. Committee on International Relations. Subcommittee on International Security and Scientific Affairs. Science, Technology and Diplomacy in the Age of Interdependence. Washington. U.S. Government Printing Office. 492 p.

Weisbrod, B. A. 1971. Costs and benefits of medical research: a case study of poliomyelitis. Journal of Political Economy 79: 527–542.

Weisbrod, B. A., R. L. Andreano, R. E. Baldwin, E. H. Epstein, and A. C. Kelly. 1973. Disease and Economic Development. Madison. University of Wisconsin Press. 218 p.

World Bank. 1975. Health. Sector Policy Paper. Washington. World Bank. 83 p.

World Health Organization. 1974. Health trends and prospects, 1950–2000. World Health Statistics Report 27: 670–706.

World Health Organization. 1975. Health Economics. Report on a WHO Interregional Seminar. Public Health Papers 64. 44 p.

World Health Organization. 1976. World Health Statistics Annual 1973-1976. Vol. I. Vital Statistics and Causes of Death. Geneva. World Health Organization. 839 p.

MEDICINE 7.

COMPARING MEDICAL CARE SYSTEMS

We can view a medical care system as an organized arrangement to provide specified medical services to designated persons, using resources allocated for that purpose. Personal medical care is everywhere the major component of health services, absorbing the vast majority of money, facilities, and personnel.

In recent years there has been a great upsurge of interest in describing and comparing health services in different countries; de Miguel (1975) lists on one page almost 150 studies in this field. Whether done by economists, sociologists, political scientists, or others, most of this work has as underlying theme the search for a better way to run a medical care system. Comparative studies may indicate what can be accomplished in effective patient care and efficient institutional operation, while at the same time warning against repetition of the mistakes of others. Faith in the existence, somewhere, of a superior system seems as widespread as dissatisfaction with the existing one. During hearings on national health insurance, a member of the U.S. Congress asked a panel of health service experts, "Taking the totality of our medical system, nonsystem, monstrosity, whatever you opt to call it, and comparing it with any other nations in the world, tell me which nation you would prefer to swap our system for, if any" (U.S. House of Representatives, 1975).

Before placing too much faith in the value of comparative studies, we must probe more deeply to see what they can and cannot tell us. On a superficial level, comparative health services research can uncover statistics on programs dealing with the numbers of specified elements making up a system (doctors, hospital beds) or put into the system (money, patient visits) over a certain period of time. It can also illustrate certain structural relationships within systems, such as the organization of divisions of a health ministry or the regionalization of hospitals, health centers, clinics, and dispensaries. Pages of tables and charts can be prepared in such studies, but to draw conclusions from these data requires great skill and care. There are two basic problems: (1) what the data show, and (2) what they do not show. Assessment of the quality and comparability of available medical and health statistics was discussed at length in Chapter 5 and need not be repeated here, except to say that what is shown on tables and charts is an interpretation of reality whose degree of verisimilitude depends upon many factors.

What is not shown on an organizational chart is, first of all, the historical context, which cannot be communicated in a simple structural model. Medical care is a continuously evolving process impossible to describe adequately in an instantaneous snapshot, any more than a single frame can exemplify a long and complex motion picture. Second, the fact that a system for medical care exists does not necessarily mean that it is used, or used properly, by the people whom it is intended to serve. The official medical care system is not necessarily *the* medical care system; all countries to some extent have informal parallel health care systems. Persons may by necessity (lack of access) or by intention (distrust, inconvenience) bypass or circumvent the formal medical care system and consult pharmacists, healers, or others whose services are not recorded on official charts and tables. In developing countries only a small minority of the population may make use of official health services. Third, whereas the elements of a system, and the resources put into it, can be counted and described, the output of the system, in terms of improved health, is very difficult to estimate and impossible to measure. But most importantly, attitudes and motivations cannot be indicated on an organizational chart. Leaders may be public-spirited, open, and responsive to the needs of the people, or dominated by self-serving professionalism in which special knowledge, ability, or association is carefully husbanded as a means for personal advancement. The degree to which the general public (the "consumers") is involved in the operation of the system also varies greatly in time and place.

Comparative anatomists can look at the skeletons of a chicken, dinosaur, fish, and man and make sense of the relationships between the various bones because they are guided by the principle of evolutionary homology of parts. They see in the unfolding of an embryo a recapitulation of the ancestral history of the species. Researchers in comparative medical care systems are not so fortunate because they have little theoretical basis for comparing structural or functional elements in countries with different historical traditions, political systems, and population structures. Furthermore, the development of today's poorer countries does not follow along the path previously taken by the wealthier nations (Chapters 2, 3). Comparisons between countries are therefore analogies, not homologies, and their utility for making predictions is thereby very much reduced.

After all these caveats, it may seem that comparison of medical care systems is a fruitless academic exercise. This, of course, is not so. Comparative studies do have value as a tool for discovering useful methods that may be profitably adopted elsewhere, and for the advancement of scholarly knowledge it is just as valid to study the historical, functional, and structural characteristics of medical care systems as of any other significant aspect of human society.

How is it possible to describe and compare the main features of more than 100 national medical care systems of extreme diversity and complexity? Here we cannot look to Ruritania for help, but must try to make sense of the real world. Tables, charts, diagrams, and written descriptions of one national system after another provide useful reference materials, but for the greatest didactic value, we must look at the basic building blocks whose proper reassembly can simulate the outlines of existing systems. The primary elements to be examined are the dyads of *usership and benefits* and *personnel and facilities*. All of these are, of course, tightly interlocked and none makes much sense without the others. The following pages should therefore be considered as one continuous story that will begin with the most basic element—those who use the system.

USERSHIP

There seems to be a common misconception in the United States that most European countries have monolithic "socialized medicine" systems under which a person need only appear on a hospital doorstep to be showered with free services. Equally widespread perhaps is the idea that most developing countries have no medical care systems at all. The truth, of course, lies somewhere between these extremes in all countries. The term *usership* is employed here to indicate, for each medical care system, those persons who have a legal right to obtain benefits and who exercise that right.

Medical care systems and subsystems, providing particular kinds of benefits (in cash or services) to specified segments of the population, are often linked, or interwoven, with programs offering other kinds of social assistance: retirement or survivorship pensions, unemployment insurance, funeral expenses, and the like. It is difficult to isolate medical care services: prenatal supervision and hospital delivery are certainly included, but what about a cash maternity bonus? Rehabilitation of a worker injured in an industrial accident seems to be medical care, but his retraining, if he is permanently handicapped, for a simpler occupation may not be so classified. We shall confine the present discussion to the conventional idea of personal medical services rendered by trained and skilled individuals to others specifically for promotion of health, prevention, alleviation and cure of illness, rehabilitation, and so forth, without further refining the definition. The primary categories of medical care systems are operated by:

1. National, state or provincial, county or municipal governments, funded by general taxation.
2. Governmental or quasi-governmental health insurance, social security, or sickness funds based on specifically earmarked financial contributions.
3. Wholly owned private organizations such as mines, factories, and plantations, primarily for their own workers.
4. Prepaid member-supported nonprofit organizations.
5. Charitable and voluntary organizations.
6. The private practice of medicine as a profit-making business (including private health insurance companies).
7. Indigenous, traditional, spiritual, empirical, or magical healers observing specific cultural practices.

These are by no means mutually exclusive. In many countries, including some in Asia, Latin America, and Africa, all of these types of systems coexist; frequently there are several subsystems in each category. For instance, the various levels of government may each operate health facilities, and where private practice exists there may be many different kinds of providers offering similar services. Alternatively, some systems may be absent or only weakly developed. An individual over a span of years may or may not make use of any, several, or all of these systems, depending primarily on his eligibility, choice, and access with respect to each.

Usership

Eligibility	Choice	Access
Age	Compulsory	Acceptability
Citizenship		Appropriateness
Dependency status	Optional	Availability
Diagnosis		Cost
Employment	Voluntary	Geographic distance
Ethnicity		Health
Income		Sociocultural distance
Residence		

Eligibility[1]

Government sources A number of governments have accepted full responsibility for the health of their citizenry and have medical care available to all at no or a trivial charge to the user. Basic costs are borne by general government revenues, but some charges (cost-sharing) may be made for certain items or to discourage overuse. These systems of socialized medicine may be found in the U.S.S.R. and some eastern European and Scandinavian countries, as well as in Cuba, the United Kingdom, and New Zealand. Several countries with substantial income from petroleum are also to be found in this category. Although politically very diverse, these governments share a common outlook, exemplified by the statement of the British National Health Service:

To ensure that everybody in the country—irrespective of means, age, sex or occupation—should have equal opportunity to benefit from the best and most up-to-date medical and allied services available ... To divorce the care of health from questions of personal means or other factors irrelevant to it and thus encourage the obtaining of early advice and the promotion of good health rather than only the treatment of ill health. (Department of Health and Social Security, 1971)

More governments have enunciated this principle than have been able to bring it to reality. For instance, the Nkrumah administration in newly independent Ghana (1957–66) tried to provide free medical care for all, but personnel, facilities, and money available were only a fraction of those needed and the program collapsed. In India, the preindependence Bhore Report (1946) specified that "medical services should be free to all without distinction and the contribution from those who can afford to pay should be through general and local taxation."

More commonly, full medical care supported directly by the central government is provided only for specific segments of the population. Almost everywhere members of the military services are in this category, usually with their immediate families. After the First World War the United States and many European countries established veterans hospi-

[1] The subsequent discussions are based upon numerous sources, including the references in the list for Chapter 7; pamphlets and brochures sent by many governments in response to requests for information about their health services; and reports and other official publications in the extensive Government Documents collection of the Stanford University libraries. Some references are comprehensive, covering many countries. Other materials are either ephemeral or not generally accessible. It would seem unproductive, as well as tedious to the reader, to cite in the text the source of each separate datum mentioned.

tals, first for treatment of war-related disabilities, then for general medical care. Sometimes dependents of veterans are also eligible. Other groups eligible for central government-supported medical care often include pensioners, inmates of prisons, and members of aboriginal or tribal populations.

The health of pregnant women, mothers, and young children is often considered a community responsibility, and direct government support of these groups, connected with maternity benefits, may exist independently of other programs. East Germany, although a socialist state, provides free, government-subsidized medical care only to pregnant women and children under three years of age. Others, if not insured, pay the full cost of care. In many countries, care, particularly preventive services, is provided for older children through the schools.

Not only are certain groups of people usually eligible for general government-sponsored medical care, but frequently all persons are eligible for specific sorts of care. Most commonly these are extensions of public health functions. In Israel, for instance, personal preventive (but not curative) services are provided free to all inhabitants directly through the Ministry of Health. In many countries certain diseases are the subjects of "monovalent" services, with preventive, diagnostic, and curative care offered free of charge. Tuberculosis, sexually transmitted diseases, leprosy, and mental illness often fall into this category. Ambulance and emergency services are also commonly provided to all by local governments.

In the United States and other countries lacking universal medical care coverage, government agencies (local, municipal, or national) may provide care for those without other means of payment. In some places such as Malaysia, Sri Lanka, and Singapore fees are adjusted by ability to pay, and they may be dispensed with altogether.

A distinction must be made between one government's policy decision to provide medical care, as a right, to all or part of its population, and the assumption by another government of the burden of medical care for the indigent, looked upon as a welfare or charity function and often performed with graceless reluctance. According to Tejeiro Fernandez (1975) the latter situation existed in prerevolutionary Cuba: "Only people in extreme hardship used the government services. Indeed when someone already beyond his first youth was not given to saving or providing for his own future or was unemployed or unmarried, it was frequently said that his unhappy person would end his days in a government hospital, as if that were the worst thing that could happen to anyone."

Social security and quasi-governmental health insurance   Although the medical care services of continental western Europe are often pictured as national health services, the fact is that they are based on the concept of health insurance, with governments playing a variable role.

The basic idea of insurance is to reduce the effects upon individuals of certain designated losses by pooling the *risk* of such losses among a group of participants, the *insured,* by whom or on whose behalf a cash *premium* is paid periodically to an *insurer.* The insurer, which may be a part of, or controlled by, a government, assumes the pooled risks and agrees to provide certain *benefits* in cash or in services to the insured or his beneficiaries upon sustaining a loss insured against.

Voluntary insurance against sickness and death has a long history in Europe, arising from early guild organizations. The working class that developed during the industrial revolution formed mutual-help groups so that by 1804 there were one million members of "friendly societies" in England, growing to seven million by the turn of the twentieth century. Similar movements for voluntary sickness insurance developed in the nineteenth century in the Netherlands, Germany, Austria, Switzerland, and Scandinavia (Abel-Smith, 1965). Coupled with these trends, from the 1880s on, were social security schemes first concentrating their medical benefits on work-related injuries and occupational illnesses. These programs spread very rapidly. In 1884 Germany passed the first modern law prescribing cash disability benefits and medical care for work-related injuries, and within 20 years every other country in western Europe except Portugal and Spain had enacted similar laws. The early laws did not set up national schemes, but only required that low-income workers must join a local insurance society, which then fell under some regulated standards. A great variety of plans for indemnification, prepayment of costs, and contracts with providers have been developed in Europe, Australia, New Zealand, and elsewhere. The first formal sickness insurance plan in a developing country was adopted in Chile in 1924, when the *Caja de Seguro Obligatorio* was established. Most other countries of Latin America followed suit in the 1930s and 1940s. Similar plans have since spread to virtually all countries, but they often cover a very small portion of the population. The Chilean health insurance program, however, continued to evolve and by 1952 covered 70% of the population.

Semiautonomous health funds or associations were often organized along occupational, religious, political, residential, or other lines. Eligibility for membership depended upon the particular funds, which came increasingly under official control and regulation.

As the sickness insurance fund movement grew, four parties emerged with major roles: members (often represented through a group such as a labor union), employers (usually when unions were involved), the medical profession, and the government. It is mainly because of the tugging and pulling of these diverse interests that few countries, at least in western Europe, have really been able to integrate or even to coordinate fully the diverse health programs accumulated over the decades. Nevertheless, there seems to be a general consensus in Europe that health care is a community responsibility, and participation in these programs has broadened in various directions. Systems have accordingly been made compulsory for employed workers, at least in specified occupations.

After the Second World War, existing insurance schemes were merged into comprehensive national programs in Belgium, France, Greece, the Netherlands, Italy, Japan, and many other countries. In some countries (e.g., Austria, West Germany, the Netherlands) membership is compulsory for those earnings less than a certain minimum wage, voluntary for others. In Denmark, persons of low income pay the local sickness fund a low premium and receive high benefits (section A), while those with high incomes (section B) pay more and receive lower benefits. About a thousand separate sickness funds in Denmark are based upon the district of residence. In Switzerland membership in sickness funds is compulsory in some cantons, or certain municipalities, for residents with income below a specified limit. For others, participation is voluntary. More than 90% of Swiss citizens are members of one or another fund.

In many countries of Europe and elsewhere, as a result of their historical development, numerous separate funds exist primarily along occupational lines: Austria has hundreds of such *Krankenkassen*; West Germany has about 1,800; Greece, about 200; South Africa, over 300; and Japan, about 1,400, just to cite a few. Many of these have become amalgamated in various countries. In Israel, for example, separate sickness funds for agricultural settlements and trade unions, established during the period of British mandate, have fused within the General Federation of Labor whose unified sickness fund, the *Kupat Holim,* covers about 70% of the population, while six smaller funds plus social welfare agencies cover the remainder. In the centrally planned economies of eastern Europe, where the government is the sole, or major, employer, historically separate funds have sometimes been merged into quasinational health service schemes while retaining their identity as social security because payments are contributed as a function of wages, not from general taxation. These are not, however, monolithic programs. In

Albania, Bulgaria, Czechoslovakia, Poland, and Romania payments to sickness and maternity insurance come from the employer and the government; in East Germany, Hungary, and Yugoslavia the individual workers also pay a percentage of their salary. Yugoslavia has more than 100 separate communal health funds, each contracting with local institutions for services.

Medical care in the People's Republic of China (P.R.C.) has been of great interest to western observers because of its many innovations in technology and personnel since 1949. Usership of modern health services has been extended from a tiny minority to the great majority of citizens. The basic system used has been medical insurance of a generally familiar kind. Hu (1975) has described the two major types of medical care insurance systems in the P.R.C. Workers in factories and state-owned firms (but not their dependents) are eligible for labor medical insurance (LMI) whose premiums are paid by the employer without an employee contribution or wage reduction (as in Albania, Bulgaria, etc., above). About 20% of the Chinese population, primarily in cities, is covered by this plan. In about 70% of rural communes (1975) poor and lower-middle income peasants are eligible to participate voluntarily in local cooperative medical services (CMS). Also, by payment of a small annual subscription fee, they can receive certain specified medical benefits, often subject to additional co-payment and charges per visit or per procedure. Welfare funds or local government subsidies may supplement insurance benefits, or complete payments for those otherwise unable to meet the full costs of medical care. The interim solution to distribution of medical care developed by the Chinese (through local insurance schemes) is quite different from the centralized, government-provided universal service adopted in Cuba and the U.S.S.R. At present, the medical care system of China is far less "socialized" than that of most western countries.

In Europe, strong political forces have often acted to maintain the independence of specific sickness funds. Most common among these are schemes for government employees, postal, railroad and communications workers, miners, and seamen. Many countries maintain independent social security funds for agricultural workers and the self-employed, for which membership is commonly voluntary. Special systems exist for journalists (Italy), "liberal professions" (Portugal), salesmen (Spain), fishermen (Norway), and so forth. Many socialized countries of eastern Europe also maintain multiple sickness-insurance funds based on occupational categories. East Germany, for example, has programs essentially indistinguishable from those in western Europe, with separate schemes for miners, railway and postal workers, workers in cooperatives, etc. Thus, the organization of medical care is not necessarily parallel to the political and economic systems.

The proportion of the population covered by health and medical insurance programs related to social security systems varies greatly. In many less developed countries, these schemes are in early stages of development, only a small percentage of people are wage earners, wages are low, and unemployment high. Workers are insufficiently organized to make many demands, employers and governments are not supportive, and medical personnel and facilities are frequently lacking anyway. Persons specifically eligible for social-insurance health benefits constitute a negligible percentage of the population in most African countries and in parts of Asia. In Latin America, by contrast, many countries have well-developed social security agencies which, as semiautonomous institutes, often spend more per capita than the government health ministries. In Guatemala in 1969, for example, the Institute of Social Security, with a health insurance program covering 113,000 wage earners and dependents and injury benefits to 578,000 others, spent an amount almost equal to the overall budget of the Ministry of Health, which was responsible for 5,000,000 people. The proportion of population eligible for services in Latin America ranges from very low (under 5%) in Bolivia, Paraguay, Honduras, Nicaragua, and other countries to substantial percentages in Argentina, Chile, and Uruguay. Here many separate systems operate through *mutuales* which, as in Europe, arose from guilds and labor unions. Even where services are very limited, they are often fragmented. In Bolivia, for instance, there are separate schemes for employees of the highway service, the petroleum social security agency, the mining corporation, the state oil company, state railroads, banking institutions, the state resettlement agency, the agricultural bank, and other entities, some with a total membership of just a few thousand persons. In Uruguay numerous *mutuales,* formed by labor unions or by religious or political groups, operate together with a complex set of public and semipublic organizations to provide or to contract for medical care. In poorer countries, coverage under any sort of health insurance program generally begins in the capital city, jumps to the larger towns, and may then be gradually extended from there.

In the United States, general medical care insurance via social security programs has not been of much importance historically. The great majority of industrial and commercial workers who are covered have participated as group or individual members in privately contracted insurance plans carried by commercial companies or by associations of providers that offer a great variety of benefits. Depending upon the plan, both employees and employers may contribute. Programs are regulated by federal and state legislation, but direct government subsidies are not a usual feature. Local and state health departments deal largely with environmental, protective, promotive, and preventive problems and do not participate in health insurance programs to a great extent. Since 1965 specified medical benefits have been available to qualifying persons aged 65 or over, and to persons with certain disabilities such as chronic kidney disease. Special national systems exist for railroad employees and for the medically indigent. Autonomous state programs determine the extent and duration of sickness and (in some states) maternity benefits.

Governments in general have played a large and increasing role in the establishment and regulation of health insurance schemes. In recent years, with medical costs rising faster than the economic base of social security receipts, many governments have been called upon to make up, from general taxation, huge deficits in medical care budgets. This has blurred the distinction between government-provided and social insurance types of programs. There is a logical progression from broadening health insurance to making compulsory health insurance universal (as in Canada, Denmark, Finland, Iceland, Norway, and Sweden) to nationalizing the entire system. It is sometimes difficult to distinguish between one and another degree of "socialization," and many national systems do not lend themselves to easy categorization. In Britain a National Health Insurance scheme came into effect in 1912, providing medical benefits for the compulsorily insured population of workers earning, at that time, under £160 per year. With the creation of the National Health Service in 1948, coverage was extended to the rest of the population, benefits were expanded, and hospitals were nationalized in order to control their size, location, and operation. Australia has gone through a similar change more recently. On July 1, 1975, their medical care system shifted from one based on compulsory membership in one of 80 voluntary health insurance funds to a general taxation-based program as in Britain. In Latin American countries it is common for the ministry of health and the *seguro social* to operate parallel and independent facilities, sometimes side by side, while large areas have no services at all. This lack of coordination has been repeatedly discussed in national and international meetings of health officials in Latin America. Resolutions of the governing bodies of the Organization of American States and the Pan American Health Organization have deplored the social discrimination, complexities, and wastefulness of duplicated and poorly integrated medical systems. "Who is hindering this coordination?" asked a working document (Pan American Health Organization, 1966) that answered its own question by pointing to the medical profession, the labor sectors, the social security agencies, and the ministries of health and other government agencies. Nevertheless, in some more progressive countries such as Costa Rica efforts are underway to merge the two partly redundant systems into one national medical care structure. Some other developing countries, having started later, have integrated (but did not merge) their social security sickness programs with their public health services from the start. This is the case, for example, in India, Burma, and Tunisia.

Private organizations Commercial development in colonial times often resulted in workers becoming concentrated in relatively remote areas and wholly dependent upon their employers for medical care as well as for other amenities of life. Entire communities developed on rubber estates in Malaysia and Liberia; tea plantations in India and Sri Lanka; and oil palm, cocoa, coffee, and other agricultural enterprises in many countries. A second group of relatively isolated workers involved miners: copper in Katanga, gold in Kivu and South Africa, tin in Bolivia and Malaysia. Some enterprises, such as Union Minière in the old Congo, had tens of thousands of employees and provided medical care to them, their dependents, and, when needed, to the nearby community if there was one.

Joubert (1972) described a modern industrial medical service at the Volta Aluminum Company (VALCO) smelter in Tema, Ghana. Before 1958 Tema was a small fishing village. By 1962 it had 20,000 people; by 1972 it had 100,000; and by 1980 it expects 150,000. The VALCO medical service began in 1964 with a compact 10-bed unit with laboratory, x-ray, and operating theatre, to serve some 3,000 construction workers. For the first three years of operation the service handled only work injuries; then it took over general health care of all employees. By 1969 service was extended to dependents of senior staff and the next year, with a work force of 2,000, the company accepted responsibility for medical care of all dependents through a contract arrangement with a local clinic. It is interesting that this sequence mirrors the historical developmental stages of many national programs.

Prepaid member-supported plans In several areas of the United States, health maintenance organizations operate on a prepaid basis, with each participating member charged a flat monthly fee in return for which he and his dependents become eligible to receive comprehensive medical care services. The largest of these programs, the Kaiser-Permanent Health Plan, which operates primarily in California, enrolls most of its participants through agreements with labor unions or employee groups, within which membership in the plan is entirely voluntary.

Charitable and voluntary organizations The role of charitable organizations in providing medical care is changing rapidly. It should be recalled that until fairly recent times in Europe all hospitals were run primarily by religious orders, and primarily for the indigent. Abel-Smith (1965) has pointed out that in Britain "where provision for the acute sick by charitable effort was inadequate to provide for all who needed care, the acute sector of hospital care was, from 1870 onwards, gradually supplemented by public authorities." It was not until 1881, he noted, that a major British hospital accommodated any paying patients at all, and until the formation of the National Health Service in 1948, charitable bodies sponsored the more costly acute hospitals. Churches, through religious orders, still control a substantial part of institutional care in Holland, Belgium, and West Germany. Their ownership and management of hospitals is declining, however, and the orders are concentrating on care for the retarded, handicapped, and disabled (Blanpain, 1973). In Latin America from the earliest days, the *beneficencia, santa casa,* and *casa de socorro* were operated by local charitable welfare boards of leading citizens (the *Junta de Beneficencia*) with heavy involvement of the Catholic church (Bravo, 1958). As time passed, government subsidies were needed to assist with the high costs of these institutions, which today "are the principal resource for medical care of the poor, especially in large cities where these institutions have been operating for the longest years" (Roemer, 1963).

The demise of colonialism in recent decades, coupled with rising nationalism and increasing numbers of local professionals, has sharply reduced the role of the medical missionary in most developing countries. In many nations, such as Tanzania, some former mission hospitals have been absorbed into the national network, sometimes with their staffs placed on salary or contract. Nevertheless, mission hospitals still provide the only curative medical care services in many remote areas: Jansen (1973) has described with incisive detail the usership of his mission hospital in Bomvanaland, South Africa.

The private practice of medicine The prevailing free enterprise system in the United States is reflected in its predominant system of private medical practice and in the large number of independent, profit-making, voluntary health insurance companies. However, private fee-for-service medical practice also exists in countries where the numbers of poor are proportionately much larger. An abundance of physicians is often available in the capitals and large cities of developing countries, for those who can afford to pay for their services. In Brazil, for example, the private sector, including hospitals and clinics, prepaid health plans, pharmacies, and physicians in private practice, accounts for two-thirds of the total national health expenditures but is really available only to a small portion of the total population. Badger (1976) has reported that a private medical consultation in Londrina, Paraná (average monthly family income equal to U.S. $231.33) cost from $25 to $45. In Palo Alto, California, U.S.A. (average monthly family income $1,250) a similar consultation cost $17.50. The obvious conclusion is that private medical practice in Londrina functions only for the small upper class. A similar situation exists in many other developing countries. However, where a very large number of physicians in private practice compete for patients, as in urban areas of the Philippines, their fees may be relatively low.

In many countries of western Europe, persons already covered by compulsory health insurance can buy additional private policies in order to obtain better coverage or amenities such as private or semiprivate hospital rooms. Physicians or specialists not on the approved list of a health insurance fund may be consulted privately, and simply paid out of pocket. Even highly organized socialist systems may permit private practice. In Czechoslovakia, for example, the state may license some specialists, dental surgeons, and retired physicians with insufficient pensions to engage in limited private practice to increase their incomes.

The 1974 reorganization of Britain's National Health Service retained private practice as a matter of policy both within and without the NHS. A very small percentage of beds is set aside for private patients "without prejudice to the needs of those—the vast majority—who wish to be treated as NHS patients and who are the hospitals' primary concern" (National Health Service Reorganisation, England, 1972), but this has been a subject of intense controversy.

Indigenous and traditional healers Despite the many systems described above, it is likely that "perhaps half of the world's people do not receive modern medical care at all..." (Bryant, 1969). It seems a safe assumption that among those receiving *some* modern medical care, many also consult traditional healers at times. Recall that the populations of North America, Europe (including U.S.S.R.), Japan, and Oceania together constitute less than 30% of the world's population and that various forms of "nonofficial" healing are practiced also in these regions. Thus, the usership of traditional medical care systems probably exceeds that of scientific or western medicine by a factor of at least 2 to 1.

Only a few countries, most notably India and the People's Republic of China, have made any efforts to integrate their indigenous medical practices with modern medicine. In the latter country, insofar as facilities permit, persons may elect to receive treatment by traditional (herbal, acupuncture, moxibustion, etc.), or modern medicine, or by a blend of both. The acceptance and integration of the traditional sector was resisted by the Chinese medical establishment following independence in 1949 and required well over a decade to achieve. It is interesting that in Cuba, another Marxist state, medical care has been organized along strictly scientific lines and folk medicine has been banned. A WHO study group that visited Cuba has reported: "It was decided not to utilize the existing traditional midwives and witch-doctors (*curanderos*). The witch-doctors were forbidden to practice, while the traditional midwives were gradually absorbed into the health services system, mostly as ancillary staff" (Djukanovic and Mach, 1975). In less developed countries generally there seems to be no move either towards integration or banishment of the traditional healers.

Choice

As we have seen, membership in some national health services (e.g., U.S.S.R.) is compulsory, without an alternative. Insofar as any use is made of medical care services, patients must use those offered by the government. Other systems offer options. In Canada, for example, health insurance is compulsory throughout the provinces, but some opting out is permitted in Ontario and Alberta. Persons of means can legally circumvent the system in Britain and in most countries with compulsory insurance.

Access

This is a key to the usership of medical care services, a problem that should keep the lights burning late in the offices of health planners. Table 7-1 shows the number of hospital admissions and outpatient attendances in several developing countries in a recent year. In the United States and other more developed countries, by contrast, the number of visits per

Table 7-1. Utilization of official health services in selected countries, 1962

Country	Population (millions)	Hospital admissions	Outpatient attendances at hospitals, health centers, and dispensaries (millions)	Average visits per person per year
Jamaica	1.7	68,828	1.1	0.6
Guatemala	4.0	136,154	0.9	0.2
Senegal	2.9	65,673	7.8	2.9
Thailand	26.0	541,000	17.5	0.7
Kenya	8.6	146,740	5.2	0.6
Tanzania	9.6	231,598	26.0	2.7
Uganda	6.7	172,279	9.6	1.5

Source: Adapted from Fendall, 1972.

capita is five or more. Much of the difference can be explained by variations in the availability of, and access to, the appropriate facilities (Table 7-2). The dilemma arises in large part from the geographic distribution of existing personnel and facilities. Figure 7-1 shows, for a number of representative countries, the concentration of physicians relative to population in the capital city. But even there, physicians do not serve the population equally. Bahadori (1975) has shown, for instance, that within Teheran 50% of the physicians serve only 10% of the population. Other categories of health personnel, laboratories, and equipment such as x-ray machines and operating theatres are usually far more disproportionately distributed than are physicians. In Bolivia, for example, La Paz, with 12% of the population, has 20% of the physicians, a not extreme discrepancy. However, while only one-third of the Bolivian population lives in towns of more than 10,000 population, 90% of the hospital facilities are found there. In Guatemala, only about 35% of persons live within two hours' travel of a health facility; in Honduras and Nicaragua, fewer than one-third are that close, and in many developing areas the proportion is far smaller.

Morley (1976) has stated the situation graphically: "Although three-quarters of the population in most developing countries live in rural areas, three-quarters of the spending on medical care is in urban areas, where three-quarters of the doctors live. Three-quarters of the deaths are caused by conditions that can be prevented at low cost, but three-quarters

Table 7-2. Hospital beds per 10,000 population, selected countries and areas, 1969–72

Number of beds	Countries and areas
0–4.9	Afghanistan, Bangladesh, Ethiopia, Mauritania, Nepal, Pakistan, Taiwan
5–9.9	Burma, Chad, Democratic Yemen, Haiti, India, Indonesia, Laos, Mali, Niger, Nigeria, South Korea, Sudan, Upper Volta
10–19.9	Benin (Dahomey), Burundi, Central African Republic, Colombia, Democratic Kampuchea (Cambodia), Gambia, Ghana, Guinea, Guinea-Bissau, Honduras, Iran, Iraq, Ivory Coast, Jordan, Kenya, Liberia, Malawi, Mexico, Morocco, Mozambique, Paraguay, Philippines, Rwanda, Saudi Arabia, Senegal, Syria, Sierra Leone, Somalia, Tanzania, Togo, Uganda
20–29.9	Algeria, Bolivia, Botswana, Cameroon, Dominican Republic, Ecuador, Egypt, El Salvador, Guatemala, Fiji, Lesotho, Nicaragua, Peru, Tunisia, Turkey
30–39.9	Angola, Brazil, Brunei, Chile, Costa Rica, Jamaica, Lebanon, Malaysia (West), Panama, Rhodesia (Zimbabwe), Sri Lanka, Swaziland, Venezuela, Zaire
40–49.9	Bahrain, Cuba, Hong Kong, Kuwait, Libya, Puerto Rico, Singapore, Surinam, Trinidad and Tobago
50–59.9	Argentina, Bahamas, Belize, Congo, Equatorial Guinea, Guyana, Israel, Spain, Uruguay, Yugoslavia
60–69.9	Albania, American Samoa, Cyprus, Greece, Portugal, New Zealand
70–79.9	Poland, Qatar, United States of America
80–89.9	Belgium, England and Wales, Hungary, Romania
90–99.9	Barbados, Canada, Denmark, France, Gibraltar, Mongolia
100–109.9	Austria, Czechoslovakia, French Guiana, Gabon, German Democratic Republic, Italy, Malta, Netherlands
110–119.9	Federal Republic of Germany, Ireland, Luxembourg, Northern Ireland, Union of Soviet Socialist Republics
120–129.9	Australia, Japan, Scotland
130–139.9	Finland, Greenland, Norway
140–149.9	Iceland
150–159.9	Panama Canal Zone, Sweden

Source: Adapted from World Health Organization, 1976.

of the medical budget is spent on curative services, many of them provided for the elite at high cost." This lament has not resulted in the magnitude of changes stimulated in the P.R.C. by the famous statement of June 25, 1965, by Chairman Mao Tse-tung:

MEDICINE

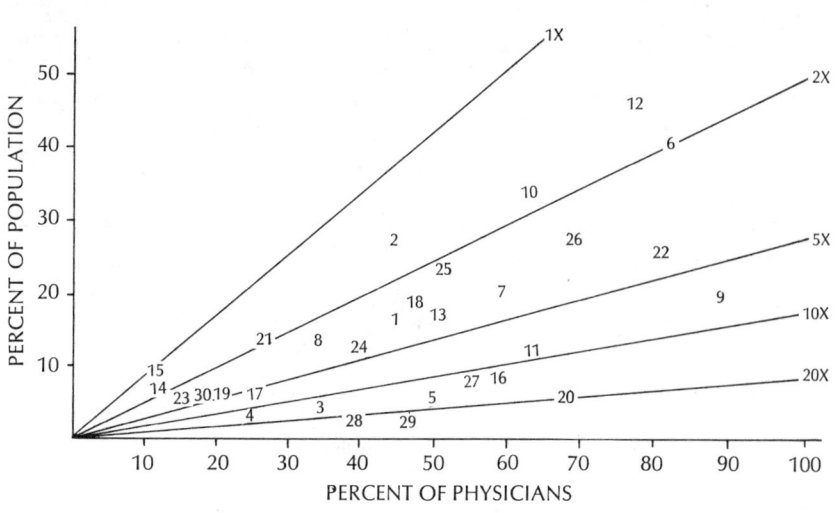

Figure 7-1

Percentage of population and of physicians in the capital city, selected countries, recent years. The diagonal lines represent a proportional concentration of physicians 1, 2, 5, 10, and 20 times that of the population. SOURCE: Adapted from data in World Health Organization, 1976.

Key to Numbers

1 Argentina	11 Haiti	21 Norway
2 Belgium	12 Iceland	22 Paraguay
3 Botswana	13 Iran	23 Poland
4 Cameroon	14 Italy	24 Senegal
5 Chad	15 Japan	25 Sri Lanka
6 Costa Rica	16 Kenya	26 Syria
7 Dominican Republic	17 Liberia	27 Thailand
8 Finland	18 Mali	28 Upper Volta
9 Gambia	19 Morocco	29 Yemen
10 Greece	20 Niger	30 Zaire

Tell the Ministry of Public Health that it only works for 15 percent of the entire population. Furthermore, this 15 percent is made up mostly of the privileged. The broad ranks of the peasants cannot obtain medical treatment and also do not receive medicine. The Public Health Ministry is not a people's ministry. It should be called the Urban Public Health Ministry, or the Public Health Ministry of the Privileged or even, the Urban Public Health Ministry of the Privileged.

Medical education must be reformed. It is basically useless to study so much... Medical education does not require senior middle school students, junior middle school students or graduates of senior elementary school. Three years are enough. The important thing is that they study while practicing. This way doctors sent to the countryside will not overrate their own abilities, and they will be better than those doctors who have been cheating the people and better than the witch doctors. In addition the villages can afford to support them ... At the present time the system of examination and treatment used in the medical schools is not at all suitable for the countryside. Our method of training doctors is for the cities, even though China has more than 500 million peasants.

A vast amount of manpower and materials have been diverted from mass work and are being expended in carrying out research on the high-level, complex and difficult diseases, the so-called pinnacles of medicine. As for the frequently occurring illnesses, the widespread sicknesses, the commonly existing diseases, we pay no heed or very slight heed to their prevention or to finding improved methods of treatment. It is not that we should ignore the pinnacles. It is only that we should devote less men and materials in that direction and devote a greater amount of men and materials to solving the urgent problems of the masses.

We should keep in the cities those doctors who have been out of school for a year or two and those who are lacking in ability. The remainder should be sent to the countryside ... In medicine and health, put the stress on the rural areas. (Quoted by Lampton, 1972)

Although the situation in many countries still resembles that described above for China, few governments are willing to make such far-reaching reforms as those demanded by Mao Tse-tung. Note that this statement was made some 15 years after establishment of the People's Republic, and that it required further years of turmoil during the Cultural Revolution from 1966 to about 1970 for China to move firmly in the directions indicated.

Morely, Mao, and many others have criticized both the distribution and appropriateness of available medical services, but there may be other barriers to access even when a clinic is located within the community. The hours of operation may be more convenient for the clinic staff than for potential users, who must often work during most daylight hours. The cost, in money or in time lost from other activities, may be considered excessive. Some persons may be too ill or too weak to get to the clinic or hospital. There is also the more subtle barrier of sociocultural attitudes and distance.

In many countries relationships between the government and the people are hardly cordial. Mistrust and negative reactions are common, the more so when people feel themselves to be treated with insensitivity. Roemer (1971) has noted that in Europe early social insurance funds of working people organized separate ambulatory care centers when it was evident that the people did not want to go to the hospital outpatient departments because of their identification with charity patients.

Why are more [people] not reached? Bryant (1969) asks in speaking of Colombia:

In the more remote areas, the obstacles are obvious: matted jungle, poor roads, high mountains, dangerous banditry. But while it is one thing for a sick person to decide against a hard trip by foot or canoe to a distant health center, it is another to decide against a short walk to a health center, as in Cali. Many decided against it. A survey of families living in the area served by one of the newest and most strongly staffed health centers in Cali showed that 40 percent used the health center, 28 percent knew of it but did not use it, and 32 percent did not know anything about it. Why people do not use health services when they are easily accessible is one of the crucial questions of medical care.

BENEFITS

Just as the usership of medical care systems is diverse and complex, so is their benefit structure:

Benefits

Types of benefits		Mode
Acute	Monovalent	Cash
Ambulatory	Outpatient	Service
Comprehensive	Preventive	
Drugs	Primary care	
Hospital	Secondary care	
Long-term	Surgical	
Medical	Tertiary care	
	etc.	

Types of benefits

Many medical care systems, by our definition, are *monovalent*; that is, they are established for a specific, limited purpose. For example, most developing countries have programs for the control of diseases such as leprosy, malaria, trachoma, yaws, schistosomiasis, or onchocerciasis. Often the specially constituted service carries out a limited function: immunization (smallpox, polio, measles); screening; or case finding and chemotherapy (trachoma, yaws); or works in a defined field such as mental health. Such a system may be temporary, activated at a special threat, as when yellow fever is reported in Latin America or Africa, and then become dormant. Many monovalent systems are permanent, having large establishments. Tuberculosis, leprosy, venereal disease, and maternal and child health services often operate networks of diagnostic and treatment centers. Monovalent systems are really extensions of public health functions: They are often largely preventive in nature, and may deal with persons who are not ill and who have little immediate incentive to come in to receive the benefit. Because these programs aim at broad participation, they are almost always directly operated by governmental agencies.

In contrast to the monovalent system, but also government run, is the all-inclusive medical care system exemplified by the British National Health Service: "To provide for all who want it, a comprehensive service covering every branch of medical and allied activity, from care of minor ailments to major medicine and surgery which would include the care of mental as well as physical health, all specialist services, all general services (i.e. by family doctor, dentist, optician, midwife, nurse and health visitor) and all necessary drugs, medicines and a wide range of appliances" (Department of Health and Social Security, 1971).

Developing countries in general are striving to extend *primary care* services to their populations, often with emphasis on common illnesses and on the health of mothers and children. Such care is offered to the population at the point of entry into the health system, ideally combining the preventive and curative, personal and community, individual and environmental aspects (King, 1966). Primary care services are provided by health workers alone or in teams, at work places, schools, homes, dispensaries, clinics, or other health facilities. Measures undertaken (again ideally) should be simple, effective, accessible, and ongoing, and they should also be an integral part of community development. Primary care should not be construed as primitive care, but as the basic level of involvement of populations with health services to prevent illness wherever possible, keep minor health problems from worsening, and refer more serious cases to the proper consultant and facility. The components of primary care services, including the providers, will be described in greater detail in the next section of this chapter. Their significance has been stated well by Mahler (1977):

I would only like to point out how crucial it is in so many countries, whatever their level of social and economic development, to ensure that essential health care is made available to all and that it complements the other elements required in the individual, family, and community environment to satisfy basic human needs and provide a minimum acceptable level of human dignity for all. Man does not live by per capita income alone. Among the most fundamental of his needs and desires is a yearning for a longer life and less illness, and for greater social opportunity so that he may have his proper enjoyment of these things. It is this that makes health improvement so powerful a lever for the genuine development of the person, the family, and the community, and that stirs people to achieve greater economic and social productivity. The essential health improvements can be achieved at such a low relative cost if the policies, priorities, strategies and tactics for primary health care are well chosen and implemented that I cannot help wondering why primary health care continues to be dismissed by the politicians of so many countries with an indifferent shrug of the shoulders.

Sometimes the framework of a monovalent system is used to develop a polyvalent primary care network. This has happened in francophone (French-speaking) West Africa where the *Service Prophylactique de la Maladie du Sommeil,* the antisleeping sickness service founded in 1931, grew through various stages by 1944 into the *Service Générale d'Hygiène Mobile et de Prophylaxie,* and then with independence in 1959 formed the basis of medical care systems in Upper Volta, Mali, Senegal, Mauritania, and Niger (Imperato, 1974).

Secondary care comprises the general hospital inpatient services and specialist consultations, often on referral from primary care providers, and in less developed countries commonly organized at municipal, county, district, or provincial levels. *Tertiary care* includes highly specialized services such as neurosurgery. In LDCs such care, if available, is often limited to university teaching hospitals or at a centralized national level.

In more developed countries, particularly in western Europe where social insurance mechanisms are highly developed, benefits are generally divided into *ambulatory or general physician care* and *hospitalization.* Depending upon the cultural background, certain conventional forms of therapy may be available to users of particular medical care systems. Czechoslovakia, for example, includes many spas as health facilities. The U.S.S.R. has sanatoria-prophylactoria providing a rustic environment, good diet, relaxation from stress, and water, mud, or parafin baths (Storey, 1972).

Mode

The philosophy of insurance schemes is different from that of national health services. The former spells out predetermined levels of compensation or idemnification for specific contingencies under a contractual arrangement, while the latter assumes responsibility for all risks. In nationalized medical care programs (as in Britain, Cuba, the Soviet Union, etc.) short-term sickness benefits are provided directly as *services,* while in other countries they may be provided as services or as *cash* (also sometimes called *indemnity*) through a variety of reimbursement schemes. Medical benefits paid as cash reimbursements must be distinguished from sickness benefits paid to replace lost wages; the latter often originate from different agencies. Where health insurance is compulsory, as in Scandinavia, these two types of systems may blend. In Norway, for example, citizens are entitled to free care in public hospitals, in obstetric clinics, and in sanatoria for treatment, convalescence, and rehabilitation without limit of time. If they choose to enter a private hospital, reimbursement is made according to a specified schedule. Because of the scattered population in Norway, transportation to a hospital, whether by helicopter, reindeer, or other means, is provided free. In Sweden free hospitalization in general wards is limited to two years. The combinations and differences in detail are virtually infinite.

Early European health insurance funds provided for service benefits to the patient and direct payment on his behalf to the physician by the sickness fund. According to Abel-Smith (1965), this arrangement was resisted by physicians' groups as they became more organized. The doctors' incomes, as well as their control of the system, was greater under cash-benefit schemes in which the patient paid the physician's fee and then presented the bill to his insurance fund for recoupment of expenses up to a specified amount. Physicians could then charge more than the stipulated reimbursement level and the patient would make up the difference out of pocket. France, New Zealand, Finland, Sweden, and parts of Canada, for example, follow this practice; in some countries higher charges are permitted only to patients from higher-income families. In countries with multiple sickness funds (Austria, Greece, West Germany, Israel, Italy, Japan, and others), benefits vary greatly depending upon the political clout and negotiating skill of the various parties involved. The same is true in the United States, where specific benefit schedules often form part of labor-management contracts in individual companies or in industry-wide negotiations. Where commercial health insurance is available on a group or individual basis, policyholders may purchase such coverages as they wish for ambulatory, hospital, surgical, indemnity, or other types of benefits.

One distinct category of benefits has to do with maternity. According to a review of 128 countries by the U.S. Social Security Administration (1976), 71 of these had some type of sickness program in 1975, but 17 countries had only a maternity insurance plan. Most maternity benefits are in the form of a percentage of the mother's salary paid, often for about six weeks before and after the birth, plus in some countries a cash grant, or a gift such as a layette. Coverage of the medical aspects of prenatal care and delivery is subject to numerous variations.

While a comprehensive international comparison of medical service benefits is not feasible in this volume, a few points may be mentioned. The first issue, sometimes considered an invisible benefit, is the "free choice" of physician by the patient. Even though the actual selection of a doctor is always limited by the realities of geography and economics, many people resent arbitrary assignment in this regard. "Free choice of private general physician," says Roemer (1969), "meets the psychological needs of patients... and satisfies the competitive entrepreneurial interests of doctors." Second, while the *quality* of all ambulatory or hospital care is roughly equivalent in developed countries (regardless of the overall system), in LDCs one can often expect private and social security programs to be of a higher standard than government care. Third, the handling of issues such as pharmaceutical benefits varies greatly and is not always predictable. In many countries, including the U.S.A. and the U.S.S.R., drugs given in hospital are commonly paid for through the hospital coverage plan, while those for use at home are bought by the patient. In Australia, Sweden, and Norway life-saving drugs are free and others must be paid for. Denmark requires partial payment for drugs on an approved list and full payment for others. In Britain there is a small flat charge for any prescription. The common practice in poorer countries of issuing very small amounts of drugs, free or at minimal cost, has both good and bad features. Wastage is prevented, overdosage minimized, and patients cannot sell their drugs to others. On the other hand, repeated visits are annoying, inconvenient, and expensive to the patient and wasteful of staff time to the service. Fourth, whereas many medical benefits have upper use limits, some countries have made special provisions for catastrophic illness. In the Netherlands residents are usually entitled to the full cost of medical care after one year of illness, and in the U.S.A. patients with particular conditions such as chronic kidney disease have special government funding or receive help from disease- or organ-related voluntary agencies. Finally, it is evident that increasing costs in all countries are acting to rationalize and centralize services and to expand governmental support and control.

PROVIDERS

Our discussion has thus far centered on the users and their relations to the medical care system. We turn now to the other indispensible component:

the providers. This term refers here not to the organizations but to the medical workers actually seen by users and to those that support their professional efforts. Just as we could not discuss users without also describing their manner of use (i.e., benefits), we cannot divorce the medical care personnel from the contexts in which they function (i.e., facilities).

Providers

Personnel			Facilities	
Vocation	Mode	Remuneration	Locus	Category
Auxiliary	Group	Capitation	Community	Clinic
Feldsher	Institutional	Contract	Home	Dispensary
Midwife	Solo	Fee	Institution	Extended care
Nurse	Split	Salary	Mobile	Hospital
Physician	Team		Workplace	Office
Technician				Surgery
etc.				

Physicians

The keystone of the medical care system in all countries is the physician, a graduate of a medical school, with professional responsibility for all aspects of patient care. In more developed countries, and for the wealthier segment of the population elsewhere, the physician is normally the point of primary contact for all curative and most preventive services. Whereas different physicians may use the same technology for diagnosis, the same surgical procedures, or the same drugs, the form of medical practice varies greatly between and often within countries.

Basically a physician may be paid a specified fee for a certain unit of service, a salary, or in both ways. In the United States, the individual entrepreneurial ("solo") practice of medicine has been the rule, in what has been called America's last great cottage industry. However, group practice under many arrangements has been developing in that country since the brothers Mayo established their multispecialty clinic in Minnesota in 1887. In recent years there has been a rapid growth of group practices in which three or more physicians work together and pool their incomes. Some large private prepaid insurance schemes, notably the Kaiser-Permanente system (mainly in California), employ numerous physicians on salary and also distribute bonus payments to them according to a predetermined schedule. Small group practices are becoming increasingly common in many countries of western Europe; in Britain over 75% of general practitioners operate in groups of two or three.

Roemer (1969, 1970) has defined *direct* and *indirect* patterns under which general physician services are provided in relation to social security in various countries. Under the former, personnel and institutions are elements of the social security system and are subject to direct control. Physicians are salaried for their time in the system. Under the indirect pattern the system contracts with independent health workers for certain services. The "indirect" countries tend to have higher levels of economic development and a lower degree of centralization in their political structure.

Salaried physicians have been used for some time in Europe. In the late nineteenth century, salaried community (general practice) doctors were engaged on a large scale to supervise public health and provide medical care to the poor. In Poland and Tsarist Russia the *zemstvo* system developed, under which physicians worked in regional polyclinics in order to save the time and cost of the home visits enjoyed by a wealthier clientele. This system was adopted by the sick funds of Jewish immigrants to Palestine, and is still used in the polyclinics of the Kupat Holim. Urban polyclinics and rural health centers on the Soviet model are a prominent feature of the Cuban medical care system and are found all over eastern Europe.

In developing countries the government medical services, and often the social security also, are based upon salaried physicians, where they are available. In Mexico, Colombia, Costa Rica, Greece, Kenya, and several other countries all new physicians must undertake a period of full-time government service in rural areas. In many other countries all physicians must spend a proportion of their time working for the government, although this can be done where the doctor wishes, usually in a city. Because of the low wages in Latin America and elsewhere (e.g., Indonesia, Egypt, Thailand), some physicians devote only part of the day to government service and maintain their private practice at other times. Government service may consist of medical school teaching, directing diagnostic laboratories, research or administration, but most commonly involves extensive patient contact in government clinics. The system of split practice is found in Europe. In Spain, for example, many physicians divide their time between government service, service under a private medical insurance plan, and their own personal practice. Even socialist countries may permit split practice; in Poland, physicians must work seven hours daily on salaried government service, but they may engage in private practice thereafter.

General practice physicians in "indirect pattern" countries operate under a variety of payment mechanisms. In Australia the doctor can bill the patient, who then claims reimbursement from the Health Insurance Commission, or he may bill the government directly (at a 15% discount). The system by which the patient pays the doctor and then seeks full or partial reimbursement is popular with physicians in many countries such as Belgium, France, Sweden, Switzerland, and (in part) Japan. This system is also found in East Germany, which although a socialist state is distinguished from other COMECON members by substantial private ownership. Under this plan physicians retain their independence and greatly simplify their bookkeeping. In Canada the same idea is used in some provinces; in others, physicians bill directly to the health plan, which then collects the full cost from the provincial and federal governments. In New Zealand the physician receives a flat government payment for each consultation, and a higher amount if called on outside of regular working hours. Often the patient pays the full bill and is then reimbursed the flat amount from the government, again simplifying life for the physician. A feature common to all of the reimbursement schemes is that a certain predetermined percentage or amount is paid by the insurance scheme or government, and the patient must pay the difference, if any, up to the amount requested by the doctor.

Two other types of payment mechanisms must be mentioned. The first is the *capitation* method, used by the British National Health Service and in Spain, the Netherlands, and to some extent in Italy and Denmark. In this plan a patient selects a general physician and becomes enrolled in his or her panel. The physician is then paid by the government according to the size of the panel, not by the number of service units performed. There is a clear incentive to minimize return visits and unneeded patient contact under this plan, and this is also true for salaried physicians. At least in theory, however, doctors paid through a capitation system have an incentive, by increasing their panel, to see more patients than those who receive a salary regardless of their productivity. The last payment mechanism to be discussed is the complex system of *Krankenkassen* or sickness funds in Austria and West Germany. Regional physicians' associations contract with these funds on a quarterly basis to provide care for fund members. Each member obtains from his fund a sickness slip (*Krankenschein*), which is valid for three months and must be presented to the physician to obtain services under the plan. Participating physicians receive a varying share of the total negotiated lump sum, depending on the services provided and weighted according to standard fee schedules. Both the capitation and negotiated-sum systems retain a measure of selection by both practitioner and patient, and they preserve the private entrepreneurial status of the doctor.

It is evident that all of these payment mechanisms and complex fee structures can, and do, influence the shape of particular medical practices such as the use of specific services, return visits, and referral to specialists. Moreover, the entire form of private practice, whether solo or group, general or specialist, is often molded by these forces.

The foregoing descriptions have dealt primarily with general medical practitioners undertaking ambulatory care of patients. For this group of physicians the major difference between western Europe and most eastern European countries is in their independence as private contractors and their location in a private office ("surgery") or a public facility (polyclinic). In hospital services, there is often much less difference. The free-choice principle in western Europe, the assignment system in eastern Europe, and the deep division between community-based and hospital-based doctors have historical antecedents extending back far beyond the 1917 Russian revolution or the development of modern medical care systems.

In the United States a community-based physician can admit a patient to a hospital (at which he or she has "hospital privileges") and continue management of that patient, dividing his practice between office-based ambulatory care and hospital-based inpatient care. In western Europe, however, these roles are generally divided to the extent that the general practitioner relinquishes care of the hospitalized patient to the separate full-time medical staff of the hospital. The patterns of hospital ownership and usage vary widely. Great Britain and the Scandinavian countries in particular have tried to rationalize their hospital systems. Sweden, for example, has a hierarchy of municipal health centers providing primary ambulatory care for about 15,000 people, local district hospitals of about 300 beds for secondary care (60–90,000 people), 28 county hospitals (*lasarett*) of 800 to 1,000 beds (250–300,000 people), and 7 regional hospitals for tertiary subspecialty care for about a million persons each. In Sweden there is little development of general family practice and the public has direct access to specialists via hospital outpatient departments. Norway has a similar system of hospital organization and also operates numerous "cottage hospitals" of 8 to 20 beds in remote areas.

These are often under the charge of the district health officer who is commonly the only physician in the area. In Scandinavia generally hospitals are operated by local authorities although there are some privately operated facilities. Elsewhere practices vary. Italy has both public *enti ospedalieri* belonging to the state, region, province, or commune and many private *cliniche* or *case di cura*. In Japan, 15% of hospitals are operated by local governments and 5% by the national government, while 80% of hospitals are private, often operated by one or a few physicians. The Netherlands, by contrast, prohibits all for-profit private hospitals. There 75% of hospitals are voluntary, operated largely by religious groups, and the other 25% are run by the government. The variety of arrangements is endless, and the few examples given should suffice to show the range.

In the U.S.S.R. the institutionalization of medical practice is virtually complete. There are no general practitioners among physicians; all are specialists, and all work in their appropriate government facility. Students in the "medical institutes" follow one of five basic tracks: medicine (including internal medicine, surgery, obstetrics, etc.), pediatrics, public health, pharmacology, or stomatology—there is no separate profession of dentistry (Storey, 1972). The basic health unit is the polyclinic, of which there are more than 40,000 in the US.S.S.R. These are generally divided into adult polyclinics, staffed by an internist (*terapevt*) and nurse for each 2,000 adults, and pediatric polyclinics with a pediatrician and one or two nurses for each 1,000 children under 14. The two may of course be under the same roof or in urban areas may share a roof with a hospital, but they are administratively separate facilities. Each *terapevt* works three hours daily in the polyclinic, three hours on home visits, and two days per month on emergency services; 70% are women. The medical services in the U.S.S.R. are highly centralized: policy is made by the Ministry of Health and Council of Ministers at national level. Each of the 15 republics has a health minister whose functions are to implement national policy and to prepare a budget. All funds come from the central government. The entire country is divided into regions (*oblasts*) of up to five million, districts (*rayons*) of up to 150,000 with hospitals, and neighborhoods (*uchastoks*) with polyclinics (Fry and Crome, 1972). A very similar system, on a much smaller scale, exists in Cuba.

A decentralized system in a socialized context is seen in Yugoslavia (Vukmanovic, 1972), where provinces enact their own basic laws regarding organization of medical services. All have polyclinics (*dom zdravlja*) with general practitioners, and the same physician might work both in a polyclinic and in a hospital. Health institutions in Yugoslavia have an elected council that includes staff and community members. A similar arrangement is found in Finland.

Other professionals

Medical care naturally involves many more people than just patients and physicians. Taylor has provided a useful table showing various categories of medical workers (Table 7-3). A more exhaustive classification is given in the World Health Statistics Annual for 1972 (World Health Organization, 1976), where almost 250 separate job titles (in English) are divided into 29 occupational groups. Once again, great variations are found from one country to another in the use of various kinds of medical and health workers. In the United States the public is accustomed to the picture described by Navarro (1975): There were in 1970 about 311,000 M.D.s, 93.1% male, and 724,000 nurses (R.N.), 97.3% female, a ratio of about 1 to 2.3. There is no reason a *priori* why such a ratio, in numbers or sex, should exist. In a great many countries in the developing world there are fewer nurses than physicians. Baker (1971) shows a ratio of 0.6 nurses per doctor in Sudan and Turkey and only 0.4 in India. Even in Japan there are only 12 nurses for each 10 doctors. The number of nurses is very low in Latin America, where nursing is often looked down upon as a low-prestige occupation, not to be followed by refined women. Sigerist (1960) quotes a cynical saying, "If a girl is pretty you should marry her, if she is not pretty but clever make her a school teacher, and if she is neither pretty nor clever make her a nurse." The restricted educational and vocational opportunities for women in most developing countries, combined in some cases with restrictive allocation of health training facilities by M.D.s, have kept the number of nurses low in many developing countries. In Europe the relative number of nurses is much higher: Sweden has over 3 R.N.s per M.D. and Finland has 3.7. However, some countries of Europe, including Austria and Italy, also have severe shortages of nurses. Considering the variety of forms of medical practice, it is difficult to specify the role of a nurse as distinct from that of a physician. Certainly some nurses are better trained and assume more responsibility for patient care than some doctors, particularly in medically underserved areas. The function of some middle-level health workers, types of health professionals generally unfamiliar in western Europe and North America, is often better defined. Of these probably the best known is the *feldsher*.

In the U.S.S.R., feldshers are among more than two million middle

Table 7-3. Classification of health auxiliaries and their relation to professionals

Function	Professional (Degree course)	Middle level (High school plus two or more years training)	Low level (Elementary or middle school with up to one year training)
Medical care			
a. Independent responsibility for treatment	Physician	Feldsher (Russia) Licentiate (India & Pakistan) Medical assistant (Pacific & Africa)	Dresser First aid men Medical corpsman (armed services)
b. Comprehensive care	Occasional physician	Health officer (Ethiopia)	Village health worker Barefoot doctor
c. Diagnostic and therapeutic specialties	Specialist	Technicians-laboratory, x-ray, physiotherapy, etc.	Technical assistants
Hospital nursing	Degree nurse	Diploma nurse Auxiliary nurse	Auxiliary nurse Ward helper
General public health	Public health physician Public health nurse	Health visitor Community nurse	Community nurse
MCH and obstetrics	Physician Midwife	Midwife Auxiliary nurse midwife	Auxiliary nurse midwife Village midwife (trained)
Sanitation Specialized functions for mass diseases	Sanitary engineer Public health specialist	Sanitarian Malaria officers (upper echelon)	Sanitary inspector Malaria sprayers, etc.

Source: Adapted from Sorkin, 1975, after Taylor.

medical workers trained in separate middle medical training institutes. There are three levels: the general, midwife, and sanitarian feldshers who take a 2 1/2 year course; the laborant, nurse, dental technician, and pharmacist feldshers with 1 year and 10 months of training; and the "dental doctor" with 2 years and 10 months (Storey, 1972). This last group, performing routine dental care, is distinguished from the stomatologist, a medical specialist giving more advanced oral care. A similar type of basic worker has functioned since 1921 in New Zealand, where school children receive their regular dental care from especially trained monovalent dental assistants. The Jamaican government has recently established such a program (Gillespie, 1973).

Feldsher training begins after 10 years of general education, about age 17. Feldshers in the U.S.S.R. do not usually work in polyclinics, which are staffed by graduate physicians and nurses. They also do not substitute for physicians except in small rural *uchastoks* where feldsher-midwife stations still exist, and here this role is declining as more physicians are trained to take over rural polyclinics. The primary functions of feldshers are to *complement* physicians in both urban and rural practice, especially in three situations that have been described by Storey (1972a). The first is for staffing of the small medical posts (*zdravpunkty*) found in most Russian cities. The second is in the *skoraya* or mobile emergency medical services. Because of the strenuous nature of this work, only 60% of skoraya feldshers are female, while the proportion of women in other feldsher roles is 90%. The third function of feldshers is in staffing forward health stations in factories, shops, and other work units. Although the U.S.S.R. has one of the world's highest ratios of physicians to population, the training of feldshers continues at a rate roughly equal to that of new doctors, about 30,000 per year in each category. Here, as in Albania, Bulgaria, and Mongolia, the use of feldshers is firmly established in the medical services. In Hungary, Poland, and Romania, by contrast, feldsher training, started after the Second World War, has been discontinued as sufficient doctors and nurses have become available (Flahault, 1973).

In contrast to the long and extensive use of feldshers in the Soviet Union, the United States in 1972 had only 585 graduate physician's assistants (Hahn, 1974), a number that increased to 2,800 by 1976, with 5,700 more expected to graduate by the end of 1977. Physician's assistants (PAs) in the U.S. can handle about 75% of common medical problems, depending upon licensing restrictions. They generally work with a particular doctor in both office and hospital, take medical histories, conduct physical examinations, and manage common emergency situations until the arrival of a doctor. By 1976 some 50 colleges and universities offered the two-year training course, and there were two job offers per graduate. Of the PAs in practice, 45% are in communities of fewer than 20,000, and 77% work in primary care (New York Times, 1976). Thus the following elements characterize the usage of PAs: (1) substantial demand; (2) brief training; (3) trend towards medically underserved rural areas; (4) concentration on primary care, routing, and emergency; (5) referral of difficult cases to a physician. Precisely the same considerations have given rise to the strong worldwide interest in medical auxiliaries in developing countries, where the degree of need can be multiplied many times over as compared with the United States.

Physicians in developing countries: the controversy

The number of medical schools in Asia, Africa, and Latin America has been increasing greatly in recent years. Yet many people remain critical and unconvinced of the overall usefulness of this effort to produce more physicians in developing countries.

What is the argument about? Why should anyone object to having more doctors where they seem most urgently needed? What are the pros and cons of medical education in developing countries?

Those who wish to maintain international standards favor the training of more doctors by scientific medical faculties on the western model. This will permit graduates to obtain advanced specialty training and experience abroad so they may practice the most modern medicine upon their return. In this view, all patients deserve first-class care, which can only be delivered by a thoroughly educated physician. Advocating this position is a large proportion of the existing medical establishment, whose prospects for career advancement may depend to a large extent upon the prestige of association with London, Paris, or Boston. Another argument for training physicians in LDCs is that medical curricula and textbooks are well established and known by local and expatriate faculty. New instructional pathways leading to "substandard" practitioners do not appeal to those who devote themselves to excellence in medical education. A third argument is that even in poor countries some people are able and willing to pay for private medical care by physicians who speak their language and understand their problems and that these people deserve to receive such treatment.

Opposing the production of larger numbers of conventionally trained physicians in developing countries are the following arguments:

1. It is economically impossible to produce enough physicians. The cost of training a doctor to international standards is often higher in poor countries than in wealthier ones (Table 7-4); maintenance of faculties and physical facilities is extremely expensive.
2. After physicians are trained it is often so difficult, if not impossible, to employ them properly in their home countries that large numbers join the "brain drain" and migrate, often permanently, to developed countries (Table 7-5). It seems paradoxical that where the proportion of doctors in the population is very low by world standards, there may still be an excess relative to the nation's economic capacity to absorb them. This is true in the major developing countries of origin ("donor countries") of physician migrants: India, Iran, Pakistan, the Philippines, South Korea, and elsewhere, to a greater or lesser extent. In part this problem stems from the realities of income distribution in LDCs. Mejia and Pizurki (1976) report that the income of working physicians in donor countries is, on average, 18 times higher than that of the general population.

    The emigration of medical graduates from poor countries is often referred to as "reverse aid," or a subsidy from LDCs to MDCs. In the United States in 1976, 30% of all interns and residents were foreign-trained; in New York state the figure was 52% overall, and in municipal hospitals, even higher (Sullivan, 1977). Not all foreign-trained doctors originated from LDCs.

    It is argued by some that increasing the number of conventional physicians trained in LDCs would only increase this attrition by emigration.
3. The conventional medical school curriculum in more advanced countries is simply not applicable to the needs of LDCs. The most telling argument against the production of more physicians in these settings is their irrelevancy. In recent years a crescendo of criticism has arisen over the common policy in LDCs of training physicians to provide sophisticated, hospital-based medical care to a population in need of the basic amenities of modern civilization. Mejia and Pizurki (1976) have stated bluntly: "The point has perhaps already been reached where the term 'international qualification' would refer to a qualification based on education that is irrelevant to the health needs of the great majority of people in the developing countries."

How has it happened that the doctor of medicine, so esteemed and respected for generations, is now the object of such criticism particularly (but not only) in the developing world? The answer cannot be given in a few simple words, but includes the following elements: As political independence, awareness, and communications have grown, so has impatience with existing conditions. Low economic status, inadequate education, high morbidity, and high infant and childhood mortality are no

Table 7-4. Comparative costs of medical education in selected countries, 1965[a]

Country	Per medical doctor graduated[a]	Per medical assistant	Per nurse graduated[b]	Per auxiliary nurse	Per health assistant	Per auxiliary sanitarian
Senegal	84,000	—	835	—	—	—
Jamaica	24,000	—	1,385	—	—	—
Guatemala	19,200	—	2,700	—	—	—
Thailand	6,600	—	1,200	—	700	350
Kenya	22–28,000	2,890	3,380	2,167	787	1,680
Pakistan	12,600	—	2,960	—	—	—
Colombia	29,000	—	3,000	1,000	—	—
United States	19,630	—	—	—	—	—

[a]In U.S. $. These figures should be viewed with some suspicion.
[b]Obtained by dividing total recurrent costs as assignable to medical education by number of students graduating.
Adapted from World Bank, 1975.

Table 7-5. Data on the migration of physicians within and between developing and developed countries (figures in thousands)[a]

Area of destination

Area of origin	Europe	U.S.S.R.	U.S.A. and Canada	Australia and New Zealand	Developed countries	Latin America	Asia	Africa	Oceania	Developing countries	World (excluding China)
Europe	9.8	—	22.9	2.7	35.3	—	0.1	1.0	—	1.1	36.4
U.S.S.R.	0.2	—	0.8	0.1	1.1	—	0.0	0.1	—	0.1	1.2
U.S.A. and Canada	0.5	—	7.1	0.2	7.9	—	0.0	0.0	0.0	0.1	8.0
Australia and New Zealand	1.5	—	0.9	0.5	2.9	—	0.0	—	—	0.0	2.9
Developed countries	12.0	—	31.7	3.6	47.2	—	0.2	1.1	0.0	1.3	48.5
Latin America	0.6	—	12.1	0.0	12.8	0.3	0.0	0.0	—	0.3	13.1
Asia	13.5	—	30.9	0.7	45.1	0.0	1.5	0.8	—	2.3	47.4
Africa	2.4	—	2.4	0.0	4.8	—	0.6	0.3	—	0.9	5.7
Oceania	0.0	—	—	0.1	0.1	—	—	—	0.0	0.0	0.1
Developing countries	16.5	—	45.4	0.8	62.8	0.3	2.1	1.1	0.0	3.6	66.3
World (excluding China)	28.5	—	77.1	4.4	110.0	0.3	2.3	2.2	0.1	4.9	114.8

[a]The figure 0.0 indicates less than 50 and a dash (—) indicates zero. Totals and subtotals may not always correspond to the sums of the figures appearing in the table, because of the rounding off of figures.
Source: Mejia and Pizurki, 1976.

longer viewed as inevitable, nor, indeed, as acceptable. At the same time, known scientific and technical advances are seen to have no beneficial impact on the lives of most people. News of the landing of men on the moon and of instruments on Mars gushes from every transistor radio, but to many an impoverished villager the intended reaction of admiration may be supplanted by one of hostility. As the economic gap between have nots and haves has widened, so has the animosity between them. "The words 'diagnose' and 'prescribe,'" says Bryant (1969) "evoke the strongest feelings of professional possessiveness." This, in turn, often evokes the strongest feelings of public resentment. Paradoxically, the very establishment of new medical schools has led to some soul-searching as to their proper function in society, and the opportunity (often missed) to plan from the start to reduce the chasms of estrangement between medical education, health services, and the needs of the people. Lastly may be mentioned the influence of revolutionary movements and writers, including Mao Tse-tung (page 286), and of the example set by new approaches to medical systems in China and elsewhere.

The primary care team

It is the current consensus that new approaches are needed to solve the health problems in poor areas of the world. No single scheme is universally applicable but the following elements are often suggested: (1) increased planning, coordination, and integration of the parts of the health services sector—e.g., education of personnel, development of facilities, provision of services, and utilization of resources—with each other and with national development planning in general; (2) stronger emphasis on primary care; (3) sustained attempts to make services more widely available, especially in rural areas; (4) greater community participation; and (5) broader development of health care teams, including various kinds of auxiliary medical workers. The implementation of each of these elements varies at present from negligible to substantial, but the general principles appear to be gaining increasingly widespread acceptance.

Functions In recent years an avalanche of studies and publications on primary care has covered every aspect of this problem in almost all countries of the world. Prominent in these are pictures of two kinds of pyramids. First is the pyramid of health services (e.g., Flahault, 1973), with the minister of health at the apex, down through the layers of bureaucracy to the many local health installations at the base. The second is the "skill pyramid" (e.g., King, 1970) at any one institution, showing the physician, or specialist at the top and proceeding through strata of nurses and clerks to the most lowly and most numerous employees. Also featured in works on primary care are diagrams resembling basket starfish, with repeatedly branched arms radiating from a central hub; these branches represent hospitals, polyclinics, health centers, satellite subcenters, dispensaries, *puestos de salud* and many other categories of medical care facilities. (It may be noted parenthetically that basket starfish are known to zoologists as the Gorgonocephalidae, named after the three hideous snake-haired sisters in Greek mythology whose terrible aspect turned beholders to stone.)

The most attention (e.g., King, 1966; Morley, 1976) has been given to the base of the pyramid or the periphery of the radii, respectively, because that is where the frontline interactions actually occur, where the users and providers of primary health care meet face-to-face. What takes place during these encounters? One hopes that all, or most, of the following will occur:

1. Flow of information, in both directions: to the user, education about sanitation, disease prevention, nutrition, family planning; from the user, hopes, fears, symptoms, observations, clues for an alert medical worker to use in planning better services.
2. Primary prevention of disease by immunization, distribution of antimalarials and other prophylactic measures.
3. Procedures for screening real or potential health problems, especially among pregnant women and young children.
4. Distribution of contraceptives to those desiring them.
5. Secondary prevention by provision of medications when needed for confirmed cases of chronic illnesses such as tuberculosis. This is also a means of primary prevention for contacts or patients.
6. Diagnosis, treatment, and follow-up of cases of common minor illnesses.
7. First aid for trauma and other accidents.
8. Arrangement for assistance with normal childbirth.
9. Referral, when necessary with transportation provided, of complex, difficult, or emergency cases to better-trained workers at better-equipped facilities.
10. Maintenance of records and vital statistics.

The planning, design and construction of the actual service sites, as well as their integration into the overall health services, is being studied by the Division of Strengthening of Health Services of the World Health Organization as well as by other groups (Kleczkowski and Pibouleau, 1976).

The person providing health care in these situations is generally a nonphysician member of the health care team, a medical auxiliary. The terms describing the various positions in the team suffer from an abundance of informal usages, but we will use the following definitions (see also Table 7-3):

Composition A *professional* on a primary care team is a person having full secondary and university education leading to an internationally recognized degree such as Doctor of Medicine or Registered Nurse. An *auxiliary* is any of a wide range of trained medical workers who have vocational and practical qualifications, with or without diploma, beyond regular schooling and who work normally under the direct or remote supervision of a professional. Both professional and auxiliary personnel are usually *credentialed,* as opposed to the traditional healers who often work in the same communities. Credentialing has several aspects: (1) *accreditation* of a specific course of study or institution to meet certain standards set by a recognized accrediting agency; (2) *certification* of individuals by an organization to record compliance with rules or standards; (3) *registration* by listing on an official roster; and sometimes (4) *licensing* by a government to permit use of a title, engage in an occupation, or perform certain functions (Selden, 1974). In some countries efforts are being made to bring some traditional health workers into the official system. Most commonly this involves the village midwife (the *empírica* or *parteira* [Latin America], *matrone* [French-speaking Africa], *dai* [India], etc.) who is given brief training in hygiene, nutrition, and basic first aid and who is often provided with a kit of supplies and instruments.

Within teams, professionals have a dual function: to use their advanced skills directly when needed for patient care; and to educate, supervise, and act as consultant to the auxiliary members of the team. The auxiliaries are "effectively used to relieve professionals of mundane tasks and to increase the outreach of primary care services at a cost that the country can afford in terms of financial and educational resources, and service facilities" (Fendall, 1973). The number of countries utilizing formally trained health auxiliaries has increased so rapidly in recent years that the World Health Organization (1976a) has issued a lengthy compendium of reference materials available for their training and use.

In many countries, various categories of medical workers have long been officially trained to less than "internationally recognized" standards precisely for diagnosis and treatment of disease. The feldsher in Russia has already been mentioned. Fiji has produced assistant medical officers since 1886, and various countries of the British Commonwealth for decades trained "licensed" medical practitioners, who were never recognized as equal to the "registered" British physicians. Between the end of the First and Second World War, both English- and French-speaking countries of Africa established schools for medical assistants or *secouristes-hygiénistes*. When Zaire (formerly Democratic Republic of the Congo) became independent from Belgium in 1960, no African physicians were present in the country. Therefore, about 200 experienced medical auxiliaries were sent to French, Swiss, or Belgian medical schools for accelerated three-year courses leading to M.D. degrees (de-Craemer and Fox, 1968). Upon their return they formed the basis of the Congolese medical services, joined later by the new physicians who emerged from six-year medical courses established in Kinshasa and Lubumbashi. This was an unusual response to an emergency situation. Generally there is no intention for auxiliary positions to be stepping-stones to subsequent education for professional posts, although this may sometimes happen. In Iran, for example, the *behdars* (auxiliary doctors) made such efforts to secure conventional medical degrees that the behdar training program was terminated. There must be respect, job satisfaction, and opportunity for growth and advancement within the auxiliary ranks in order to attract and retain effective medical care teams.

Of all types of auxiliary health workers, the *barefoot doctors* of China have received the most attention. "When the Chinese talk of 'barefoot doctors,'" said Horn (1971), "they do not mean that such a man has no shoes but that he has no special privileges, that he fully shares the life of the people among whom he works." The barefoot doctor is a product of the struggles of the Cultural Revolution of the late 1960s and represents an aspect of the politicized focus on the Chinese countryside. Barefoot doctors in the countryside, together with the urban *worker doctors* and *street doctors* (red medical workers), are part-time medical workers, "not divorced from productive labor." The selection, training and use of these workers is extremely decentralized and flexible in response to local requirements. Characteristically, young men and women in their 20s or 30s are selected by their colleagues for special training of from one to two months or more in a local institution, after which they resume their previous work, receiving frequent in-service follow-up education (Wang, 1975; New and New, 1975). These part-time medical workers are trained to diagnose and treat about 100 common ailments and to prescribe about 100 modern medicines (Sidel, 1972). Substantial reliance is also placed upon traditional remedies such as the use of herbs, moxibustion, and acupuncture, all of which are inexpensive and acceptable to the community. Barefoot doctors and other medical workers also pay attention to sanitation, vector control, and other environmental health problems as well as to family planning and a variety of functions as needed. Auxiliary medical and health workers of various kinds have been essential to the "mass patriotic health campaigns" and other disease control measures in China. The number of barefoot doctors mobilized in the decade 1966-76 has been estimated by Chen (1976) at 1.3 million, with 3.6 million other health workers and midwives in place, giving the People's Republic, in theory, more than one medical worker per 200 people.

Barefoot doctors have captured the imagination of many people throughout the world, and there has been much speculation about the relevance or transferability of the program to other countries in similar economic circumstances. Horn (1971) summarized four lessons to be drawn from the Chinese experience. First, rely on the potential talents, enthusiasms, and creative abilities of ordinary people. Second, encourage self-reliance, which can be extended to a national scale. Third, create a new type of rural health worker, one who will retain deep roots in the village community and engage in medical work on a part-time and voluntary basis. Fourth, organize the education of rural health workers to combine theory and practice at every stage, conduct it in the countryside, and adapt it to the needs of the locality. Perhaps the most important lesson to be learned from China is that it is not impossible for a poor country to mount successful efforts against the most pervasive and damaging threats to health, that large amounts of money or of medical research are not necessarily prerequisites, and that the lack of either should not be accepted as justification for official inaction.

Performance King (1970) has enunciated a general rule for employing the various members of the medical care team: "Push tasks down the pyramid to the humblest and cheapest cadre capable of doing [them] satisfactorily." With this in mind, let us compare the functioning of professional and low-level auxiliary medical workers assigned to a hypothetical village health post in a developing country. The professional is more likely to be far from home and family. Opportunities for cultural activities, professional exchanges, and career advancement are few. The auxiliary may have grown up in the village, or nearby—often a precondition of service. He or she knows the language, culture, and perhaps all the individuals in the village and is not so likely to be lonely or frustrated. Personal matters aside, how will the two individuals perform their job of providing primary medical care? How much difference will there be in outcome? The best data on this point are from Fendall (1972), who visited many outpatient clinics in a number of developing countries, observing and tabulating the patterns of complaints presented. He found that most illness was of a common and minor nature. "Possibly 5 to 10 percent of patients need more knowledgeable attention than can be given by the auxiliary and, at most, 2 to 5 percent require referral to a hospital ... In the cottage hospitals, with minimal visiting-physician supervision, the experienced medical care auxiliary arrived at a correct diagnosis in about 80 percent of the cases..." (Fendall, 1972). Citing data for Senegal, Fendall shows a "striking similarity" between the diagnoses of physicians and local *infirmiers*. If such a comparison is meaningful, one may then surmise that for diagnosis and treatment on a daily basis an auxiliary makes use of much more of his training in terms of hours and subjects studied than a professional. The additional years of study by (and investment in) the professional are put to use mainly in management, to the extent possible, of more complex cases such as diabetes or leukemia, in situations such as nonresponse to treatment, and in the recognition of outbreaks of new or unusual diseases (e.g., cholera in west Africa). In village practice a very high proportion of problems are pediatric (often readily recognizable and preventable) and there are few, if any, old people with the complex of chronic and degenerative diseases so often seen in the more developed countries. Medical care is like a water supply—in the early stages of provision the quantity available is far more important than the quality.

Acceptance How are medical auxiliaries accepted by the people? In various ways, depending upon the situation. There may be some resentment at having a "substandard" or "second-class" doctor, but in many rural areas or urban slums the auxiliary may offer the only medical care available. Auxiliaries are sometimes preferred over professionals by the local people. A working group on rural medical care in Guatemala has shown (Pan American Health Organization, 1973) that in at least one project studied, villagers responded in greater numbers for examination and immunizations by medical auxiliaries than by physicians. In India a similar phenomenon was noted: "In one instance a city-educated nurse who spent several months in a village could not persuade a single woman to undergo tubectomy, while an illiterate *dai* from the same village was able to refer 75 women for tubectomy within the same period" (Djukanovic and Mach, 1975).

Organization We can describe here only a few of the planned arrangements for provision of primary care services in medically underserved countries. While the functioning of some of these systems leaves much to be desired, their inauguration is a giant step in the right direction and it is likely that they are forerunners of many more primary care programs to come in the next decades. Let us look at a few.

Bangladesh is divided into 19 districts and more than 400 *thanas*. A rural health complex, proposed for each thana, is made up of central health centers, plus peripheral subcenters for each 12,000 to 15,000 people. At the subcenter level the staff consists of one medical officer or assistant; one assistant health inspector, four "basic health workers" (each covering about 4,000 people) and a "lady health visitor" specializing in maternal and child health. About 3,700 subcenters are planned for the country (Djukanovic and Mach, 1975).

Bolivia has a system including the *centro de salud-hospital* of 10 to 100 beds; the *puesto medico* of 10 to 20 beds, staffed by one physician and auxiliaries; the *puesto sanitario* of 1-2 beds, for childbirth and emergencies, with a nurse in attendance; and the small *centro de salud* for immunizations and preventive care, with no beds, and only auxiliary personnel in attendance.

China has both urban and rural hierarchical systems, each with four main levels (Hu, 1975). Cities have regular municipal and district hospitals, to which factory hospitals staffed by teams of doctors and worker doctors may refer patients. In neighborhoods, street health stations with street doctors can refer difficult problems to district hospitals, and in turn can receive referrals from the lane health stations where part-time public health workers offer simple care. In rural areas, county hospitals serve 400,000 to 600,000 people. *Communes* of 15,000 to 50,000 have hospitals or clinics, with or without beds. Within communes each *production brigade* of up to 3,000 has a *brigade health station* with barefoot doctors and *production teams* of 250 to 800 workers may have a barefoot doctor or other public health worker.

In Cuba there are five levels for medical services, with attempted vertical and horizontal integration of all. They are: national; provincial, (with tertiary care hospitals); regional, (with secondary care hospitals); areal, with a *basic service unit* of urban polyclinics or rural hospitals (each for 25,000 to 30,000 people); and sectoral, with peripheral units at schools, farms and communities. This last level of national service is intended to serve 3,000 to 5,000 persons with an auxiliary public health nurse (Navarro, 1972; Djukanovic and Mach, 1975).

Ghana has planned for health centers as outpatient facilities, with a dispensary and maternity services, to serve a population of about 200,000 under the direction of a nurse. Additional mobile medical field units will function for control of specific diseases such as yaws and trypanosomiasis (Sai, 1973).

The Ministry of Public Health and Social Assistance in Guatemala has announced a five-tiered plan of facilities especially designed to improve rural health. These include the national reference hospital, regional hospitals, health centers, health posts (staffed by auxiliary nurses and rural health technicians), and community-level installations. At this peripheral level reliance is placed upon native midwives and *promotores de salud,* or health promoters (Long and Viau, 1974).

In Malaysia an efficient system of rural health centers has been functioning for years. Widely distributed MCH (maternal and child health) centers, each staffed by a government midwife (*bidan kerajaan*), are much used by the rural population.

The Third Development Plan of Nigeria (April 1975) projects Basic Health Units (BHUs) for each 50,000 people. A BHU includes: 1 comprehensive health center, 4 health centers, 5 mobile clinics and 20 smaller health clinics—with a total staff of 2 physicians, 2 public health nurses, 5 nurses, 8 midwives, and 46 other auxiliary personnel (Attah, 1975).

The Philippine government has created rural health units for municipalities of 2,000 to 50,000 to provide primary care, communicable disease control, environmental sanitation, and health education, plus *puericulture centers* for MCH services.

Sri Lanka has pioneered rural health centers since the Rockefeller Foundation helped establish the first in Kalutura in 1929 for MCH services, immunizations, and health education. The League of Nations in 1931 advocated similar units elsewhere (Roemer, 1971).

Yates (1975) has reported on the *medicina simplificada* program in Venezuela, where peripheral units extend into communities. District health centers staffed by professionals and having secondary care facilities, each supervise 8 to 10 subcenters (*medicaturas rurales*) with one physician and auxiliaries providing ambulatory care to 2,000 to 5,000 people. Simple rural dispensaries, each served by one auxiliary, provide basic primary care. In publications of the World Health Organization, similar community-based approaches have been described in many other countries, including India, Indonesia, Iran, Niger, Tanzania, and Yugoslavia (Newell, 1975; Djukanovic and Mach, 1975). A bibliography of manuals and training aids from various countries has also been published (World Health Organization, 1976a).

Conjoint training In recent years a number of countries have adopted conjoint training of the various members of the health care team, on the principle that those who will work together should develop their professional relationship (and interdependence) from the start. A pioneer in this approach is the University Centre for Health Sciences (CUSS) in Yaoundé, Cameroon, which was established in 1969 "to provide university education and training for senior level health cadres (doctors, pharmacists, dentists) and for the training of all other members of the health professions (midwives, nurses, laboratory technicians, sanitary technicians, nutritionists, etc.) as well as to direct the training of auxiliary personnel at all levels" (Nchinda, 1974). Basic to the CUSS plan is a community-type teaching hospital to simulate actual conditions in urban and rural areas, with emphasis on simple and realistic care rather than international "excellence." Teams organize and operate health services in model demonstration areas and undertake research to evaluate their effectiveness. There have been many problems in introducing this concept besides developing a new multilevel-multidisciplinary-multilingual medical curriculum, not the least of which is the paucity of teachers committed to the approach, but the idea appears to be catching on, at least in Africa. Centers for integrated education in the health sciences have been launched in recent years in Bamako (Mali), Brazzaville (Congo), Freetown (Sierra Leone), Ife (Nigeria), Libreville (Gabon), Monrovia (Liberia), Niamey (Niger), and at the National University in Zaire, with as yet undetermined results.

Some basic principles

In most countries the health services, being so closely associated with vital human needs, are subjects of continuing debate. Denunciations of medical care in the United States are legion; European systems such as the British National Health Service have come in for frequent criticism. If the more developed, older countries have such difficulty in organizing acceptable medical care systems, it is hardly surprising that experiments to provide primary care to residents of underserved areas of poorer countries have often met with little success. Some ambitious schemes have been curtailed or abandoned, often without the publicity with which they were inaugurated. In Iran a "health corps" of young professionals (Dadgar and Sarouknanian, 1971) who were to serve 18 months in rural areas was considered unsatisfactory because fewer than 10% of villages were actually reached (Flahault, 1973). In Turkey, despite establishment of a nursing curriculum in 1955, physicians still exceeded nurses in number in 1972, and the lack of auxiliary staff severely impaired the country's ambitious effort to nationalize its medical care system (Brockington, 1975). In Tanzania only a small proportion of projected rural health care centers were actually built during the first and second five-year plans, according to Segall (1972). Even the barefoot doctors of rural China have been the subjects of harsh critical comment. Hsu (1974) has stated that the quality of these auxiliary workers is uneven because of their highly decentralized training and the strong emphasis upon political orthodoxy. Barefoot doctors were said to have engaged in unauthorized medical experimentation upon the people, and to be beset by a substantial degree of job dissatisfaction. Gish (1973) is broadly pessimistic: "Although much has been written about the need for medical auxiliaries, and although the need is accepted by just about everyone academically involved in problems falling under the headings of health planning or health-manpower planning, in practice no more than a handful of countries are expanding the output of medical auxiliaries."

The problems of improving the health of the world's billions are, at the least, gargantuan, and innocent trust in any simple solution will lead to disappointment. On the other hand, abandonment to despair is even more certain to be nonproductive of positive efforts. We must first believe that mankind is capable of finding ways to effect a substantial improvement in the general level of human health, and then look for the underlying principles by which this can be done.

An objective assessment shows that the current unsatisfactory situation is not basically a result of a lack of technical knowledge, as might have been said a century ago. The causes and means of prevention, and to a fair extent, the treatment are now generally known for the infectious, parasitic, and nutritional diseases that make up the majority of the world's burden of ill health. This is not to say that further biomedical research is not needed: a vaccine against malaria, for example, might save a million lives a year and prevent enormous suffering. More effective and less toxic drugs are always wanted. The prevalence of chronic diseases in both industrialized and developing countries is increasing. But in general the problem is not a technical one. Nor, despite great financial problems, is the current situation based entirely on economic causes. It is clearly imperative that more be spent for health services in poorer countries, but the expenditure of vast amounts of money (as in the United States) will still not ensure a high level of health, or even satisfactory medical care services.

It seems likely that the best means of attack against the health problems of the majority of mankind lie in the realms of motivation and organization. The health situation differs widely from one country to another because of variations in the elements that we have examined: natural, historical, economic and cultural factors, and available health and medical care services. The present chapter has described some schemes, ranging from the *Krankenschein* to the barefoot doctor, that have been devised by the ingenuity of people committed to improvement. It is not suggested that any one plan can be adopted entirely from one country to another, nor even from one time to another in the same country. But it is essential to know the experiences of others, to extract and apply lessons from their successes, and to avoid the mistakes of their failures. People are, after all, not so different that they cannot learn anything from each other.

The next chapter will consider more fully the international aspects of international health.

References[a]

Abel-Smith, B. 1965. The major patterns of financing and organization of medical services that have emerged in other countries. Medical Care 3: 33–40.

Assar, M. and Ž. Jakšić. 1975. A health services development project in Iran. *In:* K. W. Newell, Ed. Health By the People. Geneva. World Health Organization. pp. 112–127.

Attah, E. B. 1975. Health and Nigeria's third national development plan. Journal of the National Medical Association 68: 255–256.

Babson, J. H. 1972. Health Care Delivery Systems: A Multinational Survey. London. Pitman Medical. 128 p.

Badger, R. S. 1976. Health care in Brazil: a qualitative case study of government and private medicine in Londrina, Parana. Center for Latin American Studies. Stanford University. 99 p. Unpubl.

Baker, T. D. 1971. Paramedical paradoxes—challenges and opportunity. *In:* G. Wolstenholme and M. O'Connor, Eds. Teamwork for World Health. A Ciba Foundation Symposium. London. J. & A. Churchill. pp. 129–138.

[a] See footnote on p. 274.

Bahadori, M. 1975. Medical care and education in Iran. Journal of the American Medical Association 232: 966–967.

Blanpain, J. E. 1973. EEC: the founding six. *In:* I. Douglas-Wilson and G. McLachlan, Eds. Health Service Prospects. An International Survey. London. The Lancet and the Nuffield Provincial Hospitals Trust. pp. 37–54.

Bravo, A. L. 1958. Development of medical care services in Latin America. American Journal of Public Health 48: 434–447.

Bridgman, R. F. 1972. International trends in medical care organization and research. *In:* J. Fry and W. A. J. Farndale, Eds. International Medical Care. Wallingford, Pa. Washington Square East Publishers. pp. 8–23.

Brockington, F. 1975. World Health. 3rd Ed. Edinburgh. Churchill Livingstone. 345 p.

Bryant, J. 1969. Health and the Developing World. Ithaca, N.Y. Cornell University Press. 345 p.

Chen C-m. 1976. Discussion. *In:* Official Records of the World Health Organization No. 232. p. 191.

Dadgar, M. and G. Saroukhanian. 1971. The health corps in Iran: An approach to the better distribution of health resources in remote areas. *In:* G. Wolstenholme and M. O'Connor, Eds. Teamwork for World Health. A Ciba Foundation Symposium. London. J. & A. Churchill. pp. 37–50.

DeCraemer, W. and R. Fox. 1968. The Emerging Physician. A Sociological Approach to the Development of a Congolese Medical Profession. Stanford, Calif. Hoover Institution. 99 p.

deMiguel, J. M. 1975. A framework for the study of national health systems. Inquiry 12(2 Suppl.): 10–24.

Department of Health and Social Security (U.K.) 1971. The National Health Service. Summary of Early History and Main Features. Information Division, Intelligence Section. NHS Note 1. 11 p.

Djukanovic, V. and E. P. Mach, Eds. 1975. Alternative Approaches to Meeting Basic Health Needs in Developing Countries. Geneva. World Health Organization. 116 p.

Douglas-Wilson, I. and G. McLachlan, Eds. 1973. Health Service Prospects. An International Survey. London. The Lancet and the Nuffield Provincial Hospitals Trust. 346 p.

Fendall, N. R. E. 1972. Auxiliaries in Health Care. Programs in Developing Countries. Baltimore. Published for the Josiah Macy Jr. Foundation by the Johns Hopkins Press. 200 p.

Fendall, N. R. E. 1973. Auxiliaries in the health team. Pan American Health Organization Scientific Publication 278: 5–10.

Flahault, D. 1973. Review of current use of medical auxiliaries in health delivery systems. Pan American Health Organization Scientific Publication 278: 11–20.

Fry, J. and L. Crome. 1972. Medical care in the U.S.S.R. *In:* J. Fry and W. A. J. Farndale, Eds. International Medical Care. Wallingford, Pa. Washington Square East Publishers. pp. 177–203.

Fry, J. and W. A. J. Farndale, Eds. 1972. International Medical Care. Wallingford, Pa. Washington Square East Publishers. 341 p.

Gillespie, G. M. 1973. Training and use of dental auxiliaries in Jamaica. Pan American Health Organization Scientific Publication 278: 46–51.
Gish, O. 1973. Doctor auxiliaries in Tanzania. Lancet II: 1251–1254.
Hahn, J. A. L. 1974. Development of new kinds of health manpower. World Hospitals 10: 132–136.
Horn, J. S. 1971. Experiments in expanding the rural health service in People's China. In: G. Wolstenholme and M. O'Connor, Eds. Teamwork for World Health. A Ciba Foundation Symposium. London. J. & A. Churchill. pp. 77–87.
Hsu, R. C. 1974. The barefoot doctors of the People's Republic of China—some problems. New England Journal of Medicine 291: 124–127.
Hu, T-w. 1975. An Economic Analysis of Cooperative Medical Services in the People's Republic of China. U.S. Department of Health, Education, and Welfare Publication No. (NIH) 75-672. 41 p.
Imperato, P. J. 1974. Nomads of the west African Sahel and the delivery of health services to them. Social Science and Medicine 8: 443–457.
Jansen, G. 1973. The Doctor-Patient Relationship in an African Tribal Society. Assen (Neth.) Van Gorcum & Co. N.V. 224 p.
Joubert, C. 1972. Ghana—the VALCO medical service. In: J. P. Hughes. Ed. Health Care for Remote Areas. Oakland, Calif. Kaiser Foundation International. pp. 73–76.
King, M. H. 1966. Medical Care in Developing Countries: A Primer on the Medicine of Poverty and a Symposium from Makerere. Nairobi. Oxford University Press. Chaps. separately paged.
King, M. 1970. The auxiliary—his role and training. Journal of Tropical Medicine and Hygiene 73: 336–346.
Kleczkowski, B. M. and R. Pibouleau. 1976. Approaches to Planning and Design of Health Care Facilities in Developing Areas. Geneva. World Health Organization Offset Publication No. 29. 145 p.
Lampton, D. M. 1972. Public health and politics in China's past two decades. HSMHA Health Reports 87: 895–908.
Long, E. C. and A. Viau D. 1974. Health care extension using medical auxiliaries in Guatemala. Lancet I(7848): 127–130.
Mahler, H. 1977. World Health Target for Basic Human Needs. Address to the 30th World Health Assembly.
Maynard, A. 1975. Health Care in the European Community. Pittsburgh. University of Pittsburgh Press. 284 p.
Mejia, A. and H. Pizurki. 1976. World migration of health manpower. WHO Chronicle 30: 455–460.
Morley, D. 1976. Paediatric priorities in evolving community programmes for developing countries. Lancet II(7993): 1012–1014.
National Health Service Reorganisation: England 1972. Presented to Parliament by the Secretary of State for Social Services by Command of Her Majesty. Cmnd. 5055. London. Her Majesty's Stationery Office. 62 p.
Navarro, V. 1972. Health, health services and health planning in Cuba. International Journal of Health Services 2: 397–432.
Navarro, V. 1975. The political economy of medical care. An explanation of the

composition, nature, and functions of the present health sector of the United States. International Journal of Health Services 5: 65-94.
Nchinda, T. C. 1974. An integrated approach to the training of health personnel for developing countries: the Cameroon experiment. Tropical Doctor 4: 41-45.
New, P. K-m. and M. L. New. 1975. Health care in the People's Republic of China: the barefoot doctor. Inquiry 12 (2 Suppl.): 103-113.
Newell, K. W., Ed. 1975. Health By the People. Geneva. World Health Organization. 206 p.
New York Times. 1976. Doctors are slow to accept non-doctor assistants. May 11.
Pan American Health Organization. 1966. Administration of Medical Care Services. Pan American Health Organization Scientific Publication 129. 134 p.
Pan American Health Organization. 1973. Medical Auxiliaries. Proceedings of a Symposium Held During the 12th Meeting of the PAHO Advisory Committee on Medical Research, June 25, 1973. Pan American Health Organization Scientific Publication 278. 62 p.
Roemer, M. I. 1959. World trends in medical-care organization. Social Research 26: 283-310.
Roemer, M. I. 1963. Medical care in integrated health programmes of Latin America. Medical Care 1: 182-190.
Roemer, M. I. 1969. The Organization of Medical Care under Social Security: a Study Based on the Experience of Eight Countries. Geneva. International Labour Organization. 241 p.
Roemer, M. I. 1970. General physician services under eight national patterns. American Journal of Public Health 60: 1893-1899.
Roemer, M. I. 1971. Organized ambulatory health service in international perspective. International Journal of Health Services 1: 18-27.
Roemer, M. I. 1973. Political ideology and health care: Hospital patterns in the Philippines and Cuba. International Journal of Health Services 3: 487-492.
Sai, F. T. 1973. Ghana. In: I. Douglas-Wilson and G. McLachlan, Eds. Health Service Prospects. An International Survey. London. The Lancet and the Nuffield Provincial Hospitals Trust. pp. 125-155.
Selden, W. K. 1974. Accreditation. In: D. M. Pitcairn and D. Flahault, Eds. The Medical Assistant. An Intermediate Level of Health Care Personnel. Geneva. World Health Organization Public Health Papers No. 60: 131-136.
Sidel, V. W. 1972. Some observations on the health services in the People's Republic of China. International Journal of Health Services 2: 385-395.
Sigerist, H. E. 1960. On the Sociology of Medicine. Ed. by M. I. Roemer. New York. MD Publications. 397 p.
Simianis, J. G. 1975. National Health Systems in Eight Countries. U. S. Department of Health, Education, and Welfare. Social Security Administration. Office of Research and Statistics. DHEW Publication No. (SSA) 75-11924. 107 p.

Sorkin, A. L. 1975. Health Economics. Lexington, Mass. Lexington Books, D. C. Heath & Co. 205 p.

Storey, P. B. 1972. Medical Care in the U.S.S.R. Report of the U.S. Delegation on Health Care Services and Planning, May 16–June 3, 1970. U.S. Department of Health, Education and Welfare. Public Health Service. National Institutes of Health. DHEW Publication No. (NIH) 72-60. 38 p.

Storey, P. B. 1972a. The Soviet Feldsher as a Physician's Assistant. U. S. Department of Health, Education, and Welfare. Public Health Service. National Institutes of Health. DHEW Publication No. (NIH) 72-58. 25 p.

Sullivan, R. 1977. Delay asked in curb on alien physicians. New York Times. Jan. 5.

Tejeiro Fernandez, A. F. 1975. The national health system in Cuba. *In*: K. W. Newell, Ed. Health By the People. Geneva. World Health Organization. pp. 13–29.

U.S. House of Representatives. 1975. Committee on Ways and Means. Panel Discussions Before the Subcommittee on Health. 463 p.

U.S. Social Security Administration. 1976. Social Security Programs Throughout the World. U.S. Department of Health, Education, and Welfare. Social Security Administration. Office of Research and Statistics. Research Report No. 48. DHEW Publication No. (SSA) 76-11805. 255 p.

Vukmanovic, C. 1972. Decentralized socialism. Medical care in Yugoslavia. International Journal of Health Services 2: 35–44.

Wang, V. L. 1975. Training of the barefoot doctor in the People's Republic of China: from prevention to curative service. International Journal of Health Services 5: 475–488.

World Bank. 1975. Health. Sector Policy Paper. Washington. World Bank. 83 p.

World Health Organization. 1975. Health Services in Europe. 2d Ed. Copenhagen. WHO Regional Office for Europe. 299 p.

World Health Organization. 1976. World Health Statistics Annual 1973–1976. Geneva. World Health Organization. Vol. I, 839 p.; Vol. II, 303 p.; Vol. III, 340 p.

World Health Organization. 1976a. Reference Material for Health Auxiliaries and Their Teachers. Geneva. World Health Organization Offset Publication No. 28. 59 p. in English; additional 38 p. in French.

Yates, A. S. 1975. The Venezuelan *medicina simplificada* program. Public Health Reports 90: 247–253.

COMMUNITY   8.

The legal profession, looking overseas, makes a tidy distinction between comparative law and international law, the latter dealing specifically with issues between and among different countries. Borrowing the distinction, we find that the subject of international health has had little mention thus far in this book, except in the discussion of historical aspects in Chapter 2. But while the explorers of past centuries could wander for months or years in uncharted and unclaimed territories, these days every scrap of land, and much of the sea, falls within one or another sovereign jurisdiction.

The essence of things international lies in the crossing of borders, those imaginary lines on which so much of the world's energies and treasure are spent. With regard to health, what functions are served, and what sorts of events occur, at national borders? Retained within these limits is the legal jurisdiction of the government (including central and regional) with its regulations, policies, currency, and other paraphernalia of sovereign states. Concentrated, but never completely restricted here are the culture(s) of a people, including their languages and customs and, to some extent, their gene pools. Borders are rather porous filters letting various things pass through. Many of these are beyond the control of governments involved: air and water, perhaps laden with radioactivity or other pollution; migratory birds and other organisms. Subject to varying intentions and abilities to control their passage are: (1) ideas, via verbal, printed, or electronic means; (2) materials and merchandise of all sorts, from heroin to Hereford cattle, automobiles to autoanalyzers; and (3) people.

INTERNATIONAL TRAVELERS

We have discussed in Chapter 2 some historical aspects of international travel with regard to health. Here we turn our attention to the contemporary picture.

Entry of people into a country is often temporary. Nomadic groups, following historic routes, form a significant segment of the population in the Sahelian countries of northern Africa and are present to a lesser extent in some other areas (e.g., gypsies of Europe). These people may repeatedly cross national frontiers, perhaps unwittingly, and present problems in provision of health services and distribution of disease agents such as smallpox virus in the Somalia-Ethiopia-Kenya border regions. While the number of ethnic nomads is everywhere declining, there is no shortage of modern successors. Tourists, businessmen, diplomats, experts of all types, students and scholars, military personnel and dependents, volunteers, pilgrims, and missionaries, smugglers—all cross national borders.

Data on international travel and its health aspects are most readily available for the United States. From 1960 to 1974 travel to and from the United States increased about four and a half times (Table 8-1). In 1974 the average stay of American tourists in Europe was 24 days (Statistical Abstract of the U.S., 1975) from which (for the sake of this discussion) we can estimate some 185 million person-days of exposure abroad. This number of days is equivalent to the work-time of about 770,000 full-time jobs assuming a work-year of 240 days. Travelers abroad, however are travelers 24 hours a day, not just 8, but granting that some do sleep occasionally, a reasonable estimate might be 16 hours' environmental exposure per day, roughly doubling the time-person equivalency to about 1.5 million full-time jobs. This is more than the combined total of the metal and coal mining, motor vehicle manufacturing, pharmaceutical, agricultural, chemical, plastic, and synthetics industries in the United

Table 8-1. Travelers[a] to and from the United States, by world areas[b], 1960 and 1975 (in thousands)

	1960		1975	
Area	To U.S.	From U.S.[c]	To U.S.	From U.S.[c]
Europe	554	861	2,097	3,113
Asia	93	117	1,167	623
Africa	3	10	25	47
Oceania	36	24	253	173
North[b] and Central America	470	758	1,994	3,105
South America	139	71	527	362
TOTAL	1,285	1,840	6,063	7,423

[a]Excluding cruise passengers.
[b]Except Canada.
[c]U.S. citizens abroad.
Source: Travel Market Yearbook, 1976/1977.

States. When viewed in this light, foreign travel by Americans acquires the status of a very significant hidden occupation which, like any other, incurs certain occupational risks. Like most occupational groups, the travel population is not representative of the total U.S. population, particularly in the gross under-representation of children.

Risks to travelers

Travelers abroad are likely to encounter numerous infectious agents, some of which will certainly be novel to them. Being immunologically naive to such organisms, it is not surprising that they readily acquire souvenir infections, especially if stress, fatigue, jet lag, irregular and unconventional meals, sudden climatic change, and unaccustomed anonymity are considered.

Gastroenteritis, the classic complaint of travelers, called Delhi belly, Hong Kong dog, Casablanca crud, Montezuma's revenge, Turista (or worse), is well-known to voyagers and to their physicians. In one survey (Kendrick, 1972), gastroenteritis was reported by 39% of visitors to Mexico, 30% to Latin America in general, 26% to Spain, 13% to France, and 2.5% to England. Of far greater importance than simple diarrhea is the triad of *Shigella* dysentery, typhoid fever, and amebiasis found in many tropical countries. Giardiasis in the U.S.S.R. is another serious gastrointestinal infection. It is not necessary for tourists even to arrive in a foreign country to encounter enteric pathogens: An increasing number of reports describe outbreaks of gastroenteritis on cruise ships and aircraft. The thought of hundreds of hapless air passengers vomiting simultaneously boggles the mind, "puzzles the will, and makes us rather bear those ills we have than fly to others we know not of" (Shakespeare, 1603). Actual cases in which infections were acquired in transit must far exceed the number of published reports because of short flying times, rapid dispersal of passengers, and the difficulty of associating symptoms with any particular meal. In 1974, 99.2% of overseas travelers from the United States departed by air.

Upper respiratory infections are fairly common among travelers: in one survey, ten percent of American visitors to Europe reported having a cough, cold, or sore throat during their stay (Kendrick, 1972a). Contrary to popular opinion, it is quite possible to acquire a cold in the tropics, where respiratory viruses are at least as common as anywhere else. The real amount of respiratory colonization in travelers by viruses, bacteria, and other agents acquired by inhalation (e.g., fungi) can only be guessed.

Some very serious illnesses are sometimes acquired by travelers. In January 1975, a Scottish physician, feeling very ill, flew from Nigeria to London where he died two days later of Lassa fever. The incident caused a sensation in Britain because of the extreme communicability and virulence of the Lassa virus, but fortunately no secondary cases were recorded.

Sexually transmitted diseases are readily acquired by travelers although Kendrick (1972a) found only two of 8,650 travelers to Europe voluntarily reporting venereal infection (plus one case of "broken heart," possibly acquired in the same manner). International movement of persons does seem to be important in the acquisition and distribution of sexually transmitted diseases, including multiply drug-resistant strains of the agent of gonorrhea.

Vector-borne diseases are well represented among international travelers, and in North America and Europe these are effectively reported in comparison with other kinds of infections. Several hundred cases of malaria are introduced into these continents every year. Military actions in Vietnam resulted in importation into the United States of thousands of cases during the war years, with a dramatic decline of 99% among military personnel from 1970 to 1974. A similar rise and fall of malaria cases occurred during and after the Korean war 20 years earlier. Other vector-transmitted diseases appear from time to time in returned travelers, spotted by alert diagnosticians. Recent reports validate cases of scrub typhus in Connecticut and boutonneuse fever in California. Dengue fever, leishmaniasis, African trypanosomiasis, and filariasis, which surface once in a while, serve as a reminder of the smallness of our world, the continuing hazard of biting insects, and the rapidity of jet travel.

Parasites of many kinds await the unsuspecting traveler, particularly those who "go native" in tropical countries. The great majority of *Ascaris, Trichuris,* and hookworm infections acquired from contaminated food or soil are light, asymptomatic, self-limiting, and usually undetected by both the traveler and his or her physician. Schistosomiasis and other exotic diseases are occasionally acquired by tourists.

Introduced diseases

Travelers themselves are not the only potential victims of infections acquired abroad. Where conditions are receptive, an introduced agent may spread with great rapidity, as has happened innumerable times in history. For example, in 1924 two men and a boy travelled from Winnipeg,

Manitoba, to New Britain, Connecticut, via Duluth and Detroit. In their wake they left 74,100 cases of smallpox that caused 1,270 deaths. In developed countries in recent years large epidemics of disease caused by imported agents have generally been restricted to influenza, but smaller numbers of secondary cases of other illnesses have often been reported. In the United States, for instance, there have been outbreaks of typhoid fever, salmonellosis, and drug-resistant gonorrhea. Malaria has been spread to U.S. residents via native anopheline mosquitos, by blood transfusion from infected donors, and by shared syringes of narcotics addicts.

The transmission of cholera by travelers is well established. For centuries the pilgrimage to Mecca served to distribute this disease throughout the Moslem world. The El Tor quarantine station through which many pilgrims passed has even provided the name for a widespread strain of cholera. More recently the vibrio has spread by other means. An enormously destructive pandemic of cholera was carried to Conakry, Guinea, in August 1970, then spread like wildfire throughout west Africa, with tens of thousands of cases reported. As part of the same broad pandemic, cholera outbreaks occurred in Italy, Spain and Portugal. The causative organisms reached Australia and New Zealand by air, presumably via contaminated water taken on in Bahrain, but despite one fatal case the disease failed to become established in either country. Other known or suspected introductions occurred in Canada, Japan, and Sweden, also without further spread. A second introduction of cholera to Europe occurred in late 1977.

Migrant groups

The few examples given on these pages illustrate the potential for acquisition and distribution of disease by individual travelers responsible for some of the hundreds of millions of border crossings that occur annually in the world. Besides the tourists, businessmen, students, and other types of modern nomads, three categories of international travelers merit mention from a health standpoint. The first of these is migrant labor, exemplified by Mexican agricultural workers in the United States, Turkish or Yugoslav industrial workers in West Germany, and Africans from surrounding countries in the gold mines of South Africa. Characteristic of this temporary but often extended stay by large groups in a foreign country are: (1) relative poverty of the migrants compared with their hosts; (2) separation, in many cases, from wives and children; (3) communal living in a variety of substandard arrangements; (4) indifference, hostility, or exploitation by the resident population. Members of these groups often live as frugally as possible in order to send a maximum portion of their wages home. Common health problems among migrant workers in various countries relate to crowding, poor sanitation, frustration, and loneliness, not very different from those described in Chapter 3 for residents of urban slums in developing countries.

A second important group of travelers is made up of refugees. Uprooted by calamity, war, or persecution, often penniless and without either the ability or the right to earn a living in their country of residence, the world's refugees pose a difficult and poignant problem for health authorities.

The third special group consists of persons sharing some characteristics of both migrant workers and refugees but forming a distinct category of international travellers. These are the professionally trained persons who emigrate from one country to another in search of better job opportunities and conditions of life. Although engineers, educators, and others are involved in this "brain drain," the professionals of main interest here are the foreign medical graduates (FMGs). International movements of medically trained personnel are very large (Table 7-5). In Britain it is estimated that the number of physicians moving into or out of the country annually amounts to about 10% of the total number of resident medical practitioners. In the United States, one of every five physicians was an FMG by 1970, and in 1972 FMGs (excluding Canadian-trained) accounted for 46% of newly licensed additions to the medical professions (Williams and Lockett, 1975).

The problem of recognition of medical qualifications from one country to another has been solved in many ways, and there are few general rules. Some countries are highly restrictive and almost never permit a foreign medical graduate to practice. Others are more lenient and will usually permit registration if certain conditions are met. Many countries will recognize medical training for purposes of licensure to practice only if the country of origin of the candidate will do the same for the host country's graduates (principle of reciprocity). In some countries, most notably those in the Commonwealth but also in the French-speaking community, degrees are more freely recognized within the group than outside of it. Some countries have streamlined exchanges of professional personnel. Members of the Nordic Council (Denmark, Finland, Iceland, Norway, and Sweden) permit cross licensure of physicians, dentists, and pharmacists. Members of the European Economic Community, often called the "Common Market," (Belgium, Denmark, France, German Federal Republic, Ireland, Italy, Luxembourg, the Netherlands, and the United Kingdom) agreed after many delays to enact Article 48 of the Treaty of Rome permitting mutual recognition of each other's medical qualifications starting in 1977. As a result of this landmark development, the pattern of international movement of physicians is expected to change in western Europe. Specialists from Britain, disgruntled with the National Health Service, may well be lured by high salaries in private hospitals, particularly in Italy and West Germany.

ORGANIZATIONS WORKING ABROAD

Not only do individuals and commerce move across national borders, but many organizations extend their activities via the same routes. With respect to health, the following major types may be mentioned: (1) private voluntary organizations; (2) philanthropic foundations; (3) professional and technical associations and societies; (4) commercial companies; (5) official governmental agencies; (6) intergovernmental organizations.

Private voluntary organizations

Private voluntary organizations (or PVOs[1]) include both religious and secular groups. In the former category in poorer countries are the medical missions per se, a diverse group of institutions ranging from leprosaria to rural and urban hospitals. In addition to missions, many other medical and medical-related institutions (such as orphanages) are operated by religious denominations, funded primarily by contributions from the wealthier countries. Bryant (1969) summarized the situation as follows: "There are over 1,200 medical institutions related to Anglican, Orthodox and Protestant churches in developing countries, and they have combined operating budgets in excess of $100 million per year. The Roman Catholic church has more than 2,000 such institutions with expenditures of over $200 million. In some countries, these mission programs account for more than 40 percent of all health care."

As mentioned previously, the relative importance of mission hospitals has declined in many countries, where indigenous institutions and personnel are evolving. Many missions have been broadening their activities to include other aspects of community development, such as assistance in agriculture and animal husbandry. There are still some tiny, individually supported missions, but much of this work is now centralized

[1]Consult Tables 8-2 and 8-10 for decoding of abbreviations.

Table 8-2. Some abbreviations, primarily American, commonly used in international health work[a]

AID	see USAID
CDC	Center for Disease Control, U.S. Public Health Service
FY	Fiscal year
HMD	Health manpower development
IGO	Intergovernmental organization
IHR	International Health Regulations
LDC	Less developed country
LLDC	Least developed country
MCH	Maternal and child health
MDC	More developed country
MSA	Most seriously affected (countries)
NGO	Nongovernmental organization
NIEO	New international economic order
ODA	Official development assistance
OPIC	Overseas Private Investment Corporation (U.S.)
PHC	Primary health care
PL480	Public Law 480, 83rd Congress, U.S.[b]
PVO	Private voluntary organization
SHS	Strengthening health services
TNC	Transnational corporation
USAID	Agency for International Development (U.S.)

[a]See also Table 8-10.
[b]See text, p. 340.

within denominations such as the Mennonite Central Committee, Lutheran World Relief, Seventh-Day Adventist World Service, American Friends Service Committee, and Caritas International Medical Mission Board and Catholic Relief services of the Roman Catholic Church. Some denominations are members of the Evangelical Foreign Missions Association. Others may function jointly via the Church World Service, an organization encompassing some 30 Protestant and Orthodox denominations.

Among the dozens of PVOs involved in aspects of health and development assistance there is a gradation from firmly denominational organizations to those with a generally religious orientation to the many purely secular groups offering assistance to children, refugees, or other beneficiaries. In the United States, many PVOs are members of the American Council of Voluntary Agencies for Foreign Service; in the 18 other member countries of OECD the International Council of Voluntary

Agencies plays a similar role. Periodic attempts are made to collect, classify, and publish the many programs of these PVOs (Eggins, 1967; Crosby and Smith, 1971).

Philanthropic foundations

Philanthropic foundations have long been active in international health work; of the many American foundations a few may be mentioned as examples. The Edna McConnell Clark Foundation of New York, in its Developing World Program, supports laboratory research and field work on schistosomiasis in many countries. The W. K. Kellogg Foundation of Michigan is interested in developing and expanding educational programs in health and agriculture. It has funded courses for training of physicians, dentists, nurses, assistants, and technicians and has provided numerous individual fellowships for study in these fields. The Kresge Foundation of Michigan makes grants for capital construction of buildings for education of professionals, for hospitals, and for health-related services. The Milbank Memorial Fund of New York is particularly interested in the application of social and behavioral sciences to public health and preventive medicine and has supported work in demography, vital statistics, population, and general health problems. The Pathfinder Fund of Boston has devoted its efforts to the field of family planning. Each of these organizations has developed a specific field of interest in which it hopes to make a meaningful contribution towards solution of a particular aspect of health-related problems. The Ford Foundation of New York has concentrated its work in LDCs in education, economic development and planning, food production, and population and family planning and has established programs in many countries of Asia, Africa, and Latin America.

The Rockefeller Foundation Of all the private foundations in international health work, the best known and most significant has been the Rockefeller Foundation (RF). Arising from the earlier Rockefeller Institute for Medical Research (1901) and the General Education Board (1903), the Foundation began in 1909 with some 72,000 shares of Standard Oil of New Jersey stock. Its ambitious purposes were: "To promote the well-being and to advance the civilization of the peoples of the United States and its territories and possessions and of foreign lands in the acquisition and dissemination of knowledge, in the prevention and relief of suffering, and in the promotion of any and all of the elements of human progress."

The International Health Commission was set up in 1913, changed to a Board in 1916, and finally designated a Division. In its 38 years of operation, the IHD cooperated with 75 governments in campaigns on 21 separate diseases or health problems, including tuberculosis, yaws, rabies, influenza, schistosomiasis, and malnutrition, but it is best known for its work with hookworm, malaria, and yellow fever. Although these campaigns have been well chronicled by Shaplen (1964) and Williams (1969), their depth and extent seem to be insufficiently appreciated. The RF played a major part in ridding the southern United States of hookworm and malaria, which were both widespread in the early decades of this century. The 17D yellow fever vaccine was developed in RF laboratories in 1936, resulting in a Nobel Prize for Max Theiler and the saving of millions of lives. In the late 1930s the introduced African mosquito *Anopheles gambiae* was responsible for an enormous outbreak of malignant tertian malaria in Brazil, which resulted in over 100,000 cases and 14,000 deaths in 1938 alone. RF money and workers, together with the Brazilian government, eventually eradicated *A. gambiae* from that country after years of effort, demonstrating the effectiveness of vector control. In Egypt, Nigeria, India, Trinidad, and many other countries, the International Health Division of the Rockefeller Foundation established laboratories and trained local workers in methods of investigating and combatting endemic diseases.

The Rockefeller Foundation was involved in aspects of international health work other than disease control. In medical education the foundation contributed to reorganization of American medical schools following Abraham Flexner's famous report of 1910 (which had been supported by the Carnegie Foundation for the Advancement of Teaching). Overseas, RF support was given to medical schools in Bangkok, Beirut, Brussels, Brazil, and elsewhere, but none became so well known as the Peking Union Medical College (Ferguson, 1970). The PUMC was the only medical school created and operated by the Rockefeller Foundation. From establishment of the China Medical Board in 1914 to the opening of the PUMC in 1919 to its takeover by the Japanese during World War II and then by the new communist government of China in 1947, the RF spent some $47 million (under a budget separate from the IHD) on this experiment in international medical education. The emphasis at PUMC was on high quality: by 1937, there were only 166 graduates (Crozier, 1975). Although the concept of medical elitism is always questionable, it is true that a large proportion of the leaders of modern medicine in China have been PUMC graduates (Bullock, 1974). Many of the "patriotic health campaigns" in the P.R.C. were based on knowledge derived from investigations carried out by the old PUMC, and it is difficult to gauge its long-term effect upon the health of the Chinese people. It seems certain that the approach taken at PUMC can never be repeated elsewhere.

Williams (1969) has summarized the major international health activities of the Rockefeller Foundation during the period of existence of the IHD: "From 1913 through 1950, the Foundation allocated nearly $100 million to health activities, the largest amount, about $33 million being for schools of public health, schools of nursing, 2,566 fellowships, and other training expenses. More than $22 million went into the operating costs of the field staff and its offices. Aid in development of state and local health services in the United States and abroad totaled more than $8 million. The laboratories of the IHD at the Rockefeller Institute required nearly $3 million. The activities of the Rockefeller Foundation Health Commission during the Second World War took $4 million. The Health Organization of the League of Nations received nearly $1 million between the two world wars.

"In a total of $22 million spent for the control and investigation of specific diseases the four principal items were yellow fever, $8 million; malaria, $4.5 million; hookworm disease, $3.8 million; tuberculosis, $4 million." In the decades since 1950, RF support has continued in many of these and other areas, details of which may be found in their annual reports.

Many private foundations from countries other than the United States have also been active and productive in international health work. In Britain, for instance, the Nuffield Foundation and the Wellcome Trust both support fellowships and research work in LDCs.

Official connections

Institut Pasteur It is sometimes difficult to tell whether an organization is private or public. A good example of this in the health field is the Institut Pasteur of Paris. This institute was founded in the flush of the new microbiological era in the 1880s with an outpouring of funds donated by a citizenry anxious to help in the development of Pasteur's antirabies vaccine. The institute flourished, attracted many outstanding researchers, and set up a teaching program of high quality. About 1965 the privately funded Institut Pasteur began to need financial help from the French government, a dependency that has increased steadily and has led to much acrimonious debate. Our interest in this organization arises from the remarkable network of Instituts Pasteur that began to appear throughout the Francophone world within a very few years after the Paris Institut was founded and that may now be found in Abidjan, Algiers, Bangui, Casablanca, Cayenne, Dakar, Fort-de-France, Hanoi, Noumea, Point-à-Pitre, Saigon, Tananarive, Tangier, Tunis, Yaoundé, and elsewhere. These are mostly government laboratories offering diagnostic services as well as facilities for the production of sera and vaccines and for microbiological research. While their association with the Institut Pasteur in Paris may now be tenuous, they can trace their raison d'être back to the hopes and financial support of thousands of private citizens a century ago. In these outlying institutes pioneering work was done on plague by Yersin, on malaria by Laveran, and on the Bacille Calmette-Guerin (BCG) by Albert Calmette. Working with the Institut Pasteur in Algiers, a typhus team from the RF in 1943 first demonstrated the value of DDT for delousing, a technique later extensively used in postwar Europe—and a fine example of international cooperation.

Other groups With the "aid community," the PVOs, foundations, and donor government agencies often work together. Some groups receive contributions from the general public, foundations, and government agencies. In the field of population and family planning activities, for example, the USAID allocated some $200 million to PVOs from 1965 to 1975, primarily the International Planned Parenthood Federation, the Pathfinder Fund, Population Council, Association for Voluntary Sterilization, and Church World Services; AID also channels funds into many other voluntary organizations. Large projects may involve several major foundations in joint funding as in Ford-Rockefeller support of the International Rice Research Institute (IRRI) in the Philippines, the International Maize and Wheat Improvement Center (CIMMYT) in Mexico, the International Center for Tropical Agriculture (CIAT) in Colombia, and the International Institute of Tropical Agriculture (IITA) in Nigeria. All of these are intended to improve health through better nutrition.

The many professional and technical associations (Table 8-3) overlapping to some extent with PVOs serve variously in the dissemination of information; in the provision of expert consultation, training, and fellowships; in the maintenance of professional standards and conditions of employment; and so forth. They may interlock with official agencies at national and international levels. It may be noted that not all "experts" have been convinced of the importance of health programs for poorer countries. An august commission in 1969 filed a report entitled "Partners

Table 8-3. Nongovernmental organizations in official relations with WHO (January, 1977)

African Medical and Research Foundation
Biometric Society
Christian Medical Commission
Commonwealth Medical Association
Council for International Organizations of Medical Sciences
Inter-American Association of Sanitary and Environmental Engineering
International Academy of Pathology
International Agency for the Prevention of Blindness
International Air Transport Association
International Association for Accident and Traffic Medicine
International Association of Agricultural Medicine and Rural Health
International Association for Child Psychiatry and Allied Professions
International Association of Logopedics and Phoniatrics
International Association of Medical Laboratory Technologists
International Association of Microbiological Societies
International Association on Water Pollution Research
International Astronautical Federation
International Brain Research Organization
International College of Surgeons
International Commission on Radiation Units and Measurements
International Commission on Radiological Protection
International Committee of Catholic Nurses
International Committee on Laboratory Animals
International Committee of the Red Cross
International Confederation of Midwives
International Council on Alcohol and Addictions
International Council on Jewish Social and Welfare Services
International Council of Nurses
International Council of Scientific Unions
International Council on Social Welfare
International Council of Societies of Pathology
International Cystic Fibrosis (Mucoviscidosis) Association
International Dental Federation
International Diabetes Federation
International Electrotechnical Commission
International Epidemiological Association
International Ergonomics Association
International Federation of Clinical Chemistry
International Federation of Fertility Societies
International Federation of Gynecology and Obstetrics
International Federation for Housing and Planning

continued

Table 8-3.—Continued

International Federation for Information Processing
International Federation for Medical and Biological Engineering
International Federation of Medical Student Associations
International Federation of Multiple Sclerosis Societies
International Federation of Ophthalmological Societies
International Federation of Pharmaceutical Manufacturers Associations
International Federation of Physical Medicine and Rehabilitation
International Federation of Sports Medicine
International Federation of Surgical Colleges
International Hospital Federation
International Hydatidological Association
International League of Dermatological Societies
International League against Epilepsy
International League against Rheumatism
International Leprosy Association
International Organization for Standardization
International Organization against Trachoma
International Paediatric Association
International Pharmaceutical Federation
International Planned Parenthood Federation
International Radiation Protection Association
International Society of Biometeorology
International Society of Blood Transfusion
International Society for Burn Injuries

International Society of Cardiology
International Society of Chemotherapy
International Society of Endocrinology
International Society of Hematology
International Society for Human and Animal Mycology
International Society of Orthopaedic Surgery and Traumatology
International Society of Radiographers and Radiological Technicians
International Society of Radiology
International Sociological Association
International Solid Wastes and Public Cleansing Association
International Union of Architects
International Union of Biological Sciences
International Union against Cancer
International Union for Child Welfare
International Union for Conservation of Nature and Natural Resources
International Union for Health Education
International Union of Immunological Societies
International Union of Local Authorities
International Union of Nutritional Sciences
International Union of Pharmacology
International Union of Pure and Applied Chemistry
International Union of School and University Health and Medicine
International Union against Tuberculosis

International Union against the Venereal Diseases and the Treponematoses
International Water Supply Association
Joint Commission on International Aspects of Mental Retardation
League of Red Cross Societies
Medical Women's International Association
Permanent Commission and International Association on Occupational Health
Population Council
Rehabilitation International
Transplantation Society
World Association of Societies of (Anatomic and Clinical) Pathology
World Confederation for Physical Therapy
World Council for the Welfare of the Blind
World Federation of Associations of Clinical Toxicology Centres and Poison Control Centres
World Federation of the Deaf
World Federation of Hemophilia
World Federation for Medical Education
World Federation for Mental Health
World Federation of Neurology
World Federation of Neurosurgical Societies
World Federation of Nuclear Medicine and Biology
World Federation of Occupational Therapists
World Federation of Parasitologists
World Federation of Proprietary Medicine Manufacturers
World Federation of Public Health Associations
World Federation of Societies of Anaesthesiologists
World Federation of United Nations Associations
World Medical Association
World Psychiatric Association
World Veterans Federation
World Veterinary Association

Source: Based on Flache, 1977.

in Development"—commonly called the "Pearson Report"—which devoted only 27 lines out of 399 pages to health, and most of that to an overoptimistic view that malaria and other serious diseases are pretty much under control (Commission on International Development, 1969).

Private Industry

The role of commerce and industry in international health is complex and subject to many interpretations. Transnational and multinational enterprises provide much needed investment, employment, and access to markets. They often train local personnel in financial and personnel management and in some fields of technology. In more subtle ways they expose local people to the life-styles and values of their expatriate staff. Much of this has been looked upon as inappropriate to local cultures and conducive to a materialistic outlook, thereby evoking familiar sorts of criticism.

With direct relation to health the transnational enterprises most commonly discussed are the infant-formula (see Chapter 4), pharmaceutical, and medical supply companies. In a paper prepared for the Committee on Transfer of Technology of the United Nations Conference on Trade and Development (UNCTAD), Lall (1975) has presented a critical study of world pharmaceutical production and trade. Growth in this field in the 1960s and 1970s has been fast enough to double every five years or so, and international trade has grown even faster. More than 80% of the world output comes from a few countries—France, West Germany, Italy, Japan, Switzerland, Britain, and the U.S.A. The industry is highly concentrated; 10 companies account for nearly one-quarter of total world output, and 50 to 60 for more than half.

One serious problem concerning the drug industry in LDCs is the enormous proliferation of products, brands, and trade names. In India where a government committee estimated that the country's basic pharmaceutical needs can be met by 116 drugs, more than 15,000 are marketed; in Brazil there are 14,000; in Spain, 25,000. By comparison, "Sweden and Norway, with nationalized distribution systems, only deal with about 2,000 drugs in order to supply the most advanced forms of therapy to their populations" (Lall, 1975). An associated problem is the pricing policies of pharmaceutical companies under which LDCs (which together account for only 14% of world consumption) often pay a premium for their drugs. The economic power of transnational companies is often greater than that of poor countries, who have little ability to evaluate, control, or regulate them, and various kinds of influence can be exerted upon government servants at all levels. Pressure on and sometimes by physicians to use expensive new products, or to use drugs inappropriately, contributes to the LDCs' negative trade balance for pharmaceuticals of hundreds of millions of dollars annually. Some countries, such as Pakistan, have attempted to promote the use of cheaper generic products by abolishing trade names, but such regulations are difficult to enforce and may lead to a thriving industry of smuggling branded drugs.

The great bulk of drugs marketed by transnational corporations in LDCs are those developed for the health problems and marketing patterns of the wealthier countries. The actual medicinal needs of the people in LDCs may not be properly represented by such a selection, but research and development (R&D) of products by the industry in general is geared to the much larger markets in their home countries: The United States alone with 5% of the world's population is said to consume more than twice the amount of pharmaceuticals of all LDCs combined. But on the other hand, drug companies are often criticized for undertaking R&D in developing countries, where government restrictions on clinical testing may be less stringent and the principle of informed consent not so firmly established as at home. Finally, as Turshen (1976) has noted, firms that distribute medicines in LDCs also frequently deal in veterinary products, fertilizers, pesticides, chemicals, cosmetics, foods, soaps, and other classes of products extending into many aspects of daily life. These companies may also be associated in the production and especially in the marketing of all types of medical supplies, hospital and scientific equipment and apparatus, including sophisticated devices not necessarily designed for tropical climates or budgets. The problem of appropriate technology thus arises once more.

Official Agencies

Official intergovernmental agreements in the field of health exist in many forms. An example of a mutually beneficial arrangement between two developed countries may be found in the Cooperative Medical Sciences Program between the United States and Japan. This arrangement arose from a meeting in January, 1965 between (then) President Johnson and Prime Minister Sato, in which it was agreed to undertake a greatly expanded program of cooperation in medical sciences, at a high level of research competence, and concentrating upon diseases prevalent in Asia. Advisors from the two countries met in Tokyo in April 1965 and selected cholera, leprosy, parasitic diseases, tuberculosis, and viral diseases as initial subjects for joint research. Malnutrition was added the following year, and environmental mutagenesis and carcinogenesis somewhat later. The government of each country supports the costs of research by its own scientists, and funds annual joint conferences in each of the seven subjects held in alternate years in one or the other country. Over the years a substantial bond of technical cooperation, and of personal friendships, has developed between the researcher-participants on the two sides, and progress in each country has benefited from the exchanges. Similar bilateral cooperative medical science agreements are in effect between various other pairs of developed countries.

For centuries the people of wealthier countries through voluntary, charitable, professional, and commercial organizations have had an influence on the well-being and health of populations overseas. Their governments have likewise reached over national borders to become officially involved in international health in many ways. Motivations for both private and official programs vary widely in their blend of self-interest and altruism. On the government side the following motives may be cited: (1) national protection and defense against introduced diseases; (2) desire for goodwill, influence, and prestige; (3) support or protection of private investments by nationals; (4) humanitarianism; (5) furtherance of knowledge, research, and learning in medical sciences; (6) willingness to respond to specific requests or pressure from other governments. In the past, metropolitan (i.e., ruling) countries provided some health services to their colonies but from their viewpoint these were extensions of domestic programs into their overseas empires. The idea of "foreign aid" (other than to colonies) is very much a twentieth-century phenomenon, arising in part from American relief efforts in Europe after the First World War, but becoming really institutionalized in the decades following the Second World War.

It is an unfortunate fact that the bulk of "foreign aid" in the world is in the form of military equipment and armaments, primarily from the superpowers:

The information available on the international flow of military assistance is considerably more limited than for economic aid, but what is available suggests that the relative emphasis on military aid increased in recent years. Despite the crisis of economic need throughout the world, this form of aid exceeds all assistance for development purposes. In the U.S. in fiscal year 1974, foreign aid was 5 to 4 in favor of the military; in the Soviet Union in 1974, according to Western estimates, the ratio of foreign aid commitments was 2 to 1 in favor of military. (Sivard, 1976)

A portion of the total "foreign aid" flows is devoted to official development assistance (ODA), a commonly used term of imprecise meaning that embraces work in agriculture, education, infrastructure (roads, water supplies, etc.), small industry, and health. Within the health field ODA is generally spent for capital construction of facilities, manpower and institutional development (including fellowships), monovalent or limited control programs (e.g., for malaria, yaws, measles, or smallpox), disaster relief, technical and expert assistance, nutrition and family planning. The complexities of international bookkeeping and the natural interrelations of such programs make these categories difficult to compare among various donor and recipient countries. ODA programs have met with frequent criticism from both sides, and their effectiveness has often been less than optimal. Criticism on the donor side (especially in the U.S.A.) emphasizes inefficiency, corruption, excessive dependence, and ingratitude on the part of the beneficiaries. The recipient side may claim donor-country hypocrisy, excessive self-interest, export dumping and restrictive purchase agreements, exploitation, arrogance, and neocolonialism. As experience has accumulated, the solution most commonly proposed has been to increase the channeling of aid through multilateral, regional, or global institutions rather than simple country-to-country agreements. This step, it is asserted, would reduce many of the tensions and obligations implicit in bilateral arrangements, distribute aid on the basis of need rather than political loyalty, and make assistance contingent on policy reforms backed by world opinion. While this may be so, multilateralization introduces into the ODA picture at least a third bureaucracy with its inherent red-tapism, delay, and administrative expense, and it blurs the special relationships and specific mutual interests of the parties concerned. This problem was one of many taken up by a special Task Force on International Development appointed by the President of the United States in September 1969 to "provide comprehensive recommendations concerning the role of the U.S. in assistance to less developed countries in the 1970's." Its report in March, 1970, (commonly known as the "Peterson Report" after the Task Force chairman) included the following statement:

The Task Force believes that more reliance on international organizations should be built into all U.S. policies relating to international development.... This is basic to the new approach to foreign assistance we recommend. A predominantly bilateral U.S. program is no longer politically tenable in our relations with many developing countries, nor is it advisable in view of what other countries are doing in international development. (Task Force on International Development, 1970)

Within the United States government, support for international health programs directed through multilateral channels is the primary responsibility of the Bureau of International Organization Affairs; those through bilateral channels, of the Agency for International Development, both of which are in the Department of State. Certain research programs are carried out by the Fogarty International Center for Advanced Study in the Health Sciences at the National Institutes of Health, by the Comparative Studies staff of the Office of Research and Statistics of the Social Security Administration (both agencies of the Department of Health, Education and Welfare), and by other units. Coordination is provided to a great extent by the Office of International Health of HEW; its Division of Program Analysis conducts analytical studies of the relations between health and development in many countries.

We can look at the ODA budgets of the United States, as the major single donor, to see how health programs fit into the total picture. Table 8-4 shows the U.S. budget resources devoted to development in a recent year. "PL 480" refers to Public Law 480, 83rd Congress (1954), which deals with U.S.-owned foreign currencies accruing from the sale of agricultural commodities abroad. These moneys, in the purchasing country's currency, are used for various educational, scholarly, cultural, and humanitarian purposes including feeding programs. Under the Food for Peace Program, more than 80 American PVOs are also eligible to receive U.S. agricultural commodities plus funds for their transport and distribution. Table 8-5 shows the allocations within AID and Table 8-6, the categorical breakdowns within the USAID development assistance programs (not including "security supporting assistance.")

The percentage of the total U.S. ODA devoted specifically to "health" is not shown on these tables. Within the category "population

Table 8-4. U.S. budget resources devoted to development, fiscal year 1975 ($ million)

USAID	$2,486.8
PL 480	1,241.6
Peace Corps	82.4
International financial institutions	643.0
TOTAL	$4,453.8

Source: Development Coordination Committee, 1976.

COMMUNITY

Table 8-5. The USAID budget, fiscal year 1975 ($ million)

Bilateral development assistance	$ 886.8
Contributions to international organizations	139.2
Other	252.0
Total development assistance	1,278.0
Security supporting assistance	1,208.8
TOTAL	$2,486.8

Source: Development Coordination Committee, 1976.

and health" recent years have seen an emphasis on the former at the expense of the latter. In 1968, for example, AID budgeted $164 million for health and $34 million for population. By 1971, the ratio was $66 million for health and $97 million for population, out of a reduced total (Carey, 1971). It is of interest that the Peterson Report of 1970 placed emphasis on what it termed "the special problem of population." The primacy of population control problems has remained a feature of more recent AID budgets. We may assume, however, that development programs in education, agriculture, and other fields will have spillover effects on health.

Table 8-6. USAID development assistance programs, by functional categories, proposed for fiscal year 1978

Category	$ Million
Food production and nutrition	587
Population planning	177
Health	120.8
Education and human resources	95.2
Selected development activities	110.3
SAHEL development program	50
American hospitals and schools abroad	7.5
International disaster assistance	45
International organizations and programs	256
Total	1,448.8

Source: U.S. Agency for International Development, 1977.

The greater part of world ODA comes from the member countries of the Development Assistance Committee of OECD (Table 8-7). Each of these countries has an agency analogous in some ways to USAID: the Canadian, Danish, Swedish, or Norwegian International Development Agencies (CIDA, DANIDA, SIDA, NORAD, respectively), the United Kingdom's Ministry for Overseas Development (ODM), and so forth. In the case of France, the great bulk of ODA goes to former colonies, primarily in Africa. Over the past dozen years or so there have been changes in the percentage of GNP devoted to ODA in the various DAC countries (Table 8-8): relative reductions by the major western powers (the U.S., France, the United Kingdom, and West Germany) and sharp increases by some smaller countries, particularly in Scandinavia. Total financial flows

Table 8-7. Public Expenditures on official development assistance from DAC[a] countries to developing countries and to multilateral agencies, 1974

Country	As % of GNP	$ Per capita[b]	Total $ million[b]
Sweden	0.72	49.12	401
Netherlands	.63	32.05	434
France	.59	30.77	1,616
Norway	.57	32.83	131
Denmark	.55	33.27	168
Belgium	.50	27.35	268
Canada	.50	31.54	709
United Kingdom	.38	11.62	721
Australia	.37	32.23	430
Germany, Fed. Rep. of	.34	21.20	1,315
New Zealand	.31	12.87	39
United States	.25	16.44	3,483[c]
Japan	.24	10.06	1,103
Austria	.18	7.84	59
Finland	.18	8.12	38
Italy	.16	4.31	239
Switzerland	.14	10.03	65
TOTAL	.33		11,219

[a]Countries belonging to the Development Assistance Committee of OECD.
[b]U.S. dollar equivalents.
[c]Not calculated on the same base as total in Table 8-4.
Sources: UNCTAD, 1976a; World Bank, 1975a.

from DAC member countries to LDCs are summarized in Table 8-9 for 1964, 1969, and 1974. While the overall amount quadrupled in the decade, bilateral official flows did not even double in dollar volume, and fell by half as a percentage of the total; at the same time multilateral official flows increased more than sevenfold, showing a relative strengthening of multilateral agencies.

In addition to the DAC countries, ODA flows from the U.S.S.R. and the member states of COMECON (more than U.S. $1 billion in 1973), and from China. The OPEC countries have recently become substantial donors. According to UNCTAD, the internationally accepted target for aid by MDCs is 1% of GNP for total financial flows and 0.7% for ODA. By this standard, 7 of the 10 OPEC countries surpassed the 0.7% figure,

Table 8-8. Change in percentage of GNP as public expenditure on official development assistance from DAC countries to developing countries and to international agencies, 1961–62 and 1974

Country	Change in % GNP spent	Relative change, as %
Sweden	+.63	+700
Netherlands	+.16	+ 34
France	−.72	− 54
Norway	+.43	+307
Denmark	+.44	+400
Belgium	−.14	− 22
Canada	+.38	+316
United Kingdom	−.18	− 32
Australia	−.06	− 14
Germany (Fed. Rep.)	−.11	− 24
New Zealand	+.31	[a]
United States	−.31	− 55
Japan	+.07	+ 41
Austria	+.14	+350
Finland	+.18	[a]
Italy	−.01	− 6
Switzerland	+.08	+133
TOTAL	−.19	− 37

[a]ODA negligible in 1961–62
Source: Adapted from UNCTAD, 1976a

Table 8-9. Total financial flows to developing countries and territories in Asia, Latin America, and Africa and to multilateral agencies from DAC countries in 1964, 1969, and 1974 (in million U.S. $)

Type	1964 Amount	%	1969 Amount	%	1974 Amount	%
1. Official	5,592	(66.5)	6,870	(54.0)	13,213	(41.1)
Bilateral	5,168	(61.5)	5,838	(45.9)	10,169	(31.6)
ODA[a]	—		5,352	(42.1)	8,160	(25.4)
OOF[b]	—		486	(3.8)	2,009	(6.2)
Multilateral	424	(5.0)	1,032	(8.1)	3,044	(9.5)
ODA[a]	—		1,047	(8.2)	3,060	(9.5)
OOF[b]	—		-15	(-0.1)	-16	(0.0)
2. Private	2,159	(25.7)	4,056	(31.9)	9,467	(29.4)
Bilateral	2,018	(24.0)	3,637	(28.6)	9,537	(29.6)
Direct investment	1,620	(19.3)	2,753	(21.7)	6,028	(18.7)
Multilateral	141	(1.7)	419	(3.3)	-70	(-0.2)
3. Net private export credits	659	(7.8)	1,789	(14.1)	2,052	(6.4)
4. Euro-currency credits	—		—		7,452	(23.1)
TOTAL	8,410	(100.0)	12,715	(100.0)	32,184	(100.0)

[a]ODA = Official development assistance.
[b]OOF = Other official flows.
Source: UNCTAD, 1976a.

some by far: Qatar gave 11% of its GNP as ODA. The great majority of this aid was channeled bilaterally to Arab countries, and less than $650 million went elsewhere. OPEC donor countries in general have hesitated to channel their aid through existing multilateral organizations for fear of losing control over the use of the funds and instead have set up their own national institutions for international development cooperation or have created new multilateral development finance institutions (UNCTAD, 1976).

Intergovernmental Organizations

The nations of the world are enmeshed in a great variety of regional and global organizations established along geographic, political, economic, linguistic, and many other axes. Some IGOs having interests in health and development are shown in Table 8-10; most of these also have names, and acronyms, in French and Spanish, making for a virtual alphabet soup of international initials. Among the many IGOs we may examine, as examples, a small one, the SEAMEO-TROPMED project, and a large one, the World Health Organization.

SEAMEO as an example

In November 1965, the Ministers of Education of Laos, Malaysia, the Philippines, Singapore, South Vietnam, and Thailand met privately to consider the establishment of a regional organization to promote cooperation in education, science, and culture. Accordingly, an organization (SEAMEO, Southeast Asian Ministers of Education Organization) was set up with headquarters in Bangkok. Among the suggestions for cooperative projects was one for the establishment of a regional center for research and training in tropical medicine. A task force examined this idea and recommended, not a single center, but the use of existing national institutions, each to provide services to the entire region in a particular field of specialization, and all to be coordinated through a central board. Within a short time, Indonesia and the Khmer Republic (Cambodia or Democratic Kampuchea) joined the group. The cooperative project became known as TROPMED, one of seven regional arrangements through a busy SEAMEO—others being in tropical biology, educational technology, science and mathematics, agriculture, English language, and archeology and fine arts.

A major part of the work of each SEAMEO-TROPMED national

Table 8-10. Acronyms of some intergovernmental organizations having interest in health

ACAST	Advisory Committee on the Application of Science and Technology to Development[a]
ADB	Asian Development Bank
AfDB	African Development Bank
AfDF	African Development Fund
APO	Asian Productivity Organization
ASEAN	Association of Southeast Asian Nations
CACM	Central American Common Market
CEEC	Committee for European Economic Cooperation
CFNI	Caribbean Food and Nutrition Institute
CIEC	Conference on International Economic Cooperation
CGIAR	Consultative Group on International Agriculture Research
CIAP	Inter-American Committee on the Alliance for Progress
COMECON	Council for Mutual Economic Assistance
DAC	Development Assistance Committee of the OECD
ECA	Economic Commission for Africa[a]
ECE	Economic Commission for Europe[a]
ECLA	Economic Commission for Latin America[a]
ECOSOC	Economic and Social Council[a]
ECWA	Economic Commission for Western Asia
EDF	European Development Fund
EEC	European Economic Community
ESCAP	Economic and Social Commission for Asia and the Pacific[a]
FAO	Food and Agriculture Organization[b]
GATT	General Agreement on Tariffs and Trade[c]
IAEA	International Atomic Energy Agency[c]
IARC	International Agency for Research on Cancer (WHO)[b]
IBRD	International Bank for Reconstruction and Development (the World Bank)[b]
ICAO	International Civil Aviation Organization[b]
IDA	International Development Association[b]
IDB	Inter-American Development Bank
IFAD	International Fund for Agricultural Development
IFC	International Finance Corporation[b]
ILO	International Labour Organization
IMCO	Inter-Governmental Maritime Consultative Organization[b]
IMF	International Monetary Fund[b]
INCAP	Institute of Nutrition of Central America and Panama
ITU	International Telecommunications Union[b]
LAS	League of Arab States
OAS	Organization of American States
OAU	Organization of African Unity
OECD	Organization for Economic Cooperation and Development

OPEC	Organization of Petroleum Exporting Countries
PAHO	Pan American Health Organization (WHO)[b]
PASB	Pan American Sanitary Bureau (OAS)
SEAMEO	Southeast Asia Ministers of Education Organization
UN	United Nations
UNCTAD	United Nations Conference on Trade and Development[a]
UNDP	United Nations Development Programme[a]
UNDRO	Office of the Disaster Relief Coordinator (UN)[a]
UNEP	United Nations Environment Programme[a]
UNESCO	United Nations Educational, Scientific and Cultural Organization[b]
UNFDAC	United Nations Fund for Drug Abuse Control[a]
UNFPA	United Nations Fund for Population Activities[a]
UNGA	United Nations General Assembly[a]
UNHCR	United Nations High Commissioner for Refugees[a]
UNICEF	United Nations Children's Fund[a]
UNIDO	United Nations Industrial Development Organization[a]
UNITAR	United Nations Institute for Training and Research[a]
UNRWA	United Nations Relief and Works Agency for Palestine Refugees in the Near East[a]
UNSCEAR	United Nations Scientific Committee on the Effects of Atomic Radiation[a]
WFC	World Food Council
WFP	World Food Programme (FAO)[b]
WHO	World Health Organization[b]
WIPO	World Intellectual Property Organization[b]
WMO	World Meteorological Organization[b]

[a]Part of the United Nations
[b]United Nations Specialized agency, or subsidiary thereof
[c]Agency in special relation to the United Nations

center is teaching, on an annual basis, a specialized, postgraduate level course to a class made up of representatives from each of the member countries. The following distribution of subjects was made:

Indonesia	Nutrition and food science
Khmer Republic	Environmental sanitation and venereal diseases
Laos	Public health and helminthology
Malaysia	Applied parasitology, entomology, and laboratory technology
Philippines	Rural public health

Singapore	Urban health, occupational health, and family planning
S. Vietnam	Communicable disease, plague, and enteric infections
Thailand	Tropical medicine (general and clinical) and parasitology

Instruction and exchange of students got underway in Thailand in 1967, and by 1973 all centers were fully functional except for the Khmer Republic and Laos. (Since then, South Vietnam has left the group.) The SEAMEO-TROPMED program, as a model of regional international cooperation, was examined in some detail by Basch (1974), who visited each of the active centers. He has commented upon the benefits of such a plan, all of which have been well realized in the Southeast Asian region:

Financially, there are obvious economies arising from avoidance of duplication of specialized and expensive training facilities, and of the need to send candidates to distant and costly Western countries. Educational advantages arise in part because teaching can be directed towards specific regional problems, providing an immediacy and relevance not readily apparent in foreign training. Moreover, specialized faculty skills may be augmented through the stimulation of advanced-level teaching, and accumulated experience in presenting a particular topic over the years can result in the emergence of true regional centres of excellence. Psychological benefits, although perhaps less tangible, are nonetheless clear: among adjacent countries networks of professionals will develop, well known to each other and appreciative of one another's situations. The infrastructure of coordinated national centres may be utilized as a framework for regional conferences or other activities. Regional pride, independence and self-reliance are stimulated by successful local operation of complex programmes.

The World Bank Some large-scale international funding agencies have become much more aware of health in recent years. In the early 1970s the IBRD (World Bank) carried out a searching evaluation of its potential role in direct financing of basic health services, including field research, and of the cost-effectiveness of different health promotion systems. While it chose not to give specific large-scale support to health services, the World Bank did decide to "strengthen its awareness of the health consequences of the projects it supports, and of opportunities for improving health that are available under present patterns of lending." Specifically, the bank planned to:

Minimize any adverse side effects on health resulting from its lending operations in other sectors (such as projects for irrigation, drainage, land settlement, etc);
Make a number of key interventions necessary for improving the health of low-income groups (for example, projects involving water supply, sewerage, nutrition,

family planning, sites and services for low-cost housing, and training of health personnel);
Conduct field experiments to test selected elements of a reformed health-promotion system within rural development, population, and sites and services projects. (World Bank, 1975)

World Bank assistance to health-related projects is growing steadily. In November 1973 a "Memorandum of Understanding" was signed with WHO outlining the interests of the two agencies in the field of population. The World Bank and WHO have worked together in projects such as the Onchocerciasis Control Project in West Africa, for which the former is financial coordinator and the latter the executing agency (see p. 364).

The World Health Organization

History The early history of international cooperation in health work has been well documented by the World Health Organization (1958) and in the works of Goodman (1971), Brockington (1975), and Howard-Jones (1975); it need not be repeated here. A brief tabular summary (Table 8-11) is adequate to bring the story up to the creation of the present World Health Organization shortly after the end of the Second World War.

The charter of the United Nations, signed in San Francisco in June 1945, came into force in October of the same year. It contained provision for the establishment of a specialized health agency with wide powers (Article 57). A joint declaration by the delegations of Brazil and China called for the early convening of a general conference for that purpose. Little time was lost in putting the joint declaration into effect. The new General Assembly was constituted on January 10, 1946; on February 15 it adopted a resolution "to call an international conference to consider the scope of, and the appropriate machinery for, international action in the field of public health and proposals for the establishment of a single international health organization of the United Nations." The Conference was convened in New York on June 19 with delegations present from all 51 members of the U.N., 13 nonmember states, and the Allied control authorities of Germany, Japan, and Korea. Invited observers were sent by the FAO, ILO, ICAO, UNESCO, the OIHP, PASB, UNRRA (see Tables 8-10 and 8-11), League of Red Cross Societies, World Federation of Trade Unions, and the Rockefeller Foundation. The Conference set up a pro-

Table 8-11. Early official international health organizations

1851	First International Sanitary Conference, Paris. Followed the first (1828–31) and second (1847) pandemics of cholera. Convened partly because of fraudulent bills of health of ships and concealment of cholera outbreaks by many countries. Twelve states participated; convention ratified by only three, two of whom later withdrew.
1874	Fourth International Sanitary Conference, Vienna. Proposal for permanent International Commission on Epidemics, not adopted.
1881	Fifth International Sanitary Conference, Washington. The first conference attended by the U.S.; followed severe epidemics of cholera and yellow fever in North America. Proposal for an international system of notification, not adopted. Carlos Finlay suggests mosquito transmission of yellow fever.
1892	Seventh International Sanitary Conference, Venice. Limited to the Mecca pilgrimage. First effective international convention.
1893	Eighth International Sanitary Conference, Dresden. General Convention on cholera signed.
1897	Tenth International Sanitary Conference, Venice. Convention on plague signed.
1901–02	Second International Conference of American States, Mexico City. Created Pan American Sanitary Bureau.
1902	First Pan American Sanitary Conference, Washington. Formalized the PASB primarily for information exchange and reporting of quarantinable diseases.
1903	Eleventh International Sanitary Conference, Paris. Produced the International Sanitary Convention of 1903, which unified and revised the agreements relating to both plague and cholera of the four previous conferences.
1907	Rome. Conference for creation of Office Internationale d'Hygiène Publique (OIHP), also called "The Paris Office." First permanent international health organization, dealing primarily with quarantine
1923	Health Organization of the League of Nations established. Retained the independence of the Office Internationale and embodied it as General Advisory Health Council to the League, combined with a Secretariat and a Standing Health Committee. Financing from the League and the Rockefeller Foundation (until 1938). Had services in epidemiology, standardization, and technical help.
1925	Publication of Weekly Epidemiological Record was started.
1926	Thirteenth International Sanitary Conference, Paris. Set up basic modern type of health regulations.
1938	Fourteenth and last International Sanitary Conference, Paris.
1939	Last meeting of the Health Committee, League of Nations.

1943	Creation of United Nations Relief and Rehabilitation Administration (UNRRA) in Washington, with Health Division.
1946	Transfer of functions and staff of Health Organization of the League of Nations to the World Health Organization of the U.N.; termination of UNRRA. World Health Conference, New York.

tocol for taking over the remaining duties of the old OIHP, the League of Nations Health Organization, and UNRRA; established a commission to prepare for the first World Health Assembly; and produced the Constitution of the World Health Organization, which was signed on July 22, 1946, and sent to member states for ratification. The WHO had been launched.

Structure The present structure of the WHO is shown in Figures 8-1 and 8-2. Its work is carried out at headquarters in Geneva, at the six regional offices (Fig. 8-3) and at numerous projects in the field. Policy is determined at the World Health Assemblies usually held in Geneva in May of each year, attended by delegates of all member governments and observers from affiliated NGOs (Table 8-3; Flache, 1977), IGOs, and other agencies. The verbatim proceedings of these assemblies are published in the Official Records of the WHO and reveal the technical, social, and political concerns of the many parties involved. The Director-General is asked to prepare reports on subjects of current interest, the budget is discussed and approved, and many resolutions passed. The Assembly may also make recommendations to member states. An Executive Board meets at least twice a year in Geneva to prepare general work programs for the Assembly, to work on budget and financial problems of the WHO, and to undertake emergency actions in the event of calamity or epidemic. The Director-General is subject to the authority of the Board. The Executive Board consists of 30 persons, each selected by a country so authorized by vote of the Assembly, serving staggered three-year terms.

The regular budget of the WHO for 1977 was about U.S. $147 million, appropriated to general purposes and raised by assessments of member states according to the percentages given in Table 8-12. There is in addition a Voluntary Fund for Health Promotion with special accounts for research on human reproduction; community water supply; malaria, smallpox, leprosy, yaws, and cholera programs; and other purposes.

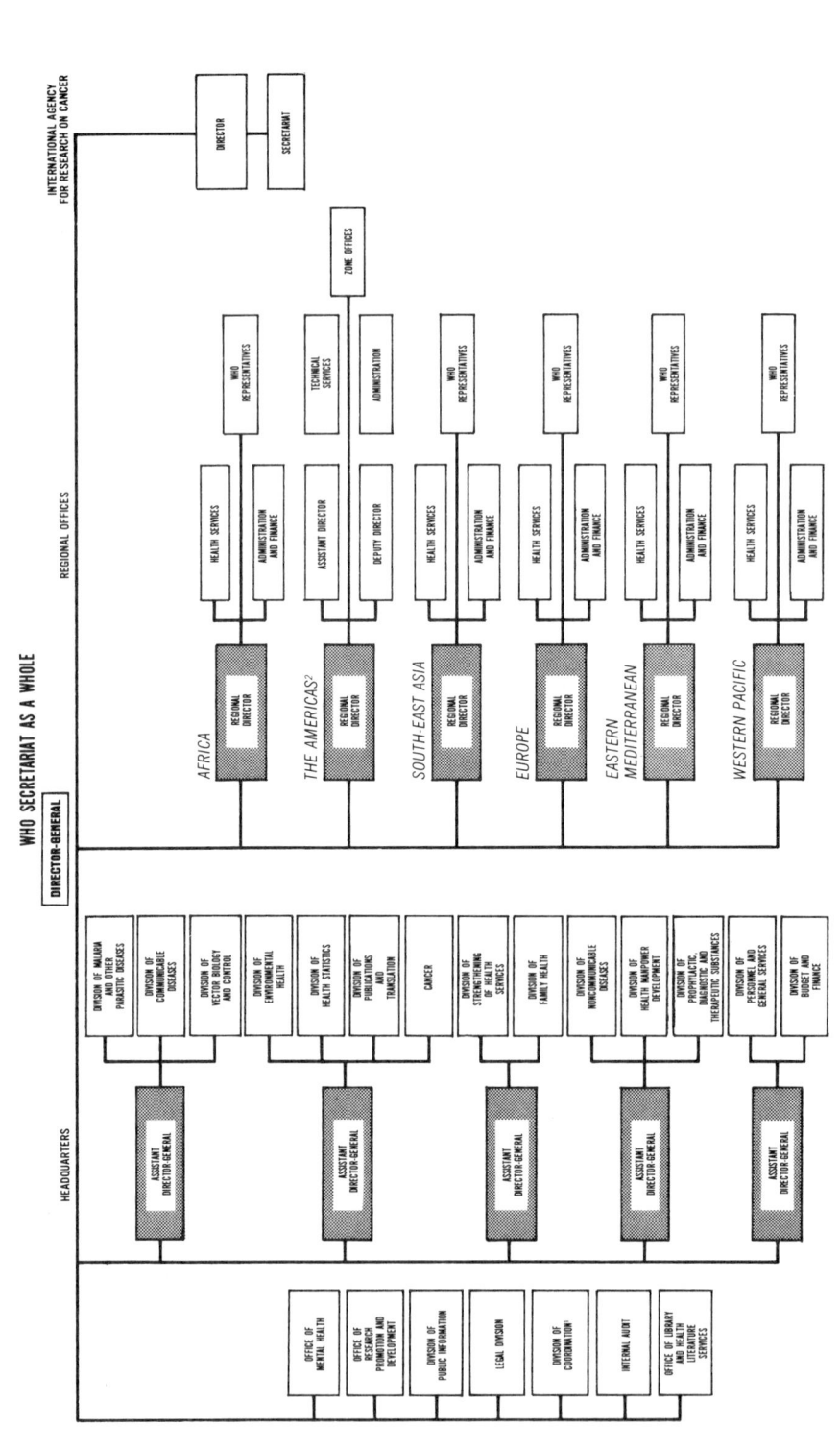

Figure 8-1 Structure of the World Health Organization at December 31, 1975. SOURCE: World Health Organization, 1976.

[1]The liaison offices with United Nations, ECA, and ESCAP, the WHO medical advisers to UNICEF (who are also responsible for liaison with UNFPA), and the WHO representative with UNRWA report to the Division of Coordination.

[2]Regional Office for the Americas/Pan American Sanitary Bureau

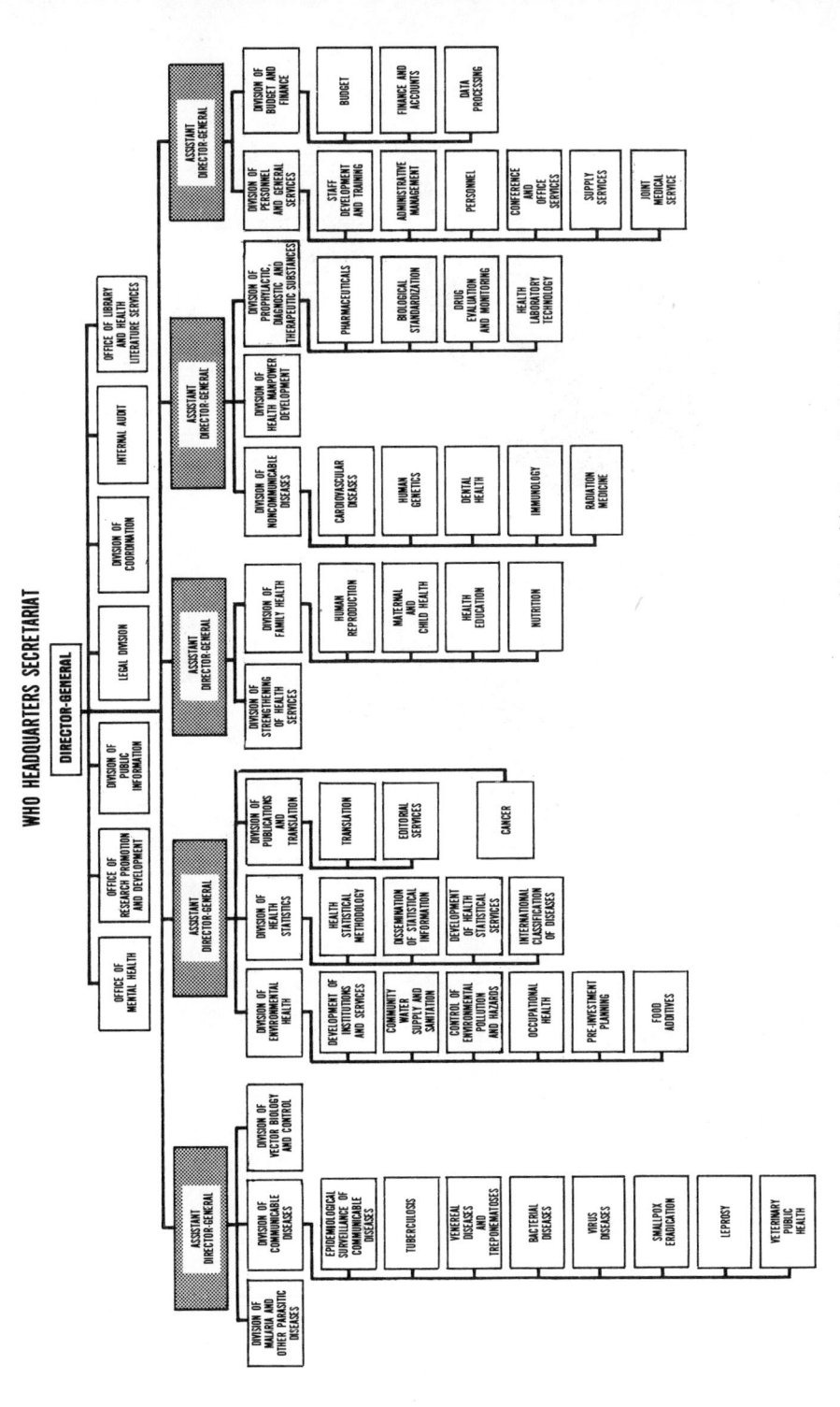

Figure 8-2 World Health Organization Headquarters Secretariat. SOURCE: World Health Organization, 1976.

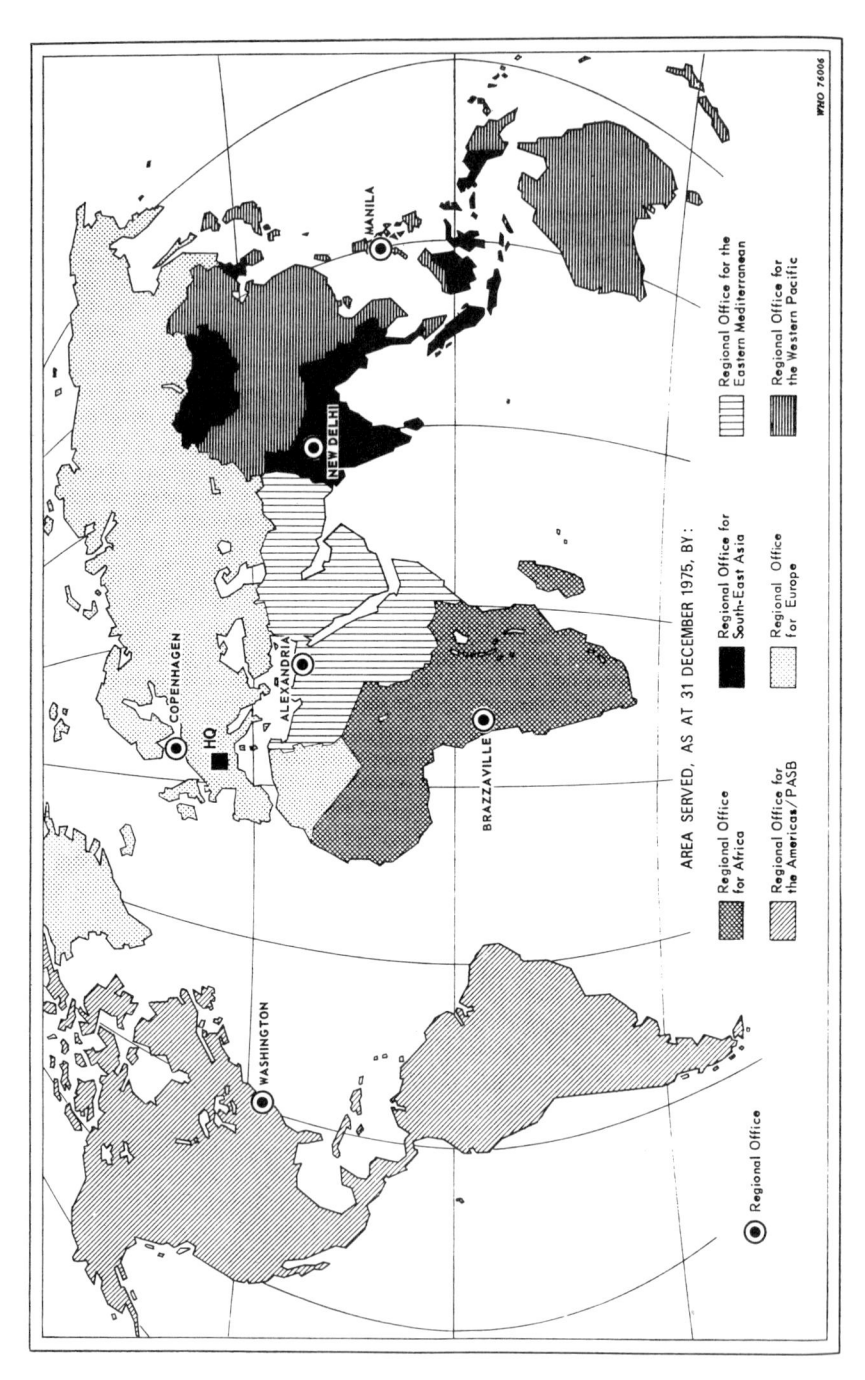

Figure 8-3 World Health Organization Regional Offices and the areas they serve. SOURCE: World Health Organization, 1976.

Table 8-12. Members of the World Health Organization and their scale of assessment for 1977

Member	Scale (percentage)	Member	Scale (percentage)
Afghanistan	0.02	Chile	0.14
Albania	0.02	China	5.40
Algeria	0.08	Colombia	0.16
Angola	0.02	Comoros	0.02
Argentina	0.81	Congo	0.02
Australia	1.41	Costa Rica	0.02
Austria	0.54	Cuba	0.11
Bahamas	0.02	Cyprus	0.02
Bahrain	0.02	Czechoslovakia	0.87
Bangladesh	0.08	Democratic Kampuchea	0.02
Barbados	0.02	Democratic People's Republic of Korea	0.07
Belgium	1.02	Democratic Republic of Viet-Nam	0.02
Benin	0.02	Democratic Yemen	0.02
Bolivia	0.02	Denmark	0.61
Botswana	0.02	Dominican Republic	0.02
Brazil	0.76	Ecuador	0.02
Bulgaria	0.14	Egypt	0.12
Burma	0.03	El Salvador	0.02
Burundi	0.02	Ethiopia	0.02
Byelorussian SSR	0.46	Fiji	0.02
Canada	2.67	Finland	0.42
Cape Verde	0.02	France	5.74
Central African Republic	0.02	Gabon	0.02
Chad	0.02	Gambia	0.02

continued

Table 8-12.—Continued

Member	Scale (percentage)	Member	Scale (percentage)
German Democratic Republic	1.19	Lao People's Democratic Republic	0.02
Germany, Federal Republic of	6.91	Lebanon	0.03
Ghana	0.04	Lesotho	0.02
Greece	0.31	Liberia	0.02
Grenada	0.02	Libyan Arab Republic	0.11
Guatemala	0.03	Luxembourg	0.04
Guinea	0.02	Madagascar	0.02
Guinea-Bissau	0.02	Malawi	0.02
Guyana	0.02	Malaysia	0.07
Haiti	0.02	Maldives	0.02
Honduras	0.02	Mali	0.02
Hungary	0.33	Malta	0.02
Iceland	0.02	Mauritania	0.02
India	1.20	Mauritius	0.02
Indonesia	0.19	Mexico	0.84
Iran	0.20	Monaco	0.02
Iraq	0.05	Mongolia	0.02
Ireland	0.14	Morocco	0.06
Israel	0.20	Mozambique	0.02
Italy	3.51	Namibia[a]	0.01
Ivory Coast	0.02	Nepal	0.02
Jamaica	0.02	Netherlands	1.20
Japan	7.01	New Zealand	0.28
Jordan	0.02	Nicaragua	0.02
Kenya	0.02	Niger	0.02
Kuwait	0.09	Nigeria	0.10

Norway	0.42	Swaziland	0.02
Oman	0.02	Sweden	1.01
Pakistan	0.14	Switzerland	0.78
Panama	0.02	Syrian Arab Republic	0.02
Papua New Guinea	0.02	Thailand	0.11
Paraguay	0.02	Togo	0.02
Peru	0.07	Tonga	0.02
Philippines	0.18	Trinidad and Tobago	0.02
Poland	1.26	Tunisia	0.02
Portugal	0.15	Turkey	0.29
Qatar	0.02	Uganda	0.02
Republic of Korea	0.11	Ukrainian SSR	1.71
Republic of South Viet-Nam	0.02	Union of Soviet Socialist Republics	12.97
Romania	0.30	United Arab Emirates	0.02
Rwanda	0.02	United Kingdom of Great Britain and Northern Ireland	5.31
Sao Tome and Principe	0.02	United Republic of Cameroon	0.02
Saudi Arabia	0.06	United Republic of Tanzania	0.02
Senegal	0.02	United States of America	25.43
Sierra Leone	0.02	Upper Volta	0.02
Singapore	0.04	Uruguay	0.06
Somalia	0.02	Venezuela	0.32
South Africa	0.50	Western Samoa	0.02
Southern Rhodesia[a],[b]	0.01	Yemen	0.02
Spain	0.98	Yugoslavia	0.34
Sri Lanka	0.03	Zaire	0.02
Sudan	0.02	Zambia	0.02
Surinam	0.02		

[a]Associate member
[b]Considered in suspension
Source: World Health Organization, 1976a.

Many of the field projects are underwritten jointly by the WHO regular budget, by the country concerned, and by funds from UNDP, UNEP, UNFPA, or UNICEF, as well as by sums from bilateral sources. These other contributions add greatly to the effectiveness of WHO programs.

The Americas represent a special case. The PASB, which had existed independently for 47 years, became the WHO's Regional office for the Americas in 1949; nevertheless it has retained some independence. The Western Hemisphere is divided into six zones by PAHO, with headquarters in Mexico City, Guatemala City, Caracas, Lima, and Rio de Janeiro, as well as overall headquarters in Washington. Terminology is confusing: the Pan American Sanitary Organization changed its name to the Pan American Health Organization in 1958, but its secretariat, the PASB, has remained the same. Through the partial merger, about 43% of PAHO's budget of $62 million (1975) comes from the WHO regular budget and from UNDP, UNFPA, and similar agencies. The WHO had a staff in 1975 of 5,577, of whom 1,239 were employed by PAHO.

Functions The objective of the WHO is spelled out very simply in Article 1 of its Constitution: "the attainment by all peoples of the highest possible level of health." Its specific functions are listed in Article 2, as follows:

(a) to act as the directing and co-ordinating authority on international health work;

(b) to establish and maintain effective collaboration with the United Nations, specialized agencies, governmental health administrations, professional groups and such other organizations as may be deemed appropriate;

(c) to assist Governments, upon request, in strengthening health services;

(d) to furnish appropriate technical assistance and, in emergencies, necessary aid upon the request or acceptance of Governments;

(e) to provide or assist in providing, upon the request of the United Nations, health services and facilities to special groups, such as the peoples of trust territories;

(f) to establish and maintain such administrative and technical services as may be required, including epidemiological and statistical services;

(g) to stimulate and advance work to eradicate epidemic, endemic and other diseases;

(h) to promote, in co-operation with other specialized agencies where necessary, the prevention of accidental injuries;

(i) to promote, in co-operation with other specialized agencies where necessary, the improvement of nutrition, housing, sanitation, recreation, economic or working conditions and other aspects of environmental hygiene;

(j) to promote co-operation among scientific and professional groups which contribute to the advancement of health;
(k) to propose conventions, agreements and regulations, and make recommendations with respect to international health matters and to perform such duties as may be assigned thereby to the Organization and are consistent with its objective;
(l) to promote maternal and child health and welfare and to foster the ability to live harmoniously in a changing total environment;
(m) to foster activities in the field of mental health, especially those affecting the harmony of human relations;
(n) to promote and conduct research in the field of health;
(o) to promote improved standards of teaching and training in the health, medical and related professions;
(p) to study and report on, in co-operation with other specialized agencies where necessary, administrative and social techniques affecting public health and medical care from preventive and curative points of view, including hospital services and social security;
(q) to provide information, counsel and assistance in the field of health;
(r) to assist in developing an informed public opinion among all peoples on matters of health;
(s) to establish and revise as necessary international nomenclatures of diseases, of causes of death and of public health practices;
(t) to standardize diagnostic procedures as necessary;
(u) to develop, establish and promote international standards with respect to food, biological, pharmaceutical and similar products;
(v) generally to take all necessary action to attain the objective of the Organization.

The work of the WHO is divided into two major categories: central technical services and services to governments. The central services include epidemiologic intelligence; work towards international conventions concerned with health aspects of travel and commerce; international standardization of vaccines and pharmaceuticals; the dissemination of knowledge through meetings and reports of expert committees, seminars, study groups, and publication of technical and similar literature on world health problems. Headquarters also coordinates the work of the WHO Collaborating Centres, several hundred laboratories and institutes throughout the world that provide expert consultation and services in any of 62 fields. A sampling of fields (and number of centers) includes: arbovirus diseases (12); cardiovascular diseases (26); environmental pollution and hazards (20); immunology (28); nutritional anemias (3); plague (1); human reproduction (29); serum reference banks (3) and water supply (34). An important contribution to international understanding is made by the WHO's fellowship program under which thousands of persons have gone for brief study tours abroad in the following fields: public health administration; environmental health; nursing, maternal and child health; other health services; communicable diseases; clinical medicine; and medical and allied education. These fellowships, administered through regional offices, have aided more than 3,000 health workers *annually* in recent years. As Brockington (1975) says: "The wise use of fellowships has continually sent new life pulsating through the world's body politic, bringing enthusiasm and keenness to banish apathy with new ideas. The same can be said for many thousands of professional men and women consultants and experts, otherwise confined within their own narrow horizons, who have been given the opportunity to learn from the experience of other lands...."

Services to governments are provided at the request of member countries—largely in the form of discrete projects established through the appropriate regional office. Some larger cooperative projects are set up on an interregional basis, for example: comparative studies of family planning and human reproduction, or applied research on immunization programs. Intercountry projects within a region may include a meeting of Deans of Faculties of Medicine in the African region, in Brazzaville; a working group on the role of nursing/midwifery in MCH care in Latin America; and a cooperative plan to control pollution of the Rhine river in Europe. But the heart of the WHO services lies in the thousands of individual country projects. It is hardly possible to summarize the extent and variety of these; a list in small type covers well over 100 pages in the Director-General's annual report. The projects are grouped within the WHO Divisions shown in Figures 8-1 and 8-2. A great proportion of them are for training, particularly in Health Manpower Development and Strengthening of Health Services, and many are concerned with organization of specific mass control programs against endemic diseases such as yaws or malaria.

WHO country representatives known as WRs are an important element in the functioning of the organization and coordination of its projects. Assigned to a specific country (or a few adjacent smaller ones) a WR normally has an office within the ministry of health and works closely with the national authorities:

The specific functions of the WHO representative include assistance to the governments in reviewing health needs and resources, and in planning, coordinating, implementing and evaluating their national health programmes and policies. He is also required to co-operate with the Resident Representatives of the United Nations Development Programme and the representatives of other agencies and sources of assistance regarding the health aspects of assistance programmes. He represents, and sometimes acts on behalf of, the regional director at the country level; gives a certain amount of common servicing and liaison facilities to project staff; and keeps the regional director informed of all relevant actions and developments. (World Health Organization, 1968)

Two programs Of the many WHO projects perhaps the best known have been the worldwide smallpox and malaria eradication programs. The former has been a great success, the latter a great disappointment. The intensified global smallpox eradication began in 1967, using the basic vaccination principle developed by William Jenner 171 years before. Early strategy, particularly in west Africa, called for mass vaccination of the entire population by use of jet injectors, but the complex immunization guns often failed under field conditions, and much money, effort and manpower were spent on the almost impossible task of locating and vaccinating every person in an area. Moreover, the delicate vaccine sometimes became impotent under tropical field conditions. As the program progressed, several significant changes occurred. First, the vaccination method was simplified by discarding the jet injectors in favor of a needle with two sharp prongs at one end, an idea borrowed from veterinarians. The bifurcated needle tip, when dipped into a vial of vaccine, picked up a precise amount of vaccine by capillarity. The prongs made a scratch of the proper depth in the vaccinee's skin and transferred the protective fluid. The needle was cheap, had no moving parts, could be used by relatively untrained personnel, caused fewer vaccine side effects and smaller scars, and saved vaccine by using much less per application. The second innovation was widespread use of freeze-dried (lyophilized) vaccine, reconstituted in the field to assure potency. The third and most important change was in the epidemiologic strategy. Work in Nigeria demonstrated that mass campaigns were less effective than pinpointed efforts to control reported outbreaks of smallpox. Therefore, efforts were directed toward case finding and reporting, quarantining those infected, and vaccinating those susceptible individuals possibly exposed. Surveillance methods included public education in schools, markets, and other gathering places and employed photographs of smallpox victims and exhortations to report any known or suspected cases. Toward the end of the Asian campaign, substantial cash rewards were often offered. House-to-house searches were conducted in suspected areas. Border monitoring stations were established. The program pushed ahead, despite local setbacks, which sometimes included false reporting of accomplishments by vaccination teams. The last case in the Western Hemisphere occurred in Brazil in 1971. In Asia, the last known case in Pakistan was reported in October 1974; in Nepal in April 1975; and in India the following month. The last report of a case of smallpox in Asia was made in Bangladesh on October 16, 1975. Some cases of variola minor, a less virulent form of the disease, were reported along the troubled border of Somalia, northern Kenya, and Ethiopia well into 1977.

The story of malaria eradication is far more complex. The spectacular effects of DDT upon the vectors of typhus and malaria created great optimism in the decade following the Second World War. Accordingly, the Eighth World Health Assembly in 1955 suggested the undertaking of a global malaria eradication program to rid the world of this burdensome disease. The strategy of malaria eradication was worked out by leading experts and spelled out most clearly in the sixth report (1957) of the WHO Expert Committee on Malaria. In principle, if interruption of transmission is maintained for three consecutive years the vast majority of malaria cases will become noninfective during this period and the remaining parasite reservoir can be eliminated by drug treatment. Malaria eradication programs were projected in several phases: pre-planning, preparation, attack, consolidation, maintenance, and certification (of eradication). The entire scheme is based upon vector control, primarily by indoor spraying of residual insecticide, chiefly DDT. This is supplemented in the attack phase by extensive case finding and chemotherapy. Later phases depended largely upon vigilant surveillance and control of localized outbreaks and introductions.

Early results of the malaria eradication effort were very encouraging. India in 1953 had had 75 million cases with 750,000 deaths. In 1968, with a much larger population, India reported only 218,000 cases. In Java and Bali in four years the number of reported cases dropped almost miraculously from 20 million to 2,000. By 1968, 651 million people (37.6% of the population at risk) were living in areas from which malaria had been eliminated, and another 715 million were in areas in the consolidation phase. But there were many reverses. Sri Lanka, a formerly highly endemic area, reported only 1,600 cases in 1959 and just 18 in 1963, whereupon total DDT spraying was relaxed. A slow increase followed until 1968–70 when 1.5 *million* cases were reported. Other resurgences have occurred in India, Pakistan, Afghanistan, Thailand, and Central America. In Bangladesh and Indonesia, civil disturbances interrupted control work, and the number of malaria cases increased greatly. In tropical Africa, the area most affected, no countrywide malaria eradication program has gotten underway (Bruce-Chwatt, 1974). It is in this region that vast majority of the world's cases occur.

The 22nd World Health Assembly, seeing difficulties with the global program, had already adopted a revised strategy in 1969. Countries were grouped into four categories based upon the degree of their success with previous malaria eradication programs. Those in which little progress was to be expected were encouraged to undertake malaria *control* activities with much reduced levels of expectation in comparison with eradication programs. But the revised strategy still failed to deal adequately with the world malaria problem, prompting the Director-General of WHO to comment:

The world community has been well aware of the unfavorable turn taken by the global programme since 1969. The World Health Assembly then adopted a new strategy against malaria. This strategy was and remains sound . . . Yet, apart from a few exceptions, nothing, or very little, has happened in terms of a renewed attack on the disease. The Organization has been unable to foster the implementation of the strategy which it has evolved. Why?

One underlying reason was the following. The global malaria eradication programme had generated such enthusiasm, enjoyed such prestige and made initially such spectacular progress that no government, national or international institution, or individual connected in any way with the programme was psychologically prepared to admit even partial failure and to break away from the past.

We all know that the concept and methods of eradication are perfectly valid in themselves and remain applicable to certain country situations where epidemiological and socioeconomic conditions permit. In future endeavours on a global scale there is room for national malaria eradication programmes. But it probably was a mistake to stipulate that 'global eradication' remained the objective when it was obviously out of reach for decades to come, with the means at our disposal. (Mahler, 1976)

Comparing the reasons for the success of the smallpox program and the breakdown of malaria eradication is an instructive exercise. Basically involved are: (1) technical factors such as immunity in man, problems of vector resistance to insecticide, and parasite resistance to drugs; (2) cost of a single effective vaccination versus lack of any method of immunization, and the need for repeated sprayings over enormous areas, including materials, vehicles, gasoline, and salaries; (3) administrative problems including lack of trained manpower, integration of a substantial monovalent malaria service with existing basic health and medical care services (themselves often inadequate), and inadequate planning and coordination.

The many problems notwithstanding, the WHO is proceeding with attacks against malaria and other parasitic diseases. Of these the most ambitious is a 20-year multimillion dollar program against onchocerciasis (river blindness) in the seven countries of the Volta River basin of west Africa—Benin, Ghana, Ivory Coast, Mali, Niger, Togo, and Upper Volta. Funds are provided by the AfDB, UNDP, IBRD, and IDA as well as by the governments of Belgium, Canada, France, the Federal Republic of Germany, Iraq, Japan, Kuwait, the Netherlands, the United Kingdom and the U.S.A. Participating donors and agencies subscribed to an Onchocerciasis Fund Agreement in May 1975. The cost of the first six-year phase of this project was estimated at U.S. $54 million.

A special program for research and training in tropical diseases was called for by the 27th World Health Assembly in 1974. Realizing that only one percent of all the money spent on medical research is devoted to the diseases of tropical countries, the WHO has attempted to take a lead in this field. Faced with the great number of tropical diseases and the vast extent of the areas in which they occur, the program has selected six diseases for attack: malaria, schistosomiasis, filariasis, trypanosomiasis, leishmaniasis, and leprosy. Africa has been chosen as the initial focus of the program; all six diseases occur there, affecting 200 million people usually in multiple infections.

Of the many other WHO programs that might be mentioned, the commitment to provide immunizations for the world's children is especially important. The 30th World Health Assembly in May 1977 voted to intensify national and international activities so that by 1990 all children would be immunized against diphtheria, pertussis (whooping cough), tetanus, measles, poliomyelitis, and tuberculosis. The Assembly noted that currently fewer than 10% of the 80 million children born annually in developing countries are adequately immunized against these diseases, and that each year some 5 million children die from them and 10 million are permanently disabled. Little biomedical research is needed for this program: effective vaccines exist against all of the named diseases and have made them a thing of the past in industrialized countries. Nevertheless, financial, technical, and managerial difficulties combine to prevent the vast majority of children in developing countries from being properly immunized.

These and other similar special programs will reinforce the goals of the WHO through special emphasis upon the countries and people in greatest need.

Policy Since the early 1950s, far-sighted officers of the WHO have realized that to concentrate efforts on specialized mass campaigns would yield only temporary results in improvement of health unless they were accompanied by effective permanent health services in the rural areas of the world. There has been a slow but definite trend toward integration of special programs with basic health services and toward the assignment of higher priorities to the strengthening of primary care. Resolutions passed by successive World Health Assemblies have progressively stressed primary care, and the number of WHO projects in all regions directly related to this field has increased enormously. Much attention has been devoted to innovative methods for meeting the health needs of the underprivileged 80% of the populations in LDCs.

Over the years and particularly in the mid-1970s, the developing countries have become more united in their demands for a greater share of world resources and world decision making. The "group of 77" countries (now much larger) was responsible for enunciating the New International Economic Order in the United Nations and has carried its principles into all major international organizations, including the WHO. The onchocerciasis, tropical diseases, and immunization programs, among many others, are attempts to narrow the health gap between rich and poor nations, but much more fundamental policy changes have been imposed upon the WHO by its third world members. A resolution (No. WHA 29.48) of the 29th World Health Assembly in 1976 noted "with deep concern the increasing allocation of resources of the Organization towards establishment and administrative costs" and directed the Director-General to cut down on expenditures at headquarters, streamline the professional and administrative cadres, and phase out projects "which have outlived their utility" (World Health Organization, 1976a). In addition, the resolution demanded that at least 60% of the 1980 budget be devoted to technical cooperation and provision of services. This challenge requires the WHO to reduce its headquarters staff by 24% by 1981 in order to devote more resources to the field. Single words can make a great difference in official resolutions, and it is no accident that the term "technical cooperation" is used in a context that some years before might have seen "technical assistance." At the Executive Board meeting in January 1977 the Director-General interpreted technical cooperation to mean "activities which have a high degree of social relevance for member states, in the sense that they are directed towards defined national health goals and that they will contribute significantly to the improvement of the health status of their populations through methods that they can apply now and at a cost they can afford now. These activities should conform to the aim of 'developing national self-reliance in matters of health.'"

When viewed in these terms, resolution WHA 29.48 may indeed presage a new orientation for the future.

THE PROFESSIONAL INTERNATIONAL HEALTH WORKER

When the PVOs, individual government agencies, and IGOs are viewed together, it is not surprising that purposes, functions, and projects often overlap. The nominal jurisdiction (the "turf") of each group is often unclear not only to a dispassionate observer, but to the agency itself, to the host (recipient) government, and to the people for whose benefit the services or merchandise or advice is presumably intended. The number of almoners in the capital cities of LDCs can grow almost without limit. Claire Stirling has vividly, if sarcastically, described the aid scene in Kathmandu:

At last count when I was there, about 700 missionaries of progress were racketing around town in their Land Rovers and Toyota jeeps, representing some fifty donor-states and agencies, all urging assorted projects on a nation the size of Arkansas. Among the foreign benefactors are USAID, the Indian Cooperation Mission, the Chinese, Russians, British, Canadians, Australians, New Zealanders, Pakistanis, and Swiss, the Japanese Overseas Cooperation Volunteers, the German Volunteer service, the Ford Foundation, the Rockefeller Foundation, the Dooley Foundation (using volunteer airline hostesses who take six months off for good works), Anglia University, Cornell University, the World Bank, the Asian Development Bank, the International Monetary Fund, the UN's Save the Children Fund, UNICEF (also for children), UNDP (development), UNIDO (international development), UNESCO (education and science), FAO (food and agriculture), WFP (food), ITU (Telecommunications), ICAO (civil aviation), WHO (health), WMO (weather), OTC (technical), UPU (postal), UNIC (informational), and IMCO (maritime), this last of the opinion that landlocked Nepal ought to own a cargo vessel moored across India, in Calcutta. (Stirling, 1976)

Considering the background discussed in this book, we may now ask what is the appropriate role for a health-related agency (and its personnel) to assume in the less developed countries of the world? Granted that every situation is different, are there not any general principles to guide international health work? Certainly there are, and at the risk of presumptuousness some of them will be discussed here. They fall into two large groupings corresponding roughly to form and substance, or to the how and the what with respect to the work to be done.

In the past it was commonplace for the more privileged groups to assume an attitude of paternalism or arrogant condescension towards non-European peoples. This attitude can be seen in a paper published by a respected psychiatric journal on "Frontal lobe function and the African" that dealt with Africans of "all degrees of sophistication and education... not feeble-minded or evil, but fair samples of their race." The African, it was said,

is in any case not used to looking very far ahead, but if he does it is merely to think that the European is all-powerful and can doubtless produce firewood somehow when he needs it and it is even possible that the sky might rain firewood at any moment... a shoe is something to be cleaned and put in a particular place, a completely incomprehensible ritual anyway, and so to be memorized by rote and performed unquestioningly... "The house-boys cannot put furniture back level with the wall, put the table at right angles to the wall, hang pictures straight, etc." This requires a type of spatial perception that is foreign to the African; it can be learned in regard to specific positions for particular items, but a general geometric orderliness is hardly attainable. His attempts to solve, for instance, the Cube Imitation performance test, which requires some spatial apperception, would be pitiful in a European child of eight.

Such remarks might have been written in the 1750s as justification for the slave trade, but in fact these lines date from the second half of our own twentieth century (Carothers, 1951). They underscore the degree of prejudice that may be found in an inappropriately educated mind, and the crucial need not only for tolerance but for respect for the dignity of other people. A humble peasant can do many things beyond the ken of many a foreign expert: he can, for example, communicate freely in his own language (often in several), make practical and attractive objects from local materials, and survive in an often hostile environment. There is no great gap or empty hole in his consciousness, waiting to be filled by an infusion of knowledge from afar, and his reluctance to change may be based not on obstinacy but on the threat of disaster following an incorrect decision.

Conditioned by the experiences of centuries, people in developing countries are wary of exploitation and may be understandably suspicious of the motives of outsiders. Mamdani (1974) has described a six-year pilot project on family planning in a village in the Indian Punjab. Through the entire period the villagers searched for a clue to what the program was "really" about, not believing that such masses of money and personnel could be devoted to its avowed purpose. The use of health and social programs as tools for accomplishing other goals (e.g., political indoctrination or evangelizing) has helped to foster such suspicions. At a different level, host country professionals are disturbed, with good reason, by well-funded foreign experts or researchers on short assignments, gathering material for publications, and gaining their personal advancement.

In developing countries today, members of the local staff may be as well trained as the representatives of overseas agencies, and they generally know more about the situation at hand. In the past, particularly in the colonial world, decisions as to where to go and what to do there were made unilaterally by the metropolitan government or agencies, and whatever health services and facilities were made available were imposed upon passive "native" populations. Today such programs must be filtered through several intermediate layers, most importantly the government of the host or recipient country, which has veto power over all projects within its jurisdiction. Even IGOs may have their projects disrupted at any time. One such event occurred early in 1975 when a mosquito genetics research unit, partially sponsored by the WHO, was severely criticized in a report by the Parliamentary Public Accounts Committee of India. The report claimed that the project, while of no utility to India, served to foster the "biological warfare" research of a project cosponsor, the U.S. Public Health Service. WHO sponsorship of the project was quickly terminated (Hanlon, 1975). The lesson is clear: any international program must respect the sensibilities of the people and governments of the areas in which it is carried out.

A model code of "ethics for an international health profession" has been proposed by Taylor (1966), who emphasized the need to develop concepts different from those of the conventional physician: a community and environmental focus, consideration of the underlying causes of social pathology, the sharing of information and skills with foreign colleagues, and a great breadth of interest. "Needs are so obvious that the temptation is great to rush in with programs that seem reasonable; but international health work is full of surprises. Each new activity needs to be carefully tested" (Taylor, 1966).

An example of such careful testing, and a possible surprise answer, may be found in the work of Scrimshaw and colleagues (1968) in three highland villages in Guatemala. Diarrheal and respiratory diseases were prevalent in all, leading to infant mortality rates of around 100 per 1,000 live births. A controlled experiment was conducted over a five-year period in these three villages. In one, a public health nurse, sanitarian, and physician were provided full-time, and a water supply system and outdoor toilets were constructed. In the second, young children were provided with a high-protein food supplement in the form of one drink five days each week. The third village was merely observed. Childhood morbidity and mortality were recorded in all three. It was found that morbidity in young children was unaffected and mortality only slightly reduced in the "medical care" village, but that both fell sharply in the "feeding" village, as compared with the control. One would wish this experiment to be repeated in other countries.

The international health worker must develop a keen awareness of: (1) the place of health among other factors in the total scheme of national development; (2) the relationship of health services to health status; (3) the place of curative medical care within health services; and (4) the likely consequences of establishing, or of not establishing, a particular health program under consideration. Inconsistencies and contradictions abound. The most advanced creations of science and technology must be weighed and, if need be, rejected, even as a gift. While the demand increases everywhere for grassroots community-based primary care, attention must also be devoted to the apex of the national health services pyramid where the crucial process of planning must be made to take place. Lives saved by development contribute to a surging population, but birth rates cannot decline so long as child mortality is high.

On the first page of this volume it was stated that in order to understand the health conditions of mankind, to see them accurately and objectively, we must be willing to cast aside preconceptions. Scrimshaw (1974) has said it more eloquently:

> We are all limited in our responses to health problems by a variety of myths, misconceptions, and, inevitably, cultural blind spots.... Myths represent man's effort to explain environmental forces that he does not understand, to develop a rationale and guidelines for living in an uncertain and confusing world. They organize the chaotic into an apparently rational system and thus may serve a very useful purpose at a given point in time. However, in a world where values and conditions are changing, people may cling to them tenaciously long after this has become disadvantageous.

These are the myths that Scrimshaw has specified: (1) Knowledge of the agent of a disease is sufficient to understand its causation and to design programs for its prevention. (2) The first health need of populations in unfavorable circumstances is medical care or, expressed another way: programs of preventive medicine and public health are a luxury until medical care has been provided for the acute conditions. (3) Modern health care is the priority need of all societies and has been responsible for the marked drop in mortality rates and the population explosion of recent decades. (4) Population growth is such a major threat to the world that family planning should have absolute priority over the other expenditures for health in developing countries. (5) The poorer a person is and the greater his need, the more time he will have to wait in clinics, bring children to health centers, make repeated visits, or attend lectures and demonstrations. And, finally, (6) a program is justified by good intentions.

It is very difficult to enter so much uncharted territory all at once, to rank priorities, to balance between factions, and to benefit the greatest number. Urgent needs and strident demands leave too few moments for contemplation, and the scientific method with its randomized controlled trials costs both time and money when these are rarely made available for the purpose.

How then are choices to be made, and what suggestions may be given? One hundred fifty experiences are better than one, and the international health professional must know and be able to interpret the global scene to those whose responsibilities end at the national border. By observing the successes and noting the failures in other countries, by adapting and refining to local conditions, through imagination, practice, evaluation, and comparison, the international health worker can become a true collaborator for the benefit of all peoples. The world is indeed full of paradoxes, but it is these that provide our most exciting challenges.

References

Basch, P. F. 1974. Regional Cooperation in Health Education: The SEAMEO-TROPMED Project. Report to the World Health Organization, Regional Office for the Americas, Washington. 38 p.

Brockington, F. 1975. World Health. 3rd Ed. Edinburgh and London. Churchill Livingstone. 345 p.

Bruce-Chwatt, L. J. 1974. Resurgence of malaria and its control. Journal of Tropical Medicine and Hygiene 77: 62–66.

Bryant, J. 1969. Health and the Developing World. Ithaca, N.Y. Cornell University Press. 345 p.

Bullock, M. B. 1974. A brief sketch of the role of PUMC graduates in the People's Republic of China. In: J. Z. Bowers and E. F. Purcell, Eds. Medicine and Society in China. New York. Josiah Macy Jr. Foundation. pp. 99–101.

Carey, H. L. 1971. Testimony. In: U.S. Congress. House of Representatives.

Committee on Foreign Affairs. Subcommittee on International Organizations and Movements. Hearings on H.R. 10042, International Health Agency Act of 1971. pp. 3–18.

Carothers, J. C. 1951. Frontal lobe function and the African. Journal of Mental Science (British Journal of Psychiatry) 97: 12–48.

Commission on International Development. 1969. Partners in Development. New York. Praeger Publishers. 399 p.

Crosby, B. and S. J. Smith, Eds. 1971. U.S. Non-Profit Organizations in Development Assistance Abroad. New York. Technical Assistance Information Clearing House of the American Council of Voluntary Agencies for Foreign Service, Inc. 1038 p.

Crozier, R. 1975. Medicine and modernization in China: an historical overview. In: A. Kleinman, P. Kunstadter, E. R. Alexander, and J. L. Gale, Eds. Medicine in Chinese Cultures. Washington. U.S. Government Printing Office. DHEW Publication No. (NIH) 75-653. pp. 21–35.

Development Coordination Committee. 1976. Development Issues. U.S. Actions Affecting the Development of Low-income Countries. Washington, D.C. Agency for International Development. 164 p.

Eggins, E., Project Coordinator. 1967. OECD-ICVA Directory. Development Aid of Non-Governmental Non-Profit Organizations. Paris. Organization for Economic Cooperation and Development. 1378 p.

Ferguson, M. E. 1970. China Medical Board and Peking Union Medical College: a Chronicle of Fruitful Collaboration 1914–1951. New York. China Medical Board. 263 p.

Flache, S. 1977. WHO and nongovernmental organizations. WHO Chronicle 31: 127–130.

Goodman, N. M. 1971. International Health Organizations and Their Work. Edinburgh and London. Churchill Livingstone. 408 p.

Hanlon, J. 1975. Germ-war allegations force WHO out of Indian mosquito project. New Scientist 68: 102–103.

Howard-Jones, N. 1975. The Scientific Background of the International Sanitary Conferences, 1851–1938. Geneva. World Health Organization. 110 p.

Kendrick, M. A. 1972. Study of illness among Americans returning from international travel, July 11–August 24, 1971 (Preliminary data). Journal of Infectious Diseases 126: 684–685.

Kendrick, M. A. 1972a. Summary of study on illness among Americans visiting Europe, March 31, 1969–March 30, 1970. Journal of Infectious Diseases 126: 685–687.

Lall, S. 1975. Major Issues in Transfer of Technology to Developing Countries. A Case Study of the Pharmaceutical Industry. United Nations Conference on Trade and Development. Committee on Transfer of Technology, Meeting of 24 November, 1975. Document TD/B/C.6/4. 63 p. + annex.

Mahler, H. 1976. Thoughts by the Director-General on the Development of the Antimalaria Programme. World Health Organization Official Records 231: 63–65.

Mamdani, M. 1974. The myth of population control. Development Digest 12: 13–18.

Scrimshaw, N. S., M. A. Guzmán, M. Flores, and J. E. Gordon. 1968. Nutrition and infection field study in Guatemalan villages, 1959-1964. V. Disease incidence among preschool children under natural village conditions, with improved diet, and with medical and public health services. Archives of Environmental Health 16: 223-234.

Scrimshaw, N. S. 1974. Myths and realities in international health planning. American Journal of Public Health 64: 792-797.

Shakespeare, W. 1603. Hamlet, Prince of Denmark. Act III, Scene 1.

Shaplen, R. 1964. Toward the Well-Being of Mankind. Garden City, N.Y. Doubleday & Co. 214 p.

Sivard, R. L. 1976. World Military and Social Expenditures 1976. Leesburg, Va. WMSE Publications. 32 p.

Stirling, C. 1976. Atlantic Report—Nepal. Atlantic Monthly. October: 14-25.

Task Force on International Development. 1970. U.S. Foreign Assistance in the 1970's: A New Approach. *In*: U.S. Congress. Joint Economic Committee. Subcommittee on Foreign Economic Policy. A Foreign Economic Policy for the 1970's. Part 3. U.S. Policies Toward Developing Countries. Hearings of May 13, 14, 18, and 19, 1970. pp. 460-502.

Taylor, C. E. 1966. Ethics for an International Health Profession. Science 153: 716-720.

Travel Market Yearbook 1976/77. Stamford, Ct. Marketing Handbooks, Inc. 128 p.

Turshen, M. 1976. An analysis of the medical supply industries. International Journal of Health Services 6: 271-294.

UNCTAD 1976. Aid from OPEC countries. Development Forum 4: 6.

UNCTAD 1976a. Handbook of International Trade and Development Statistics. New York. United Nations Publication TD/STAT. 6. 657 p.

U.S. Agency for International Development. 1977. New directions for AID. A summary of the presentation to the congress. Foreign assistance programs for fiscal 1978. War on Hunger 11: 7-22.

Williams, G. 1969. The Plague Killers. New York. Charles Scribner's Sons. 345 p.

Williams, K. N. and B. A. Lockett. 1975. Migration of foreign physicians to the United States: The perspective of health manpower planning. International Journal of Health Services 4: 213-243.

World Bank. 1975. Health. Sector Policy Paper. Washington. World Bank. 83 p.

World Bank. 1975a. World Bank Atlas. Washington. World Bank. 30 p.

World Health Organization. 1958. The First Ten Years of the World Health Organization. Geneva. World Health Organization. 538 p.

World Health Organization. 1968. The Second Ten Years of the World Health Organization. Geneva. World Health Organization. 413 p.

World Health Organization. 1976. The Work of the World Health Organization 1975. World Health Organization Official Records No. 229. 361 p.

World Health Organization. 1976a. Twenty-Ninth World Health Assembly, Geneva 3-21 May 1976. Part I. Resolutions and Decisions. Annexes. World Health Organization Official Records No. 233. 115 p.

INDEX

Abortion, 192, 224, 245
Abbreviations, meaning of, See Tables 8-2, 8-10
Acupuncture, 54, 55
Advertising, effects of, 153–55
Afghanistan, 153, 363
Africa, 20, 21, 25, 36, 62, 64, 108, 116, 135, 256, 279, 363
   Central, 157
   East, 45, 58, 64, 151, 221
   North, 31, 40, 115
   West, 20, 61, 124, 144, 151, 221, 349, 361
Age adjustment of rates, 199
Albania, 278, 301
Alcoholism, 116, 136, 148
Altitude, effects of, 9–12
Amebiasis, 3, 248, 323. See also Disease, diarrheal
Amebic meningoencephalitis, 14, 15, 221
Ancient man, 45–50
Anemia, 5, 31
   sickle cell, 31, 39
Angola, 125
Animals, as disease reservoirs, 24–25
Appropriate technology, 243, 337. See also Technology
Argentina, 5, 279
Ascaris (roundworm), 15, 35, 324
Asia, 20, 21, 25, 256, 279, 361
   Central, 57
   South, 115
   Southeast, 149
   Western, 58
Atherosclerosis, 33, 46. See also Disease, cardiovascular
Attitudes, societal, 143–44
Australia, 26, 66, 118, 152, 169, 220, 221, 280, 293, 296, 325
Austria, 276, 277, 292, 296, 299
Auxiliary medical personnel, 170, 306–14
Ayurvedic medicine, 52, 53

Bali, 362. See also Indonesia
Balkans, 20, 58
Bangladesh, 312, 362

Barefoot doctor, 163, 170, 263, 309, 310, 312, 315
Behavior and health, 141, 144–57
Belgium, 277, 282, 296
Benefits, in medical care systems, 289–93
Benin, 364
Birth, definition of, 188
Birth defects, 221
   screening for, 239
Birth rate, 40, 98, 106, 370
Bismark, Otto von, 73, 233
Blackflies, 124
Blindness, statistics on, 211–12
Blood groups and disease, 34, 35
Bolivia, 9, 63, 279, 281, 285, 312
Bomoh, 163, 172
Borneo, 49
Botulism, 34, 206
"Brain drain," 303, 326
Brazil, 7, 74, 115, 119, 123, 125, 151, 161, 162, 240, 283, 330, 336, 362
Breast-feeding, decline in, 153–55
Britain. See Great Britain
Bulgaria, 278, 301
Burkitt's lymphoma, 35, 36
Burma, 281

Cambodia, 125
Cameroon, 314
Canada, 3, 14, 160, 207, 209, 226, 280, 284, 292, 296, 324, 325
Cancer, 6, 13, 35, 52, 109, 148, 153, 199, 222, 252
Cardiovascular disease. See Disease, cardiovascular
Caribbean, 60, 122, 144
Celebes, 221
Celsus, 51
Census, data from, 173–81
Central America, 222, 362
Ceylon. See Sri Lanka
Chadwick, Edwin, 70, 71, 233
Chagas' disease, 18, 21. See also Trypanosomiasis
Childhood diseases, 94. See also Mortality, childhood; and *specific diseases*

373

Chile, 5, 154, 155, 206, 252, 276, 279
China, 12, 45, 46, 49, 50, 54, 57, 83, 84, 108, 125, 127, 140, 173, 180, 256, 278, 287, 309, 310, 312, 315
Chinese medicine, traditional, 54–55
Cholera, 3, 48, 69, 71, 74, 137, 207, 221, 238, 248, 311, 325, 338, 351
Cigarette smoking, 33, 147–48, 153
Cities, rush to, 109–19. *See also* Urbanization
Climate and health, 13–16
Colombia, 125, 154, 288, 289, 295, 332
Colonialism, 58–67, 79, 86, 127
Columbus, 60
Congo, 61, 65, 125, 281, 314
Constantinople, 57
Cook, James, 59
Costa Rica, 281
Cost-benefit analysis, 237–41
Cost-effectiveness analysis, 241–43, 348
Costs, averted future, 237
Crete, 50
Cuba, 65, 274, 275, 284, 291, 298, 312
Culture, 133–40, 202, 321
  and illness, 135
  at variance with government regulations, 187
Curandero, 163, 172
Czechoslovakia, 278, 283, 291

DDT, 332
  and malaria, 362
Dams, 123–25
Data, health-related, 167–216
  on health services, 212–16
  on morbidity, 203–12
  on mortality, 193–203
  on population, 173–81
  types of, 167–72
Death
  attitudes toward, 137
  causes of, 193–99, 227, 252
  certification of, 195, 198
  definition of, 192
Death rate. *See* Mortality
Demographic transition, 107
Dengue fever, 324
Denmark, 46, 277, 280, 293, 296
Development
  economic, 78–98
  and environment, 119–26

Development Assistance Committee, 80
Diabetes, 33, 35, 52, 199, 211, 222, 311
Dialysis, renal, 242, 262
Diphtheria, 57, 69, 94, 364
Disease
  ancient times, 45–49
  airborne, 17, 18
  cardiovascular, 6, 18, 33, 35, 36, 106, 146, 147, 150, 151, 153, 252
  categorization of, 136
  control of, 74
  cost of, 240
  and culture, 151, 157
  dental, 5, 46, 224
  diarrheal, 18, 53, 60, 62, 117, 154, 162, 207, 222, 323, 368
  distribution of, 106, 322
  and environment, 3–26
  infectious, 18, 35, 46, 52, 57, 73, 94, 121, 160, 202, 206–8, 262
  introduced, 324–27
  malignant. *See* Cancer
  mental, 140
  nidality of, 47
  notifiable, 207
  nutritional, 13, 16, 31, 69, 74. *See also* Goiter
  occupational, 51, 207
  parasitic, 121, 122, 227, 254, 315, 364, 338
  registers, 209
  renal, 242, 293
  reporting of, 206, 207
  respiratory, 15, 46, 121, 323, 468
  rickettsial, 24, 26, 324
  sexually transmitted, 24, 60, 105, 211, 275, 324, 325
  socioeconomic determinants of, 78
  surveillance, 209–11
  tropical, 233, 364
  vector-transmitted, 19–26, 35, 47, 62, 324
  viral, 18, 24, 36, 94, 124, 221, 323, 324, 338
  waterborne, 48, 124, 239
  See also specific diseases
Drugs, traditional knowledge of, 4, 52–56
Dysentery. *See* Disease, diarrheal

Easter Island, 48
East Indies, 58. *See also* Indonesia
Economic development and health, 78–98

INDEX

Economic differences between countries, 234
Economic value of individuals, 234
Ecuador, 9, 12, 63
Edna McConnell Clark Foundation, 329
Egypt, 6, 46, 50, 58, 119, 124, 240, 295, 330
Elephantiasis, nonfilarial, 5-6
England, 5, 39, 67-72, 94, 109, 125, 126, 233. See also Great Britain
Environment
  changing, 40, 41, 123-25
  and heredity, 32-40
  natural, 4
  See also Pollution
Epidemic, 46, 56, 57, 70, 125, 156, 157, 325
Epidemiology, 32, 132
Epilepsy, 51, 60
Ergotism, 57
Ethiopia, 6, 144, 362
Ethnic groups, 35-40
Europe, 62-66, 221
  Eastern, 20, 274, 297
  Western, 283, 295, 297
European Economic Community, 326
Expectation of life, 90-98, 245-46

Family planning, 107, 236, 242, 310, 329, 332, 339, 360, 367, 368
  definition of, 107-8
  See also Population
Fanon, Frantz, 79
Farr, William, 71
Favism, 32, 221
Feldsher, 301, 302
Fiji, 66, 308
Filariasis, 62, 124, 211, 324, 364
Finland, 109, 147, 210, 280, 292, 299
Finlay, Carlos, 65
Fleas and plague, 25
Food and Agriculture Organization, 99, 101
Food for Peace, 340
Food supply, world, 99-103
Ford Foundation, 329
Foreign aid, 338-345
Foreign medical graduates
  emigration, 303
  licensure of, 326
France, 45, 72, 109, 146, 206, 277, 292, 296, 331, 332

Gabon, 314
Galen, 51, 56
Gambia, 60
Gastroenteritis. See Disease, diarrheal
Genetic adaptations, 27-30
Genetic diseases, 30-32
Geological substrate, 4-7
Germany, 72, 169, 233, 276
  Democratic Republic of (East), 275, 278, 296
  Federal Republic of (West), 277, 282, 292, 296
Ghana, 16, 123-25, 274, 281, 313, 364
Goiter, 4, 132
Gorgas, William, 65
Governments, 127, 255, 338, 360, 366, 368
  role of, 127-28, 228-30, 270-370
Great Britain, 57, 89, 90, 160, 206, 241, 274, 280, 282, 283, 290, 291, 293, 295-98, 314, 327
  See also England
Greece, 4, 50, 51, 277, 293
Griscom, John, 73
Gross National Product, 80, 90, 93, 219, 248, 342, 345
Guatemala, 121, 252, 279, 285, 311, 313, 368, 369
Guevara, Che, 79
Guiana, 60
Guinea, 325
Guyana, 66

Hansen, Gerhard, 57
Hansen's disease. See Leprosy
Hawaii, 36, 221
Health
  definitions of, 204-6
  as investment, 236
  right to, 259
  value of, 234
  as wealth, 233
Health care, 158, 219, 247, 250, 255, 258, 277-81
  See also Medical care; Medical care systems
Health problems, recognition of, 219-28
Health service, functions of in Ruritania, 228-32
Health services
  policy determination, 219-55
  statistics regarding, 212-6

Health statistics, 168
Heart disease. See Disease, cardiovascular
Hemoglobin variants, 31
Herbalist, 163
Herbs, 4, 47, 51, 56
Heredity and environment, 32–40
Honduras, 279, 285
Hong Kong, 108, 211
Hookworm, 5, 15, 35, 62, 211, 248, 324, 330, 331
Hospitals, 297, 312–14, 327
　establishment of, 57, 58
Humors, balance of, 50, 139
Hungary, 278, 301
Hypertension, 33, 36, 147, 150, 153, 198, 222

Iceland, 280
Illness, 160, 161, 209, 236, 290
　concepts of, 132–40
　economic cost of, 234
Immunization, 94, 97, 156, 163, 238, 240, 243, 245, 259, 330, 331, 361, 364
Incomes, distribution of, 85–89
India, 5, 7, 18, 24, 49, 50, 52, 53, 57–59, 116, 119, 125, 127, 151, 152, 245, 274, 281, 284, 299, 311, 314, 330, 336, 362, 368
Indian medicine, traditional, 52–53
Indonesia, 24, 116, 127, 151, 295, 314, 345, 362
Industrialization, 119–23, 127
Industrial revolution, 67, 109, 119, 127
Industry, private, 336
Influenza, 57, 160, 208, 325, 330
Insects, 20, 21, 24, 25, 36, 46, 324. See also specific types
Institut Pasteur, 331, 332
Insurance, health, types of, 233, 236, 274–81
Intergovernmental Organizations, 345, 366–68
International Classification of Diseases, 194–99, 203
International comparability of data, 193–99
International Health Regulations, 207
International health worker, 366–69
International Monetary Fund, 80
International Sanitary Regulations, 208
Introduced diseases, 324–25
Investment, health as, 236–37
Iran, 125, 139, 285, 309, 314, 315

Israel, 275, 277, 292
Italy, 3, 49, 57, 206, 277, 278, 292, 296, 298, 299, 325
Ivory Coast, 125, 364

Jamaica, 108, 153, 301
Japan, 24, 26, 36, 146, 147, 206, 220–22, 277, 292, 296, 298, 299, 325
Java, 45, 48, 64, 362. See also Indonesia
Jenner, Edward, 74

Kellogg Foundation, 329
Kenya, 6, 12, 153, 154, 362
Khmer Republic, 345, 347
Korea, 24, 151
Kresge Foundation, 329
Kwashiorkor, 117

Labrador, 16
Laos, 345, 347
Lassa fever, 221, 324
Latin America, 5, 20, 66, 114–16, 144, 152, 224, 233, 279, 280, 282, 295, 299, 329
Latitude, effects of, 7–8
Lebanon, 151
Leishmaniasis, 324, 364
Leprosy, 52, 57, 275, 338, 351, 364
Leukemia, 311. See also Cancer
Liberia, 122, 281, 314
Libya, 109
Lice, 20, 24, 46, 208

Madagascar, 31, 48
Malaria, 3, 20, 31, 36, 38, 39, 46, 48, 50, 61–66, 73, 105, 122, 124, 125, 132, 171, 208, 211, 214, 243, 289, 315, 324, 325, 330–32, 351, 360, 362–64
Malawi, 135
Malaysia, 48, 63, 66, 135, 151, 221, 275, 281, 313, 345, 347
Mali, 156, 259, 291, 314, 364
Malnutrition, 16–18, 117, 158, 162, 211, 243, 248, 254, 330, 338. See also Nutrition
Malpractice, 162
Mao Tse-tung, 286–88
Marburg fever, 221
Maternal and child health, 232, 290, 292–93, 307, 312, 313. See also Primary care
Mauritania, 109, 259, 291

INDEX

Measles, 18, 24, 57, 94, 156, 157, 207, 238, 364
Medical care
  distribution of, 258–65
  organization of, 270–316
Medical care systems, 163
  definition of, 270
  comparisons between, 270–316
  usership of, 272–89
  benefits in, 289–93
  providers in, 293–314
Medical procedures, appropriateness of, 254–57
Medical research, 256
Medicine, modernization of, 74
Menarche, age at, 39
Meningitis, 207
Mental health, 252
Mental illness, 275
Mental retardation, 238, 239
Mexico, 18, 139, 154, 156, 222, 295, 332
Middle Ages in Europe, 56–58
Middle East, 31, 57, 221
Midwifery, 170, 234, 308, 310, 313
Migrants, 116, 121, 325–27
Milbank Memorial Fund, 329
Mill, John Stuart, 151
Minamata disease, 222
Mongolia, 301
Morbidity, 126, 239, 248, 303, 369
  data and statistics, 206–12
Mortality, 72, 95, 97, 106, 107, 109, 119, 127, 145, 148, 192, 199, 213, 239, 248, 254
  childhood, 40, 93, 105, 117, 127, 228, 234, 235, 303, 369
  fetal, 16, 188, 192
  infant, 16, 95, 105, 135, 182, 192, 201–3, 224, 243–45, 262
  maternal, 195
  neonatal, 202, 243
  perinatal, 105, 195, 203
  statistics, 193–201
Mosquitoes, 20, 21, 24, 34, 48, 62, 65, 66, 122, 124, 125, 171, 330
Mountain sickness (Monge's disease), 9–12
Mozambique, 125

National Health Service (Great Britain), 274, 280, 282, 283, 290, 296, 327
Native Americans, medicine of, 56–57
Nepal, 362, 366

Netherlands, 206, 276, 277, 282, 293, 296, 298
Newfoundland, 16
New Guinea, 36, 116, 126
New Zealand, 66, 207, 220, 274, 292, 296, 301, 325
Nicaragua, 279, 285
Niger, 61, 259, 291, 314, 364
Nigeria, 14, 18, 122, 124–26, 313, 314, 330, 332
Nomads, 321, 322
Nordic Council, 326
Norway, 57, 206, 278, 280, 292, 293, 297, 336
Nurses, 299, 301, 307, 315
  public health, 313, 369
Nutrition, 3, 13, 14, 16, 31, 36, 40, 48, 52, 53, 69, 72, 74, 94, 99, 101–3, 118, 121, 122, 132, 152, 171, 202, 205, 244, 307, 339, 369
  infant, 40, 152–57, 336
  See also Malnutrition

Official agencies, 337–45
Official Development Assistance, 339–45
Onchocerciasis, 124, 289, 349, 364, 365
o-nyong-nyong disease, 221
Organization of American States, 280
Organization for Economic Cooperation and Development, 328

Pakistan, 26, 125, 144, 337, 362
Paleopathology, 46, 47
Panama, 65, 66
Panama Canal, 65, 66
Pan American Health Organization, 263, 280, 358
Paraguay, 279
Parasites, 15, 20, 24–26, 35, 39, 46, 47, 62, 119, 122, 124, 158, 324. See also Disease, parasitic; and specific types
Park, Mungo, 61, 62
Pathfinder Fund, 329
Pathogens, air- and waterborne, 16–18
Pertussis (whooping cough), 94, 207, 241, 364
Peru, 9, 12, 14, 19, 47, 48, 63, 151, 155
Pettenkofer, Max von, 72
Petty, William, 167, 233
Pharmaceutical industry, 337
Pharmaceuticals, 336, 359
Philanthropic foundations, 329–36

Philippines, 24, 152, 221, 313, 332, 345, 347
Physician, 160–62, 307, 329
  distribution of, 285, 301, 302
  payment of, 294–99
  training of, 302, 303, 314
Plague, 24, 25, 57, 208, 332, 359
Poland, 278, 295, 296, 301
Poliomyelitis, 94, 208, 239, 364
Political viewpoints, 78–80, 167
Pollution
  environmental, 103, 125, 126, 172, 321
  pesticide, 122
Polyclinic, 295, 297, 298, 301, 312
Polynesia, 48
Poor Laws, 70
Population, 18, 98–109, 121, 127, 132, 171–80, 199, 201, 203, 245, 248, 254, 259, 271, 279, 283–85, 329, 336, 341
  age structure of, 173, 179–80
  control of, 106, 108, 224. See also Family planning
  distribution of, 109, 285
  growth of, 98–109
  per physician, 285, 302–3
  statistics on, 213
Portugal, 3, 58, 59, 224, 278, 325
Poverty, culture of, 86
Pregnancy, cost of, 234
Primary care, 290, 307, 308, 311–14, 365
Private Voluntary Organizations, 327–29, 332, 340
Propaganda, effects of, 153–55
Prussia, 109
Puerto Rico, 239

Quinine, 63–64, 66

Rabies, 26, 34, 330
Radioactivity and health, 7
Randomized control trial, 258
Refugees, 326
Regimen Sanitatis Salernitarium, 56
Relapsing fever, 47, 208
Rhodesia, 35, 125. See also Zimbabwe
Right to health, controversy over, 258–65
River blindness. See Onchocerciasis
Rockefeller Foundation, 205, 329–31
Rodents, 25, 47, 101
  and plague, 57
Romania, 278, 301

Rome, 50–52
Rubella, 94, 207, 221
Ruritania, 228–32
Russia, 3, 46, 295
Rwanda, 6

Sahel, 259
St. Lucia, 240
Samoa, 239
Sanitarian, 369
Sanitation, 3, 17, 56, 58, 65, 70–74, 109, 118, 125, 126, 201, 244, 250, 307, 310, 313
Sanitary reform
  in England, 70–72
  in other countries, 72–74
Saudi Arabia, 15, 39
Scandinavia, 274, 276, 297
Schistosomiasis, 18, 25, 46, 48, 62, 124, 132, 158, 211, 240, 289, 324, 330, 364
SEAMEO (Southeast Asian Ministers of Education Organization)-TROPMED, 345–48
Seat belts, use of, 152–53
Senegal, 119, 125, 259, 291, 311
Sewerage, 48, 69, 71, 73, 117, 124, 125, 348
Shaman, 163
Sicily, 50, 58
Sickle-cell trait, screening for, 211
Sickness, 157–63, 203
  preventable, 255
  insurance against, 276–82
Sick role, 159–63
Sierra Leone, 13, 314
Simon, John, 71
Singapore, 12, 13, 18, 108, 109, 119, 140, 154, 156, 221, 275, 345, 348
Slave trade, 61–62, 68
Sleeping sickness, 24, 62, 64, 65, 122
Slums, 114–19, 162
Smallpox, 3, 52, 57, 73, 207, 208, 322, 325, 351
  eradication of, 361–63
Snails and disease, 25, 48, 124
Snow, John, 72
Social Security, 264, 274–81, 293, 295
Socioeconomic development, 89–97, 246, 248
Soil and health, 4–7, 14–16

INDEX

Somalia, 362
South Africa, 18, 137, 277, 281, 282
South Korea, 108
South Pacific, 59
South Vietnam, 345, 348
Spain, 45, 58, 59, 140, 188, 278, 295, 296, 325, 336
Spengler, Oswald, 133–34
Sri Lanka, 150, 275, 281, 313, 362
Stroke, 33, 36. See also Disease, cardiovascular
Sudan, 123
Suicide, 224
Sumatra, 48. See also Indonesia
Surinam, 66, 125
Survivorship, 246
Sweden, 109, 206, 224, 245, 252, 280, 292, 293, 296, 297, 299, 325, 336
Switzerland, 17, 35, 206, 276, 277, 296
Syria, 151

Tahiti, 59
Taiwan, 5, 108
Tanzania, 6, 221, 282, 314, 315
Tapeworms, 26
Technology, 40, 103, 119–22, 134, 255
 appropriate, 337
Tetanus, 14, 238, 364
Thailand, 125, 152, 221, 295, 345, 348, 362
Tobacco, 69
 use of, 147–50, 244
Trace elements, 6–7
Trachoma, 57, 211, 289
Traditional healers, 163, 172, 284
Traditional medicine, 52–56
Traditional societies, views of health in, 134–35
Travel, 48–50, 321–27, 359
Trephining, 47
Triatoma, 21
Trichinosis, 26
Trichuris, 15, 35, 324
Trinidad, 66, 330
Trypanosomiasis, 62, 64, 65, 122, 124, 313, 324, 364. See also Sleeping sickness; Chagas' disease
Tsetse flies, 122, 124
Tuberculosis, 14, 16, 33, 46, 50, 52, 57, 69, 73, 109, 207, 211, 222, 241, 275, 330, 331, 338

Tunisia, 281
Turkey, 125, 180, 299, 315
Typhoid fever, 17, 48, 72, 207, 238, 323, 325
Typhus, 20, 24, 69, 73, 208, 332, 362

Uganda, 18, 36, 65, 125, 155
Union of Soviet Socialist Republics, 13, 24, 127, 144, 225, 274, 284, 291, 293, 298, 299, 301
United Kingdom. See Great Britain
United Nations, 80, 109, 113, 122, 173, 182, 184, 258, 365
United States, 103, 125, 145–48, 173–79, 199, 238, 242, 252, 279, 284, 293–95, 297, 299, 301, 322, 326, 328–31, 337, 340
United States Agency for International Development, 340–41
United States-Japan Cooperative Medical Sciences Program, 337
United States Public Health Service, 368
Upper Volta, 259, 291, 364
Urbanization, 112, 154
Uruguay, 206, 279

Vectors of disease. See Insects; Disease, vector-transmitted
Venereal disease. See Disease, sexually transmitted
Venezuela, 14, 125, 313
Vital statistics, 181–92, 307, 329

Wallis, Captain, 59
Water
 minerals in, 4–7
 pathogens in, 16–18, 25, 325
 supply of, 48, 51, 56, 66, 69, 71, 72, 94, 116, 117, 125, 163, 239, 244, 248, 321, 348, 351, 359, 369
West Indies, 62
"White man's grave," 60
World Bank, 80, 262, 348
World Health Organization, 17, 97, 136, 182, 184, 192, 193, 198, 203–8, 238, 258, 284, 307, 308, 314
 structure and functions, 349–66
World Medical Association, 264

Yaws, 46, 289, 313, 330, 351, 360

Yellow fever, 3, 21, 24, 48, 65, 66, 73, 208, 330, 331
Yin and *yang*, 54, 139
Yugoslavia, 238, 278, 298, 314

Zaire, 309, 314
Zambia, 124
Zimbabwe, 49, 135. *See also* Rhodesia
Zoonoses, 24–26, 46